More praise for

TOWNIE

One of *Esquire*'s Top Nine Books of 2011

One of Dwight Garner's Top Ten Nonfiction Books of 2011
(*New York Times*)

"The best first-person account of an author's life I have ever read. The violence that is described is the kind that is with us every day, whether we recognize it or not. The characters are wonderful and compassionately drawn. I sincerely believe Andre Dubus may be the best writer in America. His talent is enormous. No one who reads this book will ever forget it."
—James Lee Burke

"The most sensitive—and gripping—account of male violence imaginable."
—*Sunday Times* (London)

"[P]owerful, haunting. . . . Beautifully written and bursting with life. [Dubus's] compassionate memoir abounds with exquisitely rendered scenes of fighting, cheating, drugging, drinking and loving. A striking, eloquent account of growing up poor and of the making of a writer."
—*Kirkus Reviews*, starred review

"Dubus's novelistic storytelling combines with insightful introspection and striking, blunt prose."
—Eric Liebetrau, *People*

"Dubus relives, absent self-pity or blame, a life shaped by bouts of violence and flurries of tenderness."
—*Vanity Fair*

"In his memoir *Townie*, Andre Dubus III bravely claims all of the shadows he grew up under—his famous writer father, his parents' divorce, his newly single mother's impoverishment, the rough streets of the many working-class New England towns he called home. Fighting saved him for a while; then he put down his fists and picked up a pen. Lucky him, lucky us."
—Lisa Shea, *Elle*

"Whatever it cost Dubus to bare his soul and write this brutally honest and life-affirming memoir, it is an extraordinary gift to his readers."
—Wally Lamb, author of *The Hour I First Believed*

"*Townie* is the deeply personal exploration of one man's violence, told not with rage but with disarming vulnerability and wisdom."
—Lindsay Champion, BiblioBuffet.com

"*Townie* exquisitely explicates one writer's beginnings and his consuming need for expression—not through the delusive potency of physical violence but through the redemptive, alchemical power of words."
—Alison Hood, BookPage.com

"[Dubus III] is such a solid writer, he redeems the genre. He shows that truth can be as honest as fiction." —Mark Lindquist, *Seattle Times*

"Surprisingly, this book held me as raptly as his fiction, in Dubus's skillful words his own vulnerability and New England mill town childhood came alive." —*Largehearted Boy*

"[*Townie*] growls like an amalgam of the best work by Richard Price, Stephen King, Ron Kovic, Breece D'J Pancake and Dennis Lehane. . . . [Dubus III's] prose is clear, supple, unshowy. He gets a lot across with a few words. You'll agree with the boxing coach who said to [Dubus III] as a teenager, 'I think you got the killer instinct, kid.' "
—Dwight Garner, *New York Times*, Editors' Choice

"Dubus has an eye for searing detail that is unequaled so far this century . . . and he employs that here to maximum effect."
—Joy Tipping, *Dallas Morning News*

"In this gritty and gripping memoir, Dubus bares his soul in stunning and page-turning prose." —*Publishers Weekly*, starred review

"I've never read a better or more serious meditation on violence, its sources, consequences, and, especially, its terrifying pleasures, than *Townie*. It's a brutal and, yes, thrilling memoir that sheds real light on the creative process of two of our best writers, Andre Dubus III and his famous, much revered father. You'll never read the work of either man in quite the same way afterward. You may not view the world in quite the same way either."

—Richard Russo

"This is a memoir both disconcertingly naked and immensely careful; Dubus refrains from bitterness the way a Buddhist monk renounces worldly possessions. . . . It's tempting to get angry on the author's behalf, but *Townie* patiently teaches its readers that rage is self-poisoning. . . . There is art in abundance, in the way, for example, that Dubus's descriptions of his run-down neighborhood gradually change as the narrative goes along."

—Laura Miller, *Salon*

"Dubus has set a high water mark in this work: He shows us that the son's shadow can also be long, and can change the shape of that which came before it."   —Matthew Tiffany, *Minneapolis Star Tribune*

"You have to buy this book because once you read it, you're going to want people you know to read it, and the easiest, most efficient way to make that happen is to lend them your own copy—at least briefly."

—Gina Barreca, *Chronicle of Higher Education*

"[Dubus III's] ability to describe violence might be unmatched among contemporary writers. He understands the arcane, unspoken vocabulary of how fights start, as well as the bone-crushing details of how they end. But *Townie* is most memorable for how vulnerable Dubus seems, once he has stripped himself down to the soul for his readers."

—Doug Childers, *Richmond Times-Dispatch*

"In this powerful memoir, Andre Dubus III explores the complicated and intense relationships between siblings, mothers and sons, and fathers and sons. Growing up in hardscrabble old mill towns, Dubus learned to fight and survive and ultimately to find his own glorious voice . . . as Dubus finds his redemptive place in the world at last."

—Ann Hood, author of *The Red Thread*

"Andre Dubus III passes [the] test with the highest marks in *Townie* It's a searing memoir. . . . The passage when he picks up a pencil for the first time and feels the transformative power of storytelling is a marvel. . . . *Townie* captures the birth and evolution of [his] voice—one worth listening to by anyone who believes in the redemptive power of the written word."   —Rob Merrill, Associated Press

"*Townie* has all the rich texture, lucid characterization, compelling conflicts and narrative momentum of the best fiction. It renders heartbreaking, violent, tender and sometimes absurdly comic scenes without a trace of narcissism or sentimentality."   —John Repp, *Cleveland Plain-Dealer*

"Dubus III . . . relates the story of his childhood and young adulthood with an immediate, raw intensity—it's at times difficult to read, but it's almost impossible to turn away. His prose is unaffected in the best way possible; there's never a hint of preciousness or pretentiousness. And his depictions of the northeastern Massachusetts of the '70s are stark and evocative. . . . What's most remarkable about *Townie*, though, is the author's unalloyed emotional honesty."   —Michael Schaub, NPR

"Fluently written. . . . Dubus is aware of precisely how far he can go before falling into bathos and sentimentality—and he never crosses the line, while pushing the limits."   —Anis Shivani, *The Statesman*

"*Townie* moves with the accelerating momentum of a thriller novel, plumbs the depths of a bittersweet love affair, and rends the reader's heart in two."   —Dan Cryer, *San Francisco Chronicle*

"[A] stark and vivid new memoir. . . . *Townie* is a poignant coming-of-age story told by a man whose raw determination allowed him to endure a boyhood ruled by violence and emerge talented enough to write about it with brutal honesty."   —Amy Canfield, *Miami Herald*

"A captivating history."   —Manuela Hoelterhoff, *Bloomberg*

"What places it at the top of the heap . . . is its unflinching openness and the metamorphoses Dubus effects in his own life." —Yvonne Zipp, *Christian Science Monitor*

"Andre Dubus III's memoir, *Townie*, should be lauded. . . . [An] unsentimental portrayal (and for that reason a welcome and engrossing one)." —Oscar Villalon, *Barnes & Noble Review*

"Seamlessly and urgently written, no boast in it, no politics, no accusations, either, *Townie* is a reckoning. It is a brave insider's look at how one moves past fists toward words, past heartbreak toward compassion, past broken family to a wholeness of one's own." —Beth Kephart

"Dubus chronicles each traumatic incident and realization in stabbing detail. So chiseled are his dramatic memories, his shocking yet redemptive memoir of self-transformation feels like testimony under oath as well as hard-hammered therapy, coalescing, ultimately, in a generous, penetrating, and cathartic dissection of misery and fury, creativity and forgiveness, responsibility and compassion." —Donna Seaman, *Booklist*, starred review

TOWNIE

ALSO BY ANDRE DUBUS III

TOWNIE

· *a memoir* ·

Andre Dubus III

W. W. NORTON & COMPANY

NEW YORK · LONDON

I have tried to protect the privacy of real people here, living and dead, by changing the names of everyone except those in my immediate family and those who are already known to the public. I have also, when necessary, altered the physical descriptions of a few men and women.

Townie draws on material from three previously published essays by Andre Dubus III: "Tracks and Ties," originally published in 1993 in *Epoch*, reprinted in the *Pushcart Prize Anthology XIX* and *The Best American Essays of 1994* (New York: Houghton Mifflin); the foreword to *Andre Dubus: Tributes* (New Orleans: Xavier Press, 2001); and "Home," from *Death by Pad Thai* (New York: Three Rivers Press, 2006).

Lyrics from "Born to Run" by Bruce Springsteen. Copyright © 1975 Bruce Springsteen (ASCAP). Reprinted by permission. International copyright secured. All rights reserved.

Lyrics from "Fly Me to the Moon (In Other Words)," Words and Music by Bart Howard, TRO-© Copyright 1954 (Renewed) Hampshire House Publishing Corp., New York, NY. Used by Permission.

For information about permission to reproduce selections from this book, write to Permissions, W. W. Norton & Company, Inc., 500 Fifth Avenue, New York, NY 10110

For information about special discounts for bulk purchases, please contact W. W. Norton Special Sales at specialsales@wwnorton.com or 800-233-4830

Manufacturing by Courier Westford
Book design by Ellen Cipriano
Production manager: Anna Oler

Library of Congress Cataloging-in-Publication Data

Dubus, Andre, 1959–
Townie : a memoir / Andre Dubus III. — 1st ed.
p. cm.
ISBN 978-0-393-06466-7 (hardcover)
1. Dubus, Andre, 1959– 2. Authors, American—20th century—Biography. I. Title.
PS3554.U2652Z46 2011
813'.54—dc22
[B]
2010038029
ISBN 978-0-393-34067-9 pbk.

W. W. Norton & Company, Inc.
500 Fifth Avenue, New York, N.Y. 10110
www.wwnorton.com

W. W. Norton & Company Ltd.
Castle House, 75/76 Wells Street, London W1T 3QT

5 6 7 8 9 0

For Austin, Ariadne, and Elias

And the boys try to look so hard . . .

"Born to Run," by Bruce Springsteen

PART I

QUEEN SLIPPER CITY OF THE WORLD

I

——

I DID NOT LOOK into the mirror, not yet, not in the morning. My body
was still so small and I only looked at it right after the weights when
my muscles were filled with blood. There came the tap of my father's
horn outside. We were going running together, but what about shoes? All
I owned were a pair of Dingo boots, the square-toed kind with the brass
ring cinched in at the ankle. The horn tapped again.

I stepped into my younger brother's room. Jeb was sitting shirtless in
a chair, playing chords on his guitar in time to the metronome his teacher
had bought him. His hair was wild and there was brown fuzz across his
chin and cheeks.

"Jeb, you have any sneakers?"

He shook his head, kept playing, the metronome ticking, ticking,
ticking. I ran into Suzanne's room. My older sister was just about to turn
seventeen, and she was curled asleep, her back to me. Her room smelled
like dope and cigarette smoke. There were album covers spread on the
floor at the foot of the bed: Robin Trower, Ten Years After, the Rolling
Stones. In a swath of sunlight her blue sneakers lay side by side next to
balled-up hip-huggers.

"Suzanne, can I borrow your sneakers? I'm running with *Dad*."

She mumbled something, and I knew she wouldn't be up for another hour or two anyway. I grabbed her shoes, stole some white socks from her drawer, and ran outside.

It was a Monday in August, the sun almost directly above us in a deep blue sky. We only saw Pop on the occasional Wednesday when he saw each of us alone and on Sundays when he would drive to our house and take all of us to a movie or out to eat, but the day before, at the Carriage House just over the Merrimac line, he'd studied me over the table, his oldest son with his newly hard body I wanted to be so much bigger than it was. He looked curious about something, proud too. "You should come run with me sometime." Then he said he'd come pick me up the next day, his thirty-ninth birthday, and we'd go running together.

I waved at him behind the wheel of his old Lancer. He waved back and I stuffed my feet into Suzanne's sneakers and ran to the car and climbed in.

"Hey, man."

"Happy Birthday."

"Gracias." He pulled away from the curb. He wore running shoes, shorts, a tank top, and he'd tied a blue bandanna around his forehead. He didn't have much muscle, but he was trim. His chest and arms were covered with dark hair. He kept glancing at me as I leaned over and tied the worn laces of Suzanne's blue sneakers.

"You sure you want to do this?"

"Yep."

"It's gonna be long and hot."

I shrugged.

"Okay, man."

I sat back in my seat. I was hungry and wished I'd eaten something first, or at least drunk a glass of water. But what bothered me more were my feet. Suzanne's sneakers felt two sizes too small, my toes squeezed together, too much pressure on my heels. A few minutes later, when he pulled into the gravel parking lot and I got out and shut the door, I could feel each stone through the soles of my sister's shoes.

Pop and I were walking toward the woods and the five-and-a-half mile trail. Already there was an ache in both feet. *I should tell him. I should tell him these aren't my sneakers. They're Suzanne's and they're too small.* But when I looked over at him, the sun on his face, his trimmed beard looking brown and red in that light, he smiled at me and I smiled back and we started running.

My father had been a runner longer than he'd been my father. When he was still living with us, he'd finish his morning writing, change into sneakers and shorts and a T-shirt, and go running. He'd be gone for an hour, sometimes longer, and when he walked back in, his shirt dark and wet, his cheeks flushed, it was the most relaxed and content he'd ever look. This was the sixties and early seventies. Nobody jogged then. It was a habit he'd formed in the Marine Corps, and when he ran down the road, people would shout from their lawns and ask if he needed any help. Where was he going?

I had run with him once before when I was eight years old. It was at our old house in the woods in New Hampshire, one with land to play on, a clear brook in the trees. It was a summer day, when Mom and Pop were still married, and Pop had asked me and Jeb if we wanted to go with him. We said yes, though Jeb lost interest pretty quickly and walked back down the country road Pop and I kept running on. I lagged a few feet behind him, the sun on my face, sweat burning my eyes. At the one-mile mark, he turned around and I followed him home where he left me and set back out on a longer run. But I'd run two miles and when I stepped inside our cool, dark house, I yelled up the stairs to Mom, "I ran two miles with Daddy, Mom! I'm strong! I'm *strong*!" And I punched the wall and could feel the plaster and lath behind the wallpaper, though I had no words for them.

Now I was twice that age and hadn't run since, and even though my feet hurt with each stride, it felt good to be running outside with Pop on his birthday, spending time with him that wasn't in a restaurant he couldn't afford on a Sunday, that wasn't in his small apartment every fourth Wednesday. It was easier not having to look directly at him across a table, to have him sometimes look directly at *me*. And this was a part of town I didn't even know about. For a while it was hard to believe it was the same town as the one I spent all my time in; we were running on a wide dirt trail under a canopy of leafy branches. To our left, the trees grew on a slope and leaned over the water. To our right was a steep wooded hill, the ground a bed of pine needles and moss-covered rock, deep green ferns growing up around fallen logs and bare branches. I was in weight-training shape, not running shape, and fifteen minutes into it I could hear myself breathing harder than he was, but I didn't let myself fall behind him and I found if I relaxed my toes each time I lifted a foot, then tensed them just before it hit the ground again, the pain wasn't quite as sharp. I figured I'd have to do this another thirty minutes, maybe forty-five, just two or three times what we'd already done. I could do that, right?

The trail dropped closer to the water and for a quarter mile or so we were running on flat ground, water on both sides of us, marsh grass and lily pads and waterlogged trees that'd been there for years. Then the hills came. They were short and steep, and Pop told me to run up them hard, that it was easier that way. I did, my heart punching my ribs, my breathing coming too shallow when I was inhaling as deeply as I could. Pop was eight or ten feet ahead of me now, and I put my head down, pumped my arms and legs and tried to ignore the stabs in my soles, the vise on my toes, the metal grater on my heels.

The hill leveled off in the shade, then dropped mercifully before another rose up like a rock-strewn wave, and now my eyes were stinging from the sweat and I closed them and ran as hard as I could, my thighs burning, the air in my lungs gone for good.

There were five or six more like this, and with each one we rose higher from the water down to our left. To our right was the rise of another densely wooded hill, so shaded it looked cool, and Pop was breathing much easier than I was, his bandanna dark with sweat. He seemed to slow himself so I could pull up beside him.

"The big one's coming up."

"Big one?"

"You'll see." He laughed, and soon enough the trail cut hard to the east, and he ran ahead of me. I followed, but this was the steepest hill yet, and when I looked ahead I saw only that it kept rising and rising before it curved into more trees where it rose again.

My mouth and throat were thick and tasted like salt, my thighs hurt almost as much as my feet, and even though I was pumping my arms and legs as fast as I could I seemed to be barely moving. I couldn't see my father anymore. I closed my eyes and kept running.

POP WAS waiting for me at the top, running in place, his beard glistening in the dappled light. He was smiling at me. When I got to where he was, we ran side by side down a long winding trail in the shade.

It wasn't until we were on flat ground again, water on both sides of us, maybe a mile and a half before we were through, that he said, "You up for the second lap?"

"Yeah." I assumed the second lap meant the homestretch we were running, the same trail we'd used on the way in. I didn't know then that on his birthday every year he would double or triple his normal running distance, that the second lap meant *another* five and a half miles after I somehow got through these.

The pains in my feet felt like some territory they now lived in. Way up ahead was the clearing in the trees, green grass under the sun, the short trail back to the parking lot and Pop's car and cool water, later a shower, a chair, more cool water. But when we reached the sunlit grass, Pop turned around and ran past me back into the woods. For a moment or two, I ran in place and stared at the parking lot, the glare of the sun on the windshields, the smack and bounce of a tennis ball in the public court there, the glint of the sun off the chrome handle of the water fountain. I hadn't run even one mile since the two I'd run with Pop half my lifetime ago, and I'd just done five and a half. My own feet had become two weapons turned against me: How could I do it again? Shouldn't I just tell him about these shoes? That they were way too small, and I just couldn't do it anymore?

But my father was already disappearing into the shadows of the trail, the back of his shirt a dark V of sweat, his running shoes moving white balls. I lowered my head and I followed.

IT WAS in the ninth or tenth mile that I'd begun to hobble, pulling my feet along, pumping my arms harder to keep up any momentum. Pop kept asking if I was all right. Did I want to stop? I shook my head no, I couldn't imagine giving up after so much pain. If I did, every bruising step behind me would be wasted, right?

Three days later, it seemed, the trail came to an end and I lay down in the sunlit field of grass, my lungs raw, my feet pulsing, sweat pooling in my eye sockets. I sat up and wiped my face on my forearms and untied Suzanne's shoes. My feet were swollen and it was hard pulling them off, the skin of my heels scraping, both socks wet and red. I peeled them away to see all ten toes had split open at the sides like sausages over a fire.

Pop squatted beside me. "Jesus."

"These are Suzanne's. I think they're too small."

"Where're *your* shoes?"

I shrugged, didn't want Mom to get in trouble. I knew he gave her a lot of his monthly pay, expected her to clothe us and feed us and house us properly, three things she'd said many times she just didn't have enough money to do.

I don't know how we got to the car. I probably leaned on Pop's shoulder and tried to walk as flat-footed as I could over the gravel. But first we stopped at the water fountain and drank. It was warm and tasted vaguely like concrete and metal, but it was a liquid angel come to bless us, and even though my entire body hurt from my lungs to my feet, I couldn't remember ever feeling so good. About life. About me. About what else might lie ahead if you were just willing to take some pain, some punishment.

THREE YEARS earlier, when Suzanne was thirteen and I was twelve, when our younger brother Jeb was eleven and Nicole was eight, our mother had moved us to Haverhill, Massachusetts, a milltown along the Merrimack River. Before this, the five of us had lived in two other towns on the same river. The Merrimack originated one hundred miles north in the mountains of New Hampshire, and I imagined it was clean up there, not like where we lived where the wide, fast-moving water was rust-colored and smelled like sewage and diesel and something I couldn't name. Later, I would learn this was tanning dye from the shoe mills, that all fish died here, vegetation too. Posted down near the littered banks were signs that said no swimming or fishing, not just because of the current—the yellow industrial-waste foam of it rising off in the wind—but because the water itself was toxic.

Decades earlier, Haverhill had been named "the Queen Slipper City of the World" because the town's Irish and Italian immigrants worked endless shifts in the mills along the Merrimack churning out a lot of the country's shoes. But in the early 1900s Italy started exporting cheaper shoes and one by one the mills closed and ships stopped sailing up the river from the Atlantic. By the time we moved there in the early seventies, it was a town of boarded-up buildings, the parking lots overgrown with weeds and strewn with trash. Most of the shops downtown were closed too, their window displays empty and layered with dust and dead flies. It seemed there were barrooms on every block—the Chit Chat Lounge, the Lido, Ray and Arlene's—and they were always full, the doors open in the summertime, the cackle of a woman spilling out of the darkness, the low bass beat of the jukebox, the phlegmy cough of an old man born here when things were good.

Mom had gotten us a cheap one-story rental at the base of a hill on a street which curved around to Hale Hospital. Behind the hospital was a graveyard and there was a joke that the Hale was so bad you didn't even want to go there for a broken bone because in no time they'd put you in the cemetery out back. Our house used to be a doctor's office, and now he rented it to us. The two bedrooms and kitchen had been examination rooms, the dining room the doctor's office, and our living room was where patients sat and waited. We lived there two years. Once a month or so, in the middle of the afternoon, we four kids would be watching TV and a man or woman would open the door and walk in and sit down. One man in a trench coat and tie picked up a newspaper off the floor and sat in the chair in the corner and began reading. Suzanne was out with the friends she was making in the projects, and Jeb and Nicole and I looked at each other a while, the canned laughter of *Gilligan's Island* or *The Partridge Family* on the TV. The man was deep into his reading and we weren't sure what to do. Everyone else who'd walked in had seen right away this wasn't the doctor's office anymore—the scant furniture, the dusty carpet, no more receptionist or plastic plants, and there were these kids lying on the floor in front of a TV. I was the oldest. It was up to me, wasn't it? To tell this man to leave?

Then he glanced up from his paper. He looked around the room. He looked at us looking at him. "This *is* Dr. Deakins's office, isn't it?"

"No," I said. "He moved."

The man apologized and stood and left in a hurry. I don't know why we didn't just put up a sign and lock the door. There was a lot I didn't seem to know.

LATELY SUZANNE had been going to parties in the projects on Summer Street. It was on the other side of the cemetery, and Russ Bowman lived there. He was only fifteen or sixteen, but he had long blond hair he kept tied back in a foot-long pony tail. He had sideburns and big arm muscles he showed off in the T-shirt and biker vests he wore. I heard kids say he stabbed someone. I heard others say he raped a girl and got away with it. One night in the fall, after nine when our mother was still at work, Jeb and I went looking for Suzanne in the projects. Nicole had stayed home alone. The projects was a cluster of concrete buildings that smelled like piss and wine. There was a dark loud party, a bunch of teenagers in a hot room smoking dope while the Jackson 5 sang on the record player about ABC being as easy as 1, 2, 3. Jeb was tall for eleven, his hair long and frizzy. He put his arm around the shoulders of a cute Dominican girl, and Russ Bowman rose up out of the shadows and grabbed Jeb by the throat and backhanded his face. "She's mine, you little shit. Beat it."

I stood there. I stood there with my heart fluttering, a sick hole in my gut, and I wanted to do something, anything, but it was Russ Bowman, so I did nothing. My brother stared down at the floor like he was trying to figure out what he'd done wrong. Bowman shoved him out of the room, and I followed him onto the street.

WHENEVER THERE was a fight at school you would know it because dozens of boys and girls would be rushing to one spot like they were being pulled there by the air itself. There'd be yelling and screaming. Someone would yell "Fight!" and kids would run into the crowd. You'd see some boy getting his face punched over and over, and soon a teacher or vice principal would push his way through to break it up.

One afternoon in late spring, the last bell rang and I was in a loud moving stream of kids pushing out the front door and into the day. The air smelled like fresh-cut grass and sewage from the river. Rain clouds were gathering over it and the boxboard factory on the other side, and parked in the fire lane was a chopper Harley-Davidson, a man standing beside it, his hands on his hips. He was tall, his hair held back with a blue bandanna, his arms tattooed and sinewy. He wore ripped jeans and black biker boots and when Russ Bowman saw him, he dropped his book and turned, his face pale, his eyes as wide as a child's. He ran back through the crowd and into the school, this grown man chasing him. Somebody yelled "Fight!" And it was like watching the tide reverse itself, the ocean's waves pause, then push themselves back out to sea, all of us running back inside and down the corridors, shoulder to shoulder, some tripping and falling, chasing after the man chasing Russ Bowman.

He caught him in an empty classroom. When the rest of us spilled into it, Bowman was already flat on his back and the man was punching Russ in the face again and again.

I liked seeing this. I liked seeing Bowman's head bounce against the hard floor, I liked seeing the blood splattering across his nose and mouth and chin, and I especially liked how tightly his eyes were shut against the fear, and the pain.

Then I began to not like it.

Some kids were yelling, "Kill him! *Kill* him!" Others were quiet, watching like I was. Some of the girls covered their eyes or turned their heads away. Four cops plowed their way through us. The first one pulled his billy club and hooked it under the man's chin and jerked him off Russ Bowman. The second and third cops pushed the man face-first into a desk, and a fourth cop was reaching for his cuffs and yelling at us all to beat it. *"Beat it!"*

On my way out with the rest, I glanced back at Bowman. He was on his knees, his hair in his face, his nose and split lips dripping blood. He was staring down at the floor like he'd been waiting for this and now it had finally happened; he looked relieved.

2

——

MY MOTHER AND father were each the youngest children of their families, and they were both raised in southern Louisiana. Mom had one older sister. Pop had two. His father had worked for Gulf States Utilities Company, and when our father was old enough he'd sometimes drive out to a bayou and go surveying with him, his French father wearing high boots and a .22 pistol strapped to his belt for snakes. Pop's mother was from a big Irish family in Lafayette. Her father was a state senator descended from the Irish statesman Edmund Burke. At one time my great-grandfather had been asked to run against Huey Long, but he refused because he feared Long's political machine would try to soil his family's name. His wife, my great-grandmother, was descended from Admiral Perry, Edwin and John Wilkes Booth, and Helene DeLauné, a lady-in-waiting to Marie Antoinette who, on the day of the queen's beheading, fled with some of the silver. Over the years, it had been passed down through the male family line. When I was in my twenties, I would pull one of these spoons from my father's garbage disposal where it had slipped from the morning's cereal bowl and been mangled. "Pop," I said, "isn't this shit valuable?"

"Not to me, son."

• • •

OUR MOTHER'S father was Elmer Lamar Lowe, a man who'd never gone further than the third grade. At sixteen he'd been a foreman for a gang of gandy dancers, grown men laying railroad tracks under the sun, singing cadence as they swung sledgehammers and drove spikes into ties, fastening scalding iron rails that flashed brightly as they heaved the next length ahead of them. During the Great Depression, he was making sixty-five dollars a day setting bridge piers in the swirling depths of the Mississippi. He wore a diving bell suit, a thin air hose running from his helmet to the surface. A lot of men died doing this, but he went on to build power plants for big companies, bringing electricity to people throughout the south and even to Mexico. Our mother's mother had Welsh, Scottish, and Apache blood, a family of rice farmers and mule skinners, men who used their mules and rope to haul boats of supplies along shallow waterways.

I knew little of any of these things until I was grown. Nor did I know that in the late fifties my father's older sister Beth taught at St. Charles Academy, a convent school in Lake Charles, Louisiana, where she was a lay teacher. One of her English students was the freshman queen and homecoming queen, Patricia Lowe, a honey-haired beauty who was smart and polite and had so much presence that when she smiled at you it felt as if no one had ever smiled at you before: my future mother. As a junior she was already engaged to James Wayne, a piney woods boy from Rapides Parish, but James was in the army, and when he shipped off to Panama, Beth pulled my mother aside one day and said, "You can't marry James Wayne, you have to meet my brother Andre."

My mother had already heard of Andre Dubus. She'd read one of his articles in the local paper where he'd argued for integration, something she believed in deeply as well. She said she would meet him and when he called that winter told him she was going squirrel hunting up in Rapides Parish but that she could see him sometime after Christmas. He seemed intrigued by that, this pageant winner off in the woods with a loaded gun.

As a student at McNeese State College in Lake Charles, our father was small—barely 140 pounds—French-Irish handsome, but shy. On their

first date, my mother told him she'd just gotten a new record player so
they drove to Mueller's Department Store and he bought her two albums,
June Christy and Sammy Davis. She told him she admired his writing. He
told her he wanted to see her again. That weekend, she broke her engage-
ment with James Wayne, and the following Saturday night she was sitting with my father at a restaurant that served inexpensive oysters on the
half-shell, listening to a band of black musicians—who could only enter
and exit through the rear entrance, who could not use the same water
fountains or bathrooms as white people, who avoided looking directly at
any of the white women while they played Dixieland jazz.

The summer of 1957 my father went off to Officer Candidate School.
Like my mother, he wanted to get out of Louisiana, but that's not why he
enlisted in the United States Marine Corps. He enlisted because of two
things his father had said. On their quiet street in Lafayette, my father
had spent a lot of time playing imaginary games outside. This was during
the war, men dying over in Europe and the South Pacific. Once his father
yelled at him, "Goddamnit, all you're good for is shooting Japs in the
backyard." When my father was a teenager, my grandfather looked down
at him and said, "When are you going to grow hair on your arms? You
look like a woman."

Within a few months of meeting, my mother and father had eloped;
she had married a writer and a Marine second lieutenant, he had married
a bright beauty from the working class. A few days after the justice of the
peace had joined them for life, my mother's father said to her, "If you get
divorced, don't bother coming home. There's been no damn divorces in
our family."

IT WAS the six of us: my young parents and all four of us kids born in a
five year period beginning in 1958. We were each born on Marine bases,
delivered by Marine doctors, Suzanne at Quantico in Virginia, me and
Jeb on Camp Pendleton in California, and Nicole on Whidbey Island
in Washington State. During these years, our father spent a lot of time
aboard the USS *Ranger* off the coast of Japan. When we did see him, it
was for brief stretches in cramped Marine base housing. His head was
shaved, his face smooth and clean, but he was a man who didn't smile

much, a man who seemed locked into a car on a road he didn't want to be on. But then my father's father died in 1963, and almost immediately after that Dad retired from the Marines as a captain and was accepted into the Iowa Writers' Workshop in Iowa City.

Though I didn't have words for it, I'd never seen him happier; he laughed often and loudly; he hugged and kissed our mother at every turn; he'd let his hair grow out long enough you could actually see some on his head, thick and brown. He'd grown a mustache, too. At night before bed, he'd sit me, my brother, and two sisters down at the kitchen table or on the couch in the living room and he'd tell us stories he made up himself—adventure stories where the hero and heroine were Indians defending their families and their people from the white man. One of them was Running Blue Ice Water, a kind and brave warrior who lingered in my imagination long after we'd been tucked in upstairs in a large room all four of us children shared.

My memory of that time is the memory of parties, though we were so broke we ate canned meat and big blocks of government cheese. Once a month Pop sold blood. But the parties went on. They happened at night, the house filled with talk and laughter and cigarette smoke. There were parties during the day, too. Blankets laid out on grass under the sun. Men and women eating sandwiches and sipping wine and reading poems out loud to each other.

Some parties were at the Vonneguts' house next door. All the Vonnegut kids were older than we were, but the father, Kurt, would walk down to our house every afternoon and sit with us four kids in the living room and watch *Batman* on the small black-and-white. He smoked one cigarette after the other. He laughed a lot and made jokes, and once he squinted down at me through the smoke and said: "Who's your favorite bad guy?"

"Um, False Face."

He smiled, his face a warm mix of mustache and round eyes and curly hair. "I like the Riddler."

IN OUR bedroom floor was an air vent that overlooked the living room, and sometimes on party nights we kids would huddle around it and spy on our mother and father and their friends below, watch them dance and drink and argue and laugh, the men always louder than the women, their cigarette smoke curling up through the grate into our faces. I remember hearing a lot of dirty words then but also ones like *story, novel,* and *poem. Hemingway* and *Chekhov.*

In the morning we'd be up long before our parents. We'd get cereal and poke around in the party ruins, the table and floors of our small house littered with empty beer bottles, crushed potato chips, overflowing ashtrays, half the butts brushed with lipstick. If there was anything left in a glass, and if there wasn't a cigarette floating in it, Suzanne and I would take a few sips because we liked the taste of watered-down whiskey or gin. Once we found a carrot cake in the living room. Its sides were covered with white frosting, but the middle was nothing but a mashed crater. I remembered the cake from the night before, a mouthwatering three-layer with frosted writing on the top. I asked my mother who it was for and she said it was for one of their friends who'd just sold his novel to a publisher; they were going to celebrate. And now the cake was unrecognizable, and when my mother came down that morning looking young and beautiful, probably in shorts and one of my father's shirts, smoking a cigarette, only twenty-five or -six, I asked her what had happened to the cake. She dug her finger into the frosting, then smiled at me. "Just your father and his crazy writer friends, honey." Did that mean he was a crazy writer, too? I wasn't sure.

It was another party at our house that confirmed it for me, though, one that began with jazz on the record player, a platter of cucumbers and carrots and horseradish dip on the kitchen table, glasses set out on the counter, and in his front room on his black wooden desk were two lit candles on either side of something rectangular and about two or three inches high covered with a black cloth. As my father's friends showed up one or two couples at a time, he'd walk them into his room with a drink or bottle of beer in his hand, and he'd point at what he told them was the failed novel he was holding a funeral for. He'd laugh and they'd laugh and one of his writer friends put his hand on his shoulder and squeezed, both of them looking suddenly pained and quite serious. I knew then my father was a writer too.

When our father's first book was published in 1967, he got a job teaching at a small college in Massachusetts. We loaded up our rusted Chevrolet and drove east. For a year we lived in the woods of southern New Hampshire in a rented clapboard house on acres of pine and pasture. We had a swimming pool and a herd of sheep. There were fallen pine needles and a brook along whose banks Jeb and I found arrowheads, smooth pebbles, the bleached bones of rabbits or squirrels. We felt rich; we had all that land to play on, we had that big old house—its dark inviting rooms, its fireplaces, its fading wallpaper and floorboards fastened with square-cut nails from before the Civil War; we had that *pool.*

In 1968 we moved again, this time to a cottage on a pond on the Massachusetts-New Hampshire border. I was nine, and so it seemed like a house, but it was really a summer camp. Downstairs was the kitchen and its worn linoleum floor, the small living room with the black-and-white TV where we heard of the killing of Martin Luther King Jr.; it's where we saw X-ray photos of Robert Kennedy's brain and the .22 caliber bullet shot into it; it's where the following summer we watched a man walk on the moon, my mother sitting on the arm of the couch in shorts and one of Pop's button-down shirts, saying, "We're on the moon, you guys. We're on the fucking *moon.*"

My father, thirty-two years old then, was earning seven thousand dollars a year teaching. He had a brown beard he kept trimmed, and he ran five miles a day, a ritual he had begun in the Marine Corps a few years earlier. My mother and father rarely had money to go out to a restaurant, but they still hosted a lot of parties at our house, usually on Friday or Saturday nights, sometimes both; my mother would set out saltine crackers and dip, sliced cheese and cucumbers and carrots; they'd open a jug of wine and a bucket of ice and wait for their friends to bring the rest: more wine, beer, bottles of gin and bourbon. Most of their friends came from the college where Pop taught: there was an art professor, a big man who wore black and had a clean-shaven handsome face and laughed loudly and looked to me like a movie actor; there were bearded poets and bald painters and women who taught pottery or literature or dance. There were students, too, mainly women, all of them beautiful, as I recall, with long shiny hair and straight white teeth, and they dressed in sleeveless sweaters or turtlenecks and didn't wear bras, their bell-bottoms hugging their thighs and flaring out widely over their suede boots.

The house would be filled with talk and laughter, jazz playing on the record player—a lot of Brubeck, Gerry Mulligan, and Buddy Rich. From my bed upstairs I could smell pot and cigarette smoke. I could hear music and the animated voices of my mother and father and their loud, intriguing friends. Sometimes there'd be yelling, and there'd be words like *Saigon, Viet Cong,* and *motherfucking Nixon.*

One weeknight on the news, there was a story about Marines killed in battle. I was lying on the floor under the coffee table as the camera panned over the bodies of soldiers lying on the ground, most of them on their stomachs, their arms splayed out beside them. Pop sat straight on the couch. His hands were on his knees, and his eyes were shining. "Pat, those are boys. Oh, goddamnit, those are eighteen-year-old *boys*."

Later, sleeping in the bed beside my brother's, there was a weight on my chest and I woke to my father holding me, crying into the pillow beside my ear. "My son, my son, oh, my son." He smelled like bourbon and sweat. It was hard to breathe. I couldn't pull my arms free of the blankets to hug Pop back. Then he was off me, crying over Jeb on his bed, and there was my mother's whisper from the doorway, her shadowed silhouette. Her arm reached for our father, and he stood and looked down at us both a long while, then he was gone. The house was quiet, my room dark and still. I lay awake and thought of all the good men on TV who'd been shot in the head. I saw again the dead soldiers lying on the ground, and until Pop had cried over us, I hadn't thought much about Jeb and me having to go and fight, too. But in only nine years I'd be as old as the dead, and it'd be my turn, wouldn't it?

BUT SOLDIERS have to be brave, and I was not; I was a new kid in school again, something I would be over and over for many years, trying to find a solitary desk away from the others, dreading recess because everybody knew everyone else and threw balls back and forth and chased after each other grabbing and laughing, and I just didn't have the courage to jump in. Then some kid would see me looking and yell, "What're you lookin' at? You got a *problem*?"

Sometimes I'd get shoved and kicked and pushed to the ground. I was still trying to figure out what I'd done to make them mad, I had not yet learned that cruelty was cruelty and you don't ask why, just hit first and hit hard.

There was more fighting at home. My parents must've tried to keep it from us because it seemed to happen only late at night, both of them screaming at each other, swearing, sometimes throwing things—pots or pans, a plate or glass or ashtray, anything close by. When they fought, their Southern accents were easier to hear, especially my mother's, "God-damn you, you sonofa*bitch*." Pop's voice would get chest-deep and he'd yell back at her as if she were a Marine under his command.

Many nights my brother and two sisters and I would listen from the stairs in our pajamas, not because we enjoyed it but because it was easier to bear when we weren't hearing it alone in our beds.

But by morning, the sun shone through the trees and most of the thrown or broken dishes in the living room would be picked up, the kitchen smelling like bacon and eggs, grits and toast and coffee, the night before a bad dream already receding into the shadows where it belonged.

FOR MY tenth birthday, I got a Daisy BB gun. It had a real wooden stock and a long metal barrel, and Pop took me out to the porch and showed me how to load it. It was a warm September morning, the sun glinting off the pond through the trees, and I could smell pine needles and tree bark and Pop's Old Spice as he put one arm around me and pulled the rifle stock into my shoulder, as he reminded me how to narrow one eye down between the metal sights at my target, how to hold my breath and squeeze the trigger, not pull it. I'd shot my first gun when I was five, a long-barreled .22 pistol that was hard to grip with both hands. Pop smiled and took the pistol from me and then I was grasping the feet of the rabbit he'd shot and Pop was skinning it with his KA-BAR knife from the Marines, the dead rabbit still warm but shitting pellets down my forearms. Four years later he taught me and Jeb how to aim and fire a .22 rifle, how you rest your cheek on the wooden stock and squint your eye and line the sights on your target, how you hold your breath before you squeeze the trigger, the empty soup can flying off the stump. He'd been an expert marksman in the Marines, taught us to never point an unloaded gun at anyone, that the man with the gun always walks ahead of those without, that a gun always stays unloaded in the house.

I pointed my new BB rifle at a spruce tree. I aimed and squeezed, the tick of the BB hitting the bark, a piece of it falling to the ground. "That's it," he said. "That's it."

Soon I was taking my gun off into the woods by myself. For a while I shot dusty beer cans off of rocks, leaves hanging still on a branch, thin dead branches that would crack with the shot. But I wanted to kill something. I wanted to aim my rifle at something that was alive and make it dead.

The woods were full of birds and squirrels, but they were always moving, the birds flitting from one tree to the next, the squirrels scampering up trunks into higher branches where they disappeared. But one afternoon, just past the boarded-up summer camps not far from our house, I saw a small blackbird perched on a limb. It was looking away from where I stood, and I raised my rifle, pushed the stock into my shoulder, aimed down the sights at the bird's small black breast, held my breath, and squeezed. There was the soft recoil of the rifle's spring, then the bird falling sideways off the branch to the ground. My heart was pulsing in both hands. I'd seen what I'd done with just one shot, and as I walked to the base of the tree, I felt like some lone hunter-warrior, a man who could do something that most could not. I looked down at the bird. There was no blood, and I couldn't see where the BB had entered, but the bird lay on its back, its dead eyes open, its gray beak pointing up at me like an accusation. I felt queasy. Saliva gathered in my mouth, and I wanted to flee my own skin somehow, this boy who had killed so easily, who had enjoyed it.

SINCE IOWA City, my family had lived in the country, places where Jeb and I spent hours and hours happily outside. We raided a tackle box we found and took long sticks and tied to them fishing line, bobbers, hooks, and pea-sized lead we pinched onto the line with pliers. We dug up worms and fished off the dock, catching perch and kibbies and bass. One week we found a towering pine deep in the trees, then ran back to the garage full of our landlord's tools. We stole his handsaw and hammer and a rusty can of nails, and we built a tree house out of scrap lumber we found under the other cottages. Another time we took his pick and a spade shovel and dug a hole for us to lie down in, then we cut pine branches with the hand-saw, the blade binding in the sappy grain, and we covered the hole with them and knew it was always there for our family to hide in, just in case the Viet Cong made it up into our woods. We found an ax in the garage and cut down saplings and sawed off their branches and leaned them all together in a widening circle for our teepee. We tied the tops together with string, and for the skin we used all the pine branches we'd already cut, weaving them in and around the poles from bottom to top. When we were done, we could crawl inside and stand up in a darkened conical room, the air smelling like pine sap and sweat and dust.

In the winter we'd build an igloo. From our gravel driveway it looked like a snowbank, but if you rolled aside a snow boulder you could crawl into a snow tunnel and come out into a snow room you could stand in. We carved benches into the walls and punched a hole through the ceiling for the smoke when we made a fire.

By now we had a friend who lived in one of the cottages on the other side of the pond. His name was Dean Matheson. He was long-limbed and yellow-toothed and at eleven years old said *shit* and *fuck*. He'd stolen a bone-handled switchblade, and we took turns in our igloo throwing it down at each other's feet, trying to stick it into the packed snow as close as possible to our toes, the first to pull away a chicken shit.

One day in the fall, when all the summer cottages next to ours were boarded up for the season, we found a box of shotgun shells in the attic. Our parents and sisters were off somewhere, and Jeb and Dean and I laid the shells at the base of a pine tree, poured gasoline over them, and lit them up just to watch them explode. But there was a breeze coming in off the pond and the flames grew and leapt and in no time one of the cottages was on fire. We ran into the woods. Some adult must've seen the smoke and soon a huge pumper truck came rattling over the gravel road and there were hoses and men yelling and sparks and steam, the house saved, but its front porch gone.

Our family got home to see two police cars. As Pop talked to one of the cops, he kept glancing down at me and Jeb crouching and waiting near the pond. And he didn't look mad; he looked scared and relieved; he looked guilty.

ONE SUNLIT afternoon in the early fall our parents sat us down in the living room and told us they were getting separated. My father stood in the kitchen doorway. My mother leaned against the wall on the other side of the room. *Separated.* It was a word I'd never thought much about before, but now I pictured them being cut one from the other with a big, sharp knife. I sat in my father's chair, and I couldn't stop crying.

Then Pop was gone for weeks. One night, after Suzanne and Jeb and Nicole were asleep, I lay in bed listening to my mother crying in her room. It sounded like she was doing it into her pillow, but I could still hear it, and I got up and walked down the creaking floorboards of the hallway and knocked on her door. Her bedside lamp was on. She lifted her head, wiped her eyes, and smiled at me. I asked her if she was all right. She sat up and looked me up and down. She said, "I'm going to tell you because you're old enough to hear it. Your father left me for Betsy Armstrong. That's where he is right now, staying with her."

Betsy was one of the rich girls from the college. She had long straight hair and a pretty face. I remembered her laughing once in the kitchen with my mother. Now my mother got out of bed and leaned down and hugged me. I hugged her back.

Then Pop was home again. I woke one morning and heard his voice downstairs. I ran down there, and he hugged me. Later that day he was in the bathroom shaving. I went in there just to watch. I was ten years old, he was thirty-three. He turned from the mirror and said, "So you know about Betsy then?"

The air in the room felt thicker somehow. "Yeah."

He reached into his wallet and pulled out a small photograph. He handed it to me. "That's her."

It was of a girl I barely remembered seeing before, not the one I'd thought she was. "She's pretty."

"Yes, she is." Pop took the photo and slid it back into his wallet. I left the bathroom and walked straight to the kitchen where Mom stood at the sink washing dishes. I looked up at her face. She smiled down at me.

"Dad's girlfriend is prettier than you are, Mom." Her smile faded and she looked into the dishwater and kept scrubbing. I walked back to the bathroom and told my father what I'd said.

He was wiping shaving cream from his face with a towel. He stopped, the towel still pressed to his cheek. "No, go apologize to her. Go tell her you're sorry right now."

I ran outside and into the woods. I don't remember ever apologizing to my mother, but Pop was back, girlfriend or not, and for a while things seemed to get back to normal, and there was less fighting than before. Each night when Pop came home from teaching, Mom would be cooking in the kitchen and they'd have cocktail hour, which meant none of us kids was allowed in there while they sipped Jim Beam and our father unwound and told Mom his day and she told him hers.

Soon the hour would be over, and the six of us would sit at the rickety table in that small, hot kitchen and we'd eat. We lived in New England, but at suppertime our house smelled like any in South Louisiana: Mom fried chicken, or simmered smothered breakfast steak or cheap cuts of pork, all served up with rice and gravy and baking powder biscuits. On the side there'd be collard greens or sliced tomatoes, cucumbers, and onions she'd put ice cubes on to keep crisp. She baked us hot tamale pies, and macaroni and cheese, or vegetable soup she'd cook for hours in a chicken stock, then serve in a hollowed-out crust of French bread, its top a steaming layer of melted cheddar. But while the food was wonderful, my mother and father hardly even looked at one another anymore and instead kept their attention on us, asking about school, about the tree fort Jeb and I were building out in the woods, about the Beatles album Suzanne listened to, the drawings Nicole did each afternoon. We rarely left the table hungry, but there was a hollowness in the air, a dark unspeakable stillness, one my father would soon drive into, and away.

IT HAPPENED early on a Sunday in November. Pop was so much taller than the four of us, and we were following him down the porch stairs and along the path, Suzanne behind him in her cotton nightgown, then me and Jeb in our pajamas, Nicole last, her thick red hair and small face. We were eleven, ten, nine, and six. Ahead of us, there was the glint of frost on the gravel driveway and our car, the old Lancer, packed now with Pop's things: his clothes, his books, his shaving kit. The house was surrounded by tall pines and it was too cold to smell them, the air so clear and bright. Inside the house Mom was crying as if her pain were physical, as if someone were holding her down and doing something bad to her.

Daddy! Nicole ran past us over the gravel and she leapt and Pop turned, his eyes welling up, and he caught her, her arms around his neck, her face buried under his chin. I tried to ignore our mother's cries coming from the house. When my father looked down at me over Nicole's small shoulder, I stood as straight as I could and I hoped I looked strong.

Pop kissed Nicole's red hair. He lowered her to the gravel. His beard was thick and dark, his cheeks and throat shaved clean. He was wearing a sweatshirt and corduroy pants, and he glanced up at our house. There was only the sound of our mother's cries, so maybe he would change his mind. Maybe he would stay.

He looked down at us. "I'll see you soon. We'll go out to eat."

He hugged Suzanne, squeezed my shoulder. He tousled Jeb's hair, then he was in his car driving down the hill through the pines, blue exhaust coughing out its pipe. Jeb scooped up a handful of gravel and ran down the hill after him, "You bum! You bum! You bum!" He threw it all at once, the small rocks scattering across the road and into the woods like shrapnel.

Pop drove across the short bridge, then up a rise through more trees. Mom would need to be comforted now. Nicole too. There was food to think about. How to get it with no car. I tried to keep standing as straight as I could.

SOMETIMES WHEN the husband leaves, his friends leave with him. That's what happened to my mother; after Pop was gone, so too were his friends. And the parties. I don't know how long it was before my mother was able to buy a second car or got her first job working as a nurse's aide, or when exactly she went back to school, got her degree, and started working in social services. I do remember that we moved even more frequently now, from one cheap rented house to the next.

To be closer to Pop, we ended up in Massachusetts and moved to the first of three towns we would live in on the Merrimack River. It was 1969, and for the first time since moving East from Iowa, we lived in a house on a street with a sidewalk and other houses and there were kids to play with, and so we played.

Once more we were the new kids in school. Jeb and I had long hair and sat in the back of the bus singing Beatles songs to the girls next to us. They began to like us, which was a sweet surprise, and then a few of the boys did too. Every day after school and that summer Jeb and I played war with Craig and Danny D. and Scotty K.; it's what we knew from the TV every night. It's what grown-ups argued about and lost friendships over. And we killed all day long.

Danny D.'s father had a barn full of junk. We found a box of brass light sockets which we turned into hand grenades because you could yank the chain and hurl the socket and if one landed close to you, you were gone. We knew about the Viet Cong stabbing our soldiers' bodies after they were dead just to make sure they were dead, so when some of us were down, the others went around poking sticks into their back or ribs.

Danny D.'s big brothers, Gary and Sean, would light firecrackers and toss them at us. They'd let us come to their room and listen to the Doors and watch them smoke dope. One rainy afternoon, Sean, who was big with dull brown eyes, tied me to a utility pole out back of the barn and stacked twigs at my feet. He covered them with gas from the lawn mower and tried to light me up. But the gas was mixed with oil, and his matches were damp from his pocket, and when he ran back into the house for more I wrenched my wrists from the rope and ran for home.

In the summer, we'd catch frogs down on the muddy banks and haul them back in a coffee can. We'd stack bricks into a square prison yard and drop the frogs in, then Sean would douse them with gasoline, light a cherry bomb or M-80, and jump back for the bang and flame and smoke. Danny's brother Gary, sixteen maybe, with long brown hair and a cross around his neck, he'd tie the blackened frogs' bodies together with string, then run it to the back of his three-speed and drag them up and down the street. I'd be laughing with the rest, but that queasiness would come again.

Years later Gary would die running from the cops.

It was after midnight and it'd been a long, dangerous chase along the back roads and the police had radioed ahead for the drawbridge over the Merrimack to be raised. I don't know what Gary was driving, but he must've thought it was light and fast because when he got to the bridge it was already rising past 40 degrees and he gave the engine all it had and flew up into the air, then down into the swirling black water where he drowned.

Once I was sleeping over and Big Sean squeezed my neck in a headlock, digging his knuckles hard into my skull. I screamed, and Gary came out of his room. Jim Morrison was singing. Gary wore only underwear and a T-shirt, and he punched Sean in the back and slapped him twice in the face.

"Fuckin' leave him alone, all *right*? He's a nice kid, Sean. He's a good *kid*."

"I didn't do nothin'." Sean let go. Gary looked down at me, his dark eyes fiery and sad and kind, and he turned and walked back into his room and shut the door.

THE SUMMER of 1970 was hot and dry, and we moved to Newburyport where Mom had gotten a job working for Head Start helping poor kids. Newburyport was at the mouth of the river, the Atlantic Ocean three miles away on the other side of the salt marshes. The town was called "Clipper City" because of all the sailing ships built here in the 1800s, but when we came along the place looked abandoned. The streets of downtown were lined with empty mill buildings, their windows boarded up, some of the plywood rotted and hanging by one corner so you could walk in and step over loose papers, dusty machine parts, dog and bird shit, maybe human too. The only businesses still open were three barrooms, a diner, and a newsstand. In Market Square, two or three battered cars were left on the curb, their tires gone, a windshield caved in.

We lived three streets east of downtown on Fair in a half-house we were renting. On the other side lived another single mother. Her kids were small and dirty and she would leave her windows open and you could hear her TV all day and night, even when she was sitting on the stoop drinking a can of beer and smoking. Across the street was an empty lot with weeds, dry and yellow and high as our chests. Jeb and I thought we'd build something deep in there where no one could see you, but some drunks had gotten there first, their camp a steel barrel they sat around on broken lawn chairs and a naked mattress covered with stains so brown I was convinced they had to be blood.

Kids roamed the neighborhood like dogs. The first week I was sitting in the sun on our steps, I made the mistake of watching them go by as they walked up the middle of the street, three or four boys with no shirts, a couple of girls in shorts and halter tops. The tallest one, his short hair so blond it looked white, said, "What're you lookin' at, fuck face?"

"Nothing."

Then he was on our bottom step. He pushed me hard in the chest and kicked my shin. "You want your face rearranged, faggot?"

"No."

Maybe he walked off after that, maybe he punched me in the head, I'm not sure, but of all the places we'd lived so far it was clear this was going to be the meanest.

From our open windows, the inside of the house hot as a box, there was the day-and-night swearing and shouting of men and women fighting; we could hear the lowriders revving their engines out front of the Hog Penny Head Shop down the block; there was the constant rumble of motorcycles two streets over. On the hottest days you could smell the wood from the lumberyard on the other side of Water Street, the piss and shit of the drunks in the weeds, the engine exhaust, the sweet lead of the paint flaking off our clapboards.

Food was scarce now. Even with our father's child support payments, only a few hundred a month, my mother just didn't make enough to keep the fridge and cabinets stocked. It was hard enough keeping the rent paid on time, the electricity on, the phone. It was hard enough just to keep all four of us growing kids in at least one pair of pants, shirts, and underwear, and a pair of shoes that might last a year. It was hard enough to keep her succession of used cars gassed up and running, though I don't believe she ever filled a tank; so many times she'd pull up to the pumps, dig through her purse for change, smile at the attendant, and say something like, "A dollar and fourteen cents' worth, please."

What money she did have budgeted for food went to meals she could

cook quickly after she got home from work. Canned soup or stew, macaroni and cheese, or the one we had most often, Frito Pie. Standing there
in her earrings and work clothes—ironed pants and a blouse, maybe a
bracelet around her wrist—she'd open a bag of Fritos, spread some out on
the bottom of a casserole dish, then dump in two cans of Hormel chili,
cover it with a layer of raw onions, more Fritos, and grated cheese. She'd
bake this for thirty or forty minutes, the smell filling the downstairs like
home cooking used to, and then we'd all grab a bowlful and eat on the
floor in front of *The Waltons* or *All in the Family*. Many nights she'd come
home with grease-stained bags from McDonald's or Burger King, convenient meals she couldn't afford.

Once a week, usually a Sunday, Pop would pick us up in his old Lancer
and take the four of us to an air-conditioned movie. We'd sit in the cool
dark of the theater eating hot buttery popcorn, sipping a cold sweet Coke,
the movie stars so handsome and beautiful, and it was like being on furlough from a penal colony, the hug from Pop as he dropped us back off, the
smell of Old Spice on his cheek above his beard, his hand patting my back.

AFTER A few months, we moved to Arlington Street on the North End. It
was a street with trees on it and houses that seemed looked after, and there
were no more roaming kids or fighting sounds, and we settled in for a year
in a whole house with a fenced backyard and grass. Across the street was
the hospital, and we could hear the ambulances come and go, their sirens
starting up or winding down. Sometimes they'd come back quiet, and I
was sure whoever they'd picked up was dead inside.

The North End was districted to a different school where I was new
and the first morning a tall kid asked me what I was looking at and I said
nothing and he and his two friends pushed me down and kicked me once
or twice and after that I stayed in the dark corners and kept my head
down and my mouth shut.

Maybe we'd moved so much we didn't know how to make friends,
maybe we'd just gotten too used to keeping to ourselves, but on Arlington
Street the four of us, no matter the weather, still spent afternoons in front
of the TV. Mom would get home after dark and more and more now, her
boyfriends were coming over too. One looked like an outlaw; he had long

blond hair and a handlebar mustache, and he wore tight jeans and pretended he was interested in us. There was Maurice, a big and kind black man who, when they broke up, gave Mom a 45 record of Charley Pride's rendition of "For the Good Times." He asked her to please play it again and again. There was Dick from the South End whom she never liked but who came around all the time anyway. He was tall and had big arm muscles and short hair. Once we all had the flu and he showed up at the door with a bottle of penicillin.

"*Penicillin?*" my mother said. "Are you *crazy*? You don't just give kids *penicillin.*"

He insisted she take it from him, this nearly quart-size brown bottle of antibiotic. It looked stolen from some warehouse.

He went away, but I think he sat in his car outside a lot, waiting, hoping she'd change her mind and love him. He must've been there on a Sunday when Pop came by to get us; for a month we didn't see Dick. Then late on a weeknight, all five of us in front of the TV, a bearded man knocked on the door. He was tall with Dick's arm muscles. My mother opened the door partway.

"It's me, Patty. It's *Dickie,*" and he laughed and ran his fingers through his whiskers. "See? I got a beard, hippie style! Just like your ex. I seen you like that so I grew it. See? Hippie style."

I don't know what she said to that, but she went out to the porch and stood under the light talking to him for a long time and we didn't see him anymore after that.

THE FOLLOWING summer the landlord raised the rent and we had to move back to the South End, to Lime Street, a place many people from town called "Slime Street." It was where Suzanne and I would go to school at the Jackman, three stories of crumbling brick I would learn years later had been condemned by the city but still stayed open for the kids of the South End. We now lived in an old clapboard house so close to the street you had to be careful not to step out too quickly onto the sidewalk or you'd fall into traffic. There was a small dirt yard in back I liked because it had a solid plank fence around it and nobody could see me there. I could be outside but invisible. I was hiding all the time.

Across the street lived the Whelans. There were always three or four cars and trucks in their side yard, some on blocks, the hoods open or gone, and the father, Larry, worked on the engines every afternoon. He was short and had no front teeth and he drank from cans of Pabst he'd rest on the chassis. I don't remember how many kids lived there, but a few years later his oldest son would go to prison for raping his twenty-seven-month old niece. Another would go for some other crime. And I assume that's what happened to Clay.

At fourteen or fifteen Clay Whelan was over six feet and slope-shouldered and sullen and mean. When he first saw me—flabby, weak, and quiet—he saw a target, and for the next year he'd corner me at school and squeeze my throat till I couldn't breathe, he'd chase me the two blocks home and punch and kick me to the ground. He'd call Jeb a faggot and Suzanne and Nicole fuckin' sluts, and I did nothing but run into the house and hide.

More than ever now, the four of us stayed in every day after school and watched that one-eyed machine that would take us to other worlds. Hours and hours of it. Mom would get home between six and seven and fix us something quick and cheap, usually frozen or from a can, then the five of us would sit in the dark living room only feet from the street and watch more TV. If she looked over and asked me where I'd gotten a bruise or a cut, I'd tell her recess, playing. But recess at the Jackman was a forty-five-minute break on a square of asphalt out back where there were no balls and half the kids stood around taking drags off Marlboros then turning their heads to blow smoke away should one of the teachers see, though I don't remember many teachers being out there. And these boys were even tougher than Clay Whelan.

There was Cody Perkins, as short as I was but lean and loud. One morning in the middle of history, Mrs. Hamilton was talking about the Louisiana Purchase and he walked into the class and shouted to the back of the room, "Say it to my face, Sullivan. Say it to my fuckin' *face!*"

Sullivan was the biggest kid in school. In the sixth grade he was as tall as Clay but weighed close to 200 pounds. A month before, a wiry boy in the hallway said something to Sully he didn't like and he whirled around and punched him in the face and knocked him out. Now he was back from his suspension and Cody Perkins, half his size, was waiting for him in front of class. Mrs. Hamilton started yelling at Perkins to leave, but Perkins was breathing hard like he just ran here, his eyes on Sullivan who was up and coming for him.

I was sitting close to this. I knew Sullivan would kill Perkins and I couldn't understand how such a small kid could be so crazy, so brave.

Somebody called out, "Kill him, Sully. Beat his head in."

Cody threw himself in the air and punched Sully in the chest. It was like watching a building crumble, the way Sullivan's head dropped and his shoulders slumped and he curled forward into the air he couldn't breathe anymore, his mouth open, his face gray, and Cody Perkins was punching him in the side of the head, in both eyes, in his nose and still-open mouth. Now there were more teachers in the room, two men who pulled Perkins off and he was kicking and trying to jerk himself away and only when he was gone did I remember he'd been screaming the whole time, not words but an anguished, unrelenting sound that could only come from some raging beast.

Sully lay curled on the floor. He was bleeding and crying and still trying to breathe. He left school and I never saw him again and though I never spoke to Cody Perkins or he to me, I saw him all the time; I liked how loud he was. I liked how he walked around the Jackman or down the street with his chest out. A decade later he would become a prizefighter whose picture I would see tacked to telephone poles and the doors of barrooms. Sullivan had seemed nice enough, but I liked how Cody Perkins had destroyed him all by himself. Not like me, who hid daily from Clay and was too ashamed to tell my mother about getting chased and beat up three or four days a week, how I'd trip and fall and he would catch up to me, his eyes dark and intent, like this was something he just had to do, and the first punch was a green flash behind my eyes, the second a white shard, the third a dark mist, the fourth a muffled thud. By then I'd have curled up on the sidewalk or whatever backyard he'd found me in and he'd kick my back and head and legs, screaming or silent, breathing hard, walking away only when he was finished.

ONE NIGHT a drunk walked off Lime Street into our house. It was after ten and we were watching TV, Mom upstairs and asleep for hours already,

Nicole too. In the flickering blue light, I heard the man pissing, pissing on the floorboards of our hallway. Suzanne and Jeb and I looked at each other, then we watched him zip up and step back out onto Lime, a shadow stumbling under the streetlights.

I don't remember who cleaned it up, but the next night we sat in front of the TV eating food Mom had brought us from Burger King, and Suzanne said, "That kid across the street beats the shit out of Andre every day, you know."

"What? *Who?*"

"That kid Clay. That fuckin' moron Clay."

IT'D BEEN years since we'd seen Pop on a weeknight. It was a Tuesday or Wednesday in the spring. It was cool and the sun was going down and the last of its light made Larry's cars look etched in the air, made him look more real standing there in his dirty white T-shirt and his no front teeth talking to my father. Pop looked so out of place. He wore corduroys and a sweater and loafers. Larry hadn't shaved in two or three days, but Pop's beard was meticulously trimmed, his cheeks and throat shaved smooth. I watched all this from one of our windows facing the street, my heart pulsing dully in my neck, a sickening sweat breaking out on my chest; part of me was relieved my father was here, but the rest of me hated myself for needing his help, and now I was scared because Clay ran out of his house, his shouting mother behind him, and he went after my father the same way he went after me, his right fist up, ready to throw it, and Larry stiff-armed him in the chest and was yelling so loud I could hear it through the glass, fuckin' this and fuckin' that, Larry's face a dark hole.

Pop hadn't taken a step back, but he was pointing his finger at Clay like he was scolding him, trying to reason with him. He was talking to him like he might be a student in that place of rich kids where he taught in that green world that wasn't ours, and I just knew Clay Whelan was about to beat up my father and any hope I may have felt would be stomped and I'd be forever running and looking over my shoulder and hiding wherever there was a door and a lock and no key.

But Larry somehow sent Clay back inside. The screen door slammed behind him and his mother stood there in her sweats, her arms crossed under her heavy breasts. She eyed Pop like he was a foreigner.

Afterward, sitting in our small dusty living room, Pop told me the father had banned his son from ever going near me again.

"*Banned* him?"

"I don't think he used that word."

I knew my dad used words like that. I knew he wrote books and taught English to college kids, and it was strange having him be in our world for even this long and I was ashamed and wanted him to leave. But I was grateful to him for coming, and as he drove down Lime Street in his underpaid professor's car, Larry back at work on the engine of a Buick, Clay's house quiet in the lengthening shadows, I knew things had just gotten a lot worse.

FOR A week I saw him at the Jackman, in the halls, in the asphalt yard, in the street out front, but he stayed away from me. He was like a wolf who'd been caught and defanged and sent back out into the wild a different wolf. But on the afternoon of the fifth day, the sun high over the clustered houses of the South End, George Labelle walked into our house and the living room where I sat with my brother and sisters in front of the TV. He was as big as Sullivan but fat, as mean as Clay but subservient, and he grabbed me by the shirt and yanked me to my feet. He had the beginnings of a mustache and he smelled like B.O. and Pepsi, and I was holding on to his fists as he started dragging me to the front door, making grunting sounds, his body so much larger than mine. I had never spoken to him and knew him only by name and I knew he was going to kill me once he got me onto Lime.

Labelle's face jerked forward. His eyes began to water. He let go of me and covered his head, and that's when I saw Suzanne and the broom she held, its stiff bristles she kept jabbing at his skull. "Get out! Get the fuck *out*!"

Labelle turned and she poked him in the face. He blinked and jumped back. "*Shit!* He paid me! Clay fuckin' *paid* me!"

"I said get *out*!" Suzanne jabbed him in the ear, the neck, the back of his head. Then he was fumbling with the doorknob and running across Lime Street to Clay waiting there on the sidewalk, his face a mixture of disappointment and amusement, his hit man kicked out of the house by my sister, my big sister Suzanne.

SOMETIMES I'D have trouble breathing. I'd be standing in our small kitchen, my hands on the sink, and a big, invisible hand would squeeze my chest and rib cage. The room would start to tilt, and I'd sit on the floor awhile and stare straight ahead at the shifting wall. I'd stare at any blemish on my skin. I didn't have many, but whenever I did I was convinced I'd been bitten by something poisonous—a spider or small snake that had slithered up from the river and into our house. I'd wake in the middle of the night and walk down the creaking stairwell to the bathroom and turn on the buzzing fluorescent light; I'd stare at a small red spot on my arm, convinced since I'd gone to bed that it had moved farther up toward my shoulder where it would soon disappear into my chest and heart and kill me. Sweat would break out on my forehead and the back of my neck. My mouth would be as dry as when Whelan chased me down the street. I didn't want to give my mother something else to worry about, nor did I want her to see such fear and weakness in me, so I'd wake Suzanne in the tiny room she shared with Nicole. My older sister would climb out of bed and turn on the overhead bulb. She'd rub her eyes and squint down at the spot on my arm. "Andre, that's a fucking *zit*. Go to sleep."

SUMMER CAME and now windows were open and there was Larry's yelling, there was a woman yelling back at him or somebody else in another house, there was the canned laughter and commercial jingles of six or seven TVs, there was a bottle breaking, a drunk singing, a motorcycle or lowrider revving its engine, then peeling away from the curb, there were the smells of hot asphalt, the dusty concrete of broken sidewalks, cat shit and dog shit and gasoline, there was the wood baking in the lumberyard near the Merrimack, again the faint smell of sewage and motor oil and mud, and when the wind blew in from the east you could smell the ocean, dead seaweed and open seashell and wet sand, and it was a Saturday and Jeb and I were running from Clay and Labelle and two others I didn't even know; they'd come walking down the middle of Lime Street under the sun and seen us sitting on our stoop doing nothing.

"Get 'em!"

And we were up and running down Lime and across Water Street. We climbed a rusted chain-link fence and came down on a pallet of plywood and jumped off it to the ground. We ran past a forklift, its driver watching us under his cap, a cigarette between his lips, and my chest hurt and the air was too hot but we couldn't stop and we ran past stacks of naked two-by-fours and two-by-sixes and two-by-eights, and we climbed onto this last stack and leapt over the fence into high weeds and chunks of broken cinderblock, and we kept running.

We ended up under a pier on the river. It was cool and shaded under there. We crouched beneath heavy planks and cross timbers, their posts black with creosote, the lower ones near the water covered with white and green barnacles. Half sunk in the mud were broken glass and a couple of tires, and we could see beyond this to the sun glinting off the river. It felt safe.

Jeb, eleven and thin but taller than I was, started gathering up pieces of colored glass. Even then he was making things: little sculptures made from junk, pictures he drew, watercolors, and he was always taking things apart—fan engines, radios, once the back of our TV just to see how it worked. He needed to know how things *worked*.

I was happy to stay down here forever. Go steal some plywood and some nails and tools and build a floor and walls under the pier, make it a place only Jeb and I would know about. It was going to be hard to get back to the house without being seen. We'd have to wait till dark.

I heard the helicopter before I saw it, the *thock-thock-thock* of its massive blades, the way the water spread out smooth and rippling as it hovered over the middle of the river. Then there was an orange and white boat there too, the letters coast guard painted on its bow, two men in black wet suits and scuba gear jumping into the Merrimack.

We knew what they were looking for. People drowned in that river. It had one of the most dangerous currents in the country, especially here, at its mouth, and I wished we'd left then before the divers brought up the body. It was bloated to three times a man's normal size, the round head matted with blond hair, the face a pale pumpkin, his mouth open, dark, and bottomless.

We didn't know how we'd get back home without being found, but Jeb dropped his pieces of glass and we both crawled fast out from under that pier and ran under the sun.

THE HOUSE was almost always dirty. Whatever chores Mom would give us, we just did not do. But some days, cooped up in that small hot house, one or two of us would finally leave the TV, grab the broom, and start sweeping the floorboards, the narrow wooden stairs and hallway. We might wash the backed-up dishes in the kitchen, find the mop and scrub the floor. We'd go up to our rooms and make our beds, pick dirty clothes out of the corners, and stuff them into a garbage bag for when we went to the laundromat. Sometimes I'd go out to our tiny enclosed yard and sweep the concrete stoop. In the corner of the fence was a rusty rake and I'd use it on our dirt yard. I made straight even lines parallel to the fence. It was still a dirt yard, but standing on the concrete stoop after, looking down at it, our home seemed somehow more orderly, our lives within it more comprehensible.

NONE OF Mom's cars ever worked for long, but she was able to drive home the Head Start van and at least two Friday nights a month, she would load the four of us into it and take us on a Mystery Ride. If we asked where we were going, she'd say, "Who knows? It's a *mystery*."

Suzanne, at thirteen, wearing hip-huggers and smoking Kools in her room, acted like she was too old for this game, but I think she secretly liked it as much as Jeb, Nicole, and I did, each of us sitting on our own seat, the windows open, the radio playing rock and roll, the warm air blowing in as we drove out of the South End and the abandoned buildings of downtown. Sometimes we'd get on the highway and go fast and leave it all behind. Or else Mom would stay on the back roads near the Merrimack, winding through groves of hardwood and pines where people with enough money lived in houses you could barely see from the road.

Mom—only thirty-three years old, slender, and beautiful to men, I knew, because they were still always coming around—she nodded her head to the music and blew the smoke from her Pall Mall out the window and she sang along and tried to raise us all up out of the hole we were in.

Soon we'd be hungry and somehow the mystery ended at Skippy's, a hamburger joint built off a fast two-lane in the pine trees. The cheeseburgers were cheap and juicy, and they were served in red-and-white-checkered baskets heaped with curlicue fries. We'd sit at a picnic table spotted with squirrel and pigeon shit, and we'd eat this hot and perfect food and wash it down with cold Cokes.

Afterward, if she had the money, we'd continue our Mystery and find ourselves at the drive-in, the sun setting over a massive movie screen rising up out of scrub and weeds. Because of the van, she had to park in the far back and she'd pull it sideways so we could hook three or four speakers onto our open windows, each of us with our own bench seat to stretch out on.

Most of the movies were rated R and most were bad; I remember fast cars and naked breasts and pistol barrels flashing in the sun. Some disturbed me, like *Joe* where a father hates hippies and gets another father to go shoot up a commune where the first father accidentally kills his own daughter, her dead body lying bloody in the snow. There was *Who Is Harry Kellerman and Why Is He Saying Those Terrible Things About Me?*, Dustin Hoffman playing a hit music composer who has a split personality and ends up committing suicide in his private plane. There was Woody Allen, who talked fast and said funny things about sex I was embarrassed to hear in the van with my mother. But it was the Clint Eastwood westerns I really liked; he could shoot and kill and did it all night long to bad men who'd done bad things to him and his family. He didn't run from them. He didn't hide. He faced them, usually three or four at once, and in just a few words he told them what he thought of them, then drew his Colt and gunned them down like the pigs they were.

One Friday when there was a warm, misty rain and we had to roll the van's windows up, we watched *Billy Jack*. The lead actor wore a tight black T-shirt that showed off his chest and arm muscles, and he plays an Indian and a Green Beret who fought in Vietnam. He's also a master in some form of martial art, and he spends a lot of time alone, walking softly, his carved and handsome face shadowed beneath the brim of his black cowboy hat and its band of beads. But then his wife, a kind and pretty blonde, opens a Freedom School for Native American children on the reservation and when she drives the kids into town for ice cream, they get chased out by white racists and she ends up being staked to the ground spread-eagled where she's raped and left to the ants and the sun and Billy Jack spends the rest of the movie hunting down the men who did it and he beats them to death using roundhouse kicks to the temple, straight rights to the face and heart and groin, fast and lethal moves I'd never seen, these cruel, vicious men reduced to silent bloody heaps on the floor or in the dust.

That night I couldn't sleep; my heart wouldn't slow down. I kept seeing myself do that to Clay Whelan and George Labelle and every kid who'd ever punched or kicked or pushed me; I saw myself doing it to the drunk who'd pissed in our hallway; I saw myself doing it to the two or three boyfriends of my mother's I never liked; I saw myself doing it to anyone, everyone.

3

___

ONE SUNDAY AFTERNOON, Pop drove up to our house on Lime with Theo Metrakos. He had thinning dark hair and a thick mustache, and he was an inch or two shorter than my father but well-built. He was a first-generation Greek studying for his Ph.D. in literature, one of Pop's roommates in an apartment in Bradford, though I didn't know any of this at the time. All I knew is he had muscles like Billy Jack, that later in the day I cut my foot on a piece of broken glass in the sand and Metrakos carried me piggyback a hundred yards up the beach to the blanket where Pop had a cooler with ice and drinks. I put ice on the cut, and Metrakos ran back to the water and dived in and swam over the waves and stayed out there swimming for close to an hour.

This beach was ten or twelve miles away on the New Hampshire coast. Sometimes, if a Sunday was real hot and Pop couldn't afford a movie, he'd take us there. He'd park his Lancer across from a row of tiny beach houses and lead us over the bright sand to a wide-open place scattered with families and couples and little kids, the waves breaking softly in front of us. While we were pale and sunburned easily, he was tanned and had his shirt off right away, his chest and flat belly covered with dark, curly hair, his skin a deep red-brown. He'd lay out a blanket for us, then roll out a reed mat for himself. When I was older, I would learn this had always been his favorite season, that after a morning of writing, then a long run, he came here every afternoon to read and doze and lie in the sun. Most of the time he'd bring a girlfriend with him, though he rarely did when he was with us. Maybe because there wasn't room in the car. Maybe because he didn't want to mix his two lives, but I knew from photos he'd still sometimes show me that his girlfriends were young and rich-looking and beautiful, students he'd met at the college.

At the end of the day, the sun setting in the dunes behind us, Metrakos put on running shoes and ran the fifteen miles home. He left thirty minutes before we did but was already four miles down the road when we saw him. He wore a bandanna around his head and no shirt, his back gleaming with sweat. As we passed, Pop honked the horn and we all waved at Theo and he smiled and waved back. On both sides of us were salt marshes, acres of mudflats and sea grass, deep yellow-green under the last of the sun. I sat back in my seat and wondered how anyone could run *fifteen* miles. I also liked how kind Metrakos was, how respectful he was to everyone he talked to. And smart, too. Educated.

OUR MOTHER had a new boyfriend now, Bruce M. Her other boyfriends looked like convicts compared to him; he picked her up on a Saturday night in the summer, and as soon as he pulled to our curb on Lime Street, we knew this one was different. He didn't drive a beat-up van or a motor-cycle or a loud muscle car, he drove a sleek gray Jaguar XJ6, a car I didn't even know existed, and when he stepped out of it, we saw a slim, clean-shaven man wearing good shoes, ironed pants, and a shirt and *tie.* It was navy blue, and when he got close enough, we could see dozens of tiny peace signs sewn into it.

Mom introduced us to him and he smiled down at each of us and reached out his hand. He actually looked happy to meet us. Mom wore a skirt and earrings and as they crossed Lime in the late-afternoon light, the four of us huddled at a window and watched him open the passenger door for her. He laughed easily at something she said, then he walked around the hood of the Jaguar and climbed in behind the wheel. We must've been leaning on the curtain because the rod pulled from the window jambs and came down on us and we all hit the floor laughing, sure they saw us spying.

"I like that one," Suzanne said.

"I hope she *marries* him."

One of us said that. I don't remember who, but it could have been me.

HE SLEPT over that first night and most every weekend after that. He gave Mom money and there was food in the fridge, gas in the car, and he drove us to Schwinn Bicycles up the river and bought each of us a brand-new bike. I forget what the girls got, but Jeb picked out a yellow ten-speed and I chose a bright tangerine five-speed chopper with a banana seat and two-foot sissy bar in the back. It looked just like the motorcycle Peter Fonda rode in *Easy Rider*. It was the bike of outlaws.

That afternoon we rode those bikes up and down the streets of the South End. When the sun went down, Bruce wanted to take us all out to eat somewhere and before we left, Jeb and I went out back with our new rubber-coated chain locks and ran them through the four bike frames, locking them to a cross-brace in the fence. I checked the latch on the gate, then dragged two cinderblocks over and wedged them against it.

At the restaurant, an air-conditioned one in Andover that had white linen table cloths and rolled napkins, Bruce said we could order whatever we wanted. He and Mom sipped bourbons and laughed a lot and kept looking at each other over the table. We'd never gone out with any of her other boyfriends before. Part of me felt guilty; if there was going to be a man eating at the table with Mom and us, it should be Pop, shouldn't it? But Bruce was warm and easy to talk to and somehow whatever we said, he found interesting or funny or intelligent, and he would say so, looking us directly in the eye.

I looked away. I looked down at my plate. In our weekly dinners with Pop, he would talk with the four of us too, but he didn't look us in the eye very long. Instead, there was the feeling he had a lot to do, that this meal was something it was hard for him to take time for. But there was something else, too. Many years later, when I was in my twenties and staying for a few weeks with my father and his third wife Peggy, I'd watch her set a romantic dinner for the two of them, light candles, and complain later that he never wanted to eat that way with her. "Why?" I asked.

"Because he's shy. Don't you know that about him? Your father is actually *shy*." But Bruce wasn't, and he was looking at me in a way no adult ever had, not a man anyway.

WE GOT home from the restaurant after dark, and I walked straight through the house to turn on the outside light and look at my bike. At first I thought I was seeing dead snakes. Our cut bike chains were lying in the dirt and the rest of the yard was empty, the gate wide open.

Then I knew what I was seeing, and how could we have been so stupid? Why did we go riding those bikes in this neighborhood, advertising them like that? And I should've known you can't trust good things to stay good. I should have known that.

Lying in bed that night, Nicole crying in her room, Suzanne still trying to soothe her, Jeb silent in his bed beside mine, I pictured us getting home just as the bike thieves were putting the hacksaw to our chains. In my vision they were grown men and I was the first in the yard and I said nothing to them, just started punching and kicking until they were dead. Not hurt, but dead.

A few days later I was sitting on our front step, one eye open—the way it always was—for Clay Whelan. The sun was high over the town, and a kid on a bike came riding up from Water Street. I could see the chopper forks and the sissy bar. I could see the knob of the five-speed gear shifter, and as the rider got closer I could see the frame itself was no longer orange but a dull, spray-painted black and red and green. The kid started pedaling standing up and I saw how new the seat looked, how brightly orange it shone in the sunlight, though it'd been sliced down the middle to make it look older, its white foam protruding like guts.

My heart was punching a hole in my chest and I was about to run into the street. Then I saw who the rider was: Cody Perkins. He glanced down at me like I was not there. Like I was *not*. And I watched him pedal my new bike all the way up Lime Street and away.

THE MAILMAN came in the afternoons while the four of us sat in front of the TV. Our mailbox was rusty and hung crooked against the clapboards, and we could hear him opening it, the creak of its hinges, his footsteps walking away on the concrete. One afternoon amongst the bills was a blue envelope from Lake Jackson, Texas. It was addressed to all of us, and Suzanne opened it. It was a card from our mother's older sister, our Aunt Jeannie, and her husband, our Uncle Eddie, two people we'd heard of but barely knew. Inside it were four checks, each one made out to each of us kids for fifty dollars. The four of us looked at each other. We kept looking down at the checks in our hands, but I was drawn even more to the card and those two handwritten words: *Aunt* and *Uncle*. The fact of them, living two thousand miles south of us. Our grandfather and grandmothers, too. Mom had told us we had fifteen first cousins down there, that thirteen of them were our ages, Pop's sisters' kids, and they lived one block away from each other in Baton Rouge, Louisiana. I knew only a few of their names. Standing there with that check, there was the feeling that our family of six had been marooned up here, that our young mother and father had somehow taken a wrong turn.

JEB AND I fought a lot. He was younger by a year but taller and stronger and he almost always won. One afternoon in the house on Lime Street he had me pinned to the floor of the upstairs hall, his foot on my neck while he kicked me in the ribs. Suzanne broke it up, yelling at us, swearing, her black eyeliner looking so dark against her pale skin. She made Jeb go downstairs, then she went back into her bedroom, and I pulled from behind my door the metal stilt leaning against the wall. I don't remember where we got it or where the other one was, but it was an adjustable stilt like circus performers use and it was heavy and over four feet long.

The only bathroom in the house was at the bottom of the back stairs, and we had to walk through the kitchen and the rear landing to get to it. I knew Jeb would have to go sometime, and I stood there at the top of the stairs, the stilt resting over my shoulder like a spear, and I waited.

Thirty minutes or an hour went by. Suzanne kept playing her favorite 45 at the time, "D.O.A." by Bloodrock, the sirens wailing over and over again as the lead singer's character dies in the ambulance of an overdose. I could hear the TV voices too, then there were footsteps over the kitchen floor and I raised the stilt and pulled my arm back and there was my seven-year-old sister Nicole's red hair, and I let out a breath and lowered the stilt.

Twenty minutes later, Jeb came. Over Suzanne's record player I could hear his heavier footsteps down in the kitchen. I held my breath and when I saw his frizzy hair I hurled the stilt down the stairwell. There was the dull clank of metal on bone, his head jerking sideways as he and the stilt fell to the floor.

I thought he was dead. But he began to cry and raised both hands to his temple. Then he saw me at the top of the stairs and he dropped his hands and sprinted up the steps and he punched and kicked me and called me mother*fucker.*

ONE AFTERNOON I chased him with a butcher knife. He made it to the bathroom and slammed the door, one with slats, and I kept jabbing the blade through the cracks, trying to stab him in his wrists and hands.

IN MOVIES now, whenever a bad man would die a bloody and well-deserved death, I would feel so much pleasure I would nearly laugh. One was *Walking Tall,* the true story of Buford Pusser who single-handedly cleans up the evil that has overtaken his small town, swinging a homemade bat into the bones and skulls of criminals. Buford Pusser is who I wanted to be. Billy Jack, too. And later, Charles Bronson in the *Death Wish* movies, Clint Eastwood in *Dirty Harry.* When I thought of the word *man,* I could only think of those who could defend themselves and those they loved.

WE MOVED again, this time to Haverhill, and when the doctor evicted my mother and us four kids from his old office near the hospital, we moved to the west side of town and lived first on Marshland Ave, then, a year later, on Columbia Park. These were streets of well-maintained two- and three-story houses with hedges and real lawns fathers mowed on weekends. There were late-model cars in the driveways, and Columbia Park was really a boulevard with a long grassy center shaded by oak and elm and maple trees. Our new rented house was a Victorian with a rounded turret and a front and back porch. The yard was small, but it had grass, and in the rear corner was a tall beech tree that rose as high as the house.

Mom was working in Boston now, forcing slumlords to remove lead paint from their buildings. I knew she made $133 a week doing this, and I knew Pop's child support was $340 a month, but just the rent for this

new place was $500 a month. How would we afford it? I was expecting to
get evicted pretty quickly.

But Bruce helped. He had bought us new bikes again, a Sony color TV,
and a stereo. He gave Mom money to cover some of the bills and groceries,
and he started sleeping over not just on the weekend but weeknights too.
He was still warm and seemed interested in whatever we might say, but he
also drank a lot of bourbon at night, quietly and alone, reading a book or
watching some sport on TV. By now we knew he was separated from his
wife, that they had seven children who lived with her south of Boston.

Columbia Park was a nicer-looking street than we'd ever lived on
before, but three houses up lived a blonde stripper with large silicone
breasts. For weeks she'd climbed out of her Camaro with white gauze
taped to her cheek and jaw, and I thought she had an infection of some
kind, but then I heard the real story, that the stripper's mother, a small
chain-smoker she lived with, got mad and shot her daughter in the face.

It was the kind of thing that happened in the avenues. To get to them
I just had to follow Suzanne down Columbia Park across Main Street to
Seventh Ave, a narrow hill street of tin-sided houses behind chain-link
fences. They had no driveways and on the sidewalk or at the curb would
be a battered station wagon or Pontiac LeMans with no hubcaps, a Duster
with a sandblasted hood. Plastic children's toys would lie on the cracked
concrete among cigarette butts and empty nip bottles, and on their sides
here and there would be shopping carts for when the car wouldn't start
and the welfare checks came in and usually the mothers and wives or
girlfriends would push the carts a mile and a half away to DeMoulas and
load up with cans of Campbell's soup, eggs and milk, bags of potato chips
and cases of Coke and Budweiser, bottles of Caldwell's vodka.

Halfway down Seventh Avenue was a cluster of yellow apartment
buildings, two rows of them three-deep back from the street, each three
stories high. The ground around them was packed dirt worn smooth and
there was a gravel parking lot scarred from rain and in the back of it, up
against a field of weeds, was a green dumpster I'd never seen empty; it
was full of babies' diapers and old mattresses, dozens of beer bottles, pizza
boxes, damp condoms and instant coffee jars and plastic shampoo bottles,
a broken chair or torn lamp shade, a kitchen knife with no handle.

At night the apartments were lit up and loud, the windows open in the summer, no screens in them, maybe a fan blowing, the constant drone of TVs and radios, kids crying or laughing, a woman or man yelling, someone from another apartment shouting to shut the fuck *up!* Someone was always calling the cops, and there'd be one or two cruisers pulled up to the curb, the door open, the cab's light on, the dispatcher a static voice in the air.

I don't know when Suzanne started going down there, but I knew why. It's where you'd go to cop some brown mescaline, orange sunshine, or THC. It's where you'd go to buy an ounce of Mexican gold or a tab of four-way purple blotter acid or to sit in a dark hot room full of teenagers and grown men and women and take the joint passed your way and mooch a free hit. It's where everyone else went, to the building farthest back from the street.

There were no young families in this one, just men in their twenties and thirties who earned their rent by collecting it from everyone else, two or three going from door to door on the first of each month demanding cash. Some of them were with the motorcycle gang the Devil's Disciples, and they had long hair that fell down over the devil's insignia of their black leather jackets. They wore heavy motorcycle boots and faded oil-spotted jeans and dark T-shirts. A lot of them had beards or mustaches and they carried folded Buck knives in leather pouches at their hips. In the plywood half-wall of the top porch were three holes in a close grouping from a .38 or .45, and from that apartment there was always music blaring—Black Sabbath, Electric Light Orchestra, Alice Cooper, Led Zeppelin, and the Allman Brothers. There were always three or four motorcycles parked in the dirt or mud, and day and night people came and went.

We smoked every morning at the bus stop too. It was on the corner of Seventh Ave and Main Street right next to Pleasant Spa convenience store, a gray vinyl-sided box with dusty plate-glass windows advertising Marlboros and Borden's milk and Ajax. The owner was short and fat, his fingers brown from tobacco, a smoking cigarette forever between them or his lips. He called us punks and fuckin' assholes. To the right of his store were wooden steps leading to the apartments above, and that's where twelve or fifteen kids waited each morning.

Some of them lived down in the avenues, some on the streets across

Main, but we all looked the same: there was Glenn P., a heavy kid with
wire-rimmed glasses and thin brown hair. He wore a faded army jacket,
the inside pockets usually holding cash and the dope he sold, mainly
THC or joints at a buck apiece. In his Dingo boots, the kind I eventually
got my mother to buy me, he carried a pint of Southern Comfort and he'd
pass it around on the steps to Nicky G., Bryan F. and Chuck and Al, Anne
Marie and Dawn, my sister Suzanne, and me.

I took a sip and hated the sweet burn going down my throat. I
smoked pot, too. I drew in the smoke like everyone else, held it till my
chest hurt, then blew it out, and I hated what happened next, how a part
of me slipped inside another part of me to watch me go so dully through
the morning. But I couldn't say no, couldn't draw attention to myself and
maybe get insulted and have to fight. Only a year or so on this side of
town, and I'd begun to wear my hair tied back in a ponytail, and every
day I wore my one pair of jeans, my Dingo boots, a T-shirt, and the
brown leather jacket with the zippered sleeves my mother couldn't afford
but ended up buying for me anyway. A man driving down Main Street to
work at seven any weekday morning would see just another delinquent
drinking and smoking on the steps of Pleasant Spa, just another kid like
Nicky G. with his long hair, black as an Apache's, his sideburns like Greg
Allman's, his hard chest from the bench presses he did in his garage, the
fact he'd fucked every girl in that neighborhood at least once, including
my fourteen-year-old sister, and then he was off after some other girl and
Suzanne cried for a week in her room and I despised him, tried not to talk
to him or look at him or smile at any of his jokes, but if he passed me a
joint or Glenn P.'s Southern Comfort, I took it and said nothing.

The long yellow bus would pull up and I'd sit in the back with Suzanne
and the Heads from the avenues. Sometimes Glenn P. would pass his bottle,
sometimes he'd keep it to himself for later. We'd ride down through the
streets, the driver stopping every few blocks to pick up more kids, the girls
dressed like Anne Marie and Dawn and my sister; they wore tight hip-
huggers that went so low you could see two dimples just above their butt
cracks, and the Italian or Puerto Rican girls had that brown line in the skin
that ran from the belly button straight down past the pink and yellow rim
of panties. They wore tight tube tops and no bras, their nipples erect in the

winter behind short leather jackets dyed green or red or purple. Their hair was wild or braided, and the eyeliner around their eyes was thick and black, their lip gloss glistening.

As the bus pulled up in front of them, they'd take one last drag off a cigarette and flick it into the street. They'd climb onto the bus and make their way past the kids with lunch boxes and books and homework they'd actually done, to the back where the rest of us were.

"Mornin', Tina."

"Fuck you, Glenn. Where's the fin you owe me?"

"Blow me."

"In your dreams, faggot."

There'd be laughter and more swearing at one another, talk of a fight that was coming, of some Acapulco gold or Angel Dust due soon, who had just fucked whom and who was knocked up and who got rid of it and who wiped out his bike down to the beach and might lose a leg.

We passed the junkyard and a Catholic church, we rode down under the railroad trestle for Lafayette Square and all its barrooms around the rotary, then the package store and car dealership that year-round had Christmas lights lit up over its used and repossessed cars. We rode up Broadway past a funeral home and St. Joseph's Church and then we were out near the highway, the bus turning into the lane for the high school, a rambling one-story complex of cinderblock and glass, a statue of Michelangelo's *Lorenzo de' Medici* sitting out front, though whenever I saw it, the form of the man with his elbow on his knee looked to me like a man on a toilet.

The bus pulled around to the back lot where seniors parked their Monte Carlos and Camaros and Dusters and Trans Ams, a few motorcycles too. Facing the lot was the entrance between the M and L wings. The kids in the front of the bus, the jocks or the studious ones no one had a name for, they went inside to make it to their lockers and desks before the homeroom bell, but I followed Suzanne and the rest to the metal grates up against the walls. There were dozens of kids already there, smoking cigarettes or passing joints or dealing whatever they had, a pocket for their product, the other for cash. And there'd be a lookout for Perez, one of the narcs who wore leather and pretended he was a senior though his shaved whiskers left a dark shadow and there were lines under his eyes and he was at least thirty and a pig, what we still called cops from the antiwar days we were too young to be a part of.

BECAUSE OUR mother worked in Boston, she had to leave for her job before we got out of bed. Most mornings, only Nicole would be on time and walk herself to school a half mile north. Jeb, Suzanne, and I would sleep till we woke two or three hours later than we should have to catch the bus. Some days we'd stay home. Other days we'd go to school, which meant a four-mile walk through town across Main Street down into the avenues past the Dobermans or German shepherds chained in their dirt yards. In some were babies' toys scattered among the dog shit, the dogs barking at me behind chain-link fences. I'm sure Suzanne and I walked together many days, but I remember more clearly doing it alone, cutting across Cedar down Sixth Avenue past the auto parts store and junkyard, the battered shells of cars sitting in the weeds, many of the windshields collapsed into the front seats, the rims rusted, the lug bolts like eyes staring out at me.

But I felt watched by no one. Those weekday mornings we slept late and didn't go to school, our report cards showed as sixty to eighty absences a year, dozens and dozens of marks for tardiness. No adult at school really seemed to notice much. There'd be an occasional letter sent home to our mother, but the counselor or vice principal or whoever it was always wanted to meet during a weekday. How could she do that? She had to work.

I'd make my way through town, past the boarded-up shops on Winter Street, the gas station and used car lot, the pizza shop and Dunkin' Donuts where on summer nights old men would sit in lawn chairs in the parking lot, smoking and talking and spitting.

At Railroad Square, I'd walk under the black iron trestle covered with hot-paint graffiti: *Joey and Nina 4-ever*, *Tommy loves Denise!*, *USMC Cpl. Steve L. RIP*, *U suck!* I'd walk over broken glass and cigarette butts in my Dingo boots and leather jacket, my hair tied back. Maybe I'd thought if I looked like the toughest kids at the high school, they'd leave me alone and I wouldn't have to fight for just glancing at them a second too long. After a while it worked; because I looked like them, they didn't see me anymore. But the cops did. Especially those late weekday mornings walking through town when I should've been in algebra class, world history, gym; I'd pass more barrooms, a lock shop, St. Joe's Catholic Church, a cruiser pulling up and a cop yelling out at me, "Why ain't you in school?"

"I had a doctor's appointment."

"Where's your parents?"

"Working."

"How'd you get to the doctor?"

"Walked."

"Well, keep walkin'." And he'd drive off in his police car, his antennas swaying back and forth like a scolding finger.

It seemed that each day I got up just wanting to get through it. I didn't know if my brother and sisters felt the same way, but my mother seemed to; most weeknights, Bruce quietly drunk, sipping a bourbon and reading in the front room, she'd be stretched out on the floor in front of the TV asleep in her work clothes by eight o'clock, my brother and sisters and me free to do whatever we wanted, do homework or not do homework, fight or ignore each other, ignore the five days of dishes stacked in the kitchen sink and on the counters; ignore the overflowing garbage in the trash bucket or the mountain of bags in the garage because none of us carried any out to the curb on garbage night; ignore the dirty clothes hanging out of the full hampers in both bathrooms; ignore the fact that we each did our own laundry when we needed to, one at a time, going down into the basement and putting into the machine one pair of underwear, a pair of jeans, a pair of socks, a T-shirt and sweater, using an entire load, then drying the same outfit for an hour in the dryer, each of us doing it this way; ignore the dust everywhere, the loose hairs, the grit tracked over the linoleum floors and throw rugs; ignore that our dog, Dirt, shat regularly up on the second-floor hallway in the dark corner near the stairs up to my attic bedroom; ignore that we could walk out of that house and not come home till midnight or later; ignore that most nights Suzanne would go up to her room with a boyfriend and smoke dope and listen to her albums; ignore that twelve-year-old Nicole had installed by herself a padlock on her bedroom door, one she locked with a key she kept with her at all times; ignore that our father never called us and we never called him.

· · ·

JEB AND I had a new friend now, Cleary, whom everybody called by his last name. After the high school let out at two-thirty, I'd take the bus home and wait for my brother to walk back from the middle school, then he and I would go to Cleary's house down the dirt alley behind our garage. It was a tiny two-story of four rooms and a bathroom, the backyard just big enough for his father's Chevy, though we rarely saw him. We saw his mother a lot, a big-breasted woman who started her drinking every morning in tall plastic cups filled with vodka and Pepsi. Some afternoons we'd knock on Cleary's door, hear nothing, then walk in over the yellow linoleum of the kitchen and the living room where his mother would be passed out on the couch in front of the TV, her mouth open, a cigarette still burning in the ashtray.

We'd call our friend and he'd come leaping down the stairs smiling, always smiling, his short dark hair sticking up in a cowlick, a smattering of freckles across his cheeks. In the summer he wore cutoff shorts and a sleeveless T-shirt. In the winter it'd be fake jeans from Zayre's, a T-shirt and denim jacket covered with magic marker peace signs.

We'd walk a half mile down Main Street past houses built so close together there were no yards. Window shades were drawn and you never saw anybody sitting on a porch. Cleary walked on the balls of his feet and bounce-walked, and he was always scheming, talking about the girl he was going to screw or the Corvette he'd own one day or the real Mexican switchblades he heard you could order from a magazine. He'd shove you into a mailbox and laugh and start running, and we'd chase him, Jeb's wild frizzy hair bouncing, my ponytail slapping my back, and we'd go through GAR Park where, when the weather was warm, Dominican and Puerto Rican families laid out blankets and ate together. In the middle of the green was a statue of Hannah Duston, this woman who long ago was kidnapped by Indians along with one of her children, and late one of those first nights, after her ten captors were asleep, she crawled out from under her blanket and took a hatchet and killed every single one of them in their sleep. Then she scalped them. The statue is of her in a long dress, a hatchet in her half-raised arm, her eyes on Main Street which sloped down past the shopping plaza to the river and the Basiliere Bridge over the Merrimack. It was named for the first soldier from Haverhill to get killed in Vietnam, a war that was still going on, though we didn't think much about that.

One February morning we skipped school and went downtown. It was ten or eleven degrees and the dirty snow piled along both sides of Washington Street had become ice; the air made my lungs hurt. Our noses, ears, and fingers felt burned. The three of us had a dollar to share so we sat in a booth at Valhally's Diner and drank coffee with so much milk and sugar in it you couldn't call it coffee anymore. The Greek man behind the counter hated us; he folded his black hairy forearms across his chest and watched us take our free refills until we were giddy with caffeine. Cleary went for his seventh cup and the owner yelled something at him in Greek. On the way out Cleary stole two dollars someone had left on their check under a sugar shaker.

He paid our way on the city bus that was heated and made a loop all the way through town, along the river, up to the Westgate shopping center, then back again. We stayed on it for two hours, taking the loop six times. For a while I looked out the window at all the red brick mills, the storefronts with their dusty windows, barrooms on every block. The bus was warm, too warm. In the far rear, away from the driver, Cleary took out his black-handled Buck knife and carved a peace sign into the aluminum-backed seat in front of him.

After the bus, we made our way through the narrow factory streets, most of the buildings' windows covered with gray plywood, though Cleary's mother still worked at Cohen's Shoes, when she wasn't drinking. We walked along the railroad tracks, its silver rails flushed with the packed snow, the wooden ties gone under. The summer before we'd built a barricade for the train, a wall of broken creosote ties, an upside-down shopping cart, cinderblocks, and a rusted oil drum. We covered it with brush, then Cleary siphoned gas from a station wagon behind Cohen's and poured it on. Jeb and I lit it, air sucked by us in a whoosh, and we ran down the bank across the parking lot into the abandoned brewery to the second floor to watch our fire, to wait for the Boston & Maine, to hear the screaming brakes as it rounded the blind curve just off the trestle over the river. But a fat man in a good shirt and tie showed up at the tracks, then a cop, and we ran laughing to the first floor where we turned on the keg conveyor belt, lay on it belly-first, and rode it up through its trapdoor over and over.

As we made our way through town it began to snow. My brother and

I were hungry, but Cleary was never hungry; he was hawny, he said. One morning, as we sat in the basement of his house and passed a homemade pipe between us, his mother upstairs drunk and singing to herself, Cleary said: "I'm always hawny in the mawnin'."

Jeb and I laughed and Cleary didn't know why, then he inhaled resin on his next hit and said, "Shit, man, the screem's broken."

"The *what?*"

"The screem. You know, the *screem.* Like a screem door?"

By the time we reached the avenues the snow had blanketed the streets. On Cedar, cars spun out snow as they drove from the curb or the corner store. Cleary let out a yelp and a holler and went running after a Chevy that had just pulled away, skidding slightly as it went. Cleary ran low, bent over so the driver wouldn't see him, and when he reached the back bumper he grabbed it and squatted on his sneakers, his butt an inch or two from the road. And he skied away, just like that, the snow shooting out from under the wheels of the car, out from under his Zayre Department Store sneakers, blue exhaust coughing out its pipe beside him.

IN OUR living room stood tall pine bookshelves loaded with hardcover novels and short story collections. They were the sole objects our mother and father had ever owned, and our house seemed to be the only one in the neighborhood that had them. In Cleary's living room, there was the TV, a few glass knickknacks on the shelf beneath it. On the walls were department store prints of daisies in a vase, a kitten with sad, round eyes. Once I saw a slim hardcover lying on the coffee table, *The Illustrated Bible.*

The first time Cleary was in our house, he walked up to the shelves and ran his fingers along the spines of Faulkner, Chekhov, and Balzac, books I'd never quite noticed myself.

"Are these all real?"

"What?"

"I thought they were for looks, you know, like in a store."

"Nope."

"You read 'em all?"

I shrugged. I hadn't read any of them. "My old man has. And my mother."

Cleary kept running his fingers along all those books, shaking his head.

ON WEEKENDS at parties down on Seventh, or out in a weed lot, or up in the woods of Round Pond, we'd try whatever drugs were going around; we'd eat tabs of brown mescaline, or a quarter of LSD 25, or half a tab of four-way purple blotter acid, chemically treated paper you dissolved under the tongue. It tasted like earwax and the rush came on in twenty or thirty minutes, the feeling the world was a strange and fascinating place really, a special place. That *life* was special.

But it made your heart pound hard and fast in your rib cage and some-times we just had to get up and run, Jeb and Cleary and I flying down the dark avenues in our sneakers or boots, which seemed to be moving us, making our legs lift and our knees bend, and we could go on forever. It was long after midnight, and one of us was screaming, the wind in our faces that smelled like green leaves and motor oil and rotting wood and tin siding cool-ing off. We ran past a brick church, dark and locked up, like God's house was closed for business, had always been closed for business, and we ran past a packy and its lighted beer signs, bright blue and red neon slashing into my brain, bad to look at, and a car tore by us, some angry machine driven by no one, and we kept running and running, past the auto parts yard, all the angry machines quiet in there, a rusted hulking darkness behind a plank fence Cleary kicked himself onto sideways for a stride, the German shep-herd behind there barking, straining against his chain which sounded like jangling treasure, bad men and gold and now there were golden lights ahead, Jeb already there, his hair flapping like a small child barely connected to his head, and the gold was Christmas glowing, lighted strings of bulbs hanging over used cars with hot pink price decals on their windshields, numbers I couldn't decipher, then, without sound, the lights exploded, six or seven of them going dark, broken glass falling like snow onto the cars. Cleary was whooping and yelling, and a bottle broke against a post, brown glass spray-ing, and he ran up and down the gutter looking for something else to throw.

A cruiser pulled up, its spotlight on us brighter than the sun, but it was night and now we ran blind through the used car lot and over a chain-link fence, running through yards and side streets, a door opening and slamming, a woman yelling, her voice hoarse so maybe it was another dog yelling at us, and the cop was too slow, his cruiser shooting up all the wrong side streets, its engine angry like the others.

It was better not to go anywhere.

Sometime that year, I'd moved my room up into the attic. Our rented house had that three-story turret, and the third story was part of the attic, but it had a finished floor and light blue wallpaper and trim around the windows. It was unheated, but there were electrical outlets that worked, and there was even an old bed with a headboard. I moved my things up there, hung my blacklight posters of Janis Joplin and Jimi Hendrix. Tacked to the wall my blacklight, a birthday or Christmas present, and I got hold of some glow-in-the dark paints and painted a space galaxy on the ceiling. At night, when only the blacklight was on, Janis Joplin and Jimi Hendrix pulsing light from the walls like insistent spirits, I lay on the bed and stared at the moon and stars and distant worlds.

It was a better place to trip. No cops or dogs or angry machines. Just Bob Dylan on my record player, the expanding cosmos over our heads. But one night in winter we ate a batch of blotter cut with strychnine. Every ninety seconds or so a hot knife seemed to push through my heart, and I had to stand and hold my breath as it passed, my shoulders rounded, my chest sunken, this feeling I'd been yanked through all the decades of my life and now I was old and dying and it was my fault.

ON THE other side of the river was Bradford. It's where a lot of Jocks at the high school lived, the kids who wore corduroys and sweaters and looked clean. It's where houses had big green lawns. It's where the college was where Pop taught. It's where he lived in an apartment building with Theo Metrakos and his friend Dave Supple, a writer too.

Since leaving our mother, Pop had lived in a few places, but we rarely saw them and never slept there. Years later I would hear my father say the divorce had left him dating his children. That still meant picking us up every Sunday for a matinee and, if he had the money, an early dinner somewhere. For a few years now he was taking us to church too. He'd pull up in his rusted-out Lancer and drive us to Mass at Sacred Hearts in Bradford Square. The five of us would walk down the aisle between the crowded pews, Jeb and I with our long hair, Suzanne in her tight hip huggers, Nicole in her brace she now wore for scoliosis, Pop one of the only men in church not wearing a jacket or tie. He refused to put money in the collection basket, too. Many times I'd hear him say, "You think Jesus ever wore a fucking tie? Did Jesus spend money on *buildings*?"

One night, when we were still living at the doctor's house, I heard Mom on the phone trying to convince Pop that he should start taking out each of us one at a time, that he was never going to know us as individual people if he didn't.

I don't know if I cared then about that or not, but a cool sweat broke out on my forehead just thinking about being alone with Pop. I'd never been alone with him. What would I say? What would we talk about? What would we do?

When Mom got off the phone, she said, "I can't believe it. Your father says he'll be too shy with each of you. He's scared of his own kids!"

This made me feel better and worse, but every Wednesday night he'd drive up to the house and take one of us back to his apartment across the river. It was on the third floor of an old brick building covered with ivy. Across the street was the Bradford Green, a lawn and trees and a gazebo, and you could see it from his bedroom where his bed was always made and there were shelves of books and his black wooden desk I remembered from when he used to live with us, its surface clean and organized, notebooks stacked neatly beside his typewriter beside his humidor and pipe stand, six or eight of them each with a white pipe cleaner sticking out of the mouthpiece.

In his small kitchen we'd cook something, pasta and a quick tomato sauce and garlic bread we warmed in the oven. Maybe a bacon and cheese omelet. This was something I looked forward to the most; it seemed I was hungry all the time. At home across the river, unless Bruce had given our mother a new check, something he was able to do less and less now, there just wasn't much food in the house. Breakfast was usually a Coke from Pleasant Spa bought with change we'd found in our mother's purse or under the cushions of our wicker couch. When other kids filed into the cafeteria, we didn't have the money so drifted out back where the pot heads stood on the grates, too cool to sit with the others, passing a pipe around, a bag of potato chips, too.

Suzanne was selling dope. One afternoon I stuck my head in her bedroom doorway, and she was sitting on her mattress with Glenn P. rolling dozens of joints from a garbage bag full of Mexican gold. Edgar Winter was playing on her record player. Kids at school walked up to her with a hungry look in their eyes, and my sister had cash and after school she'd sometimes buy us subs, potato chips and Cokes and candy bars, our first real meal of the day. When Mom got home from work at close to eight o'clock, she'd open a can of Spaghettios or stew for us and heat it up on the stove. Sometimes she'd fry us Spam, or make that Frito Pie, too tired to do much else, too broke to buy much else. And Bruce didn't cook. He'd drink bourbon in the kitchen with her and talk about the new job he had in Boston doing the same thing she was, getting slumlords to rid their buildings of lead paint. She'd nod her head, moving quickly in her work clothes, a far-off look in her eyes, as if she was trying to put back together how her life had taken her here to this: this milltown, this canned food she never would have used when she was first married, these four hungry, depressed teenagers, this hovering man who wasn't their father.

Those Wednesday nights at Pop's apartment waiting to eat, he probably asked me questions about my life—school, homework, friends—but what I remember is feeling like a liar and a fake. I'd be in a T-shirt and jeans I'd washed earlier so they wouldn't smell like dope. I probably told him I was getting good grades, mostly B's, which, miraculously, I was, but I left out that I regularly skipped half my classes, slept late, and didn't go to school several days a month, that I was flunking algebra because it was the first class of the morning when I was most high, that Jeb and I and our friend Cleary spent our afternoons looking for a house party where we could get a free buzz, or we'd be downtown in one of the shops, usually the Army and Navy store distracting the man behind the register so Cleary could stuff a T-shirt or a pair of socks or wool cap down his pants. Sometimes we called the cops on ourselves. One of us would lower his voice and report kids throwing eggs at houses and we'd give them the street, then run there with eggs in our pockets and as soon as we saw the cruiser we'd pelt it and run. One time a cop stuck his head out the window and shouted, "I'll *shoot* you fuckin' assholes!"

We'd end up down by the river and stand on the railroad trestle over

58 ANDRE DUBUS III

the swirling brown water below, betting who had the balls to stay on the longest before the train came, and what would be worse? Getting hit by the Boston & Maine? Or having to jump into the Merrimack River where you'd probably be poisoned to death before you drowned anyway?

There were girls in these neighborhoods who just gave it away. One was Janice Woods, who at fifteen had cropped blonde hair and breasts and hips and liked to walk up to guys and stick her fingers down their pants just so she could feel them get hard in her hand. Lately she'd been coming around, spending afternoons with Jeb in his room.

I could have told my father about her, or her father, Daryl Woods, whom our mother got to know from her work somehow. He was short and wore tight jeans and motorcycle boots, his mustache thick and blond. One night he and my mother went out for a drink at the VFW off Monument Square. They were sitting on stools at the bar when a muscular kid with a long ponytail walked in and asked Daryl for a light. Woods looked him over and told him to get lost. The kid pushed him and Daryl Woods threw a short right into his face and dropped him.

It was winter, and when I got up for school the next morning, the house still dark, the hallway lit up Daryl Woods sleeping on the wicker couch in the living room. He was snoring, his arm over his eyes, and I could see the dried blood and stitches in his forearm from his wrist to his elbow. After their drink, my mother and Daryl had gotten back into our car, a used red Toyota. Mom said she'd just started it up when that same muscled kid with the ponytail ran up to her side of the car and yelled, "Duck, lady." Then he threw a Molotov cocktail past her face at Woods in the passenger side, the bottle smashing against his raised forearm, glass and gasoline spraying over them both. But the fuse had gone out and my mother was flooring it, downshifting and swearing, the kid in the street behind them swearing back.

The inside of the car smelled like gas for weeks.

One March afternoon, at a day party down on Seventh, Cleary and I taking the joint passed to us in the loud smoking noise, a couple of rent collectors told us to beat it and before we could stand and go, they yanked us up and pushed us down the stairs. They kicked open the door and shoved us onto the plywood porch, then off it into the mud. I remember Cleary saying, "C'mon, Ricky, we didn't do nothin'. C'*mon*."

And Ricky J., who months later would get stabbed in the same apartment he was kicking us out of, punched Cleary in the face, his head snapping back, a whimper coming out of him as Kenny V. shouldered me up against the porch, then, without a word, started throwing punches into my chest and ribs and arms. I covered up and he smacked me in the forehead and the temple and I raised my hands and then he went to work on my body. But he wasn't hitting as hard as Clay Whelan had, and a voice in my head said, *This is it? This is all?* I nearly clenched my fist and started punching back. But they both carried Buck knives and the one whaling on Cleary, Ricky J., was on top of him now, punching him over and over in the head.

Then it was done. They were on the porch breathing hard, looking down at us. Cleary was just getting to his feet, blood dripping from one eye and between his teeth.

Ricky J. lit up a cigarette and flicked the match over our heads. "No more fucking moochers. Now *screw.*"

Before we were even to the street Cleary started laughing. He turned and yelled, "Fuckin' *losers!*," and we ran up the hill and across Main Street and down the alley to his house and mother.

There were the Murphy brothers, four of them. They'd drive up to house parties where they didn't know anyone. Walk in, drink what they wanted, smoke what they wanted, eat what they wanted, grab the butt or breasts of any girl or woman nearby, and if anybody ever said anything to them about it or even looked at them wrong, they'd jump him right there, four of them on one.

Dennis was the youngest. He was tall and had dirty blond curly hair and a cracked front tooth. It was a warm afternoon in April or May, and Jeb and Cleary and I were walking back from Round Pond, a reservoir where there were woods and you could find kids smoking dope there in the trees, or passing Tall Boys around in front of a fire till somebody called the cops or the fire department and you'd run and not look back. That afternoon Cleary taught us how to get high just by breathing deep and fast for a full minute, then have someone put you in a bear hug and squeeze till you felt your brain float up and fizz out the top of your head. I was afraid to do it, it seemed dangerous to me. Bad for your heart. But I watched Jeb squeeze Cleary and dump him in the pine needles where he lay a long time, his eyes closed, his mouth open. When he came to he was pale, but he smiled and said, "That was *boss*. That was so friggin' *boss*."

We were on the sidewalk close to Monument Square. There was a sub shop there between a drugstore and convenience store. Sometimes the owners tossed out a pizza or a sub nobody ever picked up for takeout, and we'd find them in the dumpster out back, still warm and in the box or wrapped tightly in white deli paper.

"Hey, faggots!" It was Dennis Murphy. He ran across the street, then fell in step with us as if we knew him, as if we were friends. "How's it hangin'? Suckin' any hog?"

We never stopped walking and he walked with us. He had a light pine branch in his hand a foot and a half long, and he was slapping it against his palm as he walked. My heart was beating fast, and my mouth had gone gummy. We were getting close to the square, the gas stations and shops, cars driving around the statue of the Union soldier in the middle of the asphalt. An old woman was walking in our direction on the sidewalk ahead of us. She was short and small. Her hair was white. Even though the air was warm she wore a thin coat buttoned to the top, and she carried two full grocery bags, one in each arm. I started to move to the side. I remember hoping Murphy wouldn't say anything about sucking hog as we passed her. Her eyes had been on the concrete, on where it was cracked and where it was heaved and buckled, but now she looked up at us and she seemed to pull her groceries in tighter. None of us moved to the side and she had to nearly step in the street as we passed and that's when Murphy flicked his branch out and slapped her face, her eyes blinking and tearing up, and he kept walking. We all kept walking. Cleary laughed like he thought it was funny when I knew he didn't. I don't remember what Jeb said or did, but I did nothing. The old woman was yelling something at us. I could hear the shock in her voice, the outrage. She said something about the police and her dead husband. She yelled, "I hope you're *proud* of yourselves," her voice tremulous. And to walk beside Dennis Murphy for even another heartbeat felt like poison to my own blood, but I kept walking.

In my visits with Pop once a month, I could have told him that story, or the others, but why would I?

4

—

ONE WEDNESDAY IN late spring, Pop set up a hibachi grill outside on the half-wall alongside his apartment building. The air was cool and I could smell the lighter fluid he'd just lit up, the mud in the street drains. There was about an hour of daylight left and my father was throwing a ball to me on the sidewalk.

It was a baseball that belonged to one of his roommates. For a while Pop looked in his buddy's bedroom for a couple of gloves too, and I was relieved he didn't find them. I was fourteen but wouldn't know what to do with a baseball glove. What hand do you put it on? How do you catch a ball in it?

So we stood forty feet away from each other on the sidewalk and threw bare-handed. Soft arcing tosses that were fun to catch. *Fun.* At first, as the white ball sailed at me, I tensed up and jumped at it with both hands. But then, as I kept catching it, I began to look forward to catching it again, to see it spin in the air as it came, its dark stitching rotating. I had no idea how to throw it back. I have a vague memory of my father telling me to lift my leg, to throw over my shoulder, though he may not have. But I knew we were talking about something as we threw the ball back and forth, an occasional car passing in the street beside us, the charcoal glowing hotter for our burgers, and there was so much surprise in his face that I clearly had no experience with a baseball whatsoever, that I did not know one thing about it. I could see he didn't want to draw too much attention to this. In my father's eyes above his trimmed beard, I saw pity for me, and maybe I began to feel sorry for myself too, but what I remember most is being surprised that he was surprised. What did he think kids did in my neighborhood? What did he think we *did*? But how could I tell him anything without incriminating us all, especially my mother, whom he would blame? And when we sat down to eat at his tiny table in his tiny kitchen we were both quiet and ate too quickly, so much to say there was nothing to say.

ONE WEEKDAY morning, I woke late and was surprised to hear Mom's voice downstairs. She and Bruce were talking in the front room. I dressed and walked to the first floor. The sun was out and shone through the window across the dusty rug. From Suzanne's room I could hear Mick Jagger singing how beautiful Angie was. It sounded like Mom and Bruce were arguing about something, which didn't happen too often. I climbed the stairs to my sister's room.

Suzanne sat on her mattress, her back against the wall. She was smoking a cigarette, and when I walked in she looked up and stubbed it out as if she'd been waiting for me.

"You hear what happened?" She blew smoke out the side of her mouth.

"No, what?"

"Jeb tried to kill himself last night."

"*What?*"

She told me how sometime after midnight our thirteen-year-old brother had called a rock station down in Boston, how he'd requested a drum solo, how he'd crept outside with Bruce's car keys, a blanket, tape, and our vacuum cleaner's hose, how he then attached it to the exhaust pipe of Bruce's Jaguar XJ6, how he taped it airtight, then pushed the other end into the crack above the back window and stuffed the blanket around it till it, too, was airtight. How he climbed in behind the wheel, started the engine, and waited.

Maybe if Bruce hadn't been a drinker, Jeb would have died, but Bruce woke needing to piss and that's when he'd heard his engine idling out in the driveway. That's when he went out there and found Jeb half-conscious behind smoky glass. That's when he jerked open the door and pulled our brother out, switched off the Jaguar, and walked Jeb up and down the street till his head had cleared.

"Jeb wrote Mom a note. I guess Janice fucking Woods broke his heart or something."

Mick Jagger was singing on about Angie, how he still loved her. Suzanne shook her head at me. I stared down at her floor, shaking my head too. There was a twisting in the marrow of my bones, a twisting that vibrated with sound. *You should've done something. You knew Janice Woods was bad news. Why didn't you do something?*

"Where is he?"

"School. Mom's pissed at Bruce 'cause he didn't even wake her up last night to tell her about it."

THAT AFTERNOON after school I waited on the porch steps for my brother. It was a warm day in spring, and I could smell damp earth, the dry paint of the railing. Soon he was walking down Columbia Park, then he was standing on the sidewalk in front of me. He was smiling guiltily and his cheeks were pale, his T-shirt ripped under the collar. I stood. "You try something like that again, *I'll* fucking kill you."

"Sure, governor." He said this in a British accent, smiling through me as he climbed the steps and brushed past me. We both knew I was full of shit. We both knew I wasn't capable of killing anyone.

Jeb may have gone to a counselor after that, but I don't think so. The days became again what they were, and life continued as it was.

BECAUSE THERE was never a mother or father home in the afternoons, our big rented house on Columbia Park became another place for kids to gather and get high. There were some from the bus stop and the avenues, Nicky G. and Glenn P., Bryan, and Anne Marie and Dawn, but also many people I'd never seen before. Some were grown men, their motorcycles on the sidewalk leading to our porch. By three in the afternoon, the house would be thick with pot and cigarette smoke, the stereo Bruce bought us blaring in the front room: the Rolling Stones, Aerosmith, Ten Years After, Pink Floyd. In the living room, girls would be sitting on the laps of their boyfriends, some of them sharing a beer or cigarette or joint. In the dining room, at the table that came with the house and one we rarely used, five or six would be playing 45, using for an ashtray their beer cans or one of our cereal bowls.

I hadn't moved up to the attic yet, and my room was still on the second floor in the back of the house across from Jeb's. I'd go up there and shut the door behind me. I'd lie on my bed and try to ignore the weekday afternoon party voices and laughter, the yelling or loud trash-talking from Nicky G. or one of the rent collectors from Seventh who'd started coming around too. I'd lie there and imagine being a different kind of kid, one who could walk downstairs and open the front door and yell at them all to just get the fuck out. And when they wouldn't, I'd jerk the men to their feet one at a time. They'd swing at me, and I'd duck and then start hurling punches and kicks like Billy Jack, smashing bones and severing arteries, all with my hands and feet.

Instead I stayed in my room and waited for the sun to go down and for them to drift off, two or three at a time.

Still, some would come around at night. Once, close to ten o'clock, Mom lay on the floor in front of the TV in her work clothes, a pillow under her head, her cheap coat covering her like a blanket. A knocking echoed from the front door and Nicole got up and answered it. I was sitting in a wicker chair. I was half asleep, but there was a mild electrical current telling me that *I* should have gone to the door, not my ten-year-old sister.

She walked back into the room. Her back was held erect with her scoliosis brace, her chin resting on its plastic collar. "It's Glenn P. He wants to talk to Suzanne."

Mom opened her eyes. "Well you tell Glenn P. to go take a flying fuck."

Nicole turned and walked through the hall to the door. I could see her red hair pulled back over the rear collar of her brace. "Um, my mom says for you to go take a flying fuck."

If Glenn P. said something back, Nicole didn't repeat it. She locked the door and walked back into the living room and sat down with her homework.

ONE RAINY afternoon in April, I came home to another full house and I went straight upstairs and there was Kip L. and Donna H. coming down the narrow hallway. He was half a foot taller than I was but lighter, his skin white, blue veins and capillaries standing out in his arms and hands. People said he shot heroin, and I was sure that's what he and Donna H. had been doing up here, maybe in the bathroom, but her halter top was unbuttoned and beneath the flared hem of her hip-huggers were bare feet. As she passed me in the narrow hallway she smelled like sweat and Kip L.'s leather jacket.

They didn't say anything, and I didn't either. Then they were back downstairs and I walked into my room. Rain pattered against the window. The only light was gray and shadowed, and I flicked on the overhead bulb. Lately I'd been making my bed some mornings, pulling the top blanket or bedspread tight at the corners. I could see it was still made but rumpled, and there, in the middle of my mattress, was a spot of wetness the size of a quarter.

ONE WEEKDAY morning I'd somehow woken before anyone else and went down into the kitchen to see what there might be to eat. Usually the inside of the fridge was nearly empty shelves, but I was reaching for its handle anyway when I heard the hissing. I turned to see the blue flames of the front burner. It had been going all night. Inches away was a greasy Burger King bag on a stack of dirty dishes, and I rushed over and switched off the gas. The air was warm and smelled like scorched metal.

That night, long after everyone was in bed, I lay on my mattress and pictured the flames climbing the walls, thick smoke filling the hallway, snaking under our doors, blackening the glass of the windows, suffocating us before the fire even made it to where we slept. I got up and went downstairs and checked the knobs of the oven and stove. I touched each one five times, turning it to off and holding it there. But this did not seem to be enough. I moved to anything electrical and unplugged it, too. I started with the kitchen clock. I hurried to the lamps in the living room, even the stereo and TV, unplugging them all. Then I moved quickly to the front door and checked the lock, again having to touch the cool metal five times to make sure. I crept through the dark house to the back door and did the same there. Then I climbed the stairs and lay in bed and tried to sleep. I'd think of my brother wanting to die; I'd see the exhaust pipe and the vacuum cleaner hose, and I'd hear the drums on the radio, feel the carbon monoxide entering my lungs like a thief.

JEB AND I began building again. The backyard was small and square, probably thirty feet by thirty feet, but in the far corner away from the house was that tall beech tree. Tacked into its trunk at its base was the corner post for the side and rear fences, short rotting planks on rails, the one we hopped over to get to Cleary's house down the back alley to Main Street. It was the one we hauled our stolen lumber over, too.

Cleary helped us. At the bottom of the avenues on Primrose Street, not far from a Catholic church and cemetery, was a lumberyard. They kept most of their wood outside under tarps surrounded by a ten-foot chain-link fence, but there was no barbed wire at the top and lately they'd been tossing used pallets on the sidewalk outside.

At night, long after we'd eaten and Mom had dozed off, Jeb and Cleary and I would run down Seventh past the lighted noise of the apartments, the dogs barking, TVs blaring. We'd get down to Primrose where every other streetlamp was out, the lumberyard lit up with only one security light over the door to the office, and we'd check the street for a passing cruiser, then stack those pallets and climb up and over, the points of the fence sometimes catching on our pants or shirts, and we'd drop down onto a stack of plywood and head for the eight-foot two-by-fours and two-by-sixes. They were pale white in the shadows and smelled like dry wood and were hard and smooth under our hands, and we yanked them from their stack and leaned them against the fence, then pushed them up and over to the first of us down on the other side.

We needed nails, too. The office and warehouse were locked and there was that light over the office door, but lying in the black shadows around the corner were discarded sections of steel bands that had been cut away from what they'd held together. There was loose rope and spools of cable, more pallets, and all along the asphalt up against the warehouse were scattered loose screws and nails. We'd pick up as many as we could and load up our pockets. When I climbed back up over the fence, I thought it was the fence poking my thigh, but it was the nails, fifteen or twenty of them.

It seemed like we'd been in there a long time. We walked back up into the avenues where very few of the streetlights worked, most of our walk safely in shadow, and we passed the tin-sided houses with no front yards, the shades or curtains drawn, each of us carrying no more than three or four two-by-fours over our shoulders, but we walked along like men who worked, men who had actually earned what they carried.

WE WERE building a tree house in that beech in the backyard. Our landlord had a shop in the basement, and we went down there and found a couple of hammers and a handsaw. In the garage, hanging on the wall, was a wooden ladder, and within a day or two we'd built a fairly level platform fifteen feet up in the branches of the tree. For the flooring, we'd stolen a sheet of plywood from one of the stacks in the lumberyard, but it took two of us to carry it back home, and when we went back for more a few nights later, there were bright floodlights shining down into the yard and the warehouse and office.

Cleary stood there in the dark, his hair over one eye. "Holy shit." Then there was the sound of something heavy sliding over the asphalt, then a rattling, then a German shepherd charging us till the chain yanked straight. And we ran.

We needed walls and a roof. Weeknights we wandered up and down the avenues looking for scrap piles behind houses, but there seemed to be a dog chained in every third or fourth lot. Once we hopped a fence and dropped down into a packed-dirt yard. There was a motorcycle, a lawn chair, and a picnic table. In the corner a couple of bikes leaned one against the other, and Newburyport and Cody Perkins and whoever had hopped over our fence and stolen our bikes came rushing back and I began to feel like somebody I didn't want to be, an exterior light coming on and shining on the three of us. "You motherfuckers want to get shot?"

Cleary pushed open the gate and we ran up Fourth Avenue in the dark and didn't look back until we were on the other side of Main, breathing hard, sweating under our clothes, Cleary saying that was boss, "That was so friggin' *boss*."

WE GOT the rest of the materials from our basement. Before renting the house to us, our landlord had started building a recreation room.

The floors were still poured concrete, but he'd hung a ceiling to hide the
exposed subfloor and joists above, and he'd framed walls along the length
of the foundation and around the furnace and oil tank and wood shop,
tacking fake paneling to the studs. Jeb had studied the situation and seen
right away that if we went behind the wall near the furnace, we could rip
out every other two-by-four and the paneled walls would still stand and
look the same from the finished side.

It was easy to take the hammer and swing it down at the base of the
stud till it slid away from the nails that held it. Then we'd grab the bottom
and yank till the panel nails ripped free and we'd keep yanking till the top
nails gave too, and we'd carry the stud up the bulkhead steps and outside.

I did a few, but Jeb was faster, his hammer-swing more efficient. Out
in the yard, Cleary or I would pull the nails out of both ends and then
straighten them out on the concrete driveway, tapping them with a hammer until they were usable again. The sun was on us, and I could hear
the party sounds coming from inside the house—the stereo turned up
loud, some kid laughing louder, high or half drunk, and I may have felt
superior out in the yard building our new house high in the beech tree
with our stolen materials, but I hoped nobody would come out and see
us. I hoped nobody was in my room. I hoped Nicole had locked herself in
hers, as she always did, though she never talked much anymore to anyone,
and I didn't talk much to her either.

"Hey, you guys, come look." Jeb stood on the lower steps of the open
bulkhead, a cobweb in his long frizzy hair. "I found something."

We followed him back into the dark basement beyond the shop to the
oil tanks. We could hear the squeak of the living room's floorboards above
us, the bass beat of the stereo, voices and the tapping of someone's boot.

"Look."

Leaning against the wall were ten or twelve brand-new sheets of paneling, four feet wide and eight feet long, a thin layer of dust coating their
top edges.

BY THE weekend, we'd built frames for our walls, then nailed to them those
thin sheets of paneling. We had five sheets left over and we used all of them
for the flat roof, stacking one on top of the other. Now the roof was strong

enough for us to stand on and we made it a deck and took our last two-by-fours and nailed some of them lengthwise from branch to branch for railings.

Because we didn't know how to frame windows, our tree hut had none and when we crawled inside our short narrow doorway that faced Cleary's alley, we were crawling into a black hole that smelled like sawdust and basement musk, but it was our black hole, and we didn't want just anyone climbing into it either.

We got rid of the ladder and built a rope elevator. Just above the hut there was a long branch jutting out from the trunk, and into this we screwed two heavy-duty pulleys we'd found in Cleary's basement. It's where we got the rope too, coiled under a workbench.

Cleary's house didn't have a bulkhead entrance like ours and the only way in was through his kitchen and down the stairs. When the three of us walked into the house on that weekday afternoon, his mother was on the couch watching their black-and-white TV, Merv Griffin maybe, her yellow plastic tumbler in her hands on her lap. She was slow to look up at us, her eyes glazed over, the whites pink.

"Hi, honeys, you boys hungry?"

"No, Ma." Cleary was already halfway down the basement stairs. Jeb followed him, but Cleary's mother was smiling at me like I'd just said something funny to her. "You need a haircut."

I shrugged.

"How's your mom?" She took a long sip off her drink.

"Good."

"She still working down to Boston?"

"Yeah," I said, though I don't think either of them had ever met. I wanted to go downstairs but didn't want her to know I didn't want to stand there talking to her anymore, Cleary's drunk mother in her clean house, always so clean, the linoleum floors swept and mopped, the rugs vacuumed, the coffee table and TV and windowsills free of dust, even the windows looking out onto the dirt alley were as clear as if they held no glass.

Sometimes I would think how good it would be to have our mother at home all day too, to have her there to make sure we got to school, and to have her there when we came home in the afternoon, an adult who wouldn't let just anyone into her warm, clean house.

Even if she was like this.

Her attention was back on the TV now, men in shirts and ties sitting around talking, and I went down the basement stairs, ducking my head under a joist, hoping Cleary and my brother had found something useful.

TO GET up into the hut, you'd sit on a short section of two-by-four, the rope it was tied to between your legs, and you'd pull on the other rope hanging a foot away, the pulleys creaking as you rose up and up till the hut's floor was at your chest and you'd keep one hand gripping the rope, then reach out with the other and grab the inside jamb of the door, lift your knee onto the platform, then let go of the rope and hear the whistle of it through the pulleys as your two-by-four seat fell to the ground and you were inside. When all three of us were up, one of us would lean out and grip the rope and pull both ends and the seat up and nobody could get in unless he was a monkey.

But what was there to do up there? Soon it was fall, then early winter, and it was cold in the hut, and late at night we ran up and down Columbia Park stealing welcome mats from every front or side porch, our faces lit up under the exterior lights, and we hauled the mats back, tossing them one at a time up into the hut, then tacking them to the inside walls and ceiling till you couldn't see the paneling anymore. We found an orange electric cord in the garage and ran it down the trunk and along the fence to our house where Jeb pulled it through a crack in the bulkhead doors and plugged it into a socket near the washer.

Down on Seventh Avenue, on top of the trash pile in the dumpster, was an electric heater, a brown metal box, half of its safety grille kicked in but the coils looking new and untouched.

"Give me ten fingers." Cleary put both hands on the steel lip of the dumpster. He kept glancing back at the apartment houses behind us, mainly the one with the rent collectors, but there were no motorcycles out front and no music playing. Three or four times a year, the collectors went on drug runs down south somewhere. Kids talked about it at the bus stop, what was coming up here from New York and New Jersey and Florida. The mud beneath us was frozen, and from somewhere deep inside the apartments a baby cried. I squatted and knitted my fingers together and

Cleary put his cold sneakered foot into them and pushed off into the trash.

NOW THE hut was warm. We'd hung a wool blanket over the doorway, and the orange glow of the exposed heater coils gave off almost enough light but not quite. Soon we had a small lamp up there, its shade scorched in spots, and Cleary got hold of a radio too. It was old and covered with dried paint splatter, but if we kept it in the corner facing southeast, it got pretty good FM stations down in Boston, and every time we were up there it'd be playing Led Zeppelin or Aerosmith or the Stones, though sometimes it was just DJ talk and we'd switch it off.

Girls were coming up now. Girls who were strong enough to pull themselves up our rope elevator. Some of these were from Cleary's alley, and they were twelve or thirteen and wore tight hip-huggers and smoked Marlboros or Kools and swore a lot. Others came from a few streets over. One was the little sister of Ricky J., one of the rent collectors who'd thrown us out of the pot party and beaten the shit out of Cleary. She was short and thin and wore so much black eyeliner she looked like some kind of night rodent. Cleary bragged to us once that she liked to give blow jobs and that she swallowed, too. Right off she seemed to like Jeb, his wild hair, the soft brown fuzz on his cheeks and chin, his blue eyes and sweet smile.

I had sort of a girlfriend now and while Jeb and Cleary and their girls made out in the hut, I was starting to spend my afternoons at Rosie P.'s house a few blocks west and closer to the highway.

Rosie was black and quiet. She had a neat afro and a pretty face, and she wore small gold earrings like a woman. We'd met months before when we were both thirteen, at a party up in the woods at Round Pond, a Saturday night and thirty or forty kids drinking around a fire, passing joints, listening to the Alice Cooper blaring from the speakers of a Camaro somebody had driven down the trail to the clearing. I was standing next to Rosie, our backs to the dark water, and she seemed shy and kind. I offered her one of the Schlitz Tall Boys we'd brought. Cleary had stolen money from his mother's purse and we waited outside a liquor store on Cedar Street for over an hour till somebody bought some for us, a big Dominican man in a suit jacket, his Monte Carlo parked half on the sidewalk, its engine still running.

Rosie smiled and took the beer. Her older sister Laila was there too, laughing at something Cleary was saying or doing and she kept eyeing my brother.

Usually these parties got broken up by the police. From across the water, one or two cruiser spotlights would shine in our direction, lighting up the trees and casting their shadows across our faces. Then there'd be flashlights, their light paths jerking up and down as cops on foot came for us, and we'd start running.

But this night, somebody threw leafy branches on the fire and they began to smoke up right away. Someone else yelled, "That's poison *sumac,* asshole!" A few began coughing, then a few more, then the owner of the Camaro revved his engine and headed back up the trail, his headlight path rising and falling with each dip and rut, and Jeb and Cleary and I ended up at Rosie and Laila's house.

It was a freshly painted clapboard two-story with a small green lawn in front on a street with other houses just like it. Inside, the rooms were as clean as Cleary's, no dust or clutter anywhere, pillows set on the sofa, a bowl of apples on the small kitchen table, the hardwood floors gleaming under the lamplight.

Laila and Rosie were being raised alone by their mother who was working two jobs, one in an office, the other in a restaurant. In the six months I was with her daughter, I never met her mother or even saw her.

I don't know whose idea it was for the five of us to go up to the girls' bedroom, or if it was Rosie or Laila who lit the candles, or where we got the bottle of wine we began to pass around, Jeb and Laila sitting at the foot of the bed, Cleary leaning against the bureau, Rosie and me sitting side by side up near the pillows. The record player was on, Bill Withers singing "Lean On Me," and Rosie's tongue was in my mouth and we kissed a long time. Once I looked up and Laila was standing between Jeb and Cleary, kissing one, then the other, her hand rubbing Cleary's crotch.

After a while the three of them were gone, and Rosie and I stretched out on the bed on top of her covers. I was thirteen and had touched breasts before, a girl when I was eleven and she was twelve, and it was like holding a soft-boiled egg gently so it wouldn't break. Rosie let me touch

hers that way under her shirt and we never stopped kissing and soon her
jeans were unsnapped and unzipped and I was rubbing her pubic hair, so
much more than I had, and I kept expecting there to be some kind of hole
there, that if I kept rubbing, it would be like finding a button that would
open her secret compartment. She seemed to like what I was doing, but I
began to wonder if something was wrong with her, if some girls just didn't
have holes and couldn't have babies. Or maybe I couldn't find it because
she was a virgin, and it wasn't there yet.

This went on for a long time, maybe half an hour, my wrist burning
so I had to switch hands. Then Rosie arched her back slightly and my
fingers slid lower and into the warm, slippery answer to all I'd been asking
myself, my lips never leaving hers, this girl I'd just met.

A WEEK later we did it on the floor of her bedroom while up on the bed
Laila made out with Jeb or Cleary or Sal M., a handsome slow Italian
kid who lived close by. The room was dark, but I remember a nightlight
plugged in near the bureau. It was shaped like a seashell and it gave off a
dim white light over Rosie's pretty face, her eyes closed, then mine too as
something happened to me that had never happened to me, this gathering and gathering in the very center of my body that seemed to pause,
then pulse and pulse though it was like I was falling and I knew something was leaving me and going into her.

A few days later, on a bright afternoon lying clothed on her mother's
made bed, she told me that had been her first time.

"Me too."

"You know what my sister says?"

"What?"

"No protection, no affection."

She straightened her legs and reached into her front jeans pocket and
pulled out a small plastic package. She handed it to me. On the front
was the silhouette of a man and woman facing each other, sunset colors
behind them. Rosie and I looked at each other, then started kissing, and I
learned how to put that thing on and we did it on her mother's bed.

This is all we ever did. We never ate a meal together or got dropped
off at a movie, or even went walking. And she only came over to my house

a few times. Mom would be asleep on the wicker couch or the floor or maybe in her room reading a book, and Rosie and I would go to mine.

Laila had done it with Jeb and Cleary, and probably Sal M., but she was older than we were, almost seventeen, and soon enough she had a boyfriend, a white basketball player who'd pick her up in his black Mustang and they'd roar down the street and away. By now Jeb and Cleary had forgotten her and were back up in the tree hut with some of the neighborhood girls. And maybe what happened next came because Ricky J.'s little sister told someone what she'd been doing up there and with whom, told Ricky and her older brother Tommy, too.

MOST FIGHTS broke out when you didn't see it coming. I'd be walking down the crowded corridors of the school, too hot because like most of the kids from the avenues I wore my leather jacket all day long, my ponytail halfway down my back, my eyes on the backs of kids ahead of me as I moved from one class where I said nothing to the next where I said less.

"Fuckin' *ass*hole!" The slam of a locker, the slap of feet over the hard floor, the soft thudding of a fist thrown again and again into someone's face, like waxed wings flapping, then a joyous shriek of someone yelling "*Fight!*," and we'd all be running to them, crowding around the two or three bodies flailing away at each other in the center. In a school of over two thousand students, this happened once or twice a week.

It was a cool morning in October, the sky was gray and looked heavy with snow. The second bell had rung and Suzanne and I and all the dealers and smokers and loud trash-talkers from out back stepped off the grates and headed for the glass doors of the high school.

And again, it was like stepping into still water that suddenly has a current and it was pulling me forward, a bunch of us rushing for something happening on the concrete stoop in front of the doors, a big-breasted girl in a short green jacket straddling the chest of another girl, punching her in the forehead, her eyes, her nose, her teeth, yelling, "You cunt! You fucking *cunt!*"

Other kids were laughing, cheering, urging the one on top to kill her, urging the one on the bottom to fight back, her nose splattering blood on the concrete beside her ear.

Then Perez the narc pushed through us and grabbed the top girl under the arms and pulled her off and she kicked the other girl in the crotch and a knee and the girl jumped up, her eyeliner streaked, her nose and mouth bloody, hair in her face, and she charged after the girl who'd just done this to her, just like Cody Perkins had gone after Big Sully, this much smaller girl going after the bigger one Perez held, and again I felt small and weak because I knew I'd be running; if I were that girl, now was the time to run.

BUT SOME fights came with a warning. Word would get out that somebody was going to kill somebody else, beat his head in, demi him out, kick his ass for some slight; owing money he was never paying back; screwing another's girlfriend and bragging about it; telling another, "He's a pussy. My mother can take him." And then the other comes around with maybe a bat or a knife or just fists and feet to prove otherwise.

GLENN P. had just flicked his smoking roach into the gutter of Main Street. "I wouldn't want to be your brother right now."

"Why?"

"'Cause he's fucking dead, that's why."

Glenn P. hooked a strand of hair behind his ear and smiled at me like he was witnessing something that satisfied him more than he thought it would. "It was gonna be Ricky, but he got shanked in the leg so guess who's coming home on leave?" Glenn P. turned and walked into Pleasant Spa for chips and Pepsi, his usual stoned breakfast. I'd just been in there with change I'd stolen from my mother's purse, and I'd bought a Coke and a Willy Wonka bar. Now my heart was thudding in my chest, my mouth dry as the bus pulled up to the curb from Seventh. I thought of the J. brothers' little sister, her heavy black eyeliner, her skinny little body, the way she'd probably talked too much about fooling around up in the tree hut with my brother, who right now was either sleeping late or just leaving the house to walk to the middle school.

FOR A week or more, this was one of the subjects at the back of the bus, on the grates out behind the M and L wings, in day parties down on Seventh. "You hear about Tommy J.? He's coming home on leave to kill Sue's little brother. Man, you seen Tommy lately? He's fuckin' *big*."

I hadn't seen him. But I'd heard about him. People said he was crazier
than his brother Ricky who'd go after anyone for anything, that Tommy
was quiet but meaner and more dangerous, that some biker down on
Fourth looked too long at Tommy's girlfriend and he jerked him off his
parked hog and beat him till he was almost dead. That's why Tommy J.
had to join the army, they said. That or prison.

I knew he was nineteen or twenty years old, that he weighed close
to 200 pounds and was an MP in the army. I remember hoping he'd get
killed on the way home from wherever he was. Or that the army would
need him and wouldn't let him out and then months would pass, and he
and his brother would forget whatever their little sister had told them.

Jeb started taking different routes to and from school. Some afternoons his teacher would drive him home. She was thirty-five years old
and had wild frizzy hair just like Jeb. She was small and thin and wore big,
round glasses like Janis Joplin, and she drove a bright orange Z-28, sleek-
looking and low to the ground. At the middle school she'd encouraged
Jeb's natural creativity, and gave him Andrés Segovia records he would
listen to on our old record player in his room. He was starting to teach
himself classical guitar.

It was a weekday afternoon in April, and I was sitting on the front
steps of our house waiting for him to come home. An hour earlier on
the high school bus, Glenn P. tapped the back of my head, his eyes pink
behind his glasses, his long greasy hair stuck behind both ears. "Guess
who got in last night?"

I had said nothing, and he'd laughed his stoned, gleeful laugh, and now
I was waiting for my brother to come home so I could, what? I didn't know.
Maybe I was just going to tell him to get in the house and stay there. Don't
go down to the store for a Coke or anything. Don't get seen in the street.

It was a strange afternoon anyway because our mother was home,
sick with the flu, and the house was quiet, no other kids inside smoking,
drinking, cranking the stereo so loud you could always hear it out on the
sidewalk. Most of the snow had melted, but there was still a patch of it
in the front yard, the grass brown and damp, bare twigs and half a fallen
branch lying in the wet leaves nobody had raked in the fall.

Down on Main Street cars passed. It had to be after three, but I didn't own a watch and didn't want to go inside and check the clock in the kitchen. On the other side of our street, on the corner of Main and Columbia Park, was a yellow brick apartment building, and I looked past the bare branches of the trees to the flat roof and tin-colored sky above it. The air had gotten cooler. It felt like it might rain. And then I saw Jeb's teacher's sports car as it slowed down on Main, her indicator blinking yellow like an advertisement for anybody bumming at the corner of Seventh, that Sue's little brother had just gotten home. My heart started up and I stood and walked to the curb to tell him Tommy J. was home on leave, but in only seconds a man was striding up Columbia Park from Main followed by six or seven others, kids I'd seen from the avenues and on the bus, kids in leather jackets and T-shirts and Dingo boots, their long scraggly hair stuck behind their ears, though Tommy J.'s hair was so short he looked bald, and he had a trimmed mustache like a cop's. He was already halfway up the street when Jeb's teacher's car pulled up and my thirteen-year-old brother climbed out of the passenger seat, smiling and oblivious, a book or some art supplies under his arm, his hair wild, that brown fuzz on his cheeks and chin.

Somebody said, "That's him, Tommy."

The teacher was opening her door. I told Jeb to run inside. "Do it. *Go.*"

But Tommy J. was already there in front of our house. He was wearing a sweatshirt, and he was a foot taller than both of us, sixty or seventy pounds heavier, and he punched my brother in the face, Jeb's head snapping back, his book falling to the street.

"You like my little sister, mothafucka?"

Some kid laughed, the teacher was screaming something, and Jeb's nose was bleeding, his arms at his sides. "Jesus," he said.

"Tommy, come on." I stepped forward and he whirled around, his fist at his shoulder. "Shut up, Dubis, or you're fuckin' next." He punched Jeb again, his head knocking back, his hair falling in front of his face. Tommy J. was yelling something about his sister, about Jeb being dead if he even looked at her again. Jeb's eyes were welling up and there was blood in his mouth and my feet were bolted to concrete, my arms just tubes of air, my heart pounding somewhere high over my head as my sick mother came running out of the house and down the stairs. She grabbed the fallen branch off the ground and started swinging it in front of her. "Get *out* of here or I'll call the cops! *Get!*"

Tommy J. turned and raised his forearm, her swinging stick just missing it. "Fuck you, you fuckin' whore." He began walking backwards, pointing his finger at Jeb. "You heard what I said. You fuckin' *heard* me." His eyes passed over me as he turned and started walking back to Main and the avenues, the others falling in with him, and it was the same look Cody Perkins had given me as he pedaled right by me on my stolen bicycle, as if no one sat or stood where he was looking, nobody at all.

IN MINUTES the street was quiet and empty again. Jeb's teacher and my mother had walked him into the house, and I stood there on the sidewalk where Tommy J. had beaten up my brother and called my mother a whore.

And what had I done?

I'd pleaded with him. I'd called him Tommy and *pleaded*.

I stood there a long time. If there were sounds, I didn't hear them. If there was something to see, I didn't see it. There was the non-feeling that I had no body, that I had no name, no past and no future, that I simply was *not*. I was not here.

Then I was walking. Up the stairs and into the house. Through the dark foyer and into the dining room we never used. Across the back hallway and its curled linoleum into the downstairs bathroom where I shut the door behind me, though I could not be sure of that, the *me*. *Was* there a me?

I stood in front of the sink and the mirror. I was almost surprised to see someone standing there. This kid with a smooth face and not one whisker, this kid with long brown hair pulled back in a ponytail, this kid with narrow shoulders and soft arm and chest muscles and no balls. This kid had no *balls*. I looked into his eyes: *I don't care if you get your face beat in, I don't care if you get kicked in the head or stabbed or even shot, I will never allow you not to fight back ever again. You hear me?*

Ever. Not once, ever, again.

I left the bathroom and walked through the kitchen where my mother and Jeb's teacher were tending to him at the sink. They didn't look at me, and I couldn't look at them.

I ran up the back stairs and closed the door to my room. I got down on my hands and knees, straightened my back and legs, lowered my chest to the floor, and pushed back up. I did this as many times as I could, the dusty rug rising to my face, Jeb's head snapping back, his hair flying.

I may have done seven or eight push-ups. I turned over on my back and began doing sit-ups. My stomach muscles burned right away. I hooked my hands behind my head and jerked myself up for two or three more. I was sweating and breathing hard. Then I remembered the weight set in the basement.

When I was twelve and we were still living in the old doctor's office, I'd asked for it for my birthday. It seemed expensive, and I was surprised I'd gotten it, but I'd set up the bench at the foot of the bed. There was an instructional sheet of exercises for the whole body and I'd taped that to the wall and tried doing the exercises for half an hour two or three days a week. I didn't know if this was how Billy Jack had gotten started or not, but it seemed like the right place to begin except that exercises were uncomfortable and a little painful, and I wasn't sure I was doing them right anyway, and it was so much easier to stay on the floor in front of the TV.

Now, two years later, I rushed down the back stairs and through the empty kitchen into the basement. In the darkness under the stairwell I found the bench and hollow metal bar and plastic-covered concrete plates. I carried them into the paneled room on the other side of the furnace. I knew how to do bench presses, and I slid a 25-pound plate on each end of the bar, lay down, gripped the cool metal, pushed it off the forks, then lowered it to my chest till it touched and I pushed back up. But it was heavy, and I could only do five or six repetitions and barely got it back into the forks over my face.

I'd heard of guys at school who could bench-press 200 pounds, even 250. I'd heard that one of the football players could do 275, and I was struggling with *60*? Was I really this *weak*?

Yes, I was. And small. And afraid. And a *coward*.

These words about myself were not new, but today they felt less like the end and more like a beginning.

5

—

AT PLEASANT SPA, just under the rack of *Playboy, Hustler,* and *Swank* was a row of wrestling and muscle magazines. One was called *Muscle Builder.* On the cover was a man staring into the camera like we'd just interrupted his privacy and he didn't like it. His massive arms were crossed over his bare chest, and it was so muscled you could hide coins between his pectorals, a new word I was learning, others too: deltoids and trapezius, latissimus dorsi, biceps, triceps, quadriceps, and erector spinae, the muscles of a man's body that, when fully developed, made him powerful and powerful-looking.

I borrowed money from my sister and bought that magazine, rolled it up, carried it home, and studied every page. In it were men with sixty-inch chests and twenty-two-inch arms. They could bench-press 400 to 500 pounds for repetitions. They were curling more weight than my body. They looked like shaved and massive rage to me, so muscled from feet to neck that their faces and heads appeared small and out of place on top of their shoulders.

Three days later I'd already worked out three times. Every muscle I had ached. At the bus stop in the morning, I didn't talk to anyone at the corner. I didn't even look at Glenn P. When the bus pulled up, I sat in the middle and avoided the bottle getting passed around in the back. At the high school, I walked by the grate and went directly to my homeroom and waited for the bell. After school I walked home and into the basement where I started doing bench presses for my chest, overhead presses for my shoulders, bent-over rows for my back. Sometime that week, Mom had called Pop and told him about Jeb getting beat up by a grown man, and later that same night, not long after we'd eaten something in front of the TV, Pop walked in with a friend of his from the college, a poet or artist. He was tall and quiet and wore an overcoat like men who owned suits had to wear. Standing next to him, Pop looked short, and he was smiling like he was out on an adventure of some kind. He was wearing corduroys and a sweatshirt. Maybe he saw me looking at it because he said, "I wore this to hide my wrists. I don't want this guy to see my small wrists." He laughed and went up to Jeb's room to check his face.

Mom and Pop's friend chatted like they'd known each other a long time ago. Soon Pop came back downstairs and said, "Okay, let's go talk to this guy. I just hope he doesn't see my fucking *wrists*."

Then they were gone. I stood in the dark front room and watched him drive down Columbia Park to Main, my father who'd told me once that he'd never been in a fight, that he'd joined the Marines to prove to his own father he was a man, and I began to sense again that there were some things Pop just did not know, that not everybody can be reasoned with or talked to.

I don't remember if they ever found the J.s' house, but it didn't matter anyway. The only way to fight was not to have small wrists in the first place. To build so much muscle, your enemy would feel only fear before you killed him.

I turned and walked fast back down to the basement.

A FEW months later, the summer of 1975, I was working out six days a week, two hours at a time, on a split system, breaking my body parts down the way competitive bodybuilders did. I was overtraining and only ate tuna fish and eggs and the occasional steak if Mom could afford it, but by my sixteenth birthday that September, I could bench press my weight of 150 pounds; I could do fifteen straight pull-ups with a wide grip; I could curl 80 pounds for reps; and one Friday night alone in my room in the attic, I did one thousand sit ups without stopping. It took over an hour, and when I was finished, my lower back was chafed and bleeding from the floor beneath me.

It seemed no punishment was enough. In every exercise, if my muscles began to ache and burn on the seventh or eighth rep, then I'd do ten, twelve, fifteen, twenty. More than once my vision would narrow and get black at the edges, and I'd stop and breathe deeply till it passed, then I'd go right back to the barbell or dumbbells or chinning bar.

By that fall, any fat I'd had was gone. For the first time there were blue veins in my forearms and one running up my biceps. My shoulders were broader and my waist was smaller. I was getting what magazines called a V-shape, and I tried to accentuate it by always keeping my hair tied back in a tight ponytail. One afternoon, Suzanne said to me, "Girls are starting to notice you, you know."

It was an encouraging and flattering thought but oddly beside the point.

That August I ran those accidental eleven miles at Kenoza Lake with my father, and in September I went out for the high school's cross-country track team. After the last bell every day, instead of getting on the bus with Suzanne and the others from the avenues, I went to the gym and locker room with jocks, guys from Bradford who wore sweaters and boat shoes, guys who had short hair and braces on their teeth, guys who didn't swear or smoke dope or walk around the school stoned or tripping or half drunk. We changed into T-shirts and shorts and sneakers and went running.

The coach was over six feet and heavy, his mustache as blond as his hair. He had a bad limp I figured was from a motorcycle accident or maybe he was a vet, but one afternoon in the locker room as we were all changing, he changed with us, his right leg only ten or twelve inches in diameter from his groin to his ankle.

"Polio," one of the other junior varsity kids whispered to me. Coach T. could barely walk, never mind run, but still, five days a week he pulled on a jock strap and a blue nylon sweatsuit, a red stripe running down his good and bad legs, and he'd take his whistle and clipboard and we'd follow him outside to where he'd make us hurt.

Easy days would be 6-to-12-mile runs all over town. Hard days were sprints on the track, half laps, full laps, then double laps. Over and over again. On Saturday mornings I'd dress in my track uniform and walk to the high school or get a ride from my mother. I'd tie my ponytail back as tightly as I could, then run a 3.2-mile race with my team, my time medio-cre, though I thought I was running hard. Once, as I ran across the finish line behind a dark-haired kid from Revere, Coach T. shouted, "Too much left at the end, Dubus!"

He was right, and I knew it, but part of me was so surprised I was actually on a sports team of some kind, wearing a uniform like everyone else, sweating toward a common goal, that I began to *watch* myself run, happy just being there. Meanwhile, the varsity runners sprinted the entire course, coming in three to four minutes ahead of us, many of them drop-ping to their knees at the Finish Line and throwing up.

Most had cars, and I usually got a ride home with one of them. There weren't as many day parties at our house now. But once or twice a week, there'd still be five or six heads from the avenues sitting around in their leather jackets, smoking cigarettes and dope, our stereo cranked too loud, and I'd go straight upstairs and change, then take the back stairwell down through the kitchen to the basement where I'd lift weights for one to two hours. It was harder to build muscle running as much as I was, but I liked the nonstop pain of running; I liked how I almost felt high afterward.

I'd take my second shower of the afternoon, then go back up to my room in the attic and do homework. My grades were getting better. Teachers called on me in class more often. For the first time, they seemed to know I was there. And that's how I felt, too. Like I was here. Like I was somehow more on the planet with everybody else.

WITH MY new habits came new friends. Cleary still came around, but all he wanted to do was find a day party where we could get high, or else he wanted to drift downtown to steal something, or pinch a five from his mother's grocery money for a six-pack we'd ask a stranger to buy us. I'd be getting a ride home from one of the varsity runners, my hair still wet from the shower after practice, my leg muscles warm and tired, and I'd see him sitting on the steps of Pleasant Spa in his denim

jacket, his scraggly hair hanging in front of his face, a distracted glaze in
his eyes. If he walked into the house and up to my room, I'd tell him I
had homework to do.

"Homework?" He'd stare at me as if I'd just told him I was gay. Then
he'd shrug and head down the stairs to look for Jeb, but my brother preferred to stay in his room every afternoon now, practicing his guitar, or
else painting, drawing, carving images into leather with tools his teacher
had bought him. She'd be in there, too. Lying back on his bed with her
shoes off, encouraging him, laughing often, this thirty-five-year-old
woman my mother seemed to have handed her youngest son to as if she
were drowning and was simply grateful he'd be on dry land.

Sam Dolan had dark curly hair and deep-set eyes and didn't talk
much. At the high school where he was the goalie for the hockey team, he
walked the halls in a sweater, tight corduroys, and leather boat shoes, his
pec muscles straining against the wool, his upper arms so big they couldn't
possibly be real. In the spring he wore T-shirts, but he had to cut a notch
in the sleeves for his arms to fit. Other guys said he could bench over 300
pounds. Years later he would push 425 pounds off his chest, but back
then I learned he wasn't even lifting because the hockey coach believed
weight training slowed your reflexes. Instead, Sam was doing 666 push-
ups every other day in his small bedroom down on Eighteenth Avenue.
He was doing isometric curls and press-downs for his upper arms. He did
sit-ups and leg raises. He knew I'd been on the track team and asked if I
would run with him, help him get in shape for hockey.

I told him about Kenoza Lake, and three or four days a week my new
friend Sam Dolan picked me up in his black Duster, and we drove north
of town and went running together. We talked as we ran. I found out he
was an only child and adopted, that he loved the band Jethro Tull and
books by Edgar Cayce, that every night, like me, he laid out the next day's
clothes on a chair beside his bed, even his belt and socks. I told him about
my weight workouts. He asked if he could come down to the basement
and see what I had there.

It was after dark on a cool night in October. Mom was still working in Boston, or heading home on the highway in her faded red Toyota, the gasoline smell inside it finally gone. Suzanne may have been in

her room, Nicole locked in hers, Jeb practicing in his. Every light in the house seemed to be on, the floors dusty, and Sam and I were still sweating from our run, walking through the house and down into the basement. I flicked on the overhead fluorescent light.

On my last workout I'd loaded the bar with as much weight as it could hold, about 160 pounds, and I'd just barely gotten a single rep with it. Now, seeing the bar fully loaded on the forks of the bench like that, I felt a little proud of myself.

"Small bench, huh?" Sam lay down on it. He reached up, gripped the bar, popped it off the forks, and lowered it to his chest. I knew he'd be able to handle this without a problem, but I didn't think he would push it up as easily as if it were a broomstick in his hands. He could have done twenty, twenty-five repetitions with that, but after only one rep he lowered it back to the forks, sat up, and said, "Andre, that's really light."

Sometimes I forgot how far I had to go. I'd turned my body into something hard, but I still only weighed 147 pounds. I wasn't even close to being able to scare somebody away just by how I looked.

Once hockey season began, Sam and I stopped running together, but every Friday and Saturday night we'd walk from his small house on Eighteenth Avenue down Primrose Street past the Am Vets hall, its parking lot half full, music from a jukebox thumping behind the cinderblock walls. In front of the side door, four or five Harleys would be leaning on their kickstands, a black helmet hanging off a sissy bar, the red light from a neon Miller sign glinting off its surface. Beyond the Am Vets was a strip of weeds, then the parking lot for Pilgrim Lanes, a long white clapboard building where inside men and women bowled down on the floor. There'd be laughter and cigarette smoke and the clatter of candle pins, and we'd be over by the bathrooms where the pool tables were, taking turns playing eight ball with four or five others: there was Jimmy Quinn, who was six feet and could bench-press over 200 pounds for reps. One of his front eyeteeth was chipped, but he was handsome and already had a name. There were stories about him decking grown men who'd crashed house parties or some patch of woods where kids from the high school were drinking and getting high. They said he had the killer instinct, that even after a guy was down and hurt, Jimmy would keep whaling on his face and head till somebody pulled him off or the cops came and every-body started running.

There was fast-talking Kevin Daley, who played hockey with Sam and bragged often about their practice drills. "Man, we sweated bullets, didn't we, Sam? We sweated fucking *bullets*." There was gentle Jeff Chabot, who was tall and weighed over 250 pounds and was always smiling and crack-ing a joke; Greg Kelly whose cousin was the one they named the bridge after, the first kid from our town to get killed in Vietnam; and there were girls: the two April's—slim, blonde, hip-swaying April S., who was Jimmy's steady all through high school, and April C., Sam's girl, short and blonde with thick muscular legs and a cute face, and if she didn't like something you'd just said she'd smile and say, "Fuck you, you little faggot." And somehow you didn't feel less because of it. There were the twins Gina and Marie, pretty Greek girls who didn't come from down in the avenues and never seemed happy standing in the lot of brush and high weeds across from the lanes, drinking a beer and passing around a bottle of Kappy's screwdriver mix.

It's where the night always went, into the high brush across the street where we'd drink and maybe pass a joint around. Sometimes, when the weather was bad and if no one else was home, we'd end up at somebody's house, usually Sam's. His parents adopted him when they were older, and they were already in their late fifties. His father, a short, small-boned Irishman with a gravelly voice and a face like John Wayne, was the town's health inspector. Sam's mother was from a big Irish fam-ily up the river in Lowell. She was a waitress, and if she had a Saturday night off, Mr. and Mrs. Dolan usually went out with friends and didn't get home till late. We had their small two-story house to ourselves.

It was on a hill street with other small houses. The man next door drove a truck for the city. Another across the street was some kind of businessman. One July day he paid Sam and me to ride downtown in a pickup to an abandoned mill where we loaded two cigarette vending machines into the back of the truck, then rode to the man's house on Eighteenth. We carried them into his garage, and when he handed us each a twenty-dollar bill, he told us, "Don't say nothin' to nobody, all right?"

• • •

IT WAS late October, and the night was cold and wet. Sam's mother and father were out, and seven or eight of us were drinking beer inside his house. Sam had his record player going in his room, "Locomotive Breath" playing over and over, Jimmy and April making out on the couch. Daley, Kelly, Chabot, and I were playing 45 at the kitchen table, and the twins sat with us drinking and laughing and looking good in their tight sweaters and leather jackets and jeans. Sam and April were up in his room on one of his beds while the music played loud enough it would've hurt their ears if they weren't drunk and preoccupied.

This went on until Sam came down in his corduroys and white T-shirt, his hair messed up. He said it was getting late. We'd better clean up before his parents got home.

A while later, we filed outside, one of us carrying a plastic trash bag of our empties we'd stash somewhere. It was after midnight and we were standing around in the street. The air was colder and you could smell snow coming. Far off a train whistle sounded, the Boston & Maine on its last run of the night. I was drunk and didn't know it till I reached out for Marie's hand and missed.

Headlights shone on us from up the hill. The car was moving slow and every few yards the driver stepped on the brakes, his taillights flashing red. We parted for him, a small sedan, two men sitting in the front, the driver looking out at us like we'd done something to him.

"That's my neighbor," Sam said. "Let's get goin'."

April S. said she'd left her pocketbook inside the house, and she and Jimmy went back inside to get it.

Two houses down, the car jerked to a stop and parked half on the sidewalk. Both doors opened quickly and now the men were coming toward us. The light from Sam's porch glowed dimly in the street, and I could see they were forty or fifty years old, their hair thinning, one tall, the other short and wearing a parka. "Why you running? You stealing from my street? You the little shits stealing from this street? Get outta here and don'tchoofucking come back." The man was slurring his words.

The tall one behind him was weaving slightly, his eyes on Marie's breasts beneath her leather jacket.

"Mr. T., it's me, Sam Dolan. I live across the street from you."

"Don't give me that shit. It's you. Now get the hell off my street, you fuckin' punks."

I was standing close to him now, Sam on my left, Greg on my right, the others behind us, and I didn't like how this tall one kept looking at Marie. I didn't like how the short one kept insulting us, ignoring Sam, his own neighbor, swearing at us.

I stepped closer to him. "Fuck you, you ugly motherfucker."

A flash of yellow light snaked through my brain and there was black sky, then the streetlamp, then Sam's porch light again and the man who'd punched me was saying one thing more, a numbing ache in my nose, and there was the sound of running, then a fist slammed into Sam's neighbor's face, and he dropped to the street, Jimmy Quinn straddling him, punching and punching. One of the twins was screaming, and Jeff and Kevin began walking the tall man back, and Sam was trying to grab Jimmy, who was yelling, "Mother*fucker*! Piece of shit mother*fucker*!" He stood and kicked the man in the chest and back and rolled him to a parked car where he picked him up by his parka and slammed him down, his head thudding against the bumper. He picked him up and did it again, the dull clang of skull on metal. He did it again and was lifting the man to do it once more, but now Sam grabbed Jimmy around the chest and pulled him back and away.

"That's enough, Jimmy. *Enough.*"

Jimmy's shirt was ripped at the collar. He was breathing hard. He pointed at the man lying on his side in the street. "Fuck *you.*"

A man's voice called from a window. "I called the cops!"

We started running down Eighteenth Avenue, Jimmy and April ahead of me, her pocketbook jerking against her hip, her hand in his. I wished it'd been me who'd punched the man back, but as I ran drunk down the street with my friends, it felt as if something had just been revealed: Jimmy Quinn was as dangerous as everybody said he was, and even though I hadn't hit anyone, I had talked back.

I had just started something.

• • •

FOR A week or more we waited for the cops to show up at Sam's door, but nothing happened. Maybe the man woke up hurting and hungover and remembered very little, his friend either. Or, more likely, they'd probably woken to the knowledge they'd been in a fight with teenagers.

A few Saturdays later, we were back at the Lanes, shooting pool. None of us had any money for beer or even a seven-dollar bottle of Kappy's screwdriver mix, but we had enough quarters to play Eight Ball. I was no good at it, and when it was my turn to play the winner, I handed my pool cue to Big Jeff Chabot and walked past April S. sitting on Jimmy's lap, April C. beside them, chewing gum and watching the old people bowl down on the floor. I was thirsty. Earlier in the day I'd worked out in the basement for over two hours, hitting all my body parts at once, something Sam had told me to do to put on size, to work out less, not more. For a month or so now, I was doing only three workouts a week, but I could already feel my T-shirts getting tight in the shoulders and back. There was a porcelain water fountain bolted into the wall near the door, and I leaned over and drank gulp after gulp of tepid city water, every bit of it tasting good. When I straightened up, three men in ice hockey clothes walked in. I didn't know anything about hockey, but I recognized the oversized nylon shirts, all of them dark purple with orange stripes and big numbers printed on the back. The man in front had long red hair, still wet from sweating under a hockey helmet, and my heart started beating faster.

Last winter Cleary and I had been waiting outside a package store a block away from Monument Square. It was a convenience store that sold beer, and we'd stood away from the fluorescent light of the windows and waited with the money he or I had stolen from our mothers. Across the street was the used car lot we'd run through tripping so long ago, it seemed, and now all the little white bulbs were fixed again and dangled over rows of repossessed Monte Carlos and Mustangs and LeSabres. A van pulled up beside us, the radio blasting "Bennie and the Jets." The driver shut it off fast and slammed the door and stepped into the light. He had long red hair and needed a shave. He wore a dungaree jacket and didn't look like a cop or anybody's father, and Cleary said, "Hey, man, can you buy us some beers?"

He looked at us hard. For a second we thought a no was coming, the fourth of the night. But then he walked over with his hand out, and Cleary handed him a ten-dollar bill, "Schlitz Tall Boys, please."

The man took the money without a word and disappeared inside the store. A cop car was cruising down the street and we stepped back around the corner and stayed there in the darkness between the cinderblock wall and the dumpster. Behind us was a three-decker house. I could see through the second-story window the pale blue flicker of a TV behind a thin curtain. Cleary was talking about where we should go to drink our Tall Boys, maybe back to the tree hut, maybe down to Railroad Square and the abandoned brewery we knew how to get into to get warm.

An engine started up and we leapt around the corner to see the van backing fast away from the curb. We ran into the lot, shouting for him, but the redheaded man gave us the finger and stepped on it and was gone.

Weeks later, Cleary and I were walking down Main Street late on a Friday night. It was after one in the morning and the town was quiet, the boxlike houses we walked beside dark and locked up, the shades drawn. We'd been at a party at the rent collectors' on Seventh Avenue. They were fresh off a drug run down south, and the three small rooms of the apartment were wedged with people drinking and passing joints of Acapulco gold under the heart-tapping flash of a strobe light, the Stones playing "Brown Sugar."

In the bright kitchen, a man with long blond hair and an outlaw mustache sat at a table rolling joint after joint after joint. His chest was bare behind a leather vest, his arm muscles showing, and in a metal baking dish in front of him were hundreds of pot seeds he'd fingered from the dried leaf. Beside him sat two girls in tight tube tops sharing a bottle of Southern Comfort.

Cleary and I hadn't been there since we'd gotten kicked out and beat on, but there were enough people we would get lost in the crowd and the noise and the smoke. It was too crowded, though, too loud, too smoky, the windows open to let in the winter air, the radiators steaming and too hot to touch. Then Billy G., a scrawny, sunken-chested collector who had a room one story below, he took a syringe and drew blood from his thin white arm and started shooting it at whoever was closest. One girl, a frizzy-headed Dominican, ran screaming into the bathroom, Billy G.'s blood dripping off her chin, and that's when Cleary and I left.

Close to Pleasant Spa and Columbia Park, beyond the stone steps of the Jewish temple, a man was walking toward us on the sidewalk. We'd been watching him come from a long way off. He had hair that fell past his shoulders, his hands inside the pockets of his jean jacket. He wore heavy work boots and was walking fast, then he was under the streetlamp and I could see his hair was red, scruff on his cheeks and chin.

Cleary poked me in the arm. "That's the fuckin' *van* guy." Cleary picked up his pace. "Hey! 'Member us? You owe us ten *bucks*."

Everything always seemed to happen so fast, like a fuse was forever lit and you never knew when a bomb would actually blow. The man had Cleary on his back against the granite steps of the temple, one hand around Cleary's throat, a big fist raised high over his shoulder. "You want to die? Do you want to fuckin' *die* tonight?"

There was something wrong with his voice, something jagged and wired about it, and I thought he might be high on angel dust or some kind of speed. His raised fist was poised in the air where I could have just reached out and grabbed it, yanked his arm back, done something to him after that, anything. But I did nothing. Cleary said nothing. And soon the man was walking away from us down Main Street, his big hands back in his pockets, Cleary sitting up and rubbing his back.

Now, a year later, my body changed, my friends shooting pool not far away, the same man was walking in with his friends after hockey and his eyes caught mine, and I said, "Where's our ten bucks?"

I could feel my heart against my sternum, but I felt strangely calm, almost confident.

"Fuck off, kid. I don't even *know* you." And he brushed past me, looking back at me over his shoulder like I had just wronged him deeply. He looked away to order bowling shoes at the counter with his buddies, and I stood there staring at him. I believed he didn't recognize me, but

there was a nagging itch that I should go up to the counter and do more,
a slowed-time feeling a fuse was lit inside *me,* its low flame sparking at its
own pace, but this wasn't the one.

I walked back to my friends, and I could feel something coming farther down the road I just barely sensed I'd been training myself for all
along.

LIFE IS what happened between workouts. When I wasn't down in the
basement on Monday, Wednesday, and Friday afternoons working first
my chest, then shoulders, back, and arms, ignoring my legs because I
never wore shorts, even in the summer, then I was *thinking* about workouts, reading *Muscle Builder* magazine I now subscribed to, eating a lot of
eggs and tuna fish, so much my mother began to complain about the cost.
I began to think of getting some kind of job.

By the spring of 1976, I could bench-press just under 200 pounds; I
could do deep parallel-bar dips with 40- or 50-pound dumbbells hooked
to my training belt. I could do rep after rep of wide-grip chin-ups, pulling
myself so high the bar touched my chest. As the weather warmed and the
snow melted, the streets smelling like mud and rotting leaves and twigs,
I left my leather jacket at home and began to go out in a T-shirt; I had
muscles now. They weren't big, not nearly as big as Sam Dolan's, or even
Jimmy Quinn's, but enough that people glanced at my chest and upper
arms, took in my shoulders. There was the feeling that a good thing was
happening to me, that all my hard work was bringing about a good thing.

And I liked how much energy I had all the time, how I rarely got sick,
though one weekday morning in May, I woke up with a fever and stayed
in bed, and that morning Jimmy Quinn got stabbed.

Artie Doucette did it. I didn't know him well, though I'd seen him
out behind the M and L wings smoking on the grates. He wore a brown
leather jacket and had long black hair and pale skin. He was stocky-look-
ing and was always talking loud and swearing too much, and he had black
sideburns he let grow below his ears. Like a lot of people, he wore a folded
Buck knife in a snapped leather case at his belt.

Since the weekend, word had gotten around about what Doucette had
said, that Jimmy's girlfriend, April S., was a slut. This got back to Jimmy

on Monday and for three days he'd been looking all over the school for Doucette, who'd learned of this and stayed home. By Thursday, though, he could hide no longer. He had to get back to school, and that morning he took the bus. When it pulled up behind the M and L wings just before seven-thirty, the sun rising in a blue sky, hundreds of kids standing around or starting to stream inside, Jimmy was waiting. It was Daley who told me what happened next, that Doucette stepped off the bus and scanned the crowd and saw Quinn pushing past people to get to him, that Doucette ran, begging Quinn to leave him alone.

"I didn't mean nothin'! Jimmy, I didn't mean—"

Quinn grabbed the back of Doucette's leather jacket with both hands, and Doucette jerked free and spun around, the sun flashing off the five-inch blade just before he drove it into Jimmy's hip.

"*All* the way in," Daley said. "Right to the fuckin' handle."

Then Artie Doucette was running through the student parking lot, and Jimmy was down, his blood pulsing onto the concrete.

Daley helped Jimmy stand. His pant leg was soaked, blood running down his leg into his boot, and Quinn pressed his hand to the wound and limped through the crowded corridors all the way to the gym and Mr. Scanlon's office, the man who coached Jimmy on the baseball team. He called an ambulance and later we learned that Doucette's knife had just missed one of Jimmy's kidneys, that Jimmy Quinn, tall handsome crazy Jimmy Quinn, the one who had beaten up that grown man in front of Sam's house, had almost died.

For over a week Sam and Kevin Daley and Big Jeff Chabot and I walked the halls looking for any of Doucette's friends. One afternoon after lunch we found one, a skinny kid with long red hair and buckteeth. Daley backhanded his face and knocked him into a wall of lockers and the kid fell to one knee and Daley leaned close and pointed his finger an inch from his face. "You tell Doucette he's fucking *dead*, all right? You fuckin' *tell* him." Then he kicked him in the ribs, and we turned and went looking for more.

I don't know if it was having the others beside me, or that we were united in our rage, but I felt little fear, only a heart-thumping, dry-mouthed desire to hurt somebody, really *hurt* someone.

• • •

JIMMY STAYED home the rest of the school year, and it seemed a long, long time before we saw him again.

It was June, one of those hot days when you could smell the Merrimack River all over town—the faint smell of sewage and diesel and drying mud, of dead fish and creosote, of rusty iron and the melted plastic of some chemicals we couldn't name. It was after school, and Sam drove the two of us to Quinn's big family house on Main Street. His mother answered the door. She looked happy to see us and led us through cool dim rooms to the backyard where Jimmy lay in a lawn chair in the sun.

His hair was longer than I'd ever seen it, and his skin was tanned a deep brown. He wore a tank top and cutoffs. When he saw us, he smiled and grabbed the walking stick at his side and stood.

"Hey, Sam. Andre."

"Hey, Jimmy," Sam said. "You look good."

He did, and he didn't. He was handsome as ever, but he'd lost muscle in his chest and shoulders and arms. We stood there awhile. I don't remember what we talked about, just Jimmy nodding and smiling, his eyes on the sunlit trees of his backyard, the grass, his lawn chair in the middle of it. He had both hands around his walking stick, and I could see where the bark had been shaved away with a blade. If Quinn was planning to get Doucette for what he'd done to him, he didn't look it. Instead, he looked diminished by it, not by what Doucette had done, but that it could happen, that he could actually die before he got out of high school.

We didn't stay long. Sam and I had gotten jobs washing dishes, and our shift started soon. Jimmy laughed at something Sam said, then he walked back to his lawn chair, most of his limp gone, but the big stick still in his hand like something he wasn't quite ready to do without.

CAPTAIN CHRIS'S was a family restaurant overlooking the Merrimack on Water Street. On Friday and Saturday nights, it was crowded from five till closing, and it was one of the places Pop would take us to on our Sunday visits with him. It was air-conditioned, and the floors were carpeted and the tables were covered with rose-colored linens and heavy silver, Muzak playing over the sound system. From wherever you sat, you could see through the tinted windows the river moving by thirty feet below, and now I worked there in a kitchen that was hot and loud and crowded. Between the flaming stoves and the serving counter were four cooks, men in white who never stopped moving. They called out orders to each other, filled gleaming plates with baked haddock or stuffed lobster or prime rib, dropping a cruet of tomato and lemon onto the side, a sprig of parsley, then shouting for Doris or Ann Marie or Nancy to *pick up!*

And these women my mother's age, professional waitresses like Sam's mother, were dressed in a uniform of skirt and apron and white soft-soled shoes, and they would whisk the plates from under the warming lights of the counter onto loaded trays they'd heave over one shoulder, then punch open the swinging doors for the muted cool of the restaurant. Busboys would roll in a stainless steel cart, its rubber tub full of dirty dishes they'd quickly scrape, then load onto plastic trays, pushing them onto the conveyor belt for one of us to spray down before it entered the machine and came out steaming clean on the other side for another dishwasher to heave and carry back through the side doors to the busing station where he'd stack plates on a shelf, cups and glasses, sort knives and forks and spoons into the right trays, then push the empty tub into a stack of others in the corner and run back into the kitchen to do it again and again and again.

In the back were full-size stainless steel sinks for pots and pans and that's where Sam spent most of his time in an apron scrubbing bits of fish and potatoes, pasta, grease, and meat off of the bottoms and sides of massive containers. My job was to either load the machine or unload it, and I liked how hard it was to do well, how fast and efficiently you had to move, how quickly I broke out in a sweat and how much like a workout it became. That summer, the man who sprayed down the dishes and worked the machine was a drifter named Charlie Pierce.

Tall and scrawny, his arms scarred with blue tattoos, he was deep into his fifties and had thin gray hair and a coarse voice, though we never heard it much because he rarely smiled or spoke to anyone. Whenever there was a lull in the shift, he'd take a cigarette break out on the back stoop. He'd pull off his white apron and drape it over the railing, then light up a Raleigh and squint out at the river, exhaling smoke through his nose, taking his time.

One night very late, the cooks gone, the last of the waitresses too, it was just me and Sam and Charlie Pierce. Sam and I were wiping down the steel counters, and Charlie was mopping the floor. The transistor radio near the sink was playing, "Leaving on a Jet Plane."

We kept working and the singer kept singing over and over how she's leaving on a jet plane and Charlie straightened up from his mopping and shouted, "So fuckin' *leave* then!!"

Sam and I started to laugh, but Charlie was staring at us wide-eyed, like he'd just been insulted and couldn't we see that? He shook his head and went back to his mopping, swearing under his breath, mumbling to himself.

IT WAS a Saturday night in July, the place filled to capacity, and the kitchen was a loud, steaming machine of cooks calling out orders, the sizzling of hot oil, the swinging of the kitchen doors, Charlie spraying down the dishes before they went into the washer. There was the hollow clank of pots Sam was scrubbing out back, the chatter of the waitresses as they loaded their trays, some of them balancing three full platters of food up one arm, and the busboys were wheeling in carts of dirty dishes and were so backed up I had to move from the rear of the machine where I was unloading it to the front. The busboy had already run to his station to go set up recently cleared tables, and there were two full carts of food-streaked dishes, glasses, cups, and silverware, and I grabbed plates and bowls and began scraping them clean, sliding them into plastic trays and pushing them onto the belt for Charlie to spray.

"*Slow* down, kid." His voice came from behind the rack of plastic trays, and I could only see his waist and hands as he sprayed down the dishes I'd just pushed to him.

"I can't, we're backed up." I dropped a salad bowl into the loaded tray, then shoved it under the rack onto the belt and a hot sting shot across my arms and chest, water dripping from my elbows, the scalding water Charlie Pierce had just sprayed at me, and I was rushing around the corner to get him, the head cook dropping a sautée pan and jumping between us, another cook there too, then an older waitress with gray hair in a bun, Charlie saying, "I'll kill him. So help me, I will take that kid's life. I will take his life."

The head cook sent him outside to cool off. He put Sam in his place at the machine, then he turned to me and said, "And you, hothead, calm the fuck down." In seconds the kitchen was back to normal and I was pushing loaded trays to Sam, my heart still going, and even though Charlie's words were in my head, I wasn't afraid.

After smoking two or three slow cigarettes out on the stoop, Charlie came back in and relieved Sam, and we worked the rest of the shift without a word to him or from him.

Five years later, standing in my father's small campus house he shared with his third wife, I saw a photograph of Charlie Pierce in *The Boston Globe*. It was a mug shot, and he was looking into the camera with the same expression I'd seen before, as if he'd been deeply insulted and couldn't we all see that? I read the article below him, learned that he lay dying of cancer in prison and was confessing to over thirty years of murdering children. He was telling the police where he'd buried two bodies in Lawrence, one of a ten-year-old boy he said he'd raped and killed the summer of 1976, the summer he worked with us at Captain Chris's Restaurant down on Water Street overlooking the brown and swirling Merrimack River.

IN THE seventies, the only gyms were the ones we read about in *Muscle Builder* magazine, iron gyms in Southern California where the professional bodybuilders trained. There was the Y down near GAR Park, but the dues were expensive, and besides, from the outside it was a cinderblock box with few windows and looked like a prison, the only other place where I'd heard men regularly lifted weights.

Connolly's Gym was down near Railroad Square, a few blocks north of the river on Grant Street. It was on the first floor of an old shoe factory that must've been turned into a store at one time because there was no front wall, just floor-to-ceiling windows looking out onto Grant and an empty lot surrounded by a tall chain-link fence. On the other side, weeds had grown up between cracks in the asphalt, and there were a few empty oil drums, a stack of mattresses, an upside-down shopping cart.

Sam and I went down there hoping to see a weight-training gym like the kind we'd only read about, but when we walked into the hot open space, the carpet blue and commercial-thin, the walls whitewashed and still smelling like paint, we saw just two weight benches not much better than what I had in my basement. I almost turned to walk out when I saw the barbells; they were the seven-foot-long Olympics the pros used. They weighed 45 pounds and held big black iron plates. Around the corner a kid was working on a heavy bag, and he wore red Everlast hitting gloves, his wrists wrapped with tape. He looked pretty good, throwing fast punches, bobbing and weaving away from the swaying bag.

"Don't shlap it, Shtevie, punch it! *Punch* it!" Bill Connolly stood a few feet away. He was over forty and an inch shorter than I was, but he had a deep chest and thick upper arms, and we found out later that when he was younger he'd been a professional fighter up and down the East Coast. He was clean-shaven, and whenever he spoke he blinked a lot and all his *s*'s sounded like *sh*'s.

He shook our hands and showed us around. There were more weights and another bench, a couple of incline sit-up boards. He looked us up and down. "A middleweight and a welterweight. You boys gonna shign up?"

I had no desire to be a boxer. I was more interested in lifting the black iron weights I saw there, the same kind all the bodybuilders used in California. It was hard to get big if you were boxing, too. Sam may have been more interested than I was. His coach still had him off the weights, but he liked the idea of doing his push-ups and isometrics where other people were working out too.

"Yeah," he said. "We are."

The dues were cheap, and when we handed our dishwashing money over to Bill Connolly, he smiled and thanked us and took a pen and carefully wrote our names in a notebook. He blinked a lot and asked us twice about the spelling. I began to think this came from taking shots to the head, from getting punched over and over again in the brain.

WE STARTED working out there right away. Sam did his 666 push-ups, isometric curls and press-downs, pushing and pulling one hand slowly against the other, flexing his big biceps and horseshoe-shaped triceps. And I borrowed money from my mother she didn't have and sent away to southern California for an advanced bodybuilding course from Franco Columbu, a Mr. Olympia who was also a powerlifting champion and at 185 pounds could bench-press over 500.

Columbu's pamphlets were full of warnings that these were advanced routines for competitive bodybuilders, but I ignored those. Now, instead of one or two exercises for each body part, I was doing five, four or five sets each, and I moved my workouts from three times a week to six, and they were no longer one hour each but two and a half to three hours. Many times Bill Connolly would walk over and say, "Andre, you're doing too much. You want power, come hit the heavy bag."

But I didn't want to hit the heavy bag. I wanted to be as big as Franco Columbu. I wanted his flaring back, his huge bulbous shoulders, his pecs he could crush a pencil between. For weeks I ignored how tired I was getting, how I was always sore and avoided looking in the mirror because there was never much to see, even *less* than a few months earlier.

One afternoon, Bobby Schwartz walked into the gym. He was over 200 pounds and six feet tall and wanted to lose some fat around his waist. He worked for his father, Saul, who owned a police supply business up on Washington Street, his shop across from Saldana's bakery that'd been closed down because the owner hired only Puerto Ricans and Dominicans straight from their homelands and was accused of never paying them. Bobby was outgoing and good-looking, and he liked how long I worked out, how skinny I was. He asked if he could be my training partner and I said sure.

One Thursday, after a three-hour workout, we drove up to Bobby's father's store for Bobby's weekly pay. It was a small, musty shop, blue uniform pants and shirts hanging from racks. Under a glass case were silver handcuffs and black regulation billy clubs. Bobby's father was in the back office sitting at a desk cluttered with catalogues, a telephone, and Rolodex under a flickering fluorescent lamp.

Saul was talking on the phone when we walked in. He nodded at his son, his eyes passing over me, then he squeezed the receiver between his neck and shoulder and leaned back and reached into his front pocket and pulled out more cash than I'd ever seen before, fifties, twenties, tens, all in a wad three inches thick. Clipped to his belt was a semiautomatic pistol in a leather holster.

"Yeah?" he said into the phone. "Well fuck him, too." And he fingered some bills away from the fold and handed them to Bobby. He winked at him, then nodded at me as if we'd known each other a long time. He pushed the money back into his pocket. On the way out of his office, we passed another glass case, this one lined with brass knuckles and weighted black saps and boot knives.

Bobby saw me looking. "You didn't see those." He smiled. "Cops carry 'em, but they're not 'sposed to."

LATELY, EVEN though the weather was warm, I'd been wearing my leather jacket more. All I ever seemed to do was work out, but whatever muscles I'd begun to build in the last year were getting smaller. I was tired all the time and never felt like walking the two miles down to the gym or even having Bobby pull up to my house in his pickup. Still, I'd go.

One September afternoon, I had gotten to Connolly's ahead of Bobby and lay down on the incline sit up board, waiting for him. Outside there was a soft rain ticking against the glass. I could hear the transistor radio Bill sometimes played out back where he slept—talk radio, men speaking heatedly about some kind of game. Around the corner where the heavy bag hung, somebody was punching it, the shots coming hard but far apart.

"That's good," Bill's voice said. "That's good, Tommy."

My eyes were closed and I began to drift off, all the sounds becoming one sound I was floating away on.

"Hey."

I sat up. Bill was standing a few feet away looking at me, a pair of red Everlast hitting gloves in his hand. He smiled and held them up. "Get over here."

Then I was around the corner, this part of the gym unfinished, the walls naked brick, the floor concrete. It was cool and damp and smelled like sweat and rust.

"I know you want to be a muscle man, but let me show you a couple things, all right?" Bill was wrapping my wrists with two-inch-wide strips of what felt like Ace bandage. "This is sho you don't hurt yourshelf. Watch me." Bill pulled on the hitting gloves. They were made only for punching the bag, not for sparring, and they fit the hand close to the skin. Sewed inside the palm was a small iron bar. He raised his hand and shot his left fist into the bag. "That's a jab to throw 'em off balance." He threw two more, the bag jerking on its chain, then he threw a punch from his right shoulder, his back foot pivoting on his toes. There was a loud *whop* and the bag swung back three feet and Bill followed it, both hands up at his ears, and he dropped his left shoulder and got off two more quick lefts that jerked the bag to the right. He weaved to the left and shot another right, the bag jolting to a stop.

He was breathing hard, sweat breaking out just above his thick eyebrows. "Shee what I'm doin'? The jab shets you up for your combinations. I just threw three jabs, then a right crosh, a double left hook, then a shtraight right. Here, put these on."

I did. I liked the feel of the iron bar in my fists. Bill told me to raise my hands up and to turn more to the side, to put my weight on my back foot. "Now bring your elbows into your midsection and throw a jab."

I punched the bag. It was heavier than it looked. It barely moved.

"Rotate your fist as you throw it. That'll cut your opponent up good. Now jab three times, then throw a right."

I punched the bag three times, then threw the right as hard as I could, an ache jolting up my arm into my shoulder, the bag swaying away from me.

"Good power, but do it with your legs, too, Andre. Just like shwingin' a bat in baseball. You squash the bug with your back foot." I nodded like I knew what he meant. He raised his fists up. "Look at my feet." He threw a slow-motion right, his weight on his back foot, his toes corkscrewing with the punch. "A knockout comes from the legs, Andre. You try it."

I stood in front of the bag, my hands up, my body turned sideways to it.

"Put your weight on your back foot."

I did and could feel the concrete under the ball of my foot, my heel up. I threw a right, my back foot like a spring, the bag swinging away nearly as far as when Bill had punched it. It swung back and hit me in the knee. Bill steadied the bag and looked at me. He took in my chest and shoulders, my small arms. "Andre, you are deshieving. You are a lot shtronger than you look. You hit shomebody in the shtreet like that, they're going down."

I nodded and smiled. It'd felt good to hit the bag. I wanted to do it again. I wanted to find other ways to do it.

Bill said, "Give me them gloves."

For the next thirty minutes, he showed me how to throw a left hook, a right hook, the uppercut and straight right. He showed me how to weave away from the bag, then counterpunch. He showed me how to combine different shots, how to set my opponent up with pesky jabs, all while putting myself at the perfect distance to set my feet, then let go with a fight-ending right cross.

I was sweating and breathing hard, and when Bobby came in wanting to get to our chest workout, I was slow to unwrap my hands and wrists. I wanted to learn more, to keep punching that bag that began to look like Tommy J. and Cody Perkins, Clay Whelan, and Dennis Murphy and all the rest, the worn Everlast label on the canvas not letters, but eyes and a nose and a mouthful of teeth.

BOBBY GOT himself a new girlfriend. She had brown eyes and long shiny brown hair and she worked at a restaurant down the river in Newburyport. He started missing a lot of workouts, and I went back to my old routine of three days a week. Right away my energy came back. In a month my shirts were getting tight in the shoulders and upper back again, and before and after every weight workout I did three to four rounds on the heavy bag.

I was looking forward to going to the gym now. I was getting faster and trying new combinations, though I really liked going from the jab, then weaving to the left where I'd throw two left hooks to the body, then a right uppercut, a left hook to the head, then I'd find my range, set my weight down onto the ball of my foot, and throw a right cross that would shoot the bag backwards, Bill usually standing there shaking his head.

"You *are* desheivin'. A real shleeper."

This was brand new, a grown man taking note of me. It felt good, and I wanted more of it.

BY MID-FALL, Connolly had paid a carpenter to come and build a ring. It was just a plywood platform on two-by-fours on concrete, but he had the carpenter put in four posts and he padded them and ran regulation boxing rope from one to the other. In the corner was a crate of old leather boxing gloves, most of them the smaller eight ounces used in fights, but no headgear, and he told us that unless we wanted to lose some teeth we should go buy our own mouthguards.

Word got out Connolly had built a ring, and now boxers from the Y or other towns were stopping in to look at it. I was usually lifting out on the floor when they came in, their noses flattened, their eyes narrowed under punch-thickened eyebrows. One was Ray Duffy. Everybody said the Duffys were crazy as the Murphy brothers but tougher. There was the story of Ray down in a bar on Washington Street. Two men slighted him somehow and he stood there listening, then knocked them both out, one punch each.

Now Ray was coming in a few days a week. He rarely hit the heavy bag or lifted weights. Instead he'd step into the ring in his street clothes and shadowbox, his punches clean and efficient.

THE FIRST one I boxed in the ring was Bill Connolly's nephew Brent. Brent was ten or twelve pounds heavier than I was, and he had straight black hair and olive skin, acne scars on his cheeks. Except for Bill, he hit the bag better than anyone, his punches hard and crisp, his combinations fluid, his footwork and bobbing and weaving like some masculine dance. Because we were close to the same weight, and because Bill wanted to see how each of us would do, he matched us up on a gray Friday afternoon in October.

He wrapped our wrists and hands, helped us lace our gloves, made sure we had mouthguards, then ducked out of the ring. He studied his wristwatch and called, "Time!"

I expected to get beaten up, my heart pulsing hard in my temples as Brent and I raised our gloves and moved to the center of the ring. Bill had taught me to keep the right up to block any head shots, to jab, then move constantly to avoid being a target, to wait for my opening. Brent jabbed first and I blocked it with my left, then jabbed back and popped him in the forehead. His eyes blinked and I blinked too, a ripple of heat passing through my cheeks at what I'd just done. He jabbed again and as I blocked it, a right slammed into my right glove and smashed me in the eyebrow. I moved to the left and jabbed him two more times in the forehead, his eyes tearing up. His mouth looked swollen from the mouth-guard and I knew mine did too and it was harder to breathe with it. Brent stepped in and threw a straight right I weaved away from, then got off a left hook into his ribs, bright green flashing through my brain. I brought my left back up from where I'd dropped it, from where Brent had seen his opening and connected with a right.

"Shtick and move, Andre! Shtick and move! Brent, keep your right up, kid!"

I jabbed again and again, trying to do it from my feet up, putting some kind of snap into it, and maybe because I was an inch or two taller than Brent, it wasn't hard to hit him, his eyes pink and wet now, as if he was about to yell or cry, and I did not feel badly about what I was doing to him. I only wanted to keep jabbing and scoring points, to get him so frustrated he'd throw a wild punch and leave himself open for something more dangerous than a jab.

"Time!"

Brent turned and walked back to his corner, pulling at the laces with his teeth. He ducked between the ropes and yanked off his gloves, and Bill followed him. "Where're you goin', Brent? That was only one round, kid."

"I gotta go to work." Brent dropped his gloves in the crate and unwrapped his hands and walked out.

I was still in the ring, sweating, my breathing back down to normal again. Ray Duffy stood from where he'd been sitting against the wall. I hadn't known he was there. He said to Bill, "The bag don't hit back."

Bill nodded once. He smiled over at me. "That was a good shtart. I think you got the killer instinct, kid."

Which meant it didn't bother me too much to hurt somebody, that seeing his pain did not make me slow down or stop.

• • •

TWO OR three times a week I'd spar whoever was around. Many times it was Bobby, who'd come back to the gym and was doing his own lifting routine. He'd gained some weight, but he looked happy and in love, and sparring him was like fighting somebody crazy. He fought with both hands down at his sides, smiling at you even after you'd popped him in the face, then he'd shift to the side and his right would swing up hard and fast, and once I wasn't able to avoid it and it caught me in the cheek and knocked me four feet back against the ropes. Bobby moved in to finish me off, but Bill blew the whistle to stop it. He did that often because we still didn't have any headgear and now guys were climbing into the ring with others not even close to their weight, and he was afraid of getting sued. "I could lose this place, boys, sho take it eashy, all right?"

He was in danger of losing it anyway. Except for Sam and me, Bobby Schwartz and six or seven other guys from the neighborhood, his gym just didn't have that many members. He didn't have the cash to take out an ad in the paper, and he wasn't even in the phone book. He often looked worried about this, walking around the floor holding his membership notebook, its pages largely empty.

One afternoon I walked by the room where he slept. Usually a couple of sheets hung over the opening, but now they were down and I could see the mattress on the floor, the unzipped sleeping bag, a stained pillow. There was a mini-fridge and a hot plate, a jar of instant coffee, a box of Lucky Charms and a can of Campbell's soup.

By late winter, Bill Connolly's gym would go out of business, and he would close his doors and move north to Maine. Years later, we would hear he'd died, something to do with his liver or kidneys. But none of that had happened yet, and it was a Saturday morning in the fall of 1976, I'd just turned seventeen, and Bill had arranged an exhibition of his fighters and his new ring. He'd had flyers made up, and he walked all over downtown, dropping them off at shops and barrooms. That morning, he bought a coffeemaker and brewed a pot and set it on a card table beside a bucket of doughnuts. Maybe this was his way of drumming up business, or maybe he was just proud of us and his new ring and wanted to show it

off, or both, but he laughed a lot, and slapped people hard on the back,
eight or nine real boxers from real gyms in other towns along the river like
Lawrence and Lowell.

One of the first fights was Bill's nephew Brent and Sam Dolan. Sam
had his shirt off and looked like carved ice and made the rest of us look
good. Next to him Brent looked puffy, his olive skin yellow. Bill called
"Time!" and they danced around each other, trading jabs before Brent
threw a left hook and missed and Sam hit him hard in the face with two
short rights, Brent falling back, his eyes wide, his mouthguard loose, and
Bill called "Time!" though the round had just begun. "Eashy, boys, it's
just an exhibition. Andre, you go next."

"Who with?"

"Sam."

I didn't want to fight him. I was sure he would kill me, and even if
he didn't, I did not want to punch the face of my friend. But we couldn't
embarrass Bill in front of the few who had come, so I stepped into the
ring, eight-ounce gloves laced tightly over my wrapped hands and wrists,
and Bill called "Time!"

Boxing is intimate. The fighter across from you becomes nothing but
eyes. You look at nothing else. Your peripheral vision picks up his gloves,
his bare shoulders, sometimes even his footwork. But you watch his eyes
because they can show you something just before he shoots off a jab or
is trying to find his range against you, to set his feet and fire off a combination; his eyebrows may lift slightly, and you can see how his pupils
sometimes darken with emotions fighters are supposed to be above: hurt,
frustration, fear, rage, all of which can muddy your judgment, make you
swing wild when, instead, you should be minimizing damage as best you
can, waiting for your move. And so you never think how dangerous this
is, that a motivated punch from 600-pushup Sam Dolan could possibly
kill you, or at least knock you down and out.

As soon as Sam and I got within punching range, I started jabbing,
sticking and moving to keep him off balance and avoid getting hit. The
first few jabs, Sam looked surprised I was actually punching him. Then he
looked hurt. Then angry. He stepped in and threw a right hook, and when
I weaved away from it I could feel the wind behind it. If I'd thought about

that connecting, I would have stopped and walked out of the ring, but I kept jabbing. Sam's eyes blinked every time. I never realized how green they were, like mine, and now they were dark and shining and looked betrayed. He swung at me harder and I was just able to avoid his glove and pop him in the face again. Somebody yelled something from outside the ring. Another voice said, "Quit dancing. Throw a combination."

I knew he was right, but I couldn't do it. You left yourself open when you threw combinations, and I didn't want to get hit even once by Sam. I jabbed him twice in the nose, and he waded in and threw a cross that knocked my glove into my shoulder and spun me halfway around and Bill called "Time!"

He ducked into the ring. "That's good, you two. But shomebody's gonna get hurt."

Me, he meant. A couple men clapped halfheartedly. Others stood there looking at us like we'd disappointed them, that they'd come here to see a real exchange, not this. Sam and I gave our gloves to Bill to give to two more fighters, two kids from the avenues, and we stood side by side for the rest of the exhibition, but something had been wounded between us.

I knew in a fight on the street he would've beaten the shit out of me. But I'd been able to frustrate him, and standing there beside the coffee and doughnuts I tried to ignore the feeling I'd just achieved something by hurting my best friend.

6

ONE LATE FALL afternoon, I came home from the gym to the smell of cooking. The house was quiet, no day party going on, and in the kitchen Suzanne and Jeb were standing by the stove. There was the lick of blue flames under a black iron skillet, hot oil popping and spattering under the rising smoke. Suzanne glanced over at me. "We chopped these tortillas out of the freezer. They're the only thing to eat in this whole fucking house." Jeb sprinkled salt on one and handed it to me and I blew on it and ate it. Suzanne stood back from the stove and wiped her eyes, then pushed a fork into the skillet, the grease crackling, the smoke thicker now.

Jeb and I used to sit in Cleary's kitchen, his mother passed out in the front room, and eat whatever he put on the table for us: cheese and crackers, Devil Dogs, peanut butter and jelly and bread we made sandwiches with, bags of potato chips and cans of Coke or Pepsi. Most of it was junk, and we knew it but didn't care. Once he was in our kitchen and opened the fridge and saw its bright empty shelves and said, "What happened to the food?"

What could we say to that? Even when Pop had lived with us, there hadn't been enough for snacks like Cleary had. And now there wasn't enough for three meals a day either. It's something we'd all gotten used to, that hollowness in the veins, the nagging feel there was always just a bit too much air behind your ribs.

But some times in the month were better than others. Right after Mom got paid she'd go to the grocery store, and while there was never food to eat between meals, there seemed to be enough for the meals themselves. These were still the ones she could make from a can or something frozen, something quick so we didn't eat too late, but sometimes Bruce would have money to give her, too, and there might even be enough for a few days of school lunches. We hadn't sat around a table and eaten as a family since Pop had lived with us, and I no longer missed it, but our mother did. That fall when I spent so much time at Connolly's Gym, she suggested we start having breakfasts again, sit-down breakfasts together, and for a few weeks she got up every weekday morning an hour earlier to pull that off.

I'd be in the attic, lying in my bed in the early morning darkness, my breath clouding in front of me. I'd hear the door open at the bottom of the dusty stairwell and my mother's cheerful voice calling me down. Eventually the five of us would be sitting at the dining room table we rarely used, the blue light of early morning seeping through the windows: Jeb with his wild hair and downy whiskers; Nicole in the brown sweater she wore to hide the brace she endured for her scoliosis; Suzanne in her hip-hugger jeans and a T-shirt, black eyeliner around both eyes like bruises. Mom would be dressed in a blouse and scarf, earrings and makeup, dressed for this job doing good in Boston when it had never paid her enough to do the good she wanted for *us*. But it seemed she was forever too tired to look for something else. And what else could she do anyway? She was only qualified for social work. She could work two jobs like Rosie's mother, but then she'd never be home at all. Years later I would think about my father more, think about those three months off every year, his summer mornings writing and running, most every afternoon lying under the sun at the beach. But it seemed he'd chosen that job for those three months. He was as poor as we were, a condition he could endure for those ninety days it gave him back to write longer every morning than he did all year.

For a few weeks that fall, Mom served us steaming bowls of oatmeal or Cream of Wheat with cinnamon toast—bread she'd butter, then sprinkle with sugar and cinnamon and slide under the blue flames of the broiler; other mornings, it'd be buckwheat pancakes and hot bacon and orange juice. One morning we woke to eggs Benedict with hollandaise sauce and baked peaches in pools of melted butter and caramelized brown sugar.

But this didn't last. It couldn't. She ran out of money, and we were kids who went to bed late and didn't get up in the morning. Before Mom had started these breakfasts, she'd be on her way to work when we were supposed to leave the house to catch the bus around seven. Even with those wonderful smells filling the house once again, we rarely made it to the table on time, and our mother, depriving herself of a little extra sleep for this, gave up. It was like living inside a great slumbering beast who'd woken just long enough to blink its watery eyes, howl, then turn over and go back to sleep.

BUT THANKSGIVING was coming up, one of those days each year my mother always rallied for, when she seemed to shrug off the massive weight that was raising children alone, and it was like watching a night-blooming flower open its petals in the gloom: for a while holidays changed everything; she'd clean the house, and with genuine good cheer coax us into getting off our asses to clean, too. She'd put some Rolling Stones on the stereo and turn it up loud and make decorations out of construction paper and glue and yarn and glitter, taping these brilliant colors around the house. At Thanksgiving, there'd be earth tones—browns and greens and yellows. At Christmas: red, silver, and gold. On our birthdays we'd wake to presents in the living room, each of them wrapped by her; sometimes the paper would be homemade, a grocery bag she'd stenciled stars onto, then dressed with twine and a rope bow. There'd be store-bought paper, too, cut and taped perfectly around our new clothes, records, or books, these boxes laid out and stacked so that there always appeared to be more than there were. She probably spent the rent money on all this, and she put presents on layaway accounts she'd spend an entire year paying down.

For this Thanksgiving, Mom had stuffed turkey with cornbread dressing. There was baked squash and Yorkshire pudding. There was homemade cranberry relish, steaming dirty rice and mashed potatoes and rolls made from scratch. She'd decorated the house and used an ironed sheet as a linen tablecloth. She'd been playing old jazz albums on the stereo, the same music she and Pop would listen to years earlier—Dave Brubeck, Gerry Mulligan, and Buddy Rich.

Outside it was cold enough to snow, the sky gray, the front yard hard and brown. Bruce was south of Boston with his family, and Mom had put on makeup and a light sweater. She wore earrings and a bracelet like she did to work. Pop was due at three, and we'd be eating at four, and Mom worked in the kitchen, a Pall Mall smoking in an ashtray, sipping from a glass of Gallo red wine while she stirred gravy on the stove, Brubeck's West Coast piano filling the house.

It was holidays when the six of us sat down as a family again, and whenever we did, Pop sitting at the head of the table like he used to, it was as if we were each inhabiting roles to play for this brief time: Jeb was the reclusive genius; Nicole was the studious one getting good grades; Suzanne was the one just barely getting by but would; I was the newly disciplined athlete; Mom was the hardworking woman who managed to work, shop, do the bills and laundry, and cook for us too, especially on holidays like this; and Pop was the man who gave us most of whatever money he made and would sit at the head of the table like it was a throne he'd somehow left behind and was glad to reclaim two to three times a year.

Maybe we could all feel the charade, that Jeb spent way too much time in his room with his teacher, that he'd tried to kill himself once and why wouldn't he again?, that Nicole had become distant and brooding and terribly alone, that Suzanne would fall in love with one avenue boy after another, that her dealing money often bought us food we wouldn't have had otherwise, that I was methodically teaching myself how to hurt people, that Mom *was* hardworking but could never keep up with the bills, the laundry, the shopping, with feeding us, with much of any of what Pop had left her behind to do on her own, that Pop was no longer the head of the family, though he still sat at the head of the table as if he belonged there.

But I still looked forward to these dinners, to Mom's wonderful cooking, to her flirting with Pop and he flirting with her. He'd look her up and down and tell her how beautiful she still was, that nobody could cook like her. She'd say, "Oh, be quiet, Andre," and she'd reach for a spoon or knife or loaded dish, but she'd be smiling, her cheeks flushed. I looked forward to all four of us kids leaving our separate bedrooms to sit at a candlelit table and see each other over all this abundance, and for a little while we'd forget that Mom had to skip paying some bills to do this, we'd forget that this was all just temporary and everyone was an actor in a play none of us had written.

It was three-thirty and Pop wasn't here yet. Suzanne had come down from her room, Nicole too. Jeb was still up in his practicing guitar to his metronome, and Mom had me pull the turkey from the oven and set it on the counter. It was copper brown. I could smell its warm meat, the onions and cornmeal of the stuffing. Mom covered it loosely with foil and kept glancing at the clock. Pop should have been here a half hour already, sipping something in the kitchen with her like they used to. At four o'clock, she called his number and got no answer. At four-thirty, she pulled the foil off the turkey and began to carve it with a steak knife. She had me and Suzanne carry the side dishes out to the table and set them on the ironed sheet.

"Well, goddamnit," she said, "we're just going to have to start without him."

But we didn't. To start without him would be to start the play without the audience. We couldn't. We waited.

Mom tossed her wine into the sink and began washing dishes. I don't remember helping her, but I hope I did. Nicole and Suzanne ate some rolls, cool now.

Sometime between six or seven, a car pulled up to the curb. Its headlights stayed on a while, and when they finally turned off I could see from the front room that it was Pop's old Lancer. Then both doors opened. At first I thought he'd brought a girlfriend with him, but in the light from the porch I could see it was a man in an overcoat. He held a bag to his chest, and he turned and waited for Pop to walk around the hood of the car, both of them moving unsteadily up the sidewalk to the porch.

The house had been quiet for a while. I stayed in the front room long enough to lower the needle back down onto the Brubeck album, then I met them at the door. The front hallway was dark, the bulb in the ceiling fixture blown long before, and both men were shadows walking into the house smelling like booze. My father put his arm around my shoulders, and he said, "Lou, Louie, this is my boy. This is Andre."

The man said something, and I shook his hand and he pushed the bag at me, two bottles of wine I carried past the loaded dining table, half the candles still burning, out to the kitchen where Mom leaned against the counter smoking a Pall Mall, drawing deeply on it, her eyes wary.

"Pop's here. He brought a friend."

"What?"

But then Pop was behind me, his buddy too, and her face produced a smile, her eyes still wary, and Pop said, "Pat, this is Lou. Lou, Pat. He's sharing Thanksgiving with us."

Lou was taller than Pop, but his cheeks were jaundiced and under his eyes hung gray bags above a withered mustache. He moved swiftly to my mother, nearly stumbling, and he took her hand in both of his, apologized for the intrusion, said he'd brought some wine. Pop leaned close to me and whispered thickly, "He's dying, son. And, his wife just kicked him out."

I nodded. Pop took the bag from me and pulled out the bottles and soon we were all sitting in candlelight at the table, Pop at the head, me to his right, then Lou to mine. Mom sat at the opposite end, my brother and sisters across from me. The Brubeck was playing a little too loudly, the piano rhythm too fast for eating, but we'd been waiting and were hungry and we passed each other plates to fill with whatever dish was in front of us, and though a lot of the food had cooled the smells were still in the room—the celery and liver in the dirty rice, the sweet squash, the savory turkey meat and salt-drippings gravy. We all seemed to be talking at once, and Lou was drunker than I'd thought. He had a hard time holding up his plate and he kept mumbling how pretty we were, how pretty all of Andre's daughters were.

I'd seen him before, too. I'd seen him in church, and I'd seen him standing in the doorway of the framing shop he owned in Bradford Square. Pop had probably met him at Ronnie D's bar, the place he went to drink after all his work was done. And even this drunk and sick, it was clear how much he respected Pop. He kept glancing over at him with reverence and affection and gratitude. It's how so many people treated our father, as if he was not like other men, as if there was something about him that made them somehow more themselves when they were around him.

Part of it seemed to be the stories he wrote; people put him in a higher place after having read them. But Pop had always been deeply

curious about people too, from the man pumping gas into his car, to a
waitress serving us on a Sunday, to the priest standing at the church door
in his robes, Pop always lingered and asked people questions about their
work, their days and nights, questions nobody else ever seemed to ask.

This drew people to him, people like this dying man Lou, whose
hand was now on my knee under the table.

"Yurall sech pretty girlz. So pretty."

My face was hot iron. Pop was talking loudly over the jazz about the
cornbread stuffing, how it was one of the only things he missed about Louisiana. Suzanne was talking, too, her lips moving and her eyes pointed at
Pop. Mom was laughing, and Nicole was chewing, Jeb too, and now Lou's
hand moved farther up my leg and I turned to him to tell him I'm no girl,
and his lips pressed against mine, his whiskers poking my skin, his tongue
pushing into my mouth. It was like getting stabbed. I jerked back, Pop's
voice louder than ever now, "Uh-oh, uh-oh," he said. And I was up and
moving past my mother out the back door to the porch, the air a cold slap
I wanted more of. I spit over the railing. I wiped my mouth and spit again.

Pretty girls. How could he think, even shit-faced, that I was a *girl*? My
hair was cut to my shoulders now, still long but not even long enough to
tie back, and I had *changed*. I had a chest and shoulders. I had a flaring
upper back. I had learned how to throw punches. How could he even
think that? And in front of everyone, too. In front of my *father,* who was
now out on the porch with me, nearly yelling, "Andre, he doesn't want to
suck your *cock*. Lou doesn't want your cock, son, he wants your *health*."
Pop slapped my chest with the back of his hand. "He wants your youth
and your muscles and all those years ahead of you. He's dying, son, he's
fucking *dying*. He's got fucking leukemia and his wife kicked him out on
Thanksgiving *Day*. You *hear* me?"

My father was clearly as drunk as his friend, and he kept slapping my
chest, and I was crying for the first time in years, my father's reddened
face, his trimmed beard and thinning brown hair getting all blurry. Did
he think I was building muscles for my *health*? And now he wanted me to
go back in and sit down next to his friend.

I wiped my eyes and followed my father back inside. There was candlelight and Brubeck's piano, there were the smells of hot wax and this

holiday feast, but the table wasn't as loud and raucous as it had been earlier, and Lou was staring at his plate and seemed to be carrying on a conversation with himself. I sat down beside him. I did not look at my family. I lifted my fork, and I would use it if I had to, I would; I'd stick it into his dying face, for it was clear once again that nobody in this world was going to take care of you but *you*.

SUZANNE AND I discovered something called accelerated admission, where you could skip your senior year and go straight to college. I didn't want to leave my friends, but the thought of leaving the high school was cool mountain water after a long, hot run, and I took a test and somehow got into Bradford College. Suzanne was already a student there. She'd stopped wearing hip-huggers and heavy black eyeliner. She spent most of her nights studying in her room, and she began to make friends over there with the kids of doctors and bankers, and sometimes she'd spend the night in one of their dorm rooms. Because our father was a professor she just had to pay for her books, one more thing our mother had to worry about.

Bradford College was a small green campus behind stone walls and iron fences, and it held over three hundred students from around the country and the world, many of them rich. The men were only a year or two older than I was, but they drove BMWs and sports cars with names I'd never heard of. They wore khaki pants and button-down shirts and spoke ironically in classes. "Yes, Professor, but does Aristotle speak to dramaturgy in that way? It seems to me he does not."

"Yes, but how?"

"You see, Professor, that's the question, isn't it?"

There would be some appreciative laughter, a few sardonic smiles, the professor moving on to someone else.

For nearly two hundred years Bradford had been a women's college, and now it had just begun to admit men and there were far more women, roughly ten to one. So many of them were tall and slim. They had long straight hair and straight teeth and straight postures from what I imagined were childhoods spent riding horses and swimming and playing tennis. They drove convertible coupes and laughed often. Very few of them wore bras and on cool mornings I could see their nipples under their sweaters

and turtlenecks. I tried not to look, but I couldn't not look. The first week
of the first semester, I was sixteen. I walked around campus in a leather
jacket, my hair shorter now, books under my arm I was actually reading,
but around these women, who were eighteen, nineteen, and twenty, I felt
like a poor and uncultured boy.

One morning between classes I cut through the student union building, its pool table and soft chairs, its serving counter where you could
order a cheeseburger and coffee or hot chocolate. A group of them were
over by the picture window which looked out onto the raked lawn. I
heard one of them say, "That's Dubus's son. Look at him. He's such a
townie."

I'd heard the word before. They used it for the men they'd see at Ronnie D's bar down in Bradford Square, the place where my father drank
with students and his friends. It's where some men from the town drank,
too—plumbers and electricians and millworkers, Sheetrock hangers and
housepainters and off-duty cops: townies.

I enjoyed reading the books—even the biology and economics—and
usually I enjoyed the class discussions and tried to be prepared for them,
but I was surrounded by people who seemed reared from comfort, most
of whom knew where they were headed, too: law school, medical school,
business school, a few even to New York City where they would sing,
dance, and act. In the smoke room in Academy Hall, a place I walked
by often, I'd hear of their aims for the future, and I didn't have any. All I
wanted to do was bench-press 300 pounds and get so big I scared people,
bad people, people who could hurt you.

The following May, instead of going to my sociology final, I shot pool
in the student union with Sa'eed, a soft-spoken black kid who'd grown
up in the slums of Philadelphia where people shot each other regularly.
I'd just set up for the break when my sociology professor walked in for a
Coke before class. He was heavyset with a beard and glasses, and I liked
him. From the counter he smiled over at me. "That's a good way to pre-
pare for a final. Keeps you relaxed."

I smiled back. "Yep. I'll be right there."

But I didn't go and got an F in the course. The next fall I didn't go
back. I told my mother I was just taking a year off, but I didn't know if

that was true. I couldn't imagine going back to that tiny campus that felt
so foreign to me, so protected.

LAMSON'S SPA was on Winter Street, a convenience store with cardboard
in the windows, some of them cracked, duct tape holding them together.
Inside, the shelves were largely empty and half the ceiling lights were out
and everybody knew the place was a front for bookies and drug dealers.
South of it was a sub shop and American Ace Hardware, the Greek church
on one side, a Catholic church on the other, and farther down the hill were
Mediterranean Pizza and Dunkin' Donuts, their fluorescent light spilling
out the windows onto the parking lot next to the gas station where five days
a week I worked from seven to four pumping gasoline into the trucks and
vans of tradesmen. I'd take their cash and go into the tiny glass booth and
make change. I'd hand it to them, then slide the booth door shut to keep
out the cold. There was an electric space heater under the plywood shelf
the register sat on, and it was like the one we had back in the tree hut, the
one we kept going with extension cords we'd snuck into our basement, our
mother always confused as to why the electric bill had gone up so much,
and now, as I worked forty hours a week and knew how much of my day
and week and life I had to put into just making money, I felt badly about
that bill, about stealing from my hardworking mother like that.

The man who hired me was older than my father and drove a late-
model Cadillac Seville. He had dark skin and wore polyester pants, shining shoes, an overcoat, and sweet-smelling cologne. Every afternoon at
exactly four o'clock he'd drive up to the pumps to lock up and take my
deposit bag and credit card receipts. When he first hired me, he looked
me over and said, "This place gets robbed sometimes. If they got a gun,
don't try nothin'. But, there's this, too." On the booth's metal windowsill
was a homemade club. He picked it up and held it out to me. It was some
kind of hardwood, about three feet long, the length of it covered with
carved initials and ink markings. Late into my first day, tired of looking
straight out the window at the brick machine shop there, or to my left
at the black iron trestle above Winter Street, or to my right at the repossessed cars in the lot, I picked up the club and began to read who loved
whom 4-ever, who sucked, what number to call for great head, then, in

black ink, the letters neat and perfectly aligned, *Life is like a dick. If it's hard, you get fucked. If it's soft, you can't beat it.*

Just before Connolly's closed down, Ray Duffy walked up to me and asked if I wanted to buy two 50-pound plates. They were spray-painted silver and fit right onto my barbell at home and that's where Sam and I worked out together now three days a week, Sam back on the weights, his hockey career doubtful. He was so much stronger than I was, and during the bench press we had to strip 80 to 100 pounds off the bar for my sets. Still, I could push close to 250 pounds off my chest, and in the shoulder and back movements, I was almost as strong as Sam. On off days, we drove to Kenoza Lake where you could drive to the top of Kenoza Hill along a winding gravel road, but there was also a steep dirt trail through the trees. It was sixty yards long and nearly 45 degrees, and Sam and I would take turns grabbing 20-pound dumbbells and running up that trail as hard as we could. Just before the top, an invisible hand yanking the air from your lungs and the earth itself trying to pull you down, we'd reach the crest of the hill where there was an incline of open grass and we'd run on for another thirty yards. We worked up to doing this ten times each.

I'd hung a heavy bag down in the basement, too, and every day after a workout I'd wrap my hands and pull on hitting gloves and hit the bag as hard as I could. The Everlast logo was the height of a man's face, and I'd jab it, then throw a straight right to the nose, a double left hook to the ribs and temple, a right hook to the chin followed by a right cross to the forehead, that last punch rising up from my back foot and pivoting hip, the bag jerking on its chain. So many times the Everlast was Tommy J.'s face, his shaved head and small MP mustache. Other times it'd be the kid who threw the Molotov cocktail into my mother's car, or Dennis Murphy right after he slapped the pine into that old woman's face, or Clay Whelan just before he started pushing me to the ground to whale on my face and head, or Doucette stabbing Jimmy Quinn, or any of the boys and men from the avenues lounging around in our rented house, smoking and drinking and listening to the stereo Bruce bought us, calling Suzanne "Sue" and me a little pussy and Jeb a faggot. And lately, I saw myself punching Suzanne's new boyfriend, Adam Kench.

It was after ten o'clock on a weeknight and she was driving Mom's

Toyota back home from Bradford. He was hitchhiking on Main Street in a leather jacket and faded jeans, his hair past his shoulders, sunglasses on at night. She said he'd looked like Neil Young so she stopped and picked him up, but he was wearing sunglasses because the glare of the headlights was too bright for a quaalude-head, a nurse's aide who was in that line of work to steal drugs from hospitals and rehab.

He was high all the time, and she was with him for months. When they were at the house, they'd be up in her room, the door closed, Grand Funk Railroad playing, Pink Floyd, Robin Trower, the Stones. Up close you could see how sunken his chest was, how his long hair was thinning, and the skin of his face was more gray than pink, the stubble of his chin like some leveled ruin. I rarely saw his eyes because he never took off his dark sunglasses, and he was always asking Suzanne for a ride: To the hospital where he worked. To the Packy for some wine. To some low-rent neighborhood to cop some downs.

The night it happened I woke to the sound of arguing. A woman's voice, then a man's, Mom and Pop married again and I was nine, lying in my bed next to Jeb in that camp in the woods. But the voices were outside and three stories below, Suzanne and Kench. I was lying under covers in my attic bedroom. I heard the doors of Mom's Toyota open and shut, Suzanne's voice as the engine turned over and the gear shifted, the whine of the small motor as they backed out of the driveway. I had an electric clock now, and I sat up and squinted at its glowing numbers: 10:37. Where were they going this late? And why? Something felt wrong about it.

I lay awake a long time. I had no curtains in the windows, and I could see it was snowing outside, a slight wind blowing the flakes under the streetlamp. So many falling and falling, and I got tired of seeing the falling and closed my eyes.

IT WAS Suzanne who woke Mom the next morning. She called just after dawn broke. Thirty years later she told me why she waited this long but no longer, because she didn't want Mom to be awake already, getting ready for work on a Monday morning only to see her driveway empty, her car gone, her oldest daughter still out from the night before, then get angry and be pissed off when the phone rang and start yelling before

Suzanne could talk, because she knew Mom would feel guilty for that later, she'd feel guilty about yelling at her daughter on this Monday morning in February, so Suzanne called her early enough to wake her and spare her that feeling later. Save her from at least that.

She and Kench had driven forty miles to Boston for a drink. After last call, he got in behind the wheel and got them lost. They were somewhere in Dorchester or Roxbury on Blue Hill Avenue. There were row houses and broken streetlights, a few cars abandoned on the sidewalk. This was 1977, the forced busing riots still in the news, white men and women stepping in front of buses of black kids driving into their school yards, yelling, "Niggers, go home!" The previous summer, the bicentennial summer, there was a first-page photo of a white man trying to impale a black man with a pole, the American flag hanging off it, the black man a lawyer in a three-piece suit, trying to twist away from it. At the high school for a year now, there'd been talk of a race riot, of "niggers" and "spics" coming up from Lawrence and Lowell to cause trouble, so get ready, bring a blade, stick together, kick some ass.

Kench turned down a dead-end street. It was after two in the morning. He stopped the Toyota to turn around, and a beat-up sedan passed them slowly on the opposite side. Then it did a U-turn and pulled across the road and blocked it, their front bumper not far from the Toyota's exhaust pipe. Two men stepped out. They were both black and one of them knocked on the window and asked Kench for help because their car had just gotten stuck on the ice behind them.

Kench got out of the car and left Suzanne there and walked around to the rear of the sedan. One of the men got behind the sedan's wheel, the other stayed back with Kench, and they both pushed on the trunk as the big engine roared. Suzanne could hear it from inside Mom's Toyota, but she could also see the red flash of the brake lights every time her boyfriend and the other man pushed. The sedan didn't move and Kench climbed back into the Toyota and shut the door against the cold.

"Adam," she said, "he was stepping on the brakes when you guys were pushing."

"Don't worry, I got it covered. We're copasetic."

"No, we need to leave."

One of the men rapped his knuckles against the driver's window and Kench opened the door and stepped outside again and Suzanne heard the sap thump his forehead, watched him drop to the street. The one who hit him knelt over him and went through his pockets, and Suzanne's passenger door opened and the other one pulled her from the car and held a knife to her ribs and walked her to the sedan.

WHEN THEY were done with her, when they were done taking turns with her one at a time in the backseat while the other drove slowly past the steel-shuttered windows of shops, under overpasses, past the locked doors of apartment buildings—when they were done, they stopped at a corner and pushed her out. She wore only her shirt, nothing else, and as they drove off she stood there with her feet together, her arms crossed tightly. It was after three in the morning in February in Boston, ice on the sidewalk, the snowbanks along the curb dirty and frozen, her feet bare, her legs. Both of the men had held the same knife to her the whole time, and that was how she was going to die, wasn't it? But no, the cold will do it now. Maybe she was thinking that when she saw the headlights coming and she waved the car down, a taxicab, the driver older and black, looking her over, letting her climb into the back of his heated cab. She told him what had just happened to her, and he shook his head, "All that free shit thrown at them and they gotta do that."

He used his radio to call the police. She described to him the dead-end alley she'd been taken from, the streets and buildings around it. The driver took her right to it. In the glare of his headlights, Mom's red Toyota was still there, and Kench lay on his back in the low snowbank where he'd fallen. Over the rooftops, the sky wasn't quite as black, dawn not far off, a Monday in February, Valentine's Day.

NOW IT was just after seven, Mom and Bruce were in his car speeding down the highway for Boston, and I was picking up the phone to call my father.

At first, because I never called it, I couldn't remember his number. Then it came to me and I dialed, my fingers hot in the rotary holes, my body light, my tongue thick. His phone began to ring. I stood in the hall-

way near the back door, the one Suzanne had used the night before to leave.
I heard again their voices, heard the car start up, and why didn't I get up and
run down there and stop them? I knew then, wherever they were going, she
was doing it for him. I should've done something. Again, why didn't I?

Outside the sky was gray. Patches of snow lay in our neighbor's side
yard. Somewhere in our house Jeb and Nicole were awake, home because
of what had happened, though I did not know where they were or what
they were doing.

"Hello?" He sounded as if he'd been up for a long while.

"Pop?"

"Andre?"

"Yeah. I have bad news." It felt as if I were telling him to lift his chin
and hold still so I could plant my feet and raise my fists.

"What? What is it?"

And throw this right cross into his nose and mouth and trimmed
beard. "Suzanne got raped last night."

"What?"

"In Boston. Mom and Bruce are going to get her right now."

My father said more things, his voice shot through with shock and
pain. He said he'd be right over, and as I hung up, my face began to feel on
fire for what I felt right then, shame that I had not protected his daughter,
my sister, but there was something else too, something I needed to deny
but could not, this dark joy spreading through my chest at having just
done that to him, the one who should've been here all along, the one who
should never have left us in the first place.

ON THE heavy bag now, I punched it so hard my knuckles stung and my
shoulders ached. I kept seeing the men who'd done that to Suzanne; I
kept seeing them *as* they were doing it. Then I'd change what happened.
I'd stand in the middle of the street till the cruising sedan had to stop
and I'd walk around to the driver's side and set my feet and punch him in
the temple, ripping a light through his brain that would forever stop his
heart. I'd jerk open the back door and pry the knife from the one on my
sister, then hook my forearm around his forehead and pull the blade into
his throat and draw it from ear to ear, and I'd punch the bag and punch

it and punch it till I couldn't breathe anymore and my heart was charging faster than the sedan of the two men who got away and were never found, not then, not now, gone for good.

WASHINGTON STREET lay behind concrete floodwalls and ran parallel to the Merrimack River from Railroad Square all the way to the Basiliere Bridge. In the winter of 1977, it was a street of closed shops, some of their display windows covered with brown paper, squares of masking tape sticking to the glass. Other businesses had nothing covering their front windows, and beyond them lay one big dusty room. Against the wall would be shelves and a bare countertop holding a brass cash register, its drawer open and empty. The old Woolworth's building was closed up and locked, but farther down the street was Mitchell's which was still operating and where, when she could, Mom would put clothes on layaway for us. Farther west was Barrett's. Through the windows I'd see men in shirts and ties selling clothes to men who wore ties, too. I rarely saw men like that and assumed they must live across the river in Bradford.

And Washington Street was where the bars were: the Lido, the Tap, the Chit Chat Lounge. They were on the street level of the mill buildings, darkened, nearly windowless caves filled with men and women drinking and smoking, their cigarette smoke swirling through the dim lights behind the bar. There'd be music playing on the jukebox: Frank Sinatra and Sonny and Cher, Elton John, Tom Jones, and Johnny Paycheck. Near the register were jars of pickled eggs, a rack of potato chips and Slim Jims, wooden booths built into the walls, a few scattered cocktail tables, most of their bubbled Formica tops spotted with cigarette burns. Throughout downtown, along the narrow streets and alleys between the mills, there were many other bars like this: Ray and Arlene's, Smitty's, the 104 Club. There were stories of knifings or shootings in these places, of brawls with guys getting their teeth knocked out, their noses broken, their jaws splintered and having to be wired shut. The same names kept coming up, too—the Murphy boys, the Finns, the Duffys, Jon and Jake Cadell, the Wallaces, gangs of brothers who drank together down on Washington Street, then got into fights, sometimes with each other. And there were men known for just that one thing—brawling and almost always com-

ing out on top: Jackie Wright, Paul Brooks, Ray Duffy, Bobby Twist, and
Daryl Woods. Others, too. They'd work all week for the city repairing
roads, or over at Western Electric in Andover assembling circuit boards,
or on a construction crew, or in one of the quarter-running mills downtown stamping shoe soles. Then on Friday and Saturday nights they'd fold
their drinking money into the front pocket of their jeans, pull on their
leather jacket, and hit Washington Street.

IT WAS a Saturday night in winter, and we were heading downtown in
Sam's black Duster, me and Sam and my brother Jeb. For the past three
years, he'd barely left his room. He was tall and lean, and his hair was so
wild he had to stick strands of it behind his ears so he could see. He'd go
five or six days without shaving, his cheeks and chin covered with soft
brown whiskers.

He was seventeen now and a junior at the high school. When he
actually went there, he wore a denim vest and spent most of the day in
the art department, drawing and painting and sculpting. One afternoon
he found a dead cat in the snow off Columbia Park, and he carried it into
the house and cut off its tail with a kitchen knife. The next day he wore
the cat tail as a tie, the bottom half of it tucked neatly into his vest.

He practiced classical guitar hours and hours every day up in his closed
bedroom. His former teacher from the middle school would be in there with
him, and soon my brother's guitar would go silent and she'd start moaning.
After a while, Jeb's guitar would start up again. I would hear this sometimes
and think only good things, that my brother was getting regularly what
most boys could only dream of, that she was keeping him so busy with sex
and art that he couldn't possibly want to die anymore. She still bought him
guitar strings, music books, paints, canvases, but he never went out with
me on the weekends, never roamed the streets anymore like we used to. On
Saturday nights, she'd come for him in her Z-28, and he'd walk out of the
house for trips to restaurants down in Cambridge and Boston.

It was a cold night in February, two feet of snow on the ground, a
thin layer of cracked ice on the sidewalks. Somehow I'd talked Jeb into
going out with us, and it was strange having him in the backseat behind
me, but it felt good. Like it used to. Just the two of us, before there were

any friends like Cleary who was at the trade school now and had stopped coming around. We didn't see much of him at all, though we started to hear about his little brother Mike, who was making a name for himself as a martial artist, a polite and gentlemanly killer.

That night Sam and I were wearing sweaters and leather jackets, jeans and boots, but Jeb never seemed to get cold. He wore a T-shirt and loose corduroys. On his feet weren't shoes but wool slippers his teacher had knitted for him. He needed a shave.

Sam had the radio on, Rod Stewart singing about Maggie kicking him in the head. We were heading down to the Tap on Washington Street. On Saturday nights they had live music, and the place would be full of men and women, some of them from Bradford College across the river. Sam drove under the railroad bridge into Lafayette Square. We passed the bright lighted windows of Store 24 and cut around the rotary into the dark streets of downtown, tall abandoned mill buildings on both sides of us as present yet gone as dead ancestors. Every block and a half there'd be a blue or red neon glow coming from the first-floor window, another bar this town was full of, and I was looking forward to the Tap, but not to drink. Sam and I were eighteen now and legally old enough to be in these barrooms, but for months now he and I hadn't had even one sip of beer, and we weren't eating anything with sugar in it either. We were trying to get as defined as possible, to get cut.

Sam drove the Duster down the alleyway and into the asphalt lot below. It was crowded with cars and pickups. There were streetlamps along the floodwall shining down on the plowed banks, the lot salted and sanded, and out on the river was the slow dim movement of white floes on black water. Even before I stepped out of Sam's car I could hear the thumping bass of the band up in the Tap, could hear all the bar voices talking over it.

Jeb climbed out of the back. His hair was in his face. There were brown whiskers across his cheeks and chin and throat, and as we crossed the lot for the rear door of the bar, Jeb just a few steps behind us in his T-shirt and hand-knit woolen slippers, I felt I'd done him some kind of wrong by bringing him, that I was using him somehow, my little brother who'd become a kept boy, a musical recluse.

The stairwell up to the street level was dimly lit, the wooden treads wet and gritty. The music was louder here, and I heard a woman laugh over the noise. At the landing, Sam pushed open the door, the long oak bar two and three people deep, the bartenders working fast and never stopping, the band too loud, the air stuffy and smelling like damp wool and cigarette smoke, perfume and spilled beer and sweat. The bouncer sat on a stool collecting a two-dollar cover charge. Even on the stool he was taller than we were. He had curly black hair and a wool sweater and looked thirty years old.

We paid our money and made our way through the crowd. The floor was wide hardwood planks worn smooth, and the band was in the next room where the lights were dimmed and men and women sat at cocktail tables drinking and talking and laughing. A lot of them looked older than we were, married couples out for their Saturday night. The band was on a small stage, a cigarette smoke haze under the lights where the lead guitarist was singing about Amy and how he'd like to spend the night with her.

Usually Sam and I would head to the bar and order a milk, wait for the bartender to say something before he poured us the watered-down liquid they used for White Russians, but the bar was just too hard to get to, and as we stood there in the squeeze of bodies I began to recognize a face here and there, some of them girls from the high school, young women now. A lot of them worked shifts at Western Electric or in one of the mills or restaurants downtown, or maybe they were training as a nurse's aide in an old folks' home or had tried a little college like me before dropping out.

I could see a few of them drinking at the bar, talking to each other over the music. They took deep drags off their cigarettes and turned their heads to exhale, their made-up eyes glittering darkly.

Everybody was talking and nobody was even pretending to listen to the band. I was already tired of standing in the middle of it all and hoped Sam felt the same way and would want to leave soon. But he was talking to Bobby Schwartz, who I hadn't seen come in. Bobby looked big and handsome in his dress leather jacket and somehow he'd made it to the bar and had a drink in his hand. He was smiling at Sam, nodding at whatever he was saying, and something was happening up against the brick wall, Jeb slapping away the hand of Steve Lynch.

Lynch was over six feet and had curly blond hair and a deep voice and the girls liked him though he was known for being a badass, for walking the halls like some charismatic king, always three or four others trailing behind him. More than once I'd seen him push a smaller kid out of the way, or knock another's books out of his hands as he passed, and he'd laugh and call them faggots. I'd been in the same class with his older brother Dana, who wasn't much different, just a little bigger and not quite as handsome.

Lynch was here with three or four of his buddies. Now they were standing there waiting for him to do something to this little shit with the untamed hair and slippers on his feet who'd just slapped Lynch's hand aside after Steve'd scratched Jeb's chin and said, "You need a fuckin' shave."

Bobby and Sam saw what was happening, too; the three of us stepped closer as if we'd been pulled there, the four with Lynch looking us over, us doing the same to them. I was vaguely aware of a steady electric current rising up my legs and into my chest, and I wasn't afraid, just so aware, Lynch's voice somehow the only one I heard above the dozens of others, nobody looking over at us, the crowd still drinking and talking and laughing, Steve's voice, *Let's take it outside then.*

You first.

No, you.

And Jeb stepped sideways through the crowd, Lynch following him past the bouncer through the door for the long stairwell down to the parking lot where my brother would have to fight in his slippers and T-shirt, his hair swinging in front of his face, and I wanted to follow, but Bobby was holding his hand up to Lynch's boys, smiling that same smile he used to have in Connolly's ring, both gloves at his side, daring you to swing, "You stay, we stay, right, boys?"

The tallest and biggest nodded, and the seven of us stood there in the smoke haze and the noise of the crowd that didn't know we were waiting to see who'd come back in that door.

It was Lynch and it was way too soon. Less than a minute. He was smiling, looking down at me as he rejoined his friends. Sam said something, or Bobby, but I was moving through the crowd past the bouncer, then down the long stairwell, thinking *knife.* He *stabbed* him.

The steps were pockets of air under my feet. Then I was out in the

cold, the grit of salt and sand on ice under my boots, Jeb standing there
looking at me.

"You all right?"

"I had my back to him, he kicked me down the stairs, I can't find my
other slipper."

Jeb's left foot was bare, his toes naked on the iced-over asphalt.

"Where is it?"

"Up there somewhere."

I was back inside, the stairs under me like an afterthought. And I was
scanning them for my brother's wool slipper, but I wasn't looking for it.
Then I was on the landing and past the bouncer inside the noise and heat
and smoke, walking past Lynch and his boys to Sam and Bobby. *He kicked
him down the stairs. Help me find his slipper.*

Sam went first and then I did too, but there was the feeling I was
done with this, done with looking, done with everything, and I ran back
up, stepped inside the bar, turned, and there he was, Steve Lynch on the
landing, grinning down at me. My back was to the open door of the bar,
and as the words came out of my mouth I could feel my weight sink back
on my right foot, my arms go loose at my sides, and it was as if I were in a
warm bath under a blue sky, my words coming together in a question that
could only get the answer I was waiting for. "Have you seen my brother's
slipper, Steve?"

"*Slipper?* Your brother's a fuckin' faggot and so are—"

He was falling, not backwards, but straight down, as if a blade had
taken off his legs at the knees, and I was swinging and swinging but the
bouncer's arm was in the air between us and I was trying to punch over
it, my fist just missing Lynch's face which was bone-white, his lower face
wet and red, his mouth a dark hole though my fist felt nothing, and the
bouncer pushed and I was half falling, half running down the stairs and
out into the cold air where my brother waited.

"You find it?"

I was breathing hard. I shook my head. "No, but I clocked him."

"Good."

"Yeah." And we began walking through the dim parking lot for Sam's
Duster, the air strangely still and calm, the streetlamps shining down on

the parked cars, the ice floes in the river beyond barely moving. I felt light and pure and free of something. Sam's car was locked.

"Your foot cold?"

"A little."

Something was different. Everything was different. There was more quiet in the air and more noise, too. The band had stopped playing upstairs and all the voices seemed to come louder through the brick walls. The back door pushed open from the stairwell and three of Lynch's boys came walking toward us. The bigger one, the tallest one, said, "You sucker-punched my friend," and he tackled me into a snowbank, then was sitting on my chest punching me in the side of the head, in the ears, in the neck and shoulder. Then it was over. He'd done his duty, and he was walking back to his buddies, the three of them standing next to Jeb like they were in front of a fire watching it burn. The big one and his buddies walked back inside, and I was standing, dusting the snow off. That was *it*? My entire boyhood I'd been unable to talk or move or resist out of fear of *that*? My head and ears were sore, so what.

I wanted to run back up there and try again. I wanted to set my feet and throw one into the big one's face, but now couples were leaving, a few of the women lighting up, their pocketbooks swinging. Engines started to turn over and Leslie, a woman I knew from the college, another townie, was walking fast to her car. I could see her breath. "Andre, they're coming for you. Like fifteen of them. I like your face just the way it is, honey. Please, you gotta get outta here."

There was yelling inside. A door slammed out front on the street. Jeb and I looked at each other, and then we were running down the back alley along the floodwall, over iced cobblestones past dumpsters and concrete loading docks and stacked oak pallets, then up under the railroad trestle past the traffic lights onto the sidewalk of Comeau Bridge. Jeb was ahead of me, his hair bouncing, his bare arms pumping. His other slipper was loose, the sole of his foot pale in the flickering fluorescent light of the streetlamps on the bridge. A car passed us, its tires humming on the iron grid, then another, and I was waiting for the screech of brakes, for a carload of men to come get us and throw us over.

Soon we were in the bright light of the gas station on the other side, a stoner I knew from somewhere just hanging up the gas pump. His Camaro door was open, and the backseat was covered with eight-tracks and empty Marlboro cartons, Aerosmith blasting from his speakers as he drove me and my brother home.

He offered us hits off a joint, but we said no thanks. He pulled up to our house on Columbia Park, his stereo too loud, and we thanked him and heard his tires squeal on the ice behind us. Jeb went ahead of me up the path in the snow to our steps, his foot probably half frozen now. Like always, nearly every light in our house seemed to be on, each window lit up and uncovered, and I walked into it behind my brother and shut the door. *They're coming for you.* I believed that, and my first thought was to turn off the lights and darken the house. The living room was empty, Mom out maybe, or up in her room. Suzanne, too, up in hers, listening to music by herself. Nicole locked in hers, reading or doing homework on a Saturday night. There was the feeling I'd brought danger to them, but also, miraculously, that I would take care of it, that whatever was coming, I was going to take care of it.

Jeb had found a jacket and wrapped it around his foot, and I was walking straight back to the bathroom, smiling, shaking my head, only now aware that the knuckles of my right hand were stinging and had been for a while, that first punch connecting, a right cross that came up from my back foot and into Steve Lynch's sneering mouth. I ran warm water over my hands and soaped up and I looked in the mirror at the boy who hadn't backed down or run away or pleaded. I was smiling at him, and he was smiling back at me.

There were Bobby's and Sam's voices now, talking fast and excitedly. I turned off the water and rushed out to the living room where they stood telling Jeb their story, that after Lynch went down the bouncer started kicking everyone out, but Sam hadn't done anything and held his ground and the bouncer wrestled with him and Sam got low and punched him in the groin and he went down and three or four others rushed in to help and Sam gripped the doorjambs and kept yelling, "You can't push me out! You can't push *me*!"

But they finally did, right onto the sidewalk on Washington Street, the door slamming behind him. Sam walked around the corner and down the sloped alleyway into the parking lot. Bobby was there squaring off with two of Lynch's boys. His eyes caught Sam coming across the lot. *"Sam?"*

"Bobby?"

And Bobby punched the biggest one in the face, then yanked his jacket over his head and went to work on his body, the other backing off.

"And *you*." Bobby turned to me. He was smiling wider and brighter than I'd ever seen him. Our living room looked small with him in it. "You fuckin' *nailed* him."

I nodded and smiled, then I was laughing and I couldn't remember feeling this good about anything in my life ever before.

"Hey, Jeb," Sam said, "we found your slipper. It's in the car."

Jeb went outside for it. Bobby wanted to hear Sam's story again about taking on the big bouncer, and Sam was telling it when Jeb's voice came yelling from outside. "They've got sticks! You guys, they've got *sticks!*"

The three of us were pushing through the foyer and out the front door. A sedan had pulled up ahead of Sam's Duster, the back door of his car open, its interior light shining on ice patches on the asphalt and the four men closing in on Jeb in the street. Each of them carried what looked like wooden clubs or broken chair legs, the three of us already there, four against four, Dana Lynch swinging his stick and yelling, "You're dead, motherfucker!"

"I don't think so." The words came out of me, but my eyes were on the big one I'd already been in the snowbank with, the road slick under my feet, and Dana was slipping his way toward me. I could see his limp and remembered hearing months before about him getting his legs crushed between two cars at some party. Sam moved toward him, but the big one stepped in and pushed him back a step, and Bobby was calling to the others to make a move. Jeb stood in the middle holding his slipper, his foot still bare.

Sam, so used to ice under his feet, stepped around the big one and put one hand on Dana's chest and began talking him down.

"Sam, I respect you, but my brother's in the fuckin' *hospital*, man! He swallowed his two front *teeth*."

Dana swung his club at his side, and now my mother was yelling from the porch that she'd called the cops and in seconds a cruiser's spotlight was on us. The cop's window rolled down. "Break it up or every single one of you are going to jail! You hear me? Now *screw!*"

Then Lynch and his boys were gone and we were back in the house, laughing again, though not quite as hard, Jeb pulling that slipper onto his damp, pink foot.

THAT NIGHT I lay in the dark a long time and couldn't sleep. Steve Lynch would have false teeth for the rest of his life and never be quite as handsome again, and it was because of me. I knew I should probably feel bad about this, but I didn't. Not even a little. I kept seeing the pride and respect in Bobby's and Sam's eyes in the living room, the way they looked at me not only like I was one of them, but maybe even a special one of them, a guy with a gift; I only hit him once, and he was in the *hospital*?

I kept seeing his face as I punched it. I still couldn't remember feeling the impact of the right cross, just the sight of him dropping like a switch had been turned off in his brain, the blood gushing from his mouth, the shock in his eyes and how white his cheeks and forehead looked, how I kept swinging and would have hit him every time if the bouncer hadn't stopped me. How I wished he hadn't. How I wished I'd hurt Lynch even more than I did.

BECAUSE STEVE Lynch was seventeen, the town closed the Tap's doors and they stayed closed the rest of the winter. Word was out, too, that I would soon be in the hospital myself. Not just from the Lynches and their friends but their cousins, the Murphy brothers. I didn't know about this family connection till I saw them cruising by my gas station in a dented olive Chrysler, Dennis looking out the passenger window at me, his older brother Frank driving, two or three more in the backseat. My mouth dried up and I could feel my heart beating in my palms. I reached for the club and held it in my lap till the car disappeared under the railroad bridge for Lafayette Square. I stood and pulled open the slider to get some air.

Twice a day, while doing errands for his father, Bobby would pull up to the pumps in his pickup truck to check on me. Sam, too. He was a student at Merrimack College down in North Andover and at least once a day between classes he'd swing by in his Duster. I'd tell them both I was fine, that they were wasting their time. This was partly true because Dunkin' Donuts was right up the hill, and there always seemed to be at least one cruiser parked there most of the morning or afternoon. Also, I worked the day shift on a busy street, what were they going to do? But really, I was more angry than scared. I didn't like how some were still saying I'd sucker-punched Steve. A sucker punch was walking up to someone with a smile, then surprising him. Or tapping someone on the shoulder only to pop him once he turns around. Lynch had pushed my brother down the stairs and was calling me on and I gave him what he'd never expected. And since that one punch, it was as if I'd knocked a sandbag loose inside me and now a torrent of bad feeling had pushed aside all the other sandbags and I needed another place for it all to go. Another face.

SAM AND I were doing weighted dips in the basement when Suzanne came downstairs crying. She wore a dark sweater and hip-hugger jeans and her eyeliner was smeared. After her rape, no one in the family talked about it much, and neither did she. She may have gone to a counselor once or twice, but I don't think so, and now she knew for sure something she'd suspected for a long time: that Kench was cheating on her. He was living with a nurse named Denise over the state line in New Hampshire, and Suzanne wanted her things back, her record player, a turquoise ring of hers he'd liked and stuck on his finger. "Please, you guys, I don't want them in *her house*." She covered her face and Sam put his massive, sweating arm around her. In minutes we were driving north up the highway in our sweats, our muscles still pumped with blood.

The nurse lived in a trailer park in the pines. It was after ten on a weeknight and we were driving down a dirt road over exposed tree roots, a bed of pine needles running down the center. Most of the trailers were set back into the trees, their window curtains drawn, many of them dim or dark. Some of the mobile homes had small porches or decks built onto them, and there were grills and lawn chairs and a few flower boxes nailed to the rails.

"That's it," Suzanne said. "That's his car."

Sam and I were walking in the dark across a strip of grass to a white trailer. I gripped the knob, turned it, then stepped into an unlighted living room, the thin carpet wall to wall. I could see my sister's record player on the shelf across from a couch, the only light from a hallway to the left. I could hear Kench's low stoned voice talking to someone, a woman's voice, too, louder, clearer, then she was in the light of the hallway looking back at him, not seeing us at all. She was naked. I took in her breasts and hips and dark pubic hair and stepped back into the shadows beside Sam. "Kench! We're here for my sister's stuff. Get out here, you piece of shit!"

There was the slamming of the bathroom door. "Who *are* you?! Get out of my *house*!" Then she was in the hallway, knotting the belt of a blue terrycloth robe, peering into the darkness where we stood.

Sam yelled, "Be a man, Adam. Get out here!"

The back room was silent. I pictured him lying naked under a sheet in his postcoital surprise, letting his girlfriend defend him the way he never defended my sister in Boston, and I wanted to walk back there and beat him where he lay. But the woman was yelling at us to get out, and now Suzanne was pushing past us, crying and calling Kench's name, looking past her boyfriend's girlfriend as she stood there suddenly still and quiet in her lighted hallway, everything clear to her now.

Sam and I watched as Kench emerged from the bedroom. He was barefoot and his jeans were unbuttoned, his T-shirt on backwards, his long thin hair flat against his head. Suzanne was screaming now, swearing and calling him names, and she walked up to him and grabbed his wrist and jerked her ring off his finger, then was back outside, the door slamming behind her.

I grabbed her record player off the shelf and yanked the cord from the wall. Kench and his new girlfriend stood in the lighted hallway together as if they were watching something terrible happen to somebody else. "I see you again, Kench, I'll fucking kill you."

SAM DROVE over the dirt road while Suzanne cried softly in the passenger seat. I sat in the back next to her record player thinking about Kench, how he'd looked so sunken-chested and pathetic in that hallway, his nurse beside him in her robe. I meant what I said; if he came around again, I was going to pound him for doing what he did to my sister. Still, it felt wrong to have just walked into his girlfriend's trailer like that, to have seen her naked. It also felt familiar, though I'd never done something like that before. Sam's car rolled in and out of a rut, then he was on asphalt, accelerating, and I knew what it was. It was like punching Steve Lynch in the face, how you have to move through two barriers to do something like that, one inside you and one around him, as if everyone's body is surrounded by an invisible membrane you have to puncture to get to them. This was different from sex, where if you both want it, the membranes fall away, but with violence you had to break that membrane yourself, and once you learned how to do that, it was easier to keep doing it.

LATER, TWO or three in the morning on a Saturday night, a black SS Chevelle pulled up to our house, its eight-track blaring Blue Oyster Cult and waking up the neighborhood. Up on the third floor, I turned over in my bed, assumed they'd move on. But they didn't. The driver revved the engine, and I thought, *The Murphy brothers. The Lynches.* The word now was that they were going to get me when I didn't see it coming, maybe in days, maybe in months. My heart began to zip through my brain, and at the window I could see their interior light on, a woman in a leather jacket passing a joint to the driver I couldn't see. I opened my window to yell at them to quiet down, to move on, but they'd never hear over their stereo and anyway this was a street full of homeowners who called the cops all the time, had called them on us: for the afternoon parties, for the motorcycles sometimes parked out front, and one afternoon Mom was home and she came out to greet the cop and the two or three housewives who'd gathered at his car to tell him all about us, this bad element on their street. My mother calmly talked to them, explained these were just teenagers listening to music too loud, that's all, that she'd make them be more considerate about the volume in the future. After the cruiser was gone and the neighbors were walking away, one of the women—sharp-faced with the short, practical haircut of a woman who spent her days running a household—said to another, "She sounds *educated*. I'm really surprised. Aren't you?"

Now the neighbors would think these two in the Chevelle were with us, and I lay in bed waiting for the cops to pull up. But they never came, and the car got quieter anyway, the stereo off while the engine ran and ran, a sound I fell asleep to.

The next morning it was still there, a black muscle car in front of our house like an indictment. It was empty, the driver's door unlocked, and I opened it and peered inside for the keys. The interior smelled like dope. On the floor of the passenger side were three empty Haffenreffer bottles, and I slammed the door and called Sam and twenty minutes later I was behind the wheel of the Chevelle, Sam backing his Duster up to the rear bumper till the Chevelle nudged forward. I gave Sam the thumbs-up and he gave his Duster the gas. I had jerked the transmission stick down into neutral but the wheel was hard to steer and I could smell the rubber we were burning all the way up Columbia Park on a weekday morning, the sun shining bright on the trees in the median. The plan was just to get the car away from my house, but at the top of Columbia Park we waited for a van to pass by on Lawrence Street, and I could see past the chain-link fence around the reservoir, the sun flashing off Round Pond, and I eyed the rearview mirror and looked at Sam in his Duster, then raised my arm and pointed straight ahead, my neck pulling back as Sam accelerated, the tires of the Chevelle smoking, the air smelling like industry as we crossed Lawrence and headed up the lane beside the water. We passed one-story houses, their driveways vacant. In a hundred yards the road became dirt and the fence around the reservoir ended and there was an open space between its final post and where the woods began. I stepped on the brake and jerked the wheel to the left, the Chevelle pivoting around, the hood aimed at Round Pond.

I climbed out and got into Sam's car. He looked at me. I looked back at him. Then he stepped on the gas and it was only a few feet till the Chevelle dipped off the road and slipped down a short embankment into the water. It sank immediately, bubbles rising up out of the town's drinking water, only the radio antennae visible as we drove away.

Years later I would think about this, that this was the town's *drinking* supply, but that morning as we sped away, my arms and legs felt light, my fingertips buzzing electric, and it was like sweeping out the corners and shaking out the rugs and mopping the floor till it shone.

NOT LONG after, a warm day in late spring. Grass was poking up green in our small front yard and in all the other yards and the median of Columbia Park. The maple and oak trees were nearly leafed out and the air smelled like damp earth, the wooden planks of porch steps, budding flowers I couldn't name, then the exhaust of Kench's brother's motorcycle as he pulled up onto our sidewalk and blocked anyone's path to or from our porch and front door. He switched off the engine. He was smaller than Kench but had the same high forehead and long thinning hair. Sam and I were inside the house getting ready to go somewhere, and Kench's brother was standing now, pulling off his bike helmet and smiling at me as I walked down the porch steps, smiling like he was a friend here to show us his new bike, and I was yelling, swearing at him, a jolt running up my right leg, his motorcycle falling over onto the grass. I began stomping it, felt small metal pieces break under my boot, I kicked in the headlight, boot-heeled the kickstand till it was bent, squatted and grabbed the chassis and heaved and rolled it onto the front sidewalk, then kicked it again, yelling at Kench's little brother the entire time to get the fuck away from *my house. You hear me?!* **Fuck off!**

I was sweating and breathing hard, the air quiet now. Sam stood beside me as we watched Kench's brother struggle to lift his bike, his hair in his face as he fiddled with instruments I'd broken, as he bent back the kick-starter and got his motorcycle running and drove off slowly without even putting on his helmet.

"Jesus," Sam said, "you were pissed, huh?"

"Fuck him, Sam. *Fuck* him." I was looking out at the empty street. Bits of reflector glass shone on my sidewalk, and there was Kench's brother's face, the smile that had turned to surprise turned to hurt turned to fear. He'd never done anything to my sister, but that seemed to be beside the point; in the basement I was getting stronger and stronger. I could bench-press 100 pounds over my body weight. I could do ten wide-grip chin-ups with a 50-pound dumbbell hanging from my belt. I was throwing combinations at the heavy bag that rocked the joists of the house I began to feel I was defending for the first time.

7

―

IN THE SUMMER, Salisbury Beach was where you went if you had wheels, especially on Friday or Saturday night. It was a sandy strip of barrooms and open arcades, pool halls and dance clubs and carnival rides. There was a roller-coaster built entirely out of wood, bleached four-by-fours that one day would rot and they'd tear it down, but in the late seventies you could hear the rattle of the cars all night long, the cries of riders as they plummeted down one steep slope and got jerked up another. There was the bass thump of DJ music through the thin walls of the Frolics, the boxed roll and ping of steel balls in the pinball machine, the hard-cornered slap of plastic air hockey pucks, talk and yelling, little kids laughing or pleading, the creaking of gears beneath the huge lighted Ferris wheel. There were the revving motorcycle engines, their diesel-fed clacking of steel on steel. There was the electric whine of the Dodge 'Em cars, the buzz of neon lights, and the constant slap and hiss of waves breaking on the dark beach. You could smell motor exhaust and seashells and spun sugar. There was smoking beef and overheated Fry-O-Lator oil and fried dough and butter from a bottle. There was the tang of dried ketchup and mustard on the asphalt, cigarette smoke and bubble gum and suntan lotion and sweat.

It was a Sunday night, and Jeb and I were there with Sam and his girlfriend, April C. The strip was crowded with sunburned families in shorts and T-shirts, their flip-flops slapping their feet. There were tanned, bare-chested boys. Their shirts hung from their shorts pockets as they lounged around a bench or stood in a circle watching girls go by in halter tops and hip-huggers or bikini bottoms that barely covered their asses. Fifteen or twenty bikers leaned against their Harleys or Indians or Nortons, smok-ing cigarettes, their faces lined and whiskered and windburned. Most of them had long hair held back with a bandanna, and they wore black T-shirts with a neon wolf engraved across the chest, or Old Glory, or a bald eagle flying into a sunset, or no T-shirt at all, just a leather vest, some of the men muscular and tattooed, others scrawny as bar rats. Fifty yards away, a Salisbury police cruiser was parked up against the sidewalk in front of the shops selling beach towels and bathing suits and shot glasses with the wooden roller-coaster painted around it, but the cruiser was always empty, the cops walking around three or four at a time, their blue uniform shirts unbuttoned, rings of sweat under their arms.

Beyond the bikers was a gap in the pool halls and dance clubs you had to pay to get into. All these clapboard buildings along the water were built on piers, their bases covered with white barnacles, and through the gap I could see the black ocean, the dim white tops of waves curling into the sand. The Frolics was to the left. Even above all the noise I could hear the band from inside, the muffled but amplified cry of the lead singing "American Woman."

The beach sand here was cool and coarse and littered with empty cigarette packs and ketchup-streaked cardboard containers and dried sea-weed. Still, I wanted to see the ocean at night, and I stepped past the bikers onto the sand. I didn't know where Sam and April had gone, but Jeb was wandering somewhere behind me and up ahead were two girls and a guy. He wore a tight white T-shirt, his arms lean and marked with home-made tattoos. He had a crew cut, which no one but soldiers had then, and the girls with him wore tube tops and too much makeup. They looked young, fourteen or fifteen. He was talking fast, inhaling deeply on a cigarette, pointing his finger at one, then the other, "So fuck you and fuck you 'cause I'm not takin' any more a your fuckin' shit, all *right*?"

I should've kept walking. I should've minded my own business, but I

didn't like how he was talking to them, and there was the headlong pull
I'd been feeling since Steve Lynch that every moment like this was a test
and the more tests I passed the further I permanently moved myself from
the boy I'd been. "Hey, watch your mouth."

"Yeah? Let's take a fuckin' walk." He flicked his cigarette and scanned
the strip for cops and now his hand was squeezing the back of my neck
and I let him keep it there, let him think I'd be easy for him as we both
walked over the sand into the shadows under the Frolics where I twisted
away and threw one at his face, but he ducked and my fist skimmed the
top of his skull and he got low and drove me down, the sand slamming
my shoulder blades, then he was on me, swinging at my head and face,
and I arched my back and started punching him in the shoulder, the ear,
my wrist suddenly squeezed by iron, a bright light in my face, this kid
pulled off me by more bright light, my wrist being slowly vised by the
steel claw the first cop had put on me, a device that closes around bone
as tightly as it's pulled, and the big gray-headed cop was yanking me out
from under the Frolics, my eyes tearing up, the lighted strip a blur, and I
was crying, "I'll *walk*. I'll *walk*. Okay, okay, okay, I'll *walk*."

But he jerked all the harder, my arm a hot cord to my shoulder and
neck and I stumbled over the sand as fast as I could. The one I'd fought
was handcuffed in front of me, a big cop at each arm, and they were
talking to him like they knew him well. They kept calling him Jimmy,
their .38s bouncing in their belts as they hit the asphalt and the strip was
brighter than before, louder, and I could feel people looking at us, heard
Jeb call my name as the back doors of a paddy wagon opened and the
two cops ahead of me tossed in the crew-cut one and the claw let go and
I was lifted inside, the doors slamming shut, then the roll away from the
beach.

I was on a metal bench next to a sleeping drunk. The only light came
in from two high slits in the doors, neon carnival light moving by outside.
Jimmy, still cuffed, sat across from me, his hands behind his back while
my hands were free. My wrist was hot and swollen and I tried to move it
but couldn't.

"You still want to go at it, motherfucker? 'Cause I don't need hands to
kick your fuckin' head in, you piece of *shit*."

Part of me couldn't believe he was calling me on. I could start in on him with my left and he wouldn't be able to do anything about it.

He was leaning forward, a white torso and head. "You think I'm shittin' ya? Try me. Try me, mothafucka."

I felt nothing. No fear. No anger. No need to prove myself. Whatever fight had been in me was gone. So was my shirt, the metal wall of the wagon sticking to my back. I looked at him, this kid really, this angry kid all the cops knew by name. Angrier than I was, meaner, and he'd gotten the best of me back there. The same way the one did the winter before in the parking lot of the Tap, by wrestling me down. I wasn't good at it. If I couldn't throw hard fast punches I was lost. And if the cops hadn't broken up me and this Jimmy, he would've beaten the shit out of me.

I shook my head. "Say what you want. I don't have much time anyway."

"What?"

"Three months. That's it."

"What do you mean?"

"Cancer. It's in my bones. That's what the doctors say anyway. I just came here to have some fun, that's all."

"You gotta be *shittin'* me." His voice was hard, but his face was softening.

I shook my head, looked down at the scratched steel floor. I didn't know where these words came from or why I'd said them.

"Aw, *man,* but you got muscles, I mean, your health, right?"

I shook my head again. "That's just on the outside." I looked back at him, and it was like looking into the face of a small boy, his mouth opened slightly, his eyes on me but also on himself, on his own, hopefully distant, mortality. "Oh, *man.*" He leaned forward. "Listen, soon as these fat fucks open the door, you book it. Believe me, I do it all the time. They're too slow to ever get you."

I nodded. My wrist didn't hurt as much and I began to rub it, moved it up and down and side to side. I felt guilty about my lie but could see its power too, see how quickly it had disarmed him. The drunk mumbled something. The police wagon was backing up now. No light came through the slits, then there was a yellow glow.

"Lookit, I'll keep 'em busy and you take off, all right?"

"Thank you."

He nodded at me, shook his head and winced at my fate, his eyes on the doors as they opened and only one cop stood there. It was the one who'd put the claw on me. Jimmy was up off his bench. "Officer Frank," Jimmy turned his back to him, "these are a little tight tonight. Can you just loosen 'em one notch, please, that's all I ask. One notch."

"Get closer, Jimmy. Squat down."

Jimmy did, his eyes on me. He mouthed, *Go, Go.* And he motioned his head toward the open doors and the station house in electric yellow light, a short fence, then the beach, the dim white surf. I didn't move.

THE CELL was four feet wide and eight feet long, and I was in there with five other men. But not Jimmy. I was around the corner getting escorted down a short yellow hall to my cell when I'd heard it, shouting and the scuff of feet, the front door slamming back against the wall. Weeks later I heard they'd shot a kid that night, chased him down under those clubs on the beach and put one in his hip.

The cell was crowded when the cop pushed me in, so I stayed by the door and leaned against the bars where the only light was. In the gloom, three men sat on the steel bunk bolted into the wall. I didn't look long, but there was one with scraggly hair and a beard, another wearing glasses and blue Dickies work pants and janitor shoes. There was a fat one with no shirt, and using the toilet as a seat was a blond kid talking in a low voice about dust, the best you'll ever have.

The drunk I'd come in with was sitting on the floor near the bars, his back to the wall, his chin to his chest.

I leaned against the bars in the hallway light, shirtless. I hoped I looked big enough, or at least fit enough, to stay away from, and I was aware of my head now, a pulsing at my right temple, a new bruise. I knew I had a phone call coming, that I was in line for that. What I didn't know is that Jeb and Sam and April C. were in the station a wall away trying to bail me out. Jeb, with his frizzy mane and unshaven face, had asked the desk sergeant how much.

"Sixty bucks."

"Sixty *bucks*?"

"That's right."

"Where does that money go?"

"Excuse me?"

"I said where does that money go?"

"In my pocket, wise ass, now beat it."

"No, I'm not leaving." Jeb sat in a chair and crossed his arms. Two cops picked him up and hauled him to a cell not far from mine.

Out in the booking room, Sam approached the lieutenant on duty. "Please, Officer, there's no need of that. I'll get him out of here."

"You want to get arrested too?"

"No, but he didn't do anything, sir."

April tapped Sam's shoulder. "C'mon, honey. Let's go." Sam turned to leave, but his head got yanked backwards, the cop's hand in his hair. "You're going in too."

"No, I'm *not*." Sam reached up and grabbed the cop's wrist, but the cop wasn't letting go so Sam used his neck muscles to let the cop pull out his hair, and he grabbed the cop's other wrist and walked him back against the wall, pinning both hands, the cop yelling and swearing and calling for help.

"I'm going to let go and walk out that door, all right? I'm just going to let go and walk." But now there were two more cops on him, and in seconds Sam was in the cell with Jeb.

None of this I knew about. One of the men in my cell was snoring. The drunk at me feet looked dead, both palms upturned on the concrete beside his legs. In another cell, a man kept shouting through the bars for a drink. "I just need a fuckin' *drink*!"

Every fifteen minutes or so, a cop would unlock a cell door and escort a man to a pay phone. New men were being brought in too. One was young and tall and sunburned, and his escort cop ran him facefirst into the concrete wall, then tossed him in the last cell. From where I leaned against the bars, I could see the fresh blood-streak, could smell piss and sweat and old wine.

"You."

This cop was older, his hair gray. On his forearm was a U.S. Navy tattoo and he unlocked the cell and told me to stay put while he locked it again, then he gripped my elbow and walked me around the corner to a pay phone. "One call, five minutes." He handed me a dime and stepped back to where he could see the row of cells, his hands on his hips. I pushed in the dime and called my father.

Part of me was surprised I was calling him. It was my mother I lived with. My mother who knew we'd gone to the beach, my mother who would be home. And Pop had gotten married again. To a woman he'd dated back in high school in Louisiana. He'd flown down there to see his mother, heard that Lorraine was a widow now with two young kids, and he asked her to meet him at the airport for breakfast, a meal that lasted three hours, and at the end of it, after not having seen or spoken to each other in over twenty years, they were engaged. To celebrate this, Mom had him over to dinner, the six of us sitting at that table we used only for holidays, Pop at the head of it. He sat straight, his napkin in his lap, and he chewed slowly, thoughtfully.

"So you're getting married," Mom said.

He nodded. "I'm coming in from the jungle. I'm tired of being out there in that jungle." He sipped his wine, and I chewed my roast chicken and wondered what I'd missed; didn't he live on a green, walled-in campus? *What* jungle?

Jeb and I were best men at his wedding. Jeb and Pop wore jeans or corduroys, but for some reason I rented myself a white tuxedo with tails, and we walked our father to the chapel across the small campus where he lived in faculty housing. Now he lived there with Lorraine and her daughter and son.

The phone was ringing. Standing shirtless in the Salisbury jail, my wrist and knuckles and temple sore, I knew why I was calling him; I felt proud.

"Hello?" It was Lorraine. She was a small-boned woman who smoked More cigarettes one after the other, but she always seemed to wear just the right amount of makeup, her hair short and stylish, her voice tobacco-deep, her southern Louisiana accent stronger than my mother's and father's. I asked to speak to Pop.

"Honey, he's in bed."

"Can you get him, please? It's kind of important."

I waited a minute or two. The cop was looking at me. He glanced at his watch.

"Andre?" My father's voice sounded funny, as if he'd come to the phone from far away and wasn't sure of anything.

"Pop, I got in a fight and need to get bailed out of jail. I'm at Salisbury Beach."

The line was quiet. For a second I thought he might be mad, a possibility I hadn't even considered.

"Dad?"

"I took a pill, son. To sleep. You need to call your mama. I can't drive right now, man."

"Okay."

"'Kay. G'night."

I hung up. I looked at the black receiver. I was about to turn to the cop to ask for one more dime, but he had my elbow and was walking me back to the cell.

"My father can't come get me. I need to call my mother."

"One call, that's it."

"But I didn't call anyone."

"That's not my problem." The cop unlocked the cell and pulled the steel door shut behind me. I should've asked Pop to call Mom. Maybe he would. Maybe he wasn't so drugged he would. But as I leaned against the wall, I didn't think so. He was already dreaming. In the morning he'd wake up thinking he'd dreamed his son had called from jail.

But when Jeb got his one call, he called Mom and she got dressed and drove right to the beach. She worked for the state now, and she came into the station house furious, requesting names and ranks and badge numbers. She didn't have the money for bail, but she talked them into freeing us for twenty dollars apiece.

Early the next morning there was a first appearance before the judge. He began to lecture the three of us standing there before him, but Mom stood up in the back and introduced herself as our mother, said we hadn't had time to call a lawyer, then requested a continuance. The judge looked at her as if he wasn't used to this, punks with mothers who were articulate

and knew the rules of the court. He granted us this, and then she must
have called Sam's father because as soon as he found out, he went down
to the Salisbury station, introduced himself as the health inspector over
in Haverhill, and pled our case, said we were good boys, that an arrest like
this could harm our future prospects. The lieutenant agreed and weeks
later, Sam's father and Sam and Jeb and I stood in court as the judge continued the case without a finding.

Walking out of court that afternoon, Mr. Dolan in a suit jacket and
tie, there was the feel of fraternity, that we're all in this together and boys
will be boys. This was still something new, that I was one of the boys and
that what I'd done was normal. To be expected really, nothing to worry
about.

SUZANNE'S RAPE had done something to our father. Almost immediately
after it, he'd driven to the Haverhill police station and applied for a license
to carry. Now he owned a silver snub-nose .38 he kept unloaded in one of
the desk drawers. When he went out to dinner with his wife or friends, he
carried it in a shadow holster on his belt, and he covered it with his shirt
or vest. He seemed to talk about self-defense more than I'd ever heard him
talk about it before. He'd bought a weight bench and a barbell set, and in
one of our weekly dinners he reached over and squeezed my upper arm. "I
need some of that muscle. Come show me how to do it, son."

Later that week after my shift at the gas station, I walked over to his
house and guided him through a full-body workout. He'd just finished
his run and was sweating in a tank top and shorts, his bandanna damp
around his head, his beard damp too. I showed him the correct form in all
the movements, when to inhale and when to exhale. He lay on the bench
and I put on a weight I now considered light; I was surprised to see him
struggle with it; I hadn't expected that, I hadn't expected to be physically
stronger than my own father.

I pulled one of his writing notebooks from his desk, ripped out a
piece of paper, and recorded his workout program. He thanked me. He
smiled widely and gave me a sweaty hug. "Hey, man, when you coming
back to school?"

I shrugged. I was surprised to hear him ask the question. He hadn't said much at all about my having dropped out. A few weeks earlier at Ronnie D's bar, Pop turned to me and said, "I don't worry about what you're doing right now because you've already got discipline." He took in my chest and shoulders and sipped his beer.

Now I stepped away from my father and handed him his workout program. "Start light, Pop, and work your way up slowly, all right?"

ON A Friday in late August, Mike W. pulled up to the pumps in a small Japanese car. He was one of those who used to hang around our house weekday afternoons, smoking dope in our living room or kitchen. This was something people had stopped doing, not because I'd kicked them out, but because Suzanne no longer sold anything and spent most of her time across the river as a student at Bradford.

Mike W. had shoulder-length hair but was always clean-shaven and looked healthy, and he'd never been disrespectful to my sister or the rest of us. I didn't know him well, but I liked him. He stepped out of his car as I filled his tank.

He nodded at me. "Working out?"

"Yep."

"I was down in Riverside the other night. The Lynches are still talking about getting you, you know."

I glanced over at him.

"Dana's got some legal shit hanging over his head, but he says he's coming for you soon."

"Let him come." I was talking tough, but my heart was beating faster.

"I told him I heard you're a pretty good boxer, but he still thinks you sucker-punched Steve."

"Let him think that then." I topped off his tank and hung up the gas nozzle and clicked it down into place.

Mike paid me, told me he was moving down to New Jersey for college, was studying history but planned to go to Law School. I wished him luck and waved as he drove off. I watched his small car accelerate under the railroad trestle for Lafayette Square. When he drove out from under the shadows, the sun glinted off his back bumper, and I stood there in the smell of fresh gasoline feeling left behind.

8

I N THE FALL I went back to school. Back to Bradford College where my father lived and worked and where I'd fallen in love with a girl from Iran. Her name was Marjan, and as far as I knew, she did not even know I existed. She had long black hair and dark eyes and a kind smile. She wore clean, pressed clothes and had a languid, graceful walk, and I spent months trying to put myself near her just to watch her laugh or brush her hair back from her face or hear her talk, her accent sweet and exotic and from a country I'd never heard of. She smoked cigarettes and even though I did not, I would go into the smoke room if she was there and I'd listen to her chat with the others, listen to that accent, watch her puff elegantly on a Marlboro Light.

She lived in Tupelo East, one of the dorms deep in the campus away from the street and not far from where my father lived with his second family. On weekend nights, instead of cruising around with Sam and Bobby, going to bars or some house party where I kept my back to the wall and scanned the room for whomever I might have to fight, I went to Marjan's dorm instead.

I knew nothing about her. Nothing about her culture. I knew she lived with another Iranian, a short, sweet-faced girl named Parvine, that boys never went into their room. I heard they came from a strict culture and the two sexes just did not mix. I went to my classes, I read the assigned books and wrote papers and took blue book exams, but I thought mainly of workouts and her, how to get bigger and how to get closer to her.

BECAUSE THE campus was small and he lived on it, I saw more of my father than I had since I was a boy. I was eighteen and he was forty-one, and I began to learn the rhythm of his days. Every morning he got up early and drove to the Sacred Hearts church down in Bradford Square for the seven o'clock mass. He'd come home, eat breakfast, then write most of the morning. Just before lunch he'd put on running shoes and shorts and go for a run. If he had time he'd drive down through Bradford and across the Merrimack to Kenoza Lake. If he didn't, he'd run a three-to-five-mile route through the quiet residential streets off campus, and he'd take a shower and shave his cheeks and throat, then eat a light lunch while he prepared for his afternoon classes.

His favorite classroom was on the second floor of the library, a small seminar room overlooking Tupelo Pond, a tiny man-made estuary on the campus you could cross by walking over a paved stone bridge, its four-by-four rails painted white.

As a full-time faculty member Pop was expected to hold office hours, but while he had one, he was never in it. If a student needed to meet with him to discuss his or her work, he'd suggest they talk in the student union building or down in Bradford Square over a beer at Ronnie D's bar.

Before he'd married Lorraine, he might stay there quite a while, taking up a booth with four or five of his students, most of them young women, drinking and talking and flirting, maybe having a bar hotdog for supper. But since marrying Lorraine, he was expected to be home for a sit-down dinner and eat it with her and the kids at her antique dining table that took up most of the room.

"Nine thousand pounds," he'd say over and over again. "That woman owns nine *thousand* pounds of furniture." She did, and she'd had it moved up from Louisiana: carved bookcases and plush sofas, dishes and silver and shaded lamps, carpets and polished hardwood beds and bureaus and end tables.

Married housing on campus looked like small, split-level ski lodges. They had tiny kitchens and open carpeted rooms that led to sets of bedrooms at each end. There were sliding glass doors to an upper deck over-looking trees and a lawn and a paved walk to the other campus houses.

When she moved in, none of Pop's bookshelves matched hers so she asked him to make a room for himself on the second floor. It held everything he owned: a few pine bookcases of hardcover books he'd been collecting on his own for years; his clothes and record player and stack of albums, mainly jazz—Stan Getz, Charlie Parker and Dizzy Gillespie, Dave Brubeck and Cannonball Adderley. There was Dylan, too. And Kris Kristofferson and Joan Baez. He no longer owned the wooden black desk I remembered, but a metal study carrel that had come with the college. On it was his pipe collection, his humidor and ashtray, the manual type-writer he used after writing drafts longhand in bound notebooks. On the windowsill sat his collection of Akubra Australian cowboy hats he wore around campus and downtown, and in the middle of the floor was his new weight bench, the barbell lying across its upright forks. But in the rest of the house, there was little evidence of him or the life he'd lived so far, and whenever I'd stop by for a quick visit, he looked like he'd wan-dered into somebody else's house and couldn't find the door out of there.

But she didn't look so happy either. After supper she'd put her kids to bed, then sit at the kitchen table sipping black coffee, smoking a More cigarette, and staring off into the near distance as if she were completely alone in the room. I had heard she'd been content with her first husband, an affable man who one morning had died at the breakfast table in front of her and the kids.

But on weekends, Pop still went out and got drunk. It's what he'd always done, as if the disciplined rituals of the week built pressure inside him that by Friday or Saturday night just had to blow. When he began teaching at Bradford Junior College in 1967, he was thirty-one, only ten or eleven years older than his students, and because it was the sixties, there were a lot of parties with students and faculty in the same place, some at our small rented cottage in the woods in New Hampshire. But now he was in his forties, many of his colleagues older than that, and very few of them still wanted to drink and hang out with these eighteen-, nineteen-, and twenty-year-olds.

But Pop did.

One Saturday night early in my first semester back, I was sitting on the third floor of Tupelo East in the common area, hoping for Marjan to happen by. I was watching two skinny rockers from Connecticut play cards, and I could hear my father's voice in the concrete stairwell. He sounded happy and drunk and mischievous. He was with Theo Metrakos who had his Ph.D. in literature now and taught at the college and lived with his wife across the lawn from my dad and Lorraine. Pop was urging his friend to follow him, to come up and "meet the *women*."

Women. Pop always called them that, these girls from California and New York and Illinois, from New Jersey and Iran and India and England. He called them women, but I saw them as girls, and it was strange seeing him emerge from the stairwell in his jeans and cowboy boots, his cotton shirt and leather vest and trimmed beard and reddened face, his eyes scanning the hallways and common area, his reluctant friend behind him.

Pop saw me and laughed, like I'd taken a wrong turn and must be lost. I laughed too, though I didn't feel like it.

"Where's it at, man? Where's it *at*?" He came over, took me in sitting there. I caught the sweet juniper scent of gin. I shrugged and felt caught, though he was the one acting caught. A heavy girl in a T-shirt and pajama bottoms passed and he called her over and put his arm around her, said, "It's good, Marie. It's really fucking good."

She nodded and smiled. Her cheeks were flushed, but she looked genuinely pleased about something. Metrakos stood over the two boys playing cards, his hands in his corduroys. He didn't seem as loaded as Pop, though he may have been. He addressed them by their first names, asked how were they doing? Were they adjusting all right?

In less than thirty years he and my father would both be gone, but now they were still young and alive and they called themselves Butch and Sundance. They taught together, ran together, drank together, and went out on double dates with their wives. One late night, drunk and hungry for lobsters, they broke into a seafood restaurant out on the beach just to pull a few from the tank. Probably it had been Pop's idea; he'd always been the more impulsive one, the reckless leader of the two. When Pop was done with his week's work, that quality that drew people to him seemed to magnify, like life was one all-night party on the first day of some weekend-long fiesta, and I could see it was hard for people not to want to be around him then, especially those like Marie who had read his work and knew she was standing close to the man who had written such graceful stories. I had just begun to read them myself. Weeks before, on a quiet Sunday morning, I took one of his collections off the shelf and read a story called "Killings." It was set in a place like Bradford Square and was about a father planning revenge for the murder of his youngest son. The sentences were lean and lyrical and cut deeply into the people Pop was writing about; it was only twenty-one pages long but felt as strong to me as *The Grapes of Wrath,* a novel I'd just read for school and was so moved by I had to go walking after. I had to go walking after reading my father's story, too. The air was cool and smelled like rain, and I walked up the grassy median of Columbia Park. At the base of an oak I stopped and looked up at its bare branches against the sky. There was the feeling something important had just been revealed to me, that my father had created many stories like the one I'd just read and that's where most of him had been my whole life, in those pages, with people like the father who had lost his son.

Now a few other students had heard his voice and were walking up to him in the hallway; there were those parties when I was a boy, how Pop's voice was always at the center of them, how he seemed to be the axis of the wheel everyone else lounged on, spinning around what he had to say or yell or laugh about. Then the parties would end and Pop would become another man, one who worked quietly and alone, then went running alone, then left in his car alone to go teach, a man who returned to us tired and distracted and needing sleep to get ready for the next day's solitary work.

Metrakos smiled at me, then walked into the hallway where Pop was leaning close to Marie, his hand on the shoulder of a blonde girl from Long Island. Theo whispered something into my father's ear, then ushered him gently back down that concrete stairwell at Tupelo, and it was clear to me Metrakos was mellowing while my father, ten years older, was not.

WEEKS LATER, there were two feet of snow on the ground, the air so cold and dry it hurt your lungs to breathe through the mouth. There was a loud crowded party at one of the international student houses on campus across from my father's, and I was at this party hoping to see Marjan, to maybe get her alone and introduce myself and talk, but it was the kind I hated because it was full of young men in polyester shirts and pants, smelling of cologne and dancing to disco music which sounded to me synthetic and soulless, its relentless beat the echo of some narcissistic machine.

The place was small and dark and hot. Some of the women were dancing, too—an Indian girl from Bombay, one from Bahrain, another from Venezuela, their movements sweet and graceful in jeans and blouses, their gold bracelets jangling. Many were drunk, including me, sipping beer after beer, and though Sam wasn't with me, he and I had vowed to always run one mile the next day for each beer we drank. I'd begun to lose count but believed I was going to have to run seven, maybe eight miles in the morning. The Bee Gees came on, a song I hated from a movie I hated, and I drained my beer and was just about to leave when I saw Marjan dancing, her long dark hair swinging, her friend Parvine dancing beside her.

There was a banging on the bathroom door behind me. The tall girl from Bombay turned to me. "Your father's been in there with Louisa a long time. People need to use the bathroom."

"My *father's* in there?"

"Yes, with that girl from Brazil."

Louisa. She had dark skin and wore tight jeans and would walk around campus holding four or five textbooks to her chest. She was a junior or senior but didn't seem to have a boyfriend.

The music was too loud. I leaned close to the girl from Bombay, could smell her perfume and skin. "How long's he been in there?"

She shrugged. "An hour, perhaps longer."

I stepped to the door and knocked on it, could barely hear my own knocking above the party noise. "Pop. *Pop,* people need to use the toilet. Go someplace *else.*"

A line of fluorescent light shone at the bottom of the door. I tried the knob, but it was locked. I pressed my ear to the door. Heard his voice, then hers. So maybe they were just talking. Let somebody else deal with it. I shrugged at the Indian girl and made my way past the polyester boys from Turkey and Iran, Nigeria, Kenya, and New Jersey. In the candlelit gloom I caught a glimpse of Marjan dancing with two Asian girls, and I pulled the slider open and stepped out onto the frozen deck.

It felt good to be in the cold air, that disco a bit muffled behind me now. I opened another beer and drank. Across the lawn and through the bare trees not more than fifty yards away, was my father's darkened campus home. It was after one or two in the morning, and the shades were drawn, not a light on anywhere. I pictured my little stepbrother and stepsister asleep in those small rooms on the first floor. And what about Lorraine? Was she sitting up in bed, smoking a More and waiting for him? I felt complicit somehow.

I went back inside. Pop and Louisa had finally come out of the bathroom, and he looked happy to see me and gave me a big hug and soon enough he and I and students I didn't know started in on a bottle of Cuervo in the kitchen, licking the salt off the skin between our thumb and forefinger, throwing back the tequila, biting into a wedge of lemon because we could find no limes.

The disco finally ended and became something much better, some kind of African music with a lot of drums and horns. The night sky outside began to lighten, and Pop had gotten into a conversation in the corner with the tall girl from Bombay. One by one the polyester boys drifted away and the music had been off a long time and I was sweetly drunk, Marjan walking down the stairs from above. She was smiling at me. I went over and put out my hand and shook hers. It was small and cool. I told her my name. She glanced from me to my father in the corner, then back at me. She looked confused.

"Same name. I'm his son."

She nodded and let go of my hand and walked past me. Parvine followed, and I began to follow, too, but Pop was up out of the corner, his hand on my shoulder. "Shit, sun's coming up. We got to get home before Lorraine's out of bed. C'mon."

I didn't want to go to his house, but I had my mother's Toyota I shouldn't be driving now anyway, and it was a Sunday so she wouldn't need it, and Pop and I were hurrying over the shoveled walkway, the snow on both sides of us a shade of blue in the false dawn, our breath in front of us.

When we got to his front door, Pop was giggling. He whispered. "You can crash in the spare room, okay, man?"

I nodded. I hadn't slept in the same house as him since I was a boy. He gripped the knob but it wouldn't turn.

"*Shit*, she locked me out."

"You don't have a key?"

He shook his head and smiled widely, though his eyes seemed to be looking ahead in time to the trouble he was in.

Maybe it was his idea, maybe it was mine, but eight feet to the left of his door was the window to the spare room, and we pressed our hands against it and were able to slide it open. We pushed in the screen and I squatted and gave Pop ten fingers and he put his boot in my hands and pushed off and scrambled loudly through the window and down into the darkness. I grabbed the windowsill and pulled myself up and halfway in, my legs still hanging outside, kicking at air, and there was Lorraine leaning against the jamb of the doorway to the spare room, the hallway light on behind her. She wore a white nightgown and I could see the outline of her small body, her arms crossed over her breasts, and I fell in headfirst and stopped my fall with my hands, my boots hooking for a second in the window frame before I rolled all the way into her house.

Pop stood up. "Why'd you lock the door?"

"Andre."

I thought she was talking to him, but she was looking at me. "I'd like you to leave, please."

"No, he can sleep here."

"No, he can leave."

"It's okay, Pop. I've got a place to stay." I apologized to Lorraine and thought briefly of leaving the way I came in. She stepped to the side and I stepped past her and out the front door. I thought I could probably drive after all, but in my walk through the snow I saw the kitchen light still on in the international house and I knocked softly on the door and walked in.

Upstairs Marjan and the Indian girl were making breakfast. They looked neither happy nor unhappy to see me. Marjan said, "These eggs were frozen. We wanted to cook them before they were *rooned*." She smiled at me. "Would you like some?"

"Yes, thank you." I sat down at the small table. When Pop and I had left, it'd been covered with empty beer and wine bottles, the spent

Cuervo, two full ashtrays and four or five squeezed lemon wedges. Now
it was cleared away, and the Indian girl was putting on water for tea, and
there was nothing for me to do but wait, sit and wait to eat with this
lovely girl from so far away.

WE BEGAN to spend more time together, but she was an Iranian girl
so it was always in the presence of someone else, usually her roommate
Parvine, and later, in a small apartment a half mile from campus with her
mother and younger sister and ten-year-old brother. Her mother spoke
very little English and wore designer clothes and tasteful jewelry, and she
was shorter than Marjan but warm, so often smiling sincerely at whomever she addressed, and it was from her Marjan got her looks.

She called me "Andereh" and would invite me to sit and eat with
them on the *sofreh,* a wine-colored Persian carpet she had her daughters
unroll onto her apartment floor. She then covered that with a clean sheet
and set out dishes of stewing meat and tomatoes, eggplant and rice and
saffron, a yogurt dish mixed with cucumbers they would dip bread into,
and I would sit on the floor with this family and listen to them speak in
their language—Farsi, I later learned. Sometimes Marjan would look at
me and smile and I'd feel as if I'd tripped and fallen into some exotic tale.

After dinners, I would help her little brother or sister with their
homework, mainly teaching them standard rules of English I did not
know I knew. Marjan's mother would sit on the sofa with a clear glass of
tea and listen to a cassette tape of Persian music, the drums and stringed
instruments sounding thousands of years old, a woman or man singing
long mournful notes of lovers split apart and never reunited. That's what
it sounded like to me, though I had no idea what they were singing. On
the sofa Marjan would curl her feet up under her next to her mother and
the two of them would talk in a fast, heated way that in America sounded
like fighting, though they would smile often and laugh, sometimes glancing over at me, this new friend of the family.

I liked spending time with them. I liked how polite they were to
each other, how every time one addressed the other by name, it ended
with the word *jahn,* which means *dear.* So Marjan was Marjan-*jahn,* her
mother was Maman-*jahn,* and I became Andereh-*jahn.* But if they really

felt affection for you, you'd become Andereh-*joon*, Andre dearest, which is how they all began to address me, and I began to address them, too, for they had become dear to me and for the first time the idea of becoming some kind of gentleman bloomed inside my head, a man with manners and class and a good upbringing.

I WAS walking from Academy Hall. It was late on a weekend night and I'd just drunk a beer with Saeed. The air smelled like dead leaves and cashmere. I didn't own a car and sometimes walked the three miles home down through Bradford Square over the Basiliere Bridge and up the long hill of Main Street past the shopping plaza and GAR Park and the statue of Hannah Duston, her long iron dress, her raised hatchet, then up through Monument Square, walking by the sub shops and gas stations, their fluorescent light casting out over the sidewalk.

I stuck my hands in my pockets and started walking.

"Ryan, *please*. I didn't do nothin', Ryan. *C'mon*."

In the parking lot, three men stood in the near darkness next to a sedan. One was over six feet, but he was skinny, his shoulders narrow, and now he was backing away from who I thought was his friend, but then his friend stepped forward and slapped him across the face, the tall one's hair swinging.

"*Please,* Ryan." He hunched his shoulders and took another one to the face, this one a fist, and I was running toward them, could see how much bigger this Ryan was. The air was cool, but he was wearing a T-shirt that showed his rounded shoulders and wide back and thick triceps, a lifter. He punched the tall one in the cheek, the tall one flinching and beginning to cry. "C'mon, *Ryan,* what did I *do*?"

Ryan hit him again, and now I was close enough to hear it, the dulled thud of bone under flesh on bone under flesh. "Hey!" I felt my voice move through my vocal cords, watched myself stand a pace behind them, my weight on my back foot. The tall one was bent over at the waist crying, his hands cupped to his nose, and Ryan turned to me. "Mind your own fuckin' business."

"Why don't you hit me then? Hit *me*."

He rushed at me and there was a thrust in my shoulder and he fell backwards to the asphalt and lay there and didn't move.

The tall one straightened up and sniffled. He looked from me to his friend, then back at me. Someone else had been standing near the hood of the Monte Carlo, and now he ran around the car and squatted on the ground near Ryan. *"Shit."*

Ryan mumbled something. He rolled onto his shoulder, and I turned and walked through the parking lot and out the iron gates into the street for the long walk home.

TWO DAYS later I was sitting on the granite steps of Academy Hall between classes. It was a cool, gray morning, and I had a biology exam and was trying to remember what a lysosome was when Eric, one of the skinny rockers from Connecticut, sat down next to me. He had long blond hair. His cheeks always looked wind-chapped. He lit up a cigarette.

"That guy you hit had to go to the hospital."

I looked over at him. I hadn't told anyone about hitting anyone, but I'd done it in the parking lot beneath the dorm windows of Academy Hall.

"You fractured his forehead."

"How do you know that?"

"'Cause I was there. His buddy's my friend from back home."

I shrugged, though my heart was going a bit faster and I couldn't deny the warmth of pride opening up in my chest.

Eric blew smoke out both his nostrils. He nodded his head as if I'd just said something. "Yep, concussion."

"And what about his scrawny friend he was beating on? How's his nose?" I stood and gripped my biology book. Eric nodded again and took a deep drag off his cigarette, and I walked down the steps for Haseltine Hall and my biology exam. I reminded myself how big that Ryan was, that watching him punch his skinny friend was like watching a grown man hit a woman or a child.

Not far from the door to the hall, a group of girls was sitting in a circle smoking and chatting. One of them, thin and fair-skinned from Michigan, held a dead leaf to the flame of her lighter, the leaf curling away from the heat and becoming a wisp of smoke. She looked at me as I passed. I pulled open the heavy oak door of the hall and stepped inside; it was as if I'd just been warned.

9

―

P OP WAS SICK with the flu. It was spring now, and he called me and
asked if I wanted his two tickets to the game.

"What game?"

"The Red Sox."

"Baseball?"

"Yes, *baseball*."

"I guess so."

"They're playing the Yankees at Fenway."

"Where's that?"

"Boston. Take Dolan. Tell him it's the Yankees."

I'd heard of them but didn't know they were from New York or that we
were supposed to hate them. My father liked Sam Dolan, admired him for his
muscles and good manners, and I'd heard them talk sports before, using words
and terms and names I'd never heard. It was like sitting with Marjan's family
when they spoke Persian. Sometimes I listened hard for anything I might recognize, though I didn't do that the few times Sam and my father talked about
sports; I knew there was nothing in it I would know much about, these games
with balls in them that men threw at each other or bounced or hit with a bat.
I understood training for a goal, and I knew these were athletes who worked
hard at what they did. But why? Why were grown men playing *games*?

Since I was very young, I'd seen little of them and knew less. Pop had never talked to us about them; maybe if he'd stayed with us he would have. Maybe he would have had more time to, the way he did that afternoon he and I had thrown a ball to each other bare-handed on the sidewalk, the charcoals growing hotter in the hibachi on the half-wall beside us. And if he'd stayed, there may have been more money and less moving from one scrappy neighborhood to another where no one seemed to have much to do with these games either. On the TV we four kids had lived in front of, there were only three or four channels, and we would turn to those that gave us stories of escape—eccentrics stranded on a desert island, a bunch of pranksters in a concentration camp, a family of rock musicians working through all their problems in one half-hour episode every day. If we watched any games at all, it was of a woman sitting on a stool interviewing for a possible date three men she couldn't see.

One Sunday back on Lime Street, Pop had picked us up and was driving us north to the beach. Suzanne sat in the front, Jeb, Nicole, and I in the back, the windows down as we passed trailer homes in the pine trees, the smell of sap in the air. Pop turned on the radio to listen to the end of the game he said he'd been watching. His exact words were *the* game.

"What game?"

He glanced at me in the rearview mirror, his face only eyes. "The Red Sox."

"Who's that?"

He smiled as if I'd just told a joke, and he turned up the radio. But I wasn't joking. I was almost thirteen years old. It was like listening to TV newscasters talk about politics or the economy, a larger world I couldn't even begin to understand. Pop's eyes were on the road, but he was listening intently to these men, to this game, which at that moment, sitting in the back of his car, I began to understand was baseball.

When we got to our parking spot at the beach, Pop took a while to turn off the radio, and as we walked over the hot sand together he still seemed to be back there in that car and whatever it was those men were describing, their voices calm and soothing, using terms I did not know: *balls* and *strikes* and *fouls. Fastball, splitter, sinker. Double play.*

Now Sam and I were driving into Boston with Pop's tickets to a place called Fenway Park. It was a cool September night, and soon Sam and I were sitting up in the stands with thousands of other people—men, women, and kids, almost all of them wearing a Red Sox hat or jacket or sweatshirt or all three. The air smelled like mustard and popcorn and beer, and as I drank mine, I still couldn't get over how many people had come to this game. Over thirty-three thousand, Sam said, and this was the smallest park in baseball, though it looked pretty big to me, the towering banks of blinding lights that lit up the field, wide and deep green, only three players standing out in it, and there were the other men on this diamond, what Sam called the infield, the dirt path from home plate to first to second to third then back home. There was the mound the pitcher worked from, and I couldn't believe how hard and fast these men threw the ball past the batter into the catcher's mitt, another new word Sam taught me. He sat next to me, sipping his beer and patiently explaining everything: what a strike was and a ball and a foul; how the first two foul balls count as strikes, that there are different kinds of pitches and different kinds of pitchers, on and on, and as he did, he leaned close and kept his voice low, as if he didn't want to draw attention to how little I knew, that this was, in fact, the first baseball game I had ever watched.

There was a crack in the air and I watched the ball fly over the field and hit what Sam told me was "the Green Monster," a massive wall the baseball bounced off of into the glove of a Yankee who threw it to another Yankee who threw it to one at second base though our runner was safe, Sam said. That's how I felt too, safe, my best friend and me sitting deep in the stands with thousands of other people all rooting for the same team. It was like being admitted into one huge, loud and happy family you hadn't even known about.

After a while, it was the Yankees' turn to hit. Every time one of them walked up to home plate with his bat, hundreds of men and boys would yell insults at him I couldn't quite make out, just the tone, which I knew well, but it wasn't directed at me or anyone I would have to try to protect, and I felt relieved of everything, part of something far larger than I was, just one of thousands and thousands of people united in wanting the same thing, for these men from our team to beat the men from the other team, and how strange that they did this by *playing*, that one beat the other by playing a *game*.

Sam and I bought and drank a lot of beer. To get to it, we had to walk down a concrete ramp past two Boston police officers, big men with gray hair, their arms crossed over their pale blue shirts and badges, glancing at us like we might be trouble, then concluding we weren't. On the way back to our seats, we had to scoot by ten or fifteen people and every one of them stood without hesitation as we squeezed by them, trying not to spill any beer, and when we got to our seats we folded them back down and sat and drank and looked out at the bright green field and the big men playing ball in their white uniforms and their gray uniforms, a number on the back of each, and I was sweetly, happily drunk and couldn't believe I'd never come to this place before, that I'd hardly even known about it. I smiled over at Sam and he smiled over at me, though something happened in the field, and he looked up and stood and so did all the people around us, a foul ball floating fast ten feet above our heads and behind us. I turned partway around and saw the bare hands reaching for it, heard a rustling, then a *thunk*. In my seat lay the ball. I picked it up and somebody slapped me on the back, Sam too. "You should bring that home to your father."

I nodded and smiled and studied the ball in my hand. It was harder than I'd thought it'd be, but it was also just like the one Pop had thrown to me on the sidewalk four years earlier. I liked its red stitching. I stuck it in the side pocket of my jacket, Sam and I tapped our plastic beer cups, and I raised mine to the batter who'd fouled right to me, Jerry Remy, Sam said. Then Remy got a hit and made it to first base without being thrown out and I cheered for him, this man I'd never heard of in this game I'd never played or watched.

THE NEXT afternoon Sam and I stopped by my father's house to thank him for the tickets. His young stepkids were at school, and Lorraine was out somewhere, and Pop lay on one of her sofas under a light blanket. He was pale and still had a fever. Sam was telling him about the game, using language I still couldn't speak from a culture I still didn't know, but at least now I knew where the country was, had seen some of its people and smelled some of its food. I reached into my jacket pocket and pulled out the baseball. I handed it to him. "Here, you can have this."

He propped himself up on one elbow. "You got a *ball*?"

"Yep," Sam said. "It landed right in his seat."

Pop took it from me, turned it over in his hand, glanced up at me. "I've been going to games for thirty years and *never* got a ball." He said something else about it, but I kept hearing the last thing he said. *Thirty years.* He'd been going to games for thirty years? Why didn't he ever take me before? Or Jeb? Or Suzanne and Nicole? And as Sam and I left him to rest and get over his flu, as we stepped outside and walked past the faculty housing in the clear September air, I thought it must be the money. That's why he never took us before. It'd be too much money.

Lorraine was walking toward her house, a ladies' store shopping bag dangling from her hand. She smiled at us, though she looked tired and distracted and took her time walking back home.

WEEKS LATER, a cold blue October dawn, my mother's voice shot up the stairwell to my attic bedroom. "An*dre*? Tele*phone*."

It was just after six in the morning and it was Lorraine.

"Andre," she took a deep breath that seemed to catch in her throat, "your father has left me for a nineteen-year-old child. I need your help moving his things."

"Excuse me?"

"Yes, he's with her right now. In Boston." She took a deep breath, and I pictured her smoking. "Please, Andre. I need your help. Please."

IT WAS close to nine when I knocked on my father's door. I was sweating lightly from the three-mile walk through town, my French textbook in my hand. The air smelled like oak dust and dry rot, and Lorraine answered the door right away. She was in a brown velour pantsuit, barefoot and wearing no makeup, the lines in her face deeper than I'd seen them before. She hugged me to her tightly, smelled like cigarette smoke and coffee and unwashed skin. She pulled away. "Thank you for coming."

"You're welcome."

I followed her up the stairs to the second floor and my father's room.

It was clear she hadn't slept, that she'd been packing his things for most of the night. His closet doors were open, the hangers and shelves bare, as were the walls, his hat collection gone, the top of his desk empty. There were cardboard boxes stacked under the window, and I imagined her driving to some all-night grocery store to get them. But then I saw the writing on the sides, the same professional movers she'd hired to deliver her nine thousand pounds of furniture up North. She'd stacked his albums on his weight bench, some of his books too.

She was smoking now and talking. Her voice was thin, her Southern accent stronger than ever, as if the fatigue she felt had taken her down to some deeper, truer version of herself.

"Lorraine?" I was about to tell her I was sorry this was happening to her, but that it was none of my business and I would not be able to help her pack up my father's possessions. I would not be able to help her kick my father out of his own house. But the phone rang and Lorraine rushed to the other room, a feathering of smoke in the air behind her. I felt bad for her, and I wondered who this nineteen-year-old was Pop had gone to sleep with, but I had no business even standing in this room. I was just about to leave when I saw his gun.

It lay on top of the books she'd stacked on his weight bench, its leather holster unsnapped, the .38 halfway out of it. I picked it up. The holster fell away, the snub nose cool and heavy in my hand. I flipped open the chamber, and there were the brass firing pins of six .38 shells.

Had *she* loaded this? Would she know how? I looked but didn't see a bullet box anywhere, and I could hear her in the other room talking to somebody from the college, some dean whose first name I recognized as she told him how my father had left her for a child, that he had spent the night with her in Boston and Little Andre was here to help her with his things.

I upended the .38 and tapped the handle against my hand. Six rounds fell into my palm. They were hollow-points, bullets designed to fragment once they hit their target, to do the maximum damage. I knew Pop had bought these, that he imagined having to stop some rapist with them, and maybe he was keeping his gun loaded these days, though I couldn't see why. I stuffed the bullets into the front pocket of my jeans. I shoved the

.38 back into its holster and snapped the strap around the hammer, and I opened the drawers of his desk, but she'd already packed them and I saw no boxes of ammunition.

Lorraine had walked down one level to the kitchen. She stood there staring out the window as she smoked and talked on the phone to one of Pop's friends about what he was doing to her. I felt sorry for her, and I didn't feel sorry for her.

She turned and saw me heading for the stairs and the front door. She held up her hand, a More between two fingers, its smoke curling above her head. I waited as she said goodbye to the dean. She hung up the phone and stubbed out her cigarette and walked up to me.

"You can't stay, can you?"

I shook my head. "It's really none of my business. Sorry."

"No." She put her hands on my shoulders, looked into my eyes. "I shouldn't have called you." She hugged me to her and I hugged her back. Her body felt so small and I could feel her breasts against me and I began to get hard and pulled away. She kept her hands on my shoulders, looked into my eyes, hers brown and edged with pain and something I couldn't name. We stood there quite a while, it seemed. Then she thanked me again for coming, and I turned and left my father's house, six hollow-point shells, heavy as a promise, in the front pocket of my jeans.

ALL DAY long, I went to classes and carried them with me, didn't know where to put them. It didn't feel right to throw bullets in the trash. What if some kid found them and was the kind of kid I'd been? I pictured some ten-year-old squeezing the rounds in a vise and taking a hammer to the firing ends.

Later, walking across the Basiliere Bridge, I checked the traffic for a cruiser, then stopped and pulled the hollow-points from my pocket and threw them out over the railing, watched them briefly catch the sunlight as they fell into the dirty, swirling water.

It was early evening when I got to the bottom of Columbia Park. Across Main, two girls from Seventh Ave sat on the steps beside Pleasant Spa drinking Cokes and smoking. I was thirsty and told myself to drink some water before I changed and went down to the basement to work out. And maybe that's what I was thinking of as I walked up my street and saw stacked on our front lawn everything Pop owned. There was his weight bench and barbell and iron plates; there were cardboard boxes that held his books and albums, his Akubra hats and pipes and clothes and running shoes. There were two or three full garbage bags there too.

HE LIVED with us for two weeks. We didn't have a spare bedroom, and our only couch was a wicker sofa too small to sleep on, so he slept up in my room. I gave him the bed and slept on the floor, which I found I liked anyway, that cool hard surface under my back. I couldn't remember the last time I saw Pop so happy. Maybe when we were small and lived in Iowa City, when he was finally out of the Marines and going to graduate school full-time, when he was writing and taking classes and making love with his beautiful young wife, our mother, when he'd sit down on the couch with us four kids and tell us stories of Running Blue Ice Water.

Now he was forty and free again, Lorraine and her two quiet kids and her nine thousand pounds of furniture heading back South. He laughed a lot, sometimes a little too hard and a little too long, and he was in a constant mood to celebrate. Nearly every night he and I would drive down to the bars on Washington Street. It was strange going out with him this often, like having a new buddy, one I'd always known but never really knew.

I'd try to guide us to a corner table so my back would be to a wall or window and I could see who was coming in and who was leaving. I seemed to always be looking for trouble, for a husband to slap his wife, for a boyfriend to call his girlfriend a cunt or a whore, for a bigger one to lord over one smaller.

Since fracturing that bully's forehead, there'd been more fights: once, when Marjan had been in the wedding party of a friend, the reception later at an Am Vets down in East Boston. Two men in a Chrysler kept tapping the rear bumper of the limousine that held Marjan and the other bridesmaids. I was driving my mother's Toyota not far behind, and the driver of the sedan was unshaven and had dark curly hair and he leaned on the horn again and again, tapping the bumper with his. "It's

party time, bitches! Come out and fuckin' *play!*" The limo driver was
old and small. He was parked at the entrance to the hall where he was
supposed to open the back door for the girls, but he kept glancing into
his side view mirror and he wasn't getting out from behind the wheel.
Now the driver of the sedan was yelling more shit out his open window
and he bumped the limo again, and I pulled my mother's Toyota into
an empty space and was running between parked cars, the sedan driver
looking over at me just as I threw one into his face, then another and
another. A small voice inside me said, *This is wrong, he can't fight you
behind the wheel like that, you have to step away,* but I kept swinging at
him inside his window and only stepped back when he jerked open his
door and stood, staggering a second, this very big man, at least a foot
taller than I was, seventy, eighty pounds heavier, and now his friend was
hurrying around the trunk behind him and I couldn't let my adrenaline
back up on me and turn my legs to water because once you started you
couldn't stop or they'd get you so I reached up and grabbed the tall
driver's ears and yanked his face down onto my knee, then hit him with
rights again and again till somebody pulled me off, a crowd around us
now, men from inside the bar.

It was cold, but a lot of them wore T-shirts. One of them had a smoking cigarette between his lips, and he told me *cool your fuckin' jets.* The big
one was bleeding from his nose and mouth. He was telling two men how
I jumped him for no reason, that I was crazy. And now his friend, short
and thick-looking, close to thirty and wearing an Irish scully cap, was
pacing back and forth behind him, breathing hard, his fists clenched, and
I knew what he was doing. He was getting himself to where he had to be.
Because now he had a good look at me, this nineteen-year-old in a borrowed suit jacket and old corduroys, who was so much smaller than his
big friend and probably not as strong as he was either, and you couldn't
let the rush fade or there'd be nothing to fight with, and I yelled, "C'mon!
You want to go at it? You want to fuckin' go *at* it?!"

He rushed at me but two or three regulars held him back, the big one
surrounded by four more. The one smoking the cigarette pulled at my
arm. "I said *cool* it."

The bridesmaids were going inside now. A few gripped small shiny night hags, a few others bouquets of flowers, and Marjan looked over her shoulder at me as if she'd never seen me before, did not even know my name.

The function hall was smoky and dimly lit, the DJ playing loud disco. Marjan was at the head table with the bride and groom, and I sat in a chair where I could see the door. The term *sucker punch* was in my head, my face heating up with the knowledge that that's what I'd done, surprised a sitting man with a fist to the face. I kept hearing his voice out there in the parking lot calling me *fucking crazy,* and now my arms and legs felt spent and heavy and it would be bad if the two of them came in now.

"Why the fighting?"

A man sat beside me. He was five or ten years older than I was. He had long black hair tied in a ponytail. He wore a string tie with a turquoise and silver clasp at his throat, and he had narrow shoulders and dark eyes and high cheekbones.

I shook my head. I shrugged.

"Violence only leads to more violence, man."

"Yeah? What about the girls? The driver wasn't doing anything about it."

"Were they really in danger?"

"Yep." I stood and made my way through the tables for the bar and a beer. Men and women were talking and smiling at one another, laughing and drinking, and I felt like some kind of dimwitted brute.

Weeks later, drunk at Ronnie D's with Suzanne and her new boyfriend, Fred, a gentle mechanic with a bushy beard, I'd look up every time the door opened or closed; I was still expecting to see the Lynches or the Murphys coming for me, and I was tired of this, tired of the flare of adrenaline every time air from the street drifted in, and I turned to Fred and asked him if he'd give me a lift down to Riverside. It's where the Lynches and some of their cousins drank, at a bar in a Chinese restaurant in the shopping plaza next to the stadium. Fred said he would but first I needed the bathroom, and I made my way through the crowd and an opening in a partition wall and there was Pop, sitting at a table with three Bradford girls. The bar was loud with talk and laughter and you couldn't even hear the jukebox, just the dull thumping of a bass guitar, a black man singing somewhere beneath it. Pop wore one of his Akubra hats tilted back on his head, a drink in front of him, a smoking cigarette between two fingers on the table. The girls across from him were laughing hard about something, the one beside Pop laughing too, and I knew who they were but didn't know them. He saw me and waved me over.

"Want a *drink*?"

"I can't."

"What?" He cupped his hand to his ear. I walked around and leaned in close, could smell the Marlboro smoke in his hair. "I can't. I've gotta go fight somebody." It's the most I'd told him about anything, and he looked up at me, his face somber, and I squeezed his shoulder and left him for the bathroom.

In the blue light of the Chinese restaurant's bar, Dana Lynch stood there with four or five others. He was wearing a pullover sweater and I was drunker than I'd thought and walked between two men I didn't glance at. I looked up into Dana's face, saw some of Steve in it, saw the surprise. I patted his stomach, "You're getting soft, Dana." I stepped past him and walked to the men's room by a tank of goldfish treading water. I had to piss again, but I ignored the urinals, stood by the door and waited. Maybe they'd all come in, maybe just him.

I waited till I couldn't any longer and I used one of the urinals, my eye on the door. I rinsed my hands and splashed my face, then stepped back into the aquamarine darkness of where I was sure I'd be fighting more than one.

The bar was more crowded than just a few minutes earlier. More women now, most of them in ladies' leather jackets, their hair clean and feathered away from their faces like disco dancers. The air was smokier, and I walked through it past Dana Lynch and his friends. At the front door I glanced back at him. The men standing around him were not his normal crew, and he was sitting on a stool, looking at me, a still expression on his face. At his knee was a long wooden cane.

As I climbed back into Fred's car, I felt vaguely sorry for Dana Lynch. It was clear he was in no shape to fight anyone, and that he was afraid to fight me. Somebody was *afraid* of me.

It's what I'd wanted, wasn't it?

NOW POP and I were at the Tap on Washington Street raising shot glasses of Sauza tequila, toasting his new divorce and his new joy. This place had only been open a few months since Steve Lynch, and I never told my father why it had closed. I was listening to him now as he described his new woman to me, Suzanne's age exactly, an intern named Peggy he'd met at his publisher's office, the dinner they had afterward, how she was a writer and a runner.

Pop was smiling at me over his beer glass. In the smoky dim of the bar, his beard thicker and darker than it was, there was a light in his eyes that looked like pride.

"Ted told me about the Merrimack boys."

I nodded, sipped my beer, tried to hide how happy I felt about where this conversation was going. Only a week before, that fight with the boys from Merrimack College, ten or twelve of them being escorted off campus by just one security guard, Ted, a young married guy I liked because he did a good imitation of John Wayne and always had a joke. He was walking behind the last of them, and he was only armed with a flashlight.

I had just pulled up to them in Marjan's mother's car, sent there by Marjan to pick up her younger sister from a study group at the school. A couple of the men were yelling at Ted, swearing. One, bowlegged as a wrestler, yelled, "This school's full of bitches and faggots!" I pushed the gear into park, Marjan's sister saying, "No, Andre, don't, *don't*."

My headlights lit up the road, and I stepped into its light, Ted's voice in the air, telling me to get back in my "vehicle," then Gene, a slim, muscular swimmer from Indiana was standing beside me, and we were stepping into the darkness of the grass.

Pop said: "You took on *eleven* guys?"

"Gene Brock was there too."

"How do you fight eleven guys?"

"I only fought three. Gene fought the biggest one. The rest took off."

The first one ran at me and I let him bury his head in my waist and I ran backwards and dropped and let his own momentum hurl him over me onto his back and I started punching him in the face, then ran after another and got in two shots, then ran after a third and caught him in the side of the head.

Pop was squeezing my upper arm. "How'd you learn that?"

I shrugged, began to sip my beer, but I was tiring of my cowboy act and wanted to tell him everything, was aching to tell him. I looked at my father. "I figured some things out."

"Like what?" Pop raised two fingers to the bartender. It was a week-night so there was no band, but the place was loud with human voices, my eyes burning from the cigarette smoke.

"I used to think butterflies in my stomach meant I was afraid and if I'm afraid it's because I *should* be and then I'd get even more butterflies and the adrenaline would back up on me till I couldn't even move, and I'd just stand there and do nothing."

He nodded, his eyes on mine, his eyes somehow on himself.

"So, Pop, you can't let it back up on you. You have to move as soon as it comes. No foreplay. No shoving each other. As soon as you know you're in a fight, you punch him hard in the face and you keep punching."

I raised my glass and sipped my beer. A woman down the bar exhaled smoke and looked over at me and my father. I felt like a liar, like I was pretending to know more than I did. And the membrane. I wanted to tell him about that membrane around someone's eyes and nose and mouth, how you have to smash through it which means you have to smash through your own first, your own compassion for another, your own humanity.

"But where'd you learn to throw a punch?"

"Connolly's Gym."

Pop nodded again, his eyes scanning the crowd. "I've never been in a fight."

I nodded. He'd told me this before, but I said, "Not even in the Marines?"

"No, I was an officer."

"Well, just hit him first and hit him hard, Pop. And don't let the rush back up on you."

TWO OR three nights later, a woman sat alone at the bar. She was blonde and attractive, twenty years older than I was and still in her thirties. Her hair was cut straight at her shoulders and she wore a white sleeveless dress and was smoking a cigarette, a glass of white wine in front of her. She looked close to crying or walking out, and Pop and I had just come in. While we waited for our beers, he went up to her and leaned on the bar.

My father loved women. I knew that. Especially if they had pretty faces like this one. From the corner of the bar, my back to the wall, I could see him charming her, getting her to talk. Our beers came and I sipped mine and thought about bringing him his but didn't want to interrupt him. I knew he was just flirting with her anyway. He and his new girlfriend were planning to move in together, and just that day Pop had found an apartment for them across from the campus.

It was a quiet night, the place only half full, most of the crowd in the restaurant side. Every few minutes the front door would open and someone would come in, but since going to Lynch's home turf and seeing him on the stool next to his cane, I wasn't worried about him or his brother or cousins anymore. That fight was done. It was time to move on, a feeling I'd been getting more and more lately, this pull to get out of this town and go far, far away. I was eighteen, and what was there to do here but go to bars like this where I stood or sat with my back to the wall, scanning the room for trouble, scanning the room for another chance to prove myself to myself. There was the Iranian girl I loved, but I could only see her at her family's apartment, and she seemed just mildly interested in me anyway. There were more Iranian students on campus now, some of them rich and handsome. They drove sports cars and wore gold bracelets and French cologne, tennis clothes in warm weather, and I could see how comfortable she was with them all in the smoke room or walking across campus or laughing together in the student union, speaking in their mother tongue.

Pop came around the corner of the bar, his cheeks flushed. "Her fucking husband left her there."

"Left who?"

"Her." He pointed to the woman in the white dress. "She's been there for an hour and he's sitting in the restaurant with his fucking friends. An *hour*, son."

"You gonna talk to him?"

"You're damn right I am."

I watched him only a second or two before I got up and followed. The woman's husband sat at a large round table in the middle of the floor. Five or six men and two women sat with him. They looked up at my father, who stood a foot away pointing at the woman's husband and already yelling in his Marine voice words that got lost in all the bar noise. But they weren't lost on the husband, his eyes on Pop, his dark hair combed back from his face, his shoulders broad and rounded in his sweater. Even sitting down, he looked a lot bigger than Pop, and now he stood and moved fast around his friends and grabbed Pop's shirt and vest, and Pop grabbed his sweater and both seemed to pull at once so they pivoted and fell onto the table, flipping it, a woman screaming as she and the others scrambled away from their spilled drinks and broken glass and overturned chairs, the woman's husband on top of my father now, throwing punches at his head. Then the man's sweater collar was in my hands and I was yanking, a hand squeezing my shoulder and jerking me backwards, and I turned and shot a right into someone's mouth, this bearded man in a flannel shirt who dropped to the floor, and now there were other men pulling the woman's husband off my father, and in seconds he and I were out on Washington Street, laughing and breathing hard, though I wanted to get out of there before the woman's husband and his many friends came out looking for us.

We drove slowly down Main Street in my father's old Lancer. Pop kept laughing and shaking his head. He'd wanted to go to another bar somewhere, maybe Ronnie D's where some of his students might be, but we ended up buying a six-pack of Molson's at the package store next to the VFW where that kid had thrown a Molotov cocktail into my mother's car. From behind the wheel, Pop sipped his beer.

"I wanted to punch him, but man, it happened so fast."

"Yeah, it's always fast. You just have to be faster."

We were passing streetlight after streetlight, the sidewalk empty, the

tin-sided houses just blocky shadows on the other side. I drank from my
beer and saw again the face of the man I'd punched. He was twenty years
older than I was, his beard trimmed like my father's, and now I wasn't so
sure he'd been coming after me. In that flash of a second before I hit him
in the mouth, there was the light of reason in his eyes, a reasonable man
trying to break up a fight, that's all, and I'd hit him so hard he went down.

Pop reached over and squeezed my shoulder. He laughed again and I
laughed too, happy to be the object of his pride, but my knuckles stung
and there was the dark, tilting feeling I had added something to myself
that each time I used it subtracted more than it gave.

Pop took the slow right off Main up Columbia Park. I drained my
beer and knew he'd tell this story about us for a long while. I knew too
that I would not discourage him one bit from doing so.

DAYS LATER, a warm Saturday morning, I borrowed Jeff Chabot's flatbed truck to move Pop's things to his new apartment across the river in
Bradford. He was forty-one and his new girlfriend, Peggy, was nineteen
and now she stood in our front yard under the sun. She'd driven up from
Boston and had thick blonde hair and blue eyes, a dusting of freckles
across her upper cheeks. She wore shorts and sandals and looked smart
and athletic, her arms crossed under her breasts as she watched Jeb and
me tie down Pop's boxes and bags and weight bench onto Jeff's flatbed.

Pop was cheerful and laughed a lot, his eyes darting from his new girl
to his sons to his ex-wife's rented house and back again. My mother was
home, and she'd come out and introduced herself to Peggy, who'd looked
mildly surprised. Maybe because Mom was being so warm and friendly.
Maybe because she was surprised to see such a lovely first ex-wife, my
mother barefoot in shorts, her legs lean and smooth. Maybe because she
wasn't sure which ex-wife this was. The one he'd had four kids with? Or
the one he'd just left for her?

Mom teased Pop about how little he owned, about how he didn't
need a truck really, just a decent fucking car. Then she went back inside,
and now Pop's new girlfriend looked a bit bewildered. She kept looking
Jeb and me over. The fingernails of Jeb's right hand were long and tapered
for the guitar, his hair wilder than ever, his face shadowed with three or

four days of whiskers, and she seemed to take in how Pop and I talked to each other. Not like a father and son, but like pals. Like drinking buddies.

Suzanne and Nicole had come out to meet her too, but now they were back inside and Peggy seemed happy to be away from there, sitting in the middle of the front seat between me and Pop as I drove Jeff's flatbed down Main toward the river. Her bare knee was touching mine, and it was hard not to look down at her thighs.

"So," I said, "where're you from?"

"Where did I grow up?"

"Yeah."

"Manhattan."

"Where's that?"

"Manhattan?"

"Yeah, where is that?"

"You're joking, right? New York."

"New York City?"

"Yes, New York City." She laughed gracefully, as if to spare my feelings.

"Okay, so you're from New York City?"

"Yes."

"Well, I know where *that* is."

She glanced at Pop and rested her hand on his knee. He was smiling, but the ride got quiet as we rode over the Basiliere Bridge and the Merrimack River. I downshifted and gave the truck some gas. If I'd ever heard of Manhattan I couldn't remember the word, and it was like walking through the student union, three or four rich girls pointing me out, Dubus's son, the townie.

I was tired of being a townie. I was tired of this town.

FOR MONTHS I thought about becoming a long-haul truck driver, getting paid to roam the land in a thundering rig. I sent away for a brochure to the Andover Tractor Trailer Driving School, but the long sections on safety and maintenance left me cold, the same way I had felt pumping gas down on Winter Street, bored and far away from myself. Besides, when and where would I work out?

I began studying other brochures too. Glossy ones from the student services office in Academy Hall. Somewhere I heard you could transfer from one college to another, and I applied to five schools west of the Mississippi River. I'd be as far from everything I knew as I could get and once I got there, it'd be too late to change my mind and come back. These were state universities in Montana, Washington, Nevada, Colorado, and Texas. I made out the applications, sent along my B-average transcripts, and was accepted into all five.

That fall and winter I was working as a night manager in a fast food restaurant just off Monument Square, Arthur Treacher's Fish and Chips. It was owned by a Greek man named Nikos. He was short and stocky and wore thick bifocals, and he always looked distracted and concerned about money. There was Marie, too, a Greek girl who had warm brown eyes and hair as long and dark as Marjan's. Throughout our shift, we flirted, and she'd smile and ask if she could squeeze my bicep or touch my chest muscles through the polyester uniform we both had to wear. Sometimes I'd let her and feel I was betraying Marjan, but she and I rarely saw each other anymore. She was in study groups with the Iranians and Turks now, and on weekends they'd go to discos together. I was certain she was in love with somebody and it wasn't me, and I enjoyed this Greek girl's attention while I was saving the money I needed to get out of town.

Those years you could buy a two-week train pass on Amtrak and go wherever the train went, which included every state I needed to visit. Within a few months I had enough money for that ticket and then enough to move me to wherever I was going, too. One night late, when Nikos and I were closing out the register, I turned to him and said I was giving him my notice. He squinted up at me from behind his bifocals. He shook his head.

"Why do you need to do this? You're smart boy. You can make a lot of money with this business. You don't need college. I never went for college."

I nodded and listened. Then I thanked him for making me night manager and walked home. It was a damp spring night, and *college* kept sifting through my brain, Nikos's Greek accent wrapped around that word. I had to remind myself that that's where I was going, to some college far away, though I was only thinking about being far away from here, far from the stinking Merrimack River and its abandoned mills and overflowing barrooms and endless opportunities to fight. That, and what kind of gym I'd be working out in.

My last shift was a warm night in late May. Marie was wearing more makeup than she usually did, her cheeks rosy with blush, her lips too glossy. It was a slow night, just a couple of Puerto Rican or Dominican families coming in for our greasy fish and fries and tall Cokes, and I decided to close a half hour early. The dishwasher was a skinny redheaded kid who lived down in the avenues somewhere, the tattoo of a blue cross on the back of his right hand, and I told him he could go home.

While I closed out the register, Marie was mopping the floor in quick, hurried strokes, looking back at me every few seconds, hooking her hair behind one ear and smiling, though she looked melancholy and oddly eager.

I left her out front and carried the night's cash and receipts to the office, a small room on the other side of the kitchen. I sat at the desk and pushed the money and paperwork into a night deposit bag. My legs were sore. The last few weeks Sam had been coming over every morning at six o'clock to work our calves together, a body part we'd been neglecting too long. But there was no place to fit it into our workouts, so we started the day down in my basement behind the furnace doing Donkey Calf Raises, an exercise where you bend forward at a 90-degree angle and rest your elbows on a table and your partner straddles your lower back, his body weight the only resistance as you rise up and down on your toes. The day before, on my last set, the burn began on the ninth or tenth rep, and I thought, *Twenty, I'll do twenty.* Sam's sneakers were tapping my knees and hot needles were being pushed under the skin of my calves but I went for ten more, then another ten, then another, the pain barrier in my brain a flaming wall I was marching toward one scalding calf raise at a time, then I fell through it into a blue numbness and there were only sounds coming out of me, the number ninety in my head when I finally quit.

Outside, an engine revved in the parking lot. I smelled perfume and turned to see Marie standing in the doorway.

"Everything's done." She crossed her arms under her breasts and smiled at me, her chin low, one hip resting against the jamb. Now there was a rapping on the back door, loud and close together, then a muffled shouting. "*Marie*. Get out here. I know what you're doing. I know what you're fucking doing, Marie. I got Lee Paquette out here. You hear me, mother*fucker*. I got Lee *Paquette*."

Motherfucker was clearly me. Paquette was big and cut and rode around town on a Kawasaki motorcycle in short shorts and no shirt, his gym muscles oiled up, his long black hair flapping out the back of his bright red helmet. He had a rep with some for being a badass, though I'd heard more about how he liked young teenage girls, how he'd charm them, then fuck them, then tell everybody all about it.

"*Marie.*"

"That's just my boyfriend. He thinks something's going on between us."

More rapping. More yelling. I stood and stepped sideways between Marie and the doorjamb and walked through the fluorescent-lit kitchen for the back door. I opened it to see her boyfriend standing there in a white T-shirt and jeans, his hair short, his ears sticking out. Behind him Lee Paquette sat in the passenger seat of a Z-28. His eyes were on me like he was the cowboy and I was the horse, and I looked back at Marie's boyfriend. "She's almost done. You're going to have to wait quietly or I'll have to call the cops, all right?"

But he was looking past me into the kitchen, his eyes dark with something I knew nothing about. "Marie?"

"She'll be right out." I closed the door and locked it. Marie rolled her eyes at me, took her time card and punched out. She pulled her pocketbook strap over her shoulder, then slid it back off and rested it on the stainless steel counter. She looked at me.

"*Marie.*" His voice sounded farther away now, and I pictured him sitting behind the wheel of his car, Lee beside him, ready to come after me, the hired gun, which meant Marie's boyfriend was another one afraid of me, but I felt nothing about this. It was as if I'd been dropped into a story that had little to do with me.

"You have to let me kiss you." She walked closer. "C'mon, it's your last night. One kiss." She smiled, but there was a sadness in her eyes, a need of some kind I hadn't seen before, and then her lips were against mine and she parted them and flicked her tongue into my mouth and I pulled back and gave her a hug and walked to the door and opened it.

She left quickly, her pocketbook over her shoulder, her long hair swaying against her back.

"What took so fuckin' long, Marie?"

I watched her climb into the backseat. Paquette's eyes were on me. "You got a problem?"

I smiled and waved like I was in a parade. I closed the door, Marie's boyfriend firing all six cylinders. Then came the rubber-whine of his spinning tires as he laid a patch across the lot onto Main, Big Lee beside him, Marie in the back seat.

A few years later, Lee Paquette would be in a sub shop on Primrose sitting with a teenage girl when her father would walk in with a shotgun, point it behind the counter at the man who'd been fucking his wife, and pull the trigger, the man's body flying backwards into the smoking peppers and mushrooms and onions on the stove, a fist-sized hole in his chest.

The father would then look over at his daughter and Paquette, raise the shotgun and tell Lee to get on his knees. He'd press the hot barrel to Lee's forehead, and Lee would begin to cry and beg for his life. Then he'd shit his pants and maybe the man didn't shoot because of that or because his daughter was crying there beside him, too, and she'd already seen her father do enough for one afternoon. Whatever his reasons were, he lowered the shotgun and walked out the door and people still talk about Lee and how down on Primrose that day he cried and shit his pants.

THE MORNING of my train trip, Mom and Bruce drove me to South Station in Boston where Bruce insisted I borrow a navy blue sports coat for my interviews with college officials. I was nearly twenty and had hardly ever worn one before. It was tight in the upper back, but I felt like somebody in it, and I hugged Bruce and my mother goodbye, watching them pull into Boston traffic, Mom leaning out the window to wave at me, wiping under her eye and waving again. There was the feeling I was doing something more important than I'd realized.

I climbed onto the train with my duffel bag of underwear and a second pair of jeans, a sweater and socks and clothes to work out in. That's
all this trip was for me anyway. I had no intention of talking to any college officials. All I needed to see were the gyms at each school or in each
town where the school was. And I had enough money on me to buy one
meal a day plus a high-protein snack of some kind, nuts and seeds, maybe
a hard-boiled egg, but that first night, rolling fast over the rails through
New York State for the Great Lakes and Chicago, I blew fifty bucks buying beer for me and a young woman who'd been sitting beside me reading
a novel. We drank too much, and she ended up crying against my chest
under a train blanket over us both. In the morning I slept as we pulled
into the station and she left me a note with her address in Boston for
"when you ever leave that Arab girl," and I couldn't remember talking
about Marjan at all.

Nearly two weeks later, no one place had pulled me toward it, not the
mountainous ravines of Montana nor the wet, rolling green of Washington State, not the neon shine of Reno or the flat gray plains of Greeley,
Colorado. But the last stop was Austin, Texas, and when I got off the
train it was late afternoon and the air smelled like creosote and barbecue
smoke. Rising up out of weeds beside the tracks was a billboard of a
young Mexican woman, her long black hair falling over her white blouse,
and she held a platter of enchiladas and a pitcher of Lone Star Beer. She
was smiling, a red flower tucked behind one ear, and that was enough. I
was going to school here. Surely there'd be a decent gym in the capital of
Texas.

I LEFT home in September, a few days before my twentieth birthday. I'd
bought a one-way Greyhound ticket South, and the bus departed from
Railroad Square, not far from the Tap and the Lido and Ray and Arlene's,
their doors open, the jukebox already playing in one, "Bennie and the
Jets." It was a warm morning, the sun shining on the iron trestle and its
hand-painted peace sign and *Fuck U* and neon-orange cross. Cars drove
by as I carried Pop's wooden Marine trunk to the side of the bus. Once
he'd heard I was leaving town, he gave it to me, the trunk he'd used as a
young lieutenant on the USS *Ranger* off the coast of Japan. Inside it were

my clothes and Dingo boots, a dictionary and a few back issues of *Muscle Builder* magazine. I set it on the sidewalk and the driver heaved it into the belly of the bus, and I was surprised at how many people had come to see me off—Pop and Peggy, Mom and Bruce and Sam Dolan, Marjan and her mother and brother and sister. Two days before, because I was moving away, her mother allowed us time alone together. Marjan and I held each other most of the afternoon, and she kept saying she couldn't believe I was leaving, why was I leaving? And holding her, I didn't know why but I was. It was the expression the others seemed to have too, surprise that I was leaving, or maybe not that, but that I'd found a way to leave without really involving anyone else, or even telling anyone about it. It was like working out, how I found it or it found me, a private thing that saved me, something I did alone under the ongoing lives of my own family.

My mother had tears in her eyes again. It was a weekend, and she wore jeans and a light blouse and she looked young and beautiful as she stood beside her boyfriend of nine years. She wiped under both eyes with her forefinger and Sam hugged me hard and patted me on the back, and my father's girlfriend Peggy held me and kissed my cheek, then Pop said into my ear, "I'll miss you, man."

I kissed both cheeks of each member of Marjan's family I'd come to love, and I held her last, could smell the shampoo in her hair, could feel how completely she let me hold her.

She whispered, "I still can't believe you're leaving," and her voice broke and how could I have missed that she loved me? How could I have missed that they all did?

PART II

RIVER, FIST, AND BONE

10

———

TWO YEARS LATER, I was back from Texas living in a third-floor walk-up in Lynn, Massachusetts. It was a town southeast of Haverhill, a town of welfare projects and brick tenements, Cambodian and Latino street gangs, the smell of the ocean blowing in over the barrooms and alleyways and strip malls. There was a saying, "Lynn, Lynn, the city of sin, you don't come out the way you went in," but I lived contentedly alone in two rooms with no furniture and nothing on the walls, the front room echoing my footsteps each time I walked over its cracked linoleum floor to the kitchen where there was a gas stove and a small table and chair. In the back was the bedroom, and I slept there on a yoga mat my mother had made and upholstered for me years earlier. It was foam an inch thick and I laid it on the floor and put two work boots into a pillowcase for a pillow, covered up each night with a sleeping bag.

I did not own a telephone or TV, a radio or record player, and each night after working construction with my brother Jeb, I lay on my foam pad or sat at the small table in the kitchen and read Max Weber, E. F. Schumacher, Karl Marx, Friedrich Engels, and Vladimir Lenin. I was twenty-two years old, and I'd become a Marxist. That's what Texas did to me, took my hatred of bullies and bullying and institutionalized it. In Austin, I'd drifted into the social sciences where you could learn a little about a lot, but all I seemed to find was story after story of U.S. imperialism, how we had a long history of supporting dictators and Big Business at the expense of men, women, and children just trying to eat and live and be free.

I listened to lectures on Third World politics and economic policy and the fight against communism. But it looked to me like a simple fight against the poor by the rich, the strong against the weak, and I walked the campus in a constant state of outrage and grief, so much of the world's history the story of cruelty and injustice and very few people doing anything about it.

This was a campus of fifty-five thousand students, half of whom were business majors, and they went to classes in spacious, air-conditioned buildings, their roofs terracotta, their open foyers sporting exotic plants and stone fountains on cool Mexican or Italian tile. Palm trees offered shade wherever you needed it, and from the stone steps of the main building, you could stand and look over the terraced steps of the South Mall to the gold dome of the state capitol shining so bright under the Texas sun you couldn't look directly at it.

There was the tower that'd been closed since August 1966 when Charles Whitman climbed up there and calmly aimed and shot and killed fourteen people. I could see it clearly from the steps of Arrakis House on Pearl Street, the co-op I lived in with five other men and six women. It was a small two-story in the shade of oak and pecan trees. We had a fenced-in yard and a garage that had been turned into a bedroom and bathroom, and I bunked there with Dan, a tall skinny Ph.D. candidate in political science. He had a beard and long hair and wore round rimless glasses like John Lennon, and on Friday or Saturday nights he'd play his guitar on the front porch and sing how a working-class hero was something to be.

But there were other songs in the air. Across the alley from our garage apartment was a sorority house that held young women who drove brightly colored coupes and put their blonde hair in curlers at night and studied at the business school. Some nights, the tower usually glowing orange a few blocks east, new pickup trucks would pull up to the sorority, their beds full of fraternity boys in jackets and ties, their boots shining, and they'd hop out and line up on the lawn and sing some anthem to the girls who were now out on the second-story balcony, their smiling faces made up, their blue and white dresses billowing. The young men below would stand shoulder to shoulder singing of Texas and past glory and friendly señoritas, and the girls would toss single roses down to the fraternity boys, this ritual I assumed went back generations. The next morning I'd watch a Latina woman in a white cleaning uniform on the front lawn stooping to pick up the roses left behind, their red petals falling to the ground.

I'd walk the hot streets and its smells of barbecue smoke and baking asphalt, frying tortillas and eucalyptus leaves and the dried pecan shells I crushed under my feet, but I'd become brooding and reclusive and studious. When I wasn't studying, I worked out hard at the Texas Athletic Club, riding my bicycle across town to a squat cinderblock building of mainly powerlifters, some of them pushing over 400 pounds off their chests, squatting with over 600, dead-lifting even more. These were very large men, and I still strived to be one of them, but there was the growing feeling inside me that a strong body was not enough, that that kind of power was only the beginning of what you'd need to confront those who wanted to take something away from you.

ARRAKIS OWNED a rusted-out yellow Pinto wagon. It was left to us by the parents of a boy who'd killed himself the year before I arrived, and it was the model that in those days exploded into flames on rear-end collisions. We used it to go grocery shopping or take someone to the airport, or sometimes to go cool off somewhere outside of town.

It was a hot Saturday afternoon, the air still and heavy, and I was driving the Pinto into the lot of a 7-Eleven. Kourosh was sitting beside me. He was a new resident of the house, a twenty-nine-year-old Iranian who'd just moved here from London to study computer science. When I learned he was from Iran, I said hello in Persian and he smiled brightly and said hello back and soon we were studying together in the library, drinking beer together on the weekends, and every other Friday night we would sit down somewhere, and I would teach him English and he would reciprocate the following week by teaching me Persian. Because he was good with his hands, he'd become the house mechanic and he made the Pinto run smoother, and now in the back sat Molly, a large, kind woman with wide burn scars on her arms and legs. She had a problem with her hair falling out too, from stress, she said, and trauma, so she had no eyebrows or eyelashes, and half her head was bald while the other half held thin black hair from which her ears protruded.

Beside her sat Jen. She was a year younger than I was. She skipped a lot of classes and stayed in her room writing poetry and painting with watercolors or spray cans, anything she could find. She had blonde hair and wore faded cotton dresses from St. Vincent de Paul's and she'd been her high school valedictorian, though she had to explain to me what that was. Her room was next to mine on the second floor. Sometimes I'd crawl into her bed or she'd crawl into mine, and now she sat in her bathing suit next to Wei Ling, a bright and cheerful premedical student from China who laughed a lot and studied hard, smoking cigarettes in her bedroom till late at night.

The five of us were heading to Barton Creek, a spring-fed swimming hole on the other side of Austin. All we needed was beer and ice, and just as I pulled into the lot, two frat boys climbed out of their powder blue Monte Carlo. They were both tall and well-built, their button-down shirts tucked snugly into their ironed jeans, and as we pulled up in our rusted Pinto wagon, the muffler throaty, just a bit too much exhaust seeping out the back, the driver glanced over at us like we were bugs somebody should've stepped on, and that's when I noticed how he'd parked his Monte Carlo across two parking spaces, that's when I noticed the stickers on his rear bumper: *Anti-Irania Mania*, and *No Camel Jockeys*.

They weren't the first I'd seen. A month before, close to midnight, I'd walked home from the campus library to see a Cadillac parked in front of our house. Like so many of the cars in that neighborhood of fraternities and sororities, it was new, its silver hubcaps catching the dim light from our front porch. I saw the *No Camel Jockeys* sticker on the rear bumper, and I stood there looking down at it a long while.

Because of my ties to Marjan and her family, I'd studied more about Iran and its secret police, Savak, trained and supported by the United States. There were stories of men forced to watch the repeated rape of their wives, forced to watch their own children held down while fingers were broken, a hand was sawn off, or an arm. Then, on September 8, 1978, what they call Black Friday, a protesting and unarmed crowd was gunned down in Jaleh Square, and what killed them were American bullets.

In November, students climbed over the walls of the American Embassy and took control of what they called "the nest of spies for the Great Satan." I didn't see us all as being the Great Satan, but I thought it very reasonable that they did.

Back in Austin, Texas, fraternity boys got liquored up and cruised the streets looking for anyone with dark skin and eyes and hair, anyone who looked like a "camel jockey" or "sand nigger." They found Ethiopians, Mexicans, a few Egyptians and Sudanese, and they beat them up, usually three or four on one. I'd hear of these attacks, and each day I walked to and from campus hoping to see one, hoping to do what I'd learned to do.

Now in the parking lot of the 7-Eleven, my pulse was thrashing between my ears and I edged the Pinto up to the rear passenger side of the powder blue Monte Carlo and stepped on the gas and scraped metal off metal the length of both cars, Wei Ling screaming, the Monte Carlo rocking in the rear view mirror as I pulled ahead, a strip of chrome hanging from it like a broken limb.

Molly was yelling, "You have no right! You have absolutely no *right* to do that with *us* in the car. Andre. Take us home right this minute!"

"Not till they come out." My mouth was dry. I'd slipped off my seat belt so I could jump out of the car when they came back outside, those two racist, entitled pieces of shit I was going to go after. But Kourosh's hand was on my arm.

"Andre-jahn, no. No."

And it was like the man next to me in that wedding reception in East Boston, a calm voice telling me this is not the way.

FOR THE most part I was able to control myself. Every night after dinner, Kourosh and I would load our backpacks with books and notebooks and walk to the main library on campus where we'd study from seven till just after midnight. I was reading a lot of labor history now, which kept me in a dark mood, especially stories like the Ludlow Massacre in Colorado when the governor sent in the National Guard to break up a strike and they shot and burned to death twenty men, women, and children. Karl Marx said that human history is the history of class conflict, and how, I thought, could he have been anything but right. And I was tired of walking around carrying this new knowledge that only the writers of little-read books seemed to have, that only my professors had.

It was early spring in Austin and all day it had rained. You could smell the ozone, the magnolias and eucalyptus and pine. Across the alley at suppertime, the sorority's kitchen door had been open and they'd been served brisket and beans, but now it was after midnight, a Tuesday or Wednesday, and my window was open, and I lay on my mattress in the dark listening to drops of rain ticking from leaf to leaf. The house was quiet. Down the hall behind a closed door came the tapping of keys from a manual typewriter. I'd always loved that sound, was drawn to it for reasons I couldn't explain. A block or two north a college boy let out a rebel yell, some lone drunk wandering home from an outdoor bar. But then there were more voices, two or three talking loud and laughing, another one hollering, and didn't they know the whole neighborhood was asleep? Did they even *think* about that?

I closed my eyes and tried to ignore them. The voices got louder. I could hear boot steps on Pearl. A male voice was talking about a woman, how everybody knew she was a whore. "How come *you* don't know that, J.B? She's a fuckin' *whore*." And J.B. let out a boozy yell right there under my window. I sat up and looked down at three of them standing in the alley, the light from the sorority's stoop shining across the wet asphalt. They were tall, the way so many Texans seemed to be, and they wore pointed Tony Lamas and expensive cotton shirts, one of them swaying slightly as he lit a cigarette, the other two talking in loud, half-drunk voices about Dolly, the same woman they were calling a whore. The window screen was pressing against my nose. A whisper inside me said, *Ignore them. They'll wander off. Go to sleep.*

But then one of them started laughing and he let out that rebel yell again, and I said, "You want to keep it down out there, please? People are sleeping."

"Yeah? You want your *ass* kicked?"

I pulled on my jeans and T-shirt and was soon walking barefoot over the kitchen's linoleum floor, then damp ground, then the cool wet asphalt of the alley.

LATER, BACK in my bed in the dark, the boy in me kept replaying how I'd walked up to three tall men and waited for one of them to get it started, and when the tallest one asked me if I'd come out there for an ass-kicking, I dropped him with a right cross to the face, then pivoted and dropped the one next to him, then I went after the third but he was the drunkest one and he tripped and fell, then the second one was on me and we both knelt in a puddle swinging at each other till I got in more than he did and he fell back and crawled into the shadows of the dumpster.

I stood and yelled at them to get the fuck out of my alley. But the first one I'd hit wasn't moving. He lay on his back with his arms spread wide, his mouth open and bleeding, and I watched as his two friends mumbled revenge and picked him up and carried him farther down the alley to their car. They lay him in the backseat. The engine revved once, then the driver, the second one I'd punched, backed up and drove slowly away from our house.

For a while I couldn't stop replaying how well those first two punches had gone, the first a knockout, the second a knockdown. And it had happened so fast, the way it always did, so that my friends in the house I lived in didn't even know about it. That I'd protected them. For a few moments I lay in the glow of the hurt I'd caused, and I felt completely virtuous, as brave and selfless as a good father.

But then my cheeks began to burn, this voice in my head: *You did that for you.* And I saw Cody Perkins back on the streets of the South End, how he walked with his chest out and his head up, how he was always looking for a fight. At eleven and twelve years old, I could only fear and admire him; how could anyone *look* for a fight? How could anyone *want* that? But lying there on my mattress in Texas nine years later, my knuckles swelling up, the alley clear and quiet because I had cleared it, I knew why he wanted to find those fights; they were his only chance to get out what was inside him. Like pus from a wound, it was how he expressed what had to be expressed. It gave him the chance to do something for him and him only, and my shame now came from someplace I hadn't considered before, that maybe inside me there were other ways to get this pus out, other ways to express a wound.

I began to meditate. I skimmed a book on it at the campus bookstore on Guadalupe, and each night after studying at the library, I'd sit cross-legged on the floor in my room with the lights off and my eyes closed. I'd concentrate on my breathing. Every few exhalations I'd think, *Om, peace, peace, peace.*

I liked having that word in my head. It made me feel I was heading some place higher and more evolved. I'd think of Gandhi, and Martin Luther King, even Jesus, someone I'd rarely thought of; I'd breathe and begin to imagine loving all these people I'd come to hate, these wealthy white kids I was convinced would one day hold the reins of oppressive power.

But then I saw the body of Jesus Christ hanging on the cross, his chest collapsed, those spikes driven through his feet and palms. I saw the bullets shot into Gandhi's torso, his outsretched hands that could do nothing for him, and I saw Martin Luther King lying dead on that concrete motel balcony in Memphis. Now my heart was beating faster, my breathing more shallow. I thought *peace, peace, peace.* But I saw my brother's arms at his sides as Tommy J. punched him in the face, I saw my sister raped by two men who were never caught, and when I was nine and we still lived together in that house in the woods, I lay on the living room floor under the coffee table while my mother and father watched the black-and-white news, a close-up on the X-ray of Robert Kennedy's brain and the .22 caliber bullet shot into it. And now I knew by whom and why, a young Palestinian angry over Kennedy's support of Israel, and when would any of this ever end? Would we ever stop doing this to one another?

GRADUATION DAY was hot and cloudless, the Texas sky a deep blue above the terracotta-tiled roofs of campus. The steps of the South Mall were taken up with fathers in ties and mothers in dresses, and brothers and sisters and aunts and uncles and cousins watching thousands of us in our robes and tasseled mortarboards as we sat in the shade of the main building listening to a speech given by a man in a linen three-piece suit.

Somewhere in the crowd were my mother and her mother and sister, both of whom had driven to Austin from central Louisiana where my grandmother lived. My mother had flown in from St. Maarten, the island where she'd been living with Bruce for two years helping him to run a small airfreight company that flew in supplies for hotels and restaurants. My brother and sisters were up North: Suzanne had dropped out of Bradford and gotten a job tending bar at the beach. She'd met a roofer there named Keith, and they planned to get married late in the summer; Nicole was in her last year of high school and living with our father and his third wife, Peggy; and Jeb had gotten a girl pregnant. He was working construction and sharing a small rented house with her in Salem, Massachusetts. She was due to have the baby soon. He was nineteen.

Some administrator was speaking now, a tall handsome man I'd never seen before. He smiled and leaned into the microphone and declared us official graduates of the university. There were whoops of joy. Mortarboards got tossed into the air, and I turned and made my way through the crowd to look for my mother, aunt, and grandmother. I felt oddly blue. I had just begun to learn all I needed to learn. There were so many more books to read, so many more lectures to attend. How would I be completely free until I'd learned all those truths? But there was my family too; I kept feeling them inside me, an itch that could only be scratched by going North for a while: And would Jeb get married? How was he going to be a classical guitarist while working construction? Wasn't that bad for his hands? Didn't he tell me that before? That a musician has to take care of his hands?

But I wasn't just going back for my brother and two sisters. As much as I'd loved all that reading and essay-writing and test-taking, there was the instinct to walk away from it for a while, to do some kind of physical work. I could take a year before I went back to school for that Ph.D., then maybe I'd become someone with the credentials to do good, the kind of person to whom people really listened.

BY LATE fall, Jeb and I were building things together again. Our boss was Trevor D., a lanky British man who wanted to be a millionaire before he turned thirty. He had long dark hair and expected punctuality and

efficiency and the consistent execution of our tasks. These were words he
used regularly. He also said "excellence" a lot, and once or twice a week he
had to unhitch his leather carpenter's apron and lie down on the ground,
his eyes closed tight as one of his migraines passed through his head like
a silent storm.

There was the lead carpenter, Doug, and Jeb, the carpenter's helper,
and Randy the laborer, and me, who'd been demoted from carpenter to
laborer once Trevor D. saw I knew very little and could do less. I'd lied to
get the job, told him I had all kinds of experience when all I'd done was
build forts with Jeb when we were kids.

We were renovating a three-story house Trevor D. had bought down
by the water. It was in a neighborhood of two-hundred-year-old houses,
paint flaking off their clapboards, rot in their sills and doors and window
frames. There was a barroom a block away called the Hole in the Wall, a
few boarded-up shops, but from the roof of Trevor D.'s house you could
see the ocean, a gray sliver of it beyond utility poles and shingled gables.
His plan was to gut the entire structure down to its frame then rebuild it
as three condominiums, the top one a luxury unit because of the "water-
view." He said he hoped to triple or quadruple his investment.

I saw him as a tawdry capitalist.

The five of us ripped off all the clapboards, pulled out the windows
and any sheathing that may have rotted, wide pine boards nailed to studs
by men decades and decades before any of us was born. A lot of the
sheathing had to go, the roof too, including the rafters because Trevor D.
needed a flat roof for the deck we were going to build up there. It took
over a week to strip the house down to its naked frame, a week when we
all worked together doing the same thing, but now the long steel dumpster we'd filled was gone and stacks of new lumber sat in the lot, lumber
Randy and I constantly hauled to Trevor and Doug and Jeb, the men who
knew what they were doing and spoke about it in a language I did not
know.

I kept thinking Jeb shouldn't know it either. He'd spent his teenage
years in his room, practicing guitar and fucking a grown woman and
making art; then he found himself at Bradford College, drunk at a party
with a cute girl and now he was a father, and the teacher was finally gone

and how did he understand what these men were talking about? What did he know about building walls and floors and stairs to rooms with windows that worked? But somehow he did. And if he wasn't sure, he'd pretend he knew, then go learn on his own what seemed to be already there inside him, an innate knowledge of how things worked.

So many times during the day, Trevor D. and Doug and Jeb would pause to work out a problem: a support wall is needed here, but that makes the hallway on the other side too narrow; the stairs end here, but now the header's too low above the last step; if the kitchen window is framed here, there's no room for a fridge there; and on and on. I'd hear pieces of their conversation while Randy and I hauled new two-by-fours for the walls, sheets of plywood for sheathing, fifty-pound boxes of nails. Randy and I spent days pulling old ones from every stud in the house so that each one was clean and ready for twentieth-century insulation, strapping, and Sheetrock. While new construction started on the first floor, he and I continued demo work on the second and third. We knocked down partition walls. We ripped up old flooring from joists we'd then have to balance ourselves on to keep from falling through. We filled barrels with chunks of plaster and broken lathe, each one weighing well over a hundred pounds, and we'd heave them down steps and outside to the new dumpster where we'd squat on either side of the barrel, then lift it over our heads and dump it in, the plaster dust clouding back into our faces, our hair white, our eyes red-rimmed.

Randy didn't talk much, but I knew he'd dropped out of high school, that he was married and had a two-year-old son. I knew his wife had a drinking problem and was in rehab, and that Randy's mother took care of his son all day while he worked. I knew he liked cars and took pride in the black SS Chevelle he drove to the job site every morning. He kept it clean inside and out and parked it on the far side of the parking lot. Any tools he owned—a framing hammer, a sledge, a few pry bars, and a reciprocating saw—he'd lay on a blanket in the trunk. At coffee break, he and I would sit against the foundation apart from Trevor D., Doug, and Jeb, who usually stood in the middle of the lot looking up at the house, pointing things out to each other. Trevor and Doug were dressed for the weather, heavy jeans and work boots, a fleece vest and wool sweater over more wool over long underwear, the white cotton sleeves you could see at the wrists. But Jeb, his hair shorter now, his stubble catching the morning light, he stood there in jeans with a hole in one knee, his bare leg showing. He wore a T-shirt under a button-down cotton shirt that may have belonged to Bruce once. The shirttails hung out. But he didn't look cold or unhappy as he stood there and tapped a Marlboro from his pack and lit up, nodding his head at whatever Trevor D. was saying, learning his trade.

At night, alone in my apartment, I'd heat a can of soup and read Marx or Engels or Weber. The radiator hissed, and I'd read the same sentence over and over, wouldn't even see it. Later, lying on my mat in the back room, I'd thumb through catalogues for graduate schools, think about all the knowledge that would come with earning a Ph.D. in political thought, how much I would know then.

But the world didn't seem so big now, and where were the people who wanted to change it anyway? Somehow in Texas, studying all I'd studied, I'd felt like more than just one. My reading had joined my mind to the thinkers before me, to the millions of people whose lives they indirectly wrote about, these scholars who sat in a tower so high they could see everyone and I could too. But after eight to ten hours of working with my body, I was too tired to look, a capitalist plot, I thought, to keep the prole in his place. But this assumption floated away like steam; if I was a proletarian, who was Trevor D.? He had plans to be a rich bourgeois, but I saw how hard he worked every day, how two or three times a shift, he'd sit somewhere with his calculator and paper and pencil to figure out how much all this was costing, how much was left in the budget, how much would his return be? And what did I care if he made a hundred thousand dollars on this job? As long as what he built was solid and its price was fair, what was wrong with that? Did that make him an oppressor?

I didn't know. So I'd brew tea and open one of my books and keep reading, hoping one of these dead intellectuals could tell me.

FOR THE first time since I was fifteen and began to change my body with weights, I had no place to train. If there was a barbell gym in Lynn I couldn't find it, and even though I was working with my body all day long all week long, sweating and breathing hard for so much of each shift, it wasn't enough. My chest muscles felt smaller, my shoulders and arms too, and when I flexed my upper back, it didn't flare as much as it used to. Despite all my training, I had never become big, just hard and fit, but now whatever muscle I'd built was atrophying. I felt vulnerable, like a knight who has slipped off his steel-plated armor and gone back into the world without it. I was no longer the small, soft boy Clay Whelan and the others had beat up, but a cool irrational fear welled in my gut that if I didn't find a gym, I would slide back into being that boy all over again, and as soon as I did, that's when they'd come for me.

EVERY SATURDAY I'd drive forty minutes northeast to Haverhill. I'd meet Sam Dolan at the Y and he and I would work out together with rusting black iron in a dank concrete room. He was still so much stronger than I was, bench-pressing well over 300 pounds now, but I'd missed my friend, and it was good to be with him again, and for over two hours we'd push and pull and press and curl.

Sam had graduated from Merrimack College and was working as a reporter for the Lawrence *Eagle-Tribune,* something he saw himself doing for years. He'd always liked reading and writing, and now he got paid to do both. He still had his old room at his parents' house on Eighteenth Avenue, but he was engaged to marry Theresa the following August, and sometimes he'd stay over at her apartment just off Lafayette Square. Theresa worked at AT&T, which used to be Western Electric. She was kind and quiet, and she had long brown hair and a lovely face and when Sam met her at a house party, he was drawn to her right away and knew early on where they were headed together. They already had plans to one day own a house and have kids.

After our workouts and a shower, Sam and I would drive across the river on the Basiliere Bridge to Ronnie D's. The winter sun would be down, the sky casting a purple light over the brick mill buildings up the Merrimack, broken ice floes wedged hard against the granite piers beneath us. Upriver was the iron trestle the Boston & Maine would take into Railroad Square, and beyond that the bridge Jeb and I had run across three years ago. My muscles had that pleasantly flushed and tired feeling, and I was looking forward to some cold beer and two or three bar hot dogs, but as we drove into Bradford past its neon-lit fast food shops—Mister Donut, then McDonald's, the car dealership across the street—there was an emptiness somewhere behind my ribs and sternum, an airless quiet that told me I was standing still when before, in Texas, I'd been running forward.

But I liked Ronnie D's. I liked how crowded and dimly lit it always was. The only light came from amber lamps in the walls of the wooden booths and from behind the bar, and that's where Big Pat Cahill worked slow and steady tapping off glasses of beer, pouring shots of blackberry brandy and peppermint schnapps, ringing up purchases on an old brass cash register beneath the painting of a nude woman reclining on her elbow, her belly and breasts exposed, a blanket draped over her hip. Pat had a long brown beard and hair he tucked behind his ears. His voice was low and stony, and he wore black T-shirts all year long, and at closing when the lights would come up, the bar crammed with drunk men and women in a smoky haze, another bartender would yell, "You don't have to go home, but you can't stay *here!*" This was a line people ignored, but then Pat would bellow, "Everyone the fuck out! *Now!*" And we'd drain our drinks and beers and head for the door.

By nightfall, the place would be full of people I'd known and not known for years. Faces from high school, or men and women I'd seen in the streets. They stood crowded at the bar or sat at the cocktail tables or in the booths against the wall that Sam and Theresa and I preferred. We'd drink and laugh and talk. Because he'd lived in this town his entire life, Sam knew far more people than I did. Men from his old hockey team, maybe a coworker from the paper, or a friend of his parents or one of his many aunts and uncles and cousins. Now and then, one or two would sit in the booth with us for a while as we drank beer after beer. Every half hour or so, the cocktail waitress would come by to take another order and she'd start to clear the table, but we'd ask her to leave the empty bottles where they were; for some reason we liked to see evidence of all we drank, as if we were measuring just how much fun we were having.

And it *was* fun, though back in Texas all that book-learning had seemed to open doors inside me that led to a higher part of myself, one that was more evolved and thoughtful, reasonable and idealistic; in the

Northeast again, working construction in Lynn, trying to study at night but losing interest, lifting and drinking with Sam, I was at the mercy of something; every time a man laughed too loudly or yelled above the crowd, I'd sit up and look over there, expecting to see trouble and ready to jump back into the heart of it. Most of the time it was nothing, though; Ronnie D's was a friendlier bar than those across the river in Haverhill. The customers were regulars who knew each other, and besides, there was Pat to deal with.

Sometimes I'd go home with a woman. Wake up in an apartment or house I didn't recognize. Turn to see the sleeping face of someone I did not know, her brown curly hair on the pillow, or red, or straight and blonde, my clothes on the rug, hers too, once a leopard-skin outfit I stepped over on my way out the door.

But most nights I'd leave with Sam and Theresa, and the three of us would drive down along the river past the closing bars and men and women milling on the sidewalks, smoking cigarettes, laughing, and we'd head under the railroad bridge up River Street past pawnshops and sub shops, a machine shop, a car dealership of repossessed cars, then along the black Merrimack to the highway and Howard Johnson's where we'd wait for a table and order eggs and home fries, toast and pancakes and coffee.

One night at Ronnie's, the last-call lights up and shining on us like a cop's, Sam and Theresa and I were in a crowd close to the door. Pat had switched off the jukebox and now there were only loud, drunken voices, so much cigarette smoke in the air my eyes burned. Theresa was wearing a short leather jacket and tight jeans, her back to the booth behind her. A man sat there against the wall, one leg up, his arm resting on it, and his eyes were on Theresa's ass. There was another man sitting across from him, but I was seeing only this one. He had long black hair and wore a black sweater, his sideburns shaved off halfway across his jaw. He reminded me of Kenny V., who years ago had walked me and Cleary out of a pot party on Seventh and started whaling away on my head and rib cage. The waitress had cleared all the bottles away, so now I held a glass of beer and sipped from it. Theresa was talking to somebody, laughing, and the man in the booth said something to the other, then raised his eyebrows and nodded in the direction of Theresa's ass, and I leaned forward and dumped my beer in his face.

It was like pushing the button to some rusty old machine whose functions were simple but automatic: the man in the booth was standing up now, yelling, his face dripping, but he was the first moving part that touched the next moving part that touched the next. I don't remember punching him or his friend, but Sam had gotten into it with a tall man in a light windbreaker at the bar and with one hand under the man's chin, Sam pushed him up and over it. Then Pat was moving fast and hollering and we were all outside, two cruisers pulling up to move us along, this raucous band of people I only saw when drunk.

The next morning I lay in bed thinking about it. The shock in the man's face, then the outrage. And why shouldn't he feel that? What was so wrong about just looking at Theresa's ass? As long as he was quiet about it, and she didn't see him do it and so didn't feel objectified and violated, what was wrong with that? Didn't I look at women like that all the damn time? So who was I to do what I did? Again, there was this almost electric hum in my bones that I had somehow gotten myself wired wrong, that now I was stuck with impulses I could not control, ones that could lead to nothing but deeper and deeper trouble.

SOMETIMES I'D sleep in Pop's spare bedroom. When I was in Texas, he and Peggy had gotten married, and they moved back into the same campus house Pop had shared with Lorraine. Since marrying Peggy he seemed happier now. He said it was because they lived the same way; they were both writers and readers and runners. Each morning after he attended the 7 a.m. Mass down at the Sacred Hearts church, he would write at the desk in their bedroom, and she would work in the study upstairs. Then they'd each go for a run or fast walk, sometimes alone, sometimes together with their dog, a big golden retriever named Luke. The rest of the day, she worked on her graduate degree in writing and Pop taught his classes. It was like seeing him live with one of his buddies, the ones like Metrakos who wrote or studied, then worked out, but now he had this in his wife, and I was happy for him. It looked like this time he'd be able to stay married.

Since Suzanne's rape, my father had begun to acquire an arsenal of handguns. Besides the .38 snub-nose, he now owned a .380 semiautomatic, a .45, a 9-millimeter, and a .22 caliber derringer that easily fit into the front pocket of his jeans. He even bought Peggy a lady's-size nickel-plated Saturday Night Special, a revolver he insisted she keep with her whenever she drove up to the University of New Hampshire for her classes. On his birthday the August before, Jeb and I pitched in and bought him a replica of a .22 Colt six-gun. It was silver and had smooth maple handgrips, and he kept it in a leather holster on a closet shelf with the others.

One weekend that fall, Pop and Peggy were invited by the novelist Thomas Williams and his wife to spend the night at their cabin up in the White Mountains. Pop asked me if I wanted to come along, and I said yes. Maybe that weekend I wanted to get away from the pull of the barrooms and their warm, smoky noise, the beer-by-beer sinking into mindlessness, the naked body I'd sometimes wake up to; maybe I wanted to get away from the possibility of another fight, or perhaps it was just clarity I was looking for, a little distance from the hard physical labor of the week, my distracted efforts at reading abstract political theory at night, my low-down yearnings come Friday and Saturday.

On the two-hour drive north, I sat in the back of Peggy's Subaru while Pop drove and she sat beside him, and they talked. I learned more about Thomas Williams, that he won something called a National Book Award for his novel *The Hair of Harold Roux,* that with his own hands he had built this cabin one summer with his wife of many years.

After a while we left the highway and drove miles down a rutted dirt road, thick stands of pine and hardwood on either side of it. At the end was the Williamses' place, a shaved-timber cabin with a steeply pitched gable roofed with cedar shingles, and beyond it a sloping field of wild grass, then deep woods that rose into a mountain ridge. In the last light of the afternoon, it was purple and blue on the horizon, and Thomas and Elizabeth Williams stepped off the porch to greet us. They were warm and welcoming and right away I liked them both. Tom Williams wore a faded work shirt and jeans and work boots. His face was clean-shaven, deeply lined and handsome, and when he shook my hand it was like shaking the hand of

Trevor D. or Doug or Jeh, the thick pad of calluses just beneath the base of the fingers, the kind you get from swinging a hammer.

Pop had brought up a few handguns, and soon he and Thomas Williams and I were taking turns shooting at a playing card Williams had clamped to some brush with a clothespin. We were using the .380, a semiautomatic with a hair trigger that allowed you to empty the clip in seconds, your hand kicking back, the smell of cordite in the air. But when it was my turn I didn't want to look young and impulsive, so I shot it slowly and deliberately. I aimed it with one arm and sighted down its short barrel, the playing card a white rectangle in green, and I held my breath, then squeezed the trigger, the card fluttering.

"He could've been a Marine, too," Williams said. He and Pop were behind me, Williams sitting on a homemade picnic table smoking a pipe. The sun on the trees had darkened, and I felt pride from what Williams had said. I took my time with my next five shots, hitting the card with three of them.

I lowered the .380, released the magazine, then pulled back on the slide and checked the chamber to make sure it was empty. I handed it to Pop handle-first, the safe way he'd taught me when I was a boy, and I could see the pride in his eyes too, but it was as if there was a fishhook lodged in my skin somewhere: Williams's words, *could've been a Marine*. They echoed up against something inside me I hadn't been aware of, that even though I had plans for graduate school in less than a year, there was the feeling I had done very little with my life so far and still wasn't doing much. *Could've been*. Like it was too late. Like I'd been letting chances to do things slip by.

My father reloaded the .380, stepped past me, and said, "Rape who, motherfucker?" Then he raised the weapon and fired six rounds in seconds, the reports echoing out over the field of wild grass into the trees.

"Hello? *Hello?*" A man in hiking boots and shorts was waving at us thirty feet to the right, our target just on the other side of what was a trail. Pop lowered the pistol and Williams apologized to the man and we gathered up our guns and ammo and went inside.

We ate at a weathered oak table on a small deck overlooking the field and mountain ridge, black now against a red sky. Dinner was grilled steaks and French bread and tossed green salad. I sat beside Pop and Peggy, who sat across from the Williamses. The conversation was warm and relaxed, though a lot of it was between Peggy and Elizabeth, and Williams and Pop, and there were glasses of red wine, and we passed around the bread and broke it off with our hands. I kept looking at Elizabeth and Tom Williams. They were a good-looking couple, their kids grown already, and I thought about them building this cabin together one summer, the sharing of all that work, the joy in it. I ate the tender meat and sipped my wine; so many of the writers from my parents' early days in Iowa City had gone on to sleep with other people, their marriages cooling piles of ash they left behind. It was something my father had been writing about for years. But the Williamses were obviously different, and I did not know till that moment that I had assumed writers just could not stay married, that something inside them—maybe the dark side of their creativity—simply made them unstable.

Before dessert I thanked Thomas and Elizabeth Williams for dinner and excused myself to go sleep outside somewhere. Elizabeth insisted I take their guest room and Tom said something about bears, but I said good night, borrowed one of their flashlights, and carried my rolled sleeping bag down the path into the trees.

The trail descended alongside the field for a while, then cut south and rose steeply into the pines. The beam from the flashlight bounced ahead of me, and I was breathing hard and had no idea why I was doing this. The trail began to level off onto a small clearing of flat rocks. Between two of them was a patch of dirt. A young pine sprouted there, and it looked as good a place as I would find in the dark, and I set my flashlight on one of the rocks, unrolled my sleeping bag, untied my work boots, and climbed in. I lay back, but when the moist earth touched my head, I grabbed one of my work boots and set it on its side, then rested back against it. I reached up and switched off the flashlight.

The air was cool. It smelled like moss and pine needles and through the trees I could hear my father laugh, then Peggy or Elizabeth. They had to be at least a half mile away, but they sounded much closer than that. I closed my eyes and listened to the voices in the trees. Only the men's now. Pop and Thomas Williams, two people who, when they were young, had both found something they were good at and then just kept doing it. They seemed more whole to me because of that. But what was *I* good at? Why was I even here? Not in the White Mountains but here, on *earth*?

Then I saw Steve Lynch go down with one punch, the two frat boys in the alley. There was Bill Connolly's nephew I seemed to hit at will in the ring, Sam Dolan too, his eyes tearing up each time I jabbed.

Maybe I was meant to be a boxer. The signs were there, weren't they? What was stopping me? I'd learned that to hesitate was to freeze and to freeze was not to fight, and so now I never hesitated; my body responded the way I had somehow taught it to, but lying there in my sleeping bag between two stretches of rock, it was clear it was time my head got involved in all this again, that there had to be a fine balance between passivity and reckless action, and maybe the place to find it was back in the ring.

THE LYNN Boys Club was a mile or so from my street, a brick building that when I first entered it smelled like cotton and sweat, glove leather and canvas and hair oil. From the front desk I could hear men's voices, the chugging slappity-slap of a speed bag, then a heavy bag jerking on its chain, the shuffle of feet, a man calling "Time!"

I walked down concrete steps into the basement training room. It was dimly lit and crowded, the walls covered with fight posters. Beneath three bare bulbs, two boxers sparred in the ring. One was black, the other white, and when the black one lashed out with a quick jab or straight right or left hook, the white one would counterpunch instantly, his eyes two shadowed slits under puffy eyebrows, his blue mouthguard visible between his lips. They wore no headgear and the gloves were fight-size and both were young and fast and small, featherweights probably. Around the ring were six or seven folding chairs, half of them taken by other fighters, their hands wrapped. Against the left wall were four speed bags. A big man in a gray sweatsuit was working one of them in a steady rhythm, the inflated rubber bag bouncing up and back in triple time. On the concrete floor two boxers skipped rope, another was doing incline sit-ups, his hands locked behind his head, and two more were doing push-ups side by side, one going down while the other came up. To the right, in the fluorescent glare of an open doorway, hung three heavy bags, each one heavier than the last. A Latino boy was working on the smallest. He'd throw a body shot, then weave away from the swaying bag and come up on it with an uppercut or left hook. His hair was wet black ringlets he kept out of his face with a red bandanna, and I was turning my attention to a man on the heaviest heavy bag. He wasn't much taller or bigger than I was, but he was throwing one-two combinations that rocked the long Everlast, the iron beam above vibrating. A knockout punch for sure.

There was the smack of leather on flesh, the hiss of air through the nostrils of the fighters every time they threw a punch, the scuff and squeak of their rubber soles, the *tip-tip-tip* of the skip rope, men grunting and breathing hard, the muffled pops of punches connecting with the heavy bags, and behind all this the constant staccato of the speed bag in the corner. The air smelled like testosterone and damp cotton and muscle liniment. I was about to walk to the lighted doorway when someone tapped my arm.

It was a short man in his seventies. He wore a thin brown sweater and his nose was a smudge on his face, his eyes deeply lidded. But it was his ears it was hard not to stare at; sticking to each side of his head was a gnarled clump of flesh.

"Who are you?"

"Andre."

"French?"

"Yep."

"You wanna fight?"

"Yeah, I do."

He offered his hand, his knuckles twice the size of mine. "Tony Pavone." He waved his arm at the room. "I train all these kids. We got the Gloves coming up down to Lowell. What're you, a middleweight?"

I smiled and shrugged.

"Yeah, we need a middleweight. You want to start right now?"

I was still in my construction clothes and work boots, but I told him I'd be back the next night, and I was.

TONY PAVONE had been the New England Champion in his weight class back in the thirties, and he trained everyone the same way. The workout

started with three rounds of shadowboxing in the ring. At first no one
was in there but me, throwing combinations at the air under the lights,
bobbing under imaginary counterpunches, weaving into some hopefully
evasive footwork before going back in and throwing more punches. I'd
never done it before, and I felt silly till I saw four or five others doing the
same thing. One climbed into the ring and worked alongside me. The
others shadowboxed in the center of the concrete floor. A few times Tony
would shout from the darkness beyond the ropes, "Keep your right up.
Throw more jabs."

After only three rounds I was breathing hard and my sweatshirt was
sticking to my back. Now it was time for two rounds on the small heavy
bag, then two on the medium, then two more on the heaviest. Earlier
I'd wrapped my hands and it felt good to have those hitting gloves back
on, that leather-sewn iron bar against my palms. Pavone walked around
the gym in his wool sweater and worn gray dress pants and scuffed black
shoes. He studied each fighter for a half minute or so. Whether they were
in the ring or shadowboxing or working one of the bags, he'd offer a tip or
he'd stay quiet. With me he was quiet till I got to the heavy bag, my eyes
burning from the sweat, my shoulders sore from holding up my hands. I'd
been trying to remember some of the combinations I'd learned from Bill
Connolly, and I threw a jab, then a double left hook, weaved away from
the bag, set my feet, and threw a right cross that sent an ache up my arm
into my shoulder.

"That's good power. That's good."

He walked away, and that's all I needed to hear, though it was a surprise to me that I did; I already knew I had something good with my right
cross, that it might be a knockout punch in the ring too, but it was just
having a man older than my father take me in and say something about
what he saw that felt like cool water on a dry tongue, one I hadn't known
was so dry.

Sam often talked about his own growing up, how his father had
driven him to hundreds of practices and games, the coaches or ex-
teachers or uncles he would sometimes go to for advice. But I'd had no
coaches and until college had done my best to be invisible in the classroom. Whatever uncles I had were in Louisiana and they were uncles

by a marriage that had ended years ago anyway. Somewhere, sometime I'd stopped expecting my father to father; maybe if he'd stayed with us, it would have been different, but even then there was the feeling that writing and running and teaching is where he seemed to put the truest part of himself. After those things, there seemed to be little extra energy or time for anything else. When I saw him now, it was usually at Ronnie D's on the weekends and when I walked in his eyes would light up and he'd call me over to the bar and buy me a beer, put his arm around me as if we both knew more about the other than we did.

I finished my rounds on the heavy bag, then followed old and slightly hunched Tony Pavone to the ring.

11

LIZ WAS IN one of my father's fiction writing classes. She was from Maine and had brown hair and bright hazel eyes and whenever she blinked a tiny indentation appeared above her nostrils. Pop told me she was a good writer, one of his most talented, and one night at Ronnie D's I sat across from her in one of the booths. Under the bar noise we talked and sipped beer, then went for a drive where we kept talking, and now on weekends it was in her room I slept.

It was in Academy Hall on the Bradford College campus. She had a suite and a roommate, a small living room between the two bedrooms. On Saturday nights, Sam and Theresa and Liz and I would meet there, then go down to Ronnie D's or one of the bars on the river in Haverhill. We'd drink till last call, then end up at Howard Johnson's.

One Friday in the loud smoky noise, we four sat in a booth when Pop walked over from the bar. He only came down to Ronnie's after all his disciplined rituals and duties were over, when he'd felt he'd earned the drinking he did there, and he usually looked relaxed and glad to be among some of his students, a few lawyers and off-duty cops he'd gotten to know, men from the mills he never would've met otherwise, and now his oldest son.

But tonight he walked over looking pained about something, angry, his cheeks red above his trimmed beard. I immediately thought of Peggy. Marriage trouble.

Sam stood up in the booth and offered Pop his hand. Pop shook it, said hello to Liz and Theresa, then asked me if we could talk over at the bar for a minute. I said yeah and followed him. We stood at the corner of the bar, the entire length of it thick with men and women two or three deep, their talk and laughter a constant sound, the jukebox playing a Stones song. Most of the women were smoking, blowing it out their nostrils or the sides of their mouths as they told stories or listened to stories or laughed at stories or looked pissed off about something. The air smelled like cigarette ash and smoke, sour beer, perfume and leather and the oak bar Pop and I leaned our elbows against, our shoulders touching. Pat Cahill's big hands rested two glasses of beer in front of us. "These are on Jimmy." Then Pat was back at the register, and Pop raised his glass to a man at the opposite end of the bar fifty people away, a small face in the neon light of the Budweiser sign in the window. In a few years he'd be dead from cirrhosis of the liver. Pop raised his glass to him in thanks, set it back on the bar, and said, "He hit her."

"Jimmy? Who'd he hit?"

"No, Suzanne. Her fucking husband hit her."

There was no sound, no voices or thumping music, no laughter or rattling ice in so many glasses, no empty beer bottles tossed into a box— there was the open back porch Suzanne got married on, a small wedding to this man she'd met at Hampton Beach. He was a roofer with a red beard and shoulder-length hair, and he liked her right away and she liked him and then the two families and a few friends were on an uncut lawn on a warm September afternoon witnessing their marriage. I watched from a picnic table I sat on with a few others, and I tried to push aside my concerns but there was something wrong with what I was seeing; Suzanne, twenty-three years old, was in a denim skirt and a white blouse. She'd lost some weight and looked pretty and hopeful standing there on the porch looking up into her groom's face, smiling as the justice of the peace spoke. She held a small bouquet of flowers.

Keith was in jeans too and a light windbreaker, and maybe he wasn't conscious they were even on his face, a pair of mirrored aviator sunglasses so that as Suzanne looked into his eyes and recited her vow, she was seeing only herself looking back.

And then at the reception, a fish fry at Pop and Peggy's house on campus, the place overflowing with people, at the end of the night Sam and Theresa and I had decorated my Subaru for them, covered it with shaving cream and flowers, tied a dozen empty cans to the bumper, wrote with soap on the rear window *Just Married*. I met Keith in the downstairs bathroom to give him the keys. He stood at the sink trimming his beard. Maybe for the fancy hotel they were going to for the night, I didn't know. But as he looked into the mirror at his own face, he appeared to me unburdened of something, a man just given a second chance.

"Your sister and me are gonna have such a good life together. Our kids'll have everything they ever wanted. My son's gonna get a fucking Maserati on his sixteenth birthday."

How? I wondered. *And why?*

Last I'd heard they'd moved from Florida to California, that they'd rented a cabin up in the mountains and she was working in a fast food restaurant while he was roofing houses along the Pacific.

Now he hit her.

"She tell you this?"

"Wrote me a letter." Pop's eyes were on me, and it was then I could tell why he was telling me; he wanted to know what we were going to do about it.

My mouth was air, the rest of me too, my heart humming sickly. "In the *face?*"

Pop nodded. "She thinks he broke her eardrum."

Now I was moving, my body solid again, stepping sideways between men and women in the loud happy haze to the bathroom, the stall door behind me, its wooden surface covered with inked initials and *fuck*s and *shit*s and *dick*s and phone numbers and crossed-out hearts. There were the smells of piss and deodorizer, of wet filter tips and varnished wood, and I saw Suzanne standing on the porch smiling up into Keith's mirrored sunglasses, her bouquet, her clasped hands; then I saw her jabbing the broom straw into George Labelle's face, kicking my attacker out of our house, and there was a pinch in my vocal cords, my yelling lost in all the barroom noise, my palms pushing against the stall till it pulled from its fasteners, the door wobbling as I hurried back to the bar and my father and the retribution that must now be delivered.

POP AND I stood in his tiny kitchen lit only by the fanlight above the stove. Peggy and Nicole were downstairs asleep. He picked up the phone and called his old friend in San Francisco, a writer and bar owner, and told him the story and asked if he knew anyone there he could hire to break Keith's legs. His friend said he'd make a few calls and get right back to him. I was pacing back and forth. "Let's just fly out there and do it ourselves, Pop. Let's just fuckin' go out there tonight."

Pop shook his head. "A pro will get there faster."

The phone rang, and he picked it up. It was as if his friend had hung up and found someone standing right there at his bar.

"I'll call you back." Pop set the phone in its cradle, looked at me. "Five hundred."

"For what?"

"To have his kneecaps broken."

"Good, *fuck* him, I'll pay for half."

Pop still had his hand on the phone. He looked as if he were considering something.

"Call him back."

He was looking at the window. Maybe he saw our reflections in it, or maybe he was thinking of Keith. I knew he liked him. In the months leading up to the wedding, he had spent a lot of time with him, drinking and shooting the shit. Many nights he'd invited him and Suzanne over to share a meal. When I'd called from Austin earlier that spring, he said, "Suzanne's fallen in love with a red-bearded carpenter. He's a good man, and he treats her well."

And he'd seemed to, calling her honey and listening to her whenever she spoke, his eyes lit with a seeming gratitude at the world for bringing her to him.

Pop said: "We call him and give him one warning. Just one."

"No, no fucking warnings."

Pop was dialing their number. My fingertips and toes were buzzing, my mouth dry as paper; this was the time to set my feet and throw a right cross, no talk, no warning, just physical action, the only thing I'd ever found to work.

I did not want to hear this warning. I opened the kitchen's back door and stepped out onto the porch. It was small and uncovered and I pissed over the side. There was a thin stand of trees, then the street and houses. Through the branches I could see lighted windows, the numbing flicker of a TV.

I finished and grasped the doorknob, but it was self-locking, and I had to take the steps and run around to the front. Luke barked once, then I was climbing the stairs back to the kitchen. Pop held the receiver to his ear, his eyes on the floor but not on the floor. His cheeks above his beard were a deep red. I was holding out my hand.

"You don't sound like you're listening, Keith. You'd better be fucking *listening*." He pushed the phone at me. The receiver had no weight of any kind and my first words were just sounds coming out of my throat, but I knew what I'd promised him. "You under*stand*, Keith? Six feet under the leaves in some fucking woods somewhere, motherfucker."

"That's cool." His voice was relaxed, like he was lying in a warm bath with a cold beer talking to good, good friends.

"Did you hear me, you piece of shit?"

"Yep, you too. Give our love to everybody. Bye now."

In the hum of the dial tone Pop stood in the shadows of their small dining room looking at me. I hung up the phone, felt that old feeling again, that I was small and weak and invisible. His reaction the kind of non-reaction given to a nobody who can and will do nothing.

Many years later, Suzanne told me she was there with him when we called, that he spoke to us like we were phoning him just to shoot the shit. But for weeks afterward, I imagined shooting *him,* then digging a deep hole and rolling his body into it, filling it back up with dirt and broken rock and the roots I'd had to sever from any tree close to me.

THE FOLLOWING morning Pop pushed aside his writing and wrote a short story in one sitting. It was called "Leslie in California." When he handed it to me and I read the first line, I remembered again how good at this Pop was, that he wrote beautifully every time he tried. I was standing in his kitchen holding the typed manuscript in my hands. He stood there in his tank top and shorts and running shoes, a bandanna tied around his head. Luke was beside him, his tail wagging. But Pop's face was like I'd rarely seen it, his eyes expectant and hopeful yet mournful, too. As if he were both proud and ashamed. It was a feeling I knew well, and he nodded and left the house for his workout. I sat at his and Peggy's table and read this story of a young wife the morning after her drunk husband hits her, his remorse, her dawning awareness that she is in a permanently dangerous place.

I finished reading the last line, and I too felt proud and ashamed. Proud because my father was an artist at this, a man who had just written deeply and poetically from a woman's point of view. But ashamed because he had done that. It felt like thievery to me. Like he had just stolen Suzanne's experience and made it his own, and meanwhile Keith was still walking the earth untouched, unpunished, his in-laws' warnings some distant echo in his head. And now this story for strangers to read.

How did this help my sister? What *good* did this do?

After his run, Pop asked me what I'd thought of the story. His bandanna was drenched. He pulled it off and ran his forearm along his hairline.

"It's a good story."

"I'm going to send it to her."

"Good." I nodded. It was a Sunday, and it was time to drive back to my apartment in Lynn. I gave Pop a half hug, tapped his sweaty back, and stepped out into the cold. I felt like a liar and a chickenshit.

MY MOTHER sat across from me at Village Square, a breakfast place in Bradford set into a row of shops between Ronnie D's and the Sacred Hearts church. It was midwinter on Saturday morning, and in front of us were plates of eggs and bacon, hot weak coffee, and she looked better than she had in years. Gone was the look of constant financial worry. Gone was the look that she was under a great weight she just could not hold much longer. Gone was the look, blue and still surprised, that she'd been left behind.

Instead, she was tanned, and her hair was nearly blonde again.
She'd lost weight and her eyes were bright and if I'd ever seen her happier, I couldn't remember when. She was talking of their life down in St.
Maarten, Bruce's work for his brother-in-law's airfreight business, how
much she enjoyed helping deliver food to restaurants, the white sand and
green sea, the ice-cold Heinekens in the salt breeze.

I was glad for her. She seemed free of something, and she kept smiling
at me. "Are you excited about graduate school?"

I sipped my coffee, shook my head.

"Why not?"

"I don't know." The place was crowded, people eating and talking
and laughing, the waitresses delivering plates of waffles and sausage, the
smell of hot coffee and syrup in the air. "It seemed like a plan for a while,
but—I don't know."

"Why don't you write?"

"Write?"

"Yes, honey. Go *write*."

"Why do you say that?"

"Because you were good at it in school."

"What good does writing do, Mom? Who cares about making up
stories? I want to do something important for people."

It was as if I'd reached over and slapped her face with a damp rag. "I
can't believe you just said that, Andre. I won't tell anyone you just said
that."

I didn't say anything. She said more, but I was thinking of my father,
of the story he wrote about Suzanne when he should have done something for her in *this* world, not the one in his head.

I changed the subject. We talked about Suzanne and her marriage
to this man I still wanted to kill. We talked about Jeb and his baby son,
Nicole and her last year of high school, the schools out West she was looking into. Our breakfast ended soon after that. I hugged my mother on the
sidewalk, thanked her for the eggs. Sam and I were to meet at the Y in an
hour, and I climbed into my Subaru and went driving. I drove over the
Basiliere Bridge and the Merrimack, up the hill of Main Street past the
shopping plaza and library, GAR Park and the statue of Hannah Duston

and her raised hatchet. I drove through Monument Square past the Exxon station and insurance company and the VFW hall.

It was a cold bright day, and I headed east past Kenoza Lake where I'd run with my father, then under the highway, the same back road Mom used to drive us on in that Head Start van, those Mystery Rides when joy was something she willed herself to show us, something she raised from deep inside herself as a promise for what could be. Now her life seemed to have opened up into it as if it had been waiting for her.

What waited for me? I knew she was right to chastise me for what I'd said, but I did not yet know why she was right: How could art truly help people? Did it feed them? Clothe them? Keep them warm in the winter? Did it put a gun in their hands to fend off their oppressors?

Up ahead was a roadhouse. It wasn't even noon yet, but in the gravel lot were parked five or six motorcycles, a neon Miller sign glowing in the sun-streaked window. I downshifted, pulled into the lot, then turned around and headed back to Haverhill and the long workout with Sam that always cleared my head, that always made me feel ready for whatever was coming next.

TREVOR D. promoted me from laborer to carpenter's helper and he bumped my pay to five dollars an hour. Instead of hauling debris and fresh lumber and tools all day with Randy, I got to wear a tape measure on my belt and stick a pencil behind my ear. I was made the cut man for all the partition walls they were building.

It was a cold dry week, the sun heavy and bright in a deep sky, and first thing every morning I set up my cut station in the parking lot down below. I took three eight-foot two-by-fours, set them across two sawhorses, then laid a full sheet of plywood over them and carried over the chop saw and unrolled a cord and plugged it in.

"Hey, *Ratchet.*" Doug called down from the second-story window. He stood in the naked wood frame, a big grin on his face. He always wore a dark wool sailor's cap down around his ears, and in the early morning sun I could see the sawdust in it. "Here's your list." He tossed a foot-long section of two-by-six out into the air and Randy ran and caught it over his shoulder, but Doug was already inside, and I said, "Nice catch, Randy."

"Nice list, Ratchet."

They'd been calling me that ever since Doug and I went up to the new flat roof and started lagging the perimeter joists to four-by-four posts in the corners. We each had a ratchet wrench, something I'd never used before. Doug was on the east side of the frame, I was on the west, and I could hear him cranking the galvanized lag bolts into wood, the *clickety-clickety-click* his ratchet made, but I couldn't figure out how he could work his hand so fast; once I pushed the lag bolt into its predrilled hole and set the ratchet head on its end, I could crank it only half a turn before the ratchet handle hit the perimeter joist, then I'd have to pull the ratchet head free and set it on the bolt for another half crank again and again.

Doug was on his third bolt while I was still on my first. He looked over at me. He stood and walked across the roof. "The fuck you doin'? That's a *ratchet* wrench." He squatted and cranked the ratchet back and forth, the lag bolt sinking all the way into the wood without his once having to pull it away and reset it on the head of the lag. "See, numb-nuts. It fuckin' *ratchets*." He straightened up and laughed. "That's it, man. When we come to one of your fights, I'm calling you 'the Ratchet Kid.'" He laughed again and shook his head. "See what college did to you? Unfuckin'believable, the Ratchet Kid."

Jeb had told them I was boxing. The five of us were standing around the vending truck, sipping hot coffee, warming our hands on the Styrofoam cups. Jeb nodded in my direction and said, "Andre's a boxer." I could see the pride in my younger brother's eyes, and it surprised me; what seemed to move and impress him most were artistic pursuits—a perfectly executed painting, a flawlessly played fugue, anything that came from the rosewood guitar of Andrés Segovia.

"Yeah," Trevor said, "but can you build a *box*?"

The conversation turned to furniture-building, fine-finish work, but when coffee break was over, Doug tossed his cup into the dumpster and said, "We should all get shit-faced and go watch Andre fight."

We went back to the job, but it was like hearing they wanted to come watch me read political theory at night, this private thing I was doing to weigh who I was and where I should be going. And my first official fight wouldn't come until late winter anyway, the Golden Gloves down

in Lowell, another milltown on the Merrimack River, the one Jack Ker-
ouac had made famous. I'd been doing well enough in the ring that Tony
Pavone handed me an application form, and a few days later I got my
AAU number in the mail. At the Gloves you had to have it pinned to your
shirt or trunks for each bout, and each one was single-elimination, a term
I'd never heard before. Pavone was standing in the fluorescent light of his
office doorway when he said it. Behind me the gym was crowded with
fighters working out, the place smelling like sweat and mildew.

"What's that mean, Tony?"

"You know, like in playoffs. It means you can't lose. You do, and
you're out."

Playoffs. Another word I barely knew. But I learned a Golden Gloves
champion sometimes fought as many as ten fights in two days. And he
had to win them all.

In the ring, even after an hour of shadowboxing and working on
the heavy bags and now the speed bag I'd finally learned how to control,
I kept coming out ahead. Not in a big way; I never knocked anyone
down or out, and I was often too afraid of dropping my guard to plant
my feet and throw combinations, so I jabbed and jabbed and jabbed.
I never stopped jabbing. These years of consistent workouts hadn't put
much muscle on me, but I had stamina. It's what seemed to come more
naturally to me than power, and I felt as if I could throw jabs for hours,
my opponent's eyes tearing up as I popped him in the forehead, the upper
cheek, his nose and mouth.

Every few jabs I'd let go with a straight right or a cross, and I'd feel
the itch to weave and step in close with an uppercut I could follow with
a left hook to the ribs or ear, but I was worried about the rain of counterpunches from these fighters, some black, some white or Latino. Most
of them were only eighteen or nineteen but had over a hundred fights
behind them already. One black kid, an eighteen-year-old welterweight
I'd sparred for three rounds, told me he'd been training with Tony Pavone
since he was six.

Tony had big plans for him, said openly, "This kid's gonna be the
welterweight champ at the Gloves. You watch."

Tony would sometimes match up fighters from different weight

classes. Bigger boxers could learn speed from the smaller ones. Small boxers learned how to evade. The night Tony put me in the ring with the
welterweight, I felt sure it was to warm the kid up for a better, more experienced fighter after he was done with me.

The welterweight had a lean, muscled torso, his skin a burnished
brown, and when Tony called "Time!," the kid and I tapped gloves in the
center of the ring, and I chomped down on my mouthpiece and wished
for headgear.

But I never let him get close to me. I jabbed him in the face for most
of the three rounds. A few times he weaved away and got off a hook or
a right, but his feet weren't set and his range was off so the punches only
glanced my gloves. After three rounds, the kid ducked fast through the
ropes and looked frustrated and I felt mildly proud of myself. Tony talked
to him awhile in the light of his office. Two heavyweights stepped into the
ring, and I ducked between the ropes and unlaced my gloves and started
doing incline sit-ups, my feet hooked beneath an iron bar. After a while,
Tony came over. "You're good with that jab but you gotta throw more
combinations. You don't want to win on points, you want to *fight*."

I nodded and thanked him. I knew he was right. I *was* too careful in
the ring, and I wasn't sure why, but his last word hung between my ears—
fight. Is that what I was supposed to be doing? Because a boxing match
just did not feel like a real fight to me; something was missing from it, the
way maybe love is missing from an act that then becomes fucking. Something was missing, but I wouldn't know what it was till later that winter
close to dawn in a diner in Monument Square.

WE WERE all in a celebratory mood. Sam and Theresa were now officially
engaged. They asked me to be best man, and the wedding was set for
late August, just a few days before I'd be driving west to the University
of Wisconsin at Madison and their Ph.D. program in Marxist social science. The letter had come in the mail just a few days before. That night
Liz was happy too. She'd just written something she was proud of, and
now she and Sam and Theresa and I were in her room, listening to music
and telling stories and drinking beer and playing cards. After his shift,
Vinny T. came up and joined us, too. Vinny T. was the head of security

at Bradford College. He was a short, small-boned ex-Marine with olive skin and a mat of curly black hair, his cheeks and jaw forever darkened by whiskers he kept shaved as close to the skin as possible. Vinny always had a good joke and liked to go drinking after his shift. Partly because he'd been in the Marines, he and Pop hit it off and Vinny spent a lot of time at Pop's campus house, the two of them drinking till very late. Soon he was sitting on the couch very close to one of Liz's girlfriends who'd wandered in, his hand on her knee, his handsome Italian face just inches from hers as he told her a dirty joke and she laughed too hard and spilled her drink. There was the feeling that good things were happening, that life wasn't so directionless anymore and that hard work and focus could bring about something like Sam and Theresa getting married. I still wasn't sure why I was going back to school, but just knowing I was really going had lifted something off me.

Liz sat close to Theresa on the couch, the two of them laughing and looking like sisters with their brown hair and wool sweaters and tight jeans. Then it was after three in the morning and Liz's friend had wandered off and there was a plan to go to Vinny's house out on Lake Attitash. He was going to cook the five of us omelets. Sam and Theresa wanted to get home, though, and I hugged them at the back door of Academy Hall, quiet now, the red-carpeted floor soft and gritty under our feet. I watched the two of them walk out to the parking lot holding hands, the light from a security lamp shining dully on Sam's black Duster as they pulled away.

Vinny had some last-minute paperwork to get done so Liz and I sat on the couch in Vinny's office. The only light came from a fluorescent desk lamp, and Vinny sat in it entering something into the shift log, his eyes squinting, the slight static of the dispatch radio in the air. Liz was smoking a cigarette. The couch was wobbly but deep and maybe I dozed a few minutes. Maybe I didn't. But it was as if Sam and Theresa had never driven off because now they were hurrying through the back door, Theresa looking pale as she held the door for her fiancé, his beard dripping blood.

DRIVING THERESA home to where she lived with her mother down in the avenues, Sam had slowed for the right he'd have to take at the corner of

Fifth and Cedar, but there was a massive oak tree at the corner, its roots having buckled the sidewalk long ago, and he had to edge up almost into Cedar Street and that's when a car shot in front of his hood, nearly clipping it. The car slowed immediately and Sam saw the flashing blue light on the dashboard, an unmarked police car. It pulled over, and the cop was sitting there, Sam thought, studying him, the black Duster that almost hit him.

Instead of turning right for Sixth Avenue, Sam turned left and eased up behind the unmarked car. He was ready to explain himself, to explain the big oak he couldn't see around. Inside the car, the blue light was still flashing, and Sam waited for the cop to step out first, but when he didn't, Sam did, and now the cop stepped out too, a young guy in a leather jacket and dark pants and motorcycle boots standing in the path of Sam's headlights. He had stringy black hair and he just stood there looking at Sam, then past him to the Duster. Maybe he could see Theresa, maybe he couldn't. Then the front and back passenger doors opened and three more guys climbed out, all of them in denim or leather jackets, and a white light rocked through Sam's head, his chin a numbing burn, the kid who'd just punched him standing there like it was Sam's move now.

"Yeah?" Sam jerked down the zipper of his jacket and yanked it off his shoulders and dropped it to the ground. "I'll fight all you pieces of shit, let's *go*."

Sam was wearing a short-sleeve polo shirt, and maybe if he hadn't worn that one, maybe if he'd worn a loose sweater or work shirt, the kid who'd punched him wouldn't have seen so clearly Sam's deeply muscled chest, his impossibly thick shoulders and upper arms, and he wouldn't have pulled the knife he now waved in front of him, the base of the blade between his thumb and forefinger, the handle in his palm. Like this was something he did all the time, pulled knives on people in fights, people he'd just pulled over in his phony unmarked cruiser.

"Fine," Sam said, "fine. We're going to call this one over, all right?" He could feel his chin bleeding, the liquid itch of it, and he walked backwards to his Duster, the four of them standing there in his headlights. One of them laughed and another stepped closer. The kid's knife blade glinted dully in his hand, and the blue light still flashed, and Sam climbed in behind his wheel and pulled the door shut after him, and Theresa said, "I got their plate number, Sam."

Sam put the Duster in reverse. He rolled his window down and yelled out into the cold air. *"Remember this face. You hear me? Remember this face."*

THE KID with the knife must've had a big ring on his hand; behind the black whiskers of Sam's beard a chunk of flesh was missing from his chin, and somebody—Theresa or Liz—had gotten him a damp paper towel from a bathroom and he was pressing it to the wound. He'd told us their story that way, his hand pressed to his chin in the dim fluorescent light of Vinny's small office. There were droplets of blood on Sam's shirt, and I kept thinking of that kid and his sucker punch and his knife. I pictured my best friend stabbed and bleeding to death down in the avenues, his fiancée no longer his fiancée, and then what would they have done to her? What were they hoping to do with their phony police flasher and their knives?

Vinny had Sam pull the paper towel from his chin. "You're gonna have to get that stitched up, Sam."

Liz and Theresa were already at the door. There were the words *hospital* and *Let's go,* but Theresa had given Vinny the license plate number and Sam and I stood in front of Vinny's desk as he called the Haverhill police. Sam had left his jacket back on Cedar Street. He stood there in his shirt, blood drops all down his chest, the damp paper towel at his side, and he was looking into my eyes like we'd both just come to the threshold of something. I nodded; the last few years he'd talked about being big, how that had always kept him from ever having to fight or throw that first punch and he wasn't sure he ever could.

Theresa called from the hallway to hurry up. "Someone needs to look at that, Sam." Vinny was talking to a cop on the phone, but he wasn't telling him about the dummy cruiser or the assault, just said he needed help running the tag on an illegally parked car on campus; he needed an address. In seconds Vinny was writing it down on a notepad he stuffed into his jacket pocket. He glanced up at Sam and me and we said nothing and left his office and Academy Hall, Theresa and Liz walking ahead of us.

It was a quiet ride down through Bradford Square, the five of us in Sam's Duster. I was in the back with Liz and Theresa, and none of us spoke as Sam drove us down empty South Main Street by the Sacred Hearts church, then under the flashing yellow traffic light past Village Square Restaurant and Ronnie D's, their windows dark, the vacant lots of McDonald's and Mister Donut and the bank. Now we were crossing the Merrimack, Sam picking up speed, then slowing once we got to the Haverhill side, and that's when he should've turned right for Water Street and Captain Chris's Restaurant, that's when he should've gone on for another half mile to Buttonwoods and the Hale and the doctor who would stitch him up.

But instead Sam drove straight up Main, and we all stayed quiet. None of us said anything. My heart was a restless old acquaintance in my chest, and I tried to breathe evenly and keep my hands and feet still. There was a new restaurant in Monument Square, a franchise diner called Sambo's. It was close to four in the morning but its parking lot was full, a white halogen haze cast out over all the Pontiacs and Chryslers, Ford pickups and Chevy vans. Sam accelerated past it and its walls of windows. Inside, nearly every booth was filled with men and women from the barrooms and maybe a dance club down in Lawrence or up at the beach. The counter was filled too. One woman sat there in a silver rayon dress, a smoking cigarette between her fingertips. The man beside her was in jeans and a dark sweatshirt, his back to the street. At his waist was a biker chain and a Buck knife, and she was laughing at something he must've just said. Then we were on Main, Sam steering left down one of the avenues.

In a low voice Vinny said something to him, a sentence with numbers in it, but it was as if both my ears were pressed to seashells, the cupped silence that becomes the crash of ocean waves, far away and against your skin.

Liz rested her hand against my leg. We were near Primrose and the lumberyard Jeb and Cleary and I used to steal from. Then we were parked in front of a house, a two-story with asphalt siding made to look like brick. There was no light on over the front stoop, none in the windows, and the aluminum storm frame was empty of glass and hung away from the door and its two dead bolts above a dented knob. To the right of the stoop was a rutted dirt alleyway between this house and the next, but there was nothing there but a motorcycle with no rear tire, its axle on a shopping cart on its side.

Let's keep looking.

Vinny may have said it, or Sam, these words the first about what we were actually doing, and now we were driving up and down the avenues, Sam's headlights most of the only light there was. Sometimes there'd be a streetlamp flickering at a corner, or in a window the muted blue of a TV, even this late when there was nothing on, and I pictured a drunk passed out on a couch. In a second-story window there glowed an electric Virgin Mary, her robes as bright as a hundred-watt bulb, her palms clasped in prayer. But I didn't want her praying for me or the ones I was beginning to fear we wouldn't find, that they'd get away like all the worst seemed to—like Clay Whelan and Dennis Murphy and Tommy J., like the two men in Boston who did what they did to my sister and left her where she could have frozen to death, and now these young motherfuckers who had come close to stealing my friend from me, the first person who had seemed to see me as something more than I was.

But these thoughts were not in my head, they were only mute spaces of air between heartbeats I was trying to calm with steady breathing. If we didn't find them, what would I do with this nearly gut-sick readiness? Where would it go?

Sam turned right onto Main, the lights of Sambo's ahead in Monument Square. It was an hour before dawn, but as we rode slowly by, the place seemed even more crowded than before, every booth filled now, every counter stool occupied. Beyond the counter, waitresses worked swiftly, pouring coffee, pulling plates of food from the serving shelf to the kitchen where I could see the hurried movement of cooks in white. There was cigarette smoke in the air, a man in a black shirt and thin red tie leaving the bathroom. I looked to my left, past Liz. In the center of the square, the statue of the Union soldier was a granite silhouette against the fluorescent glare of the gas station on the other side, and I could feel it all begin to back up on me, my arms and legs starting to feel heavy now, Liz's hand a weight on my knee.

Theresa's voice was in the air—*That's them. Sam, that's **them**.* She sounded as if she'd been holding her breath, her words coming out on released air. *They're in that first booth. Did you **see** them? They're right **there**.*

We were steering fast into the lot of Sambo's, Sam pulling into a space between a pickup and a small sedan. *That's their car.* Under the security light, it was a dull green, like it had been sandblasted and spray-painted that color, and in the backseat a boy and girl were kissing. My body was light again. If my heart had a sound it would be an electronic thumping in the air. I reached for the door handle, but this was a two-door and Vinny wasn't opening his fast enough—*Go, go, **go**.* Then there was cold air and I was pushing the seat against Vinny's back, his voice a warning, and I had one leg out the door, my hand squeezing Sam's shoulder; he turned to me, his face as still as a photograph. *Just throw that first punch,* these words I left behind as I ran across the lot for the glass doors. I could feel how far ahead of everyone I was, but the doors swung open from their centers and grasping the handles were hands that looked like mine, small hands, and there'd been no weight to those doors, no surface to the rust-colored porcelain tiles of the entryway under my boots, no resistance as I pushed open the final doors, thick commercial glass on double hinges that swung back and forth behind me. There were the smells of bacon and eggs and coffee, of maple syrup and dried ketchup and cigarette smoke. There were men and women in their party clothes, their barroom clothes, their dance-club clothes, none of them looking up at me as they smoked and sipped and laughed and talked and chewed; all of this made sounds but none of it was understandable, voices without words lost in wind off the ocean that was my head. I was moving to the first booth, had been all along.

It was a silent, well-lighted island, and it held three men, young I could see now, younger than I was. One of them sat facing the door, the two others across from him, a smear of skin and hair and leather and wool. It was hard to see them clearly, only what was in front of each: a ceramic coffee cup on a white saucer, the cups empty, and now I was standing at their booth, their faces turning slowly my way as words came out of me, *friend knife my best **friend**? **My** friend?* And the one who sat alone, the one with the stringy black hair whose eyes were on mine, he began to smirk, and I knew it was him who'd pulled the knife, and then his cup was in my hand and I was breaking it across his nose and cheeks and I grabbed the next cup and pushed it into the face of the one at the window, my elbow shooting into the chin of the one closest to me, his head snapping back, and I could see it was a big head on a big body that was trying to stand. There was more movement and noise, human shouts and cries, the one near the window being jerked out of the booth, Vinny's voice, *Mother**fucker**,* and Sam's wide back, then the kid who'd pulled the knife dragged off his bench, and there was the constant thud and jolt of my right hand and shoulder as I kept punching the big one's wincing face, his head not moving enough, his neck thick, a lifter, much bigger than I was, much stronger than I was, and *look what I'd started, this is what will kill me, this is who will do it if I stop hitting him, if I ever stop hitting him he'll rise up and beat me to death, but look how he falls to the tiled floor, look how he curls up on his side and covers his face and squirms for the door,* and I straddle him and keep punching him in the skull, the ear, the temple, his bare hands, his neck. My throat burns from vibration, the wind in my head a sound, *my* sound, the wind shrieking through barbed wire, *Fuck you, you piece of shit you fuckin' piece of **shit**.* And I'm standing and kicking him in the head, my work boots doing it, the boots with the steel toes that when it's cold freeze your feet that feel nothing now, and his head keeps bouncing back and rolling forward, bouncing back and rolling forward, but he can still get up and if he does he will kill me, he will kill me, he will kill me.

Liz's face there now, so strange to see it. She is kneeling, her hands in the air, and she looks up at me, her eyes shining, and words are coming out, but they're lost in mine which don't stop, have never stopped. There is the cry of wind through the wire and now it's her wind but she seems to be whispering, her eyes so shiny, "You're killing him. Stop, you're killing him. Please, stop."

His hands have fallen and no part of him moves. The last kicks have gone under Liz's fingers, but his eyes are closed as if in sleep, his mouth a bloody hole in his face, the wind in my legs now, pulling me to Sam's voice.

*You pull a knife on **me**? You pull a **knife**?*

The kid, the driver, the smirker and sucker puncher, is on his knees and elbows, and Sam's hand is in his hair and he pulls till the kid's face shows, his eyes squeezed shut, and Sam punches it, then pushes it back to the floor, then does it again and again. A muffled voice there. "I'm only *sixteen*. I'm only *sixteen*." A wire turning in the wind, my boot toe sinking into his ribs, then off his hip, then into his ribs again, and what are all these people doing here? These seated men and women who stare at us and do not move? At the far end of the counter, there is a flurry of movement, Vinny's dark hair, his arm punching someone I can't see, and the wind pushes me through this painting of a diner of people dressed in red and black and denim, this haze of cigarette smoke, these perfumes and colognes and coffees, and my hand reaches behind the lady in the silver rayon dress, a sound from her as I grab a full ketchup bottle, its neck in my fist, and I'm at the end of the counter and my arm swings the bottle down on it, an explosion of glass, but Vinny is on the third one now, punching him over and over again, this face with whiskers, a punch-smudged face I hold the broken bottle to, but my hand throws it down and I punch the face Vinny punches, I kick the man's hip, his thigh, his knee, the wind louder than it's ever been, my face burning, and it's the burning that sends me back to Sam and the two others on the floor, Liz kneeling there by the big one who doesn't move, and beyond, in the brighter light of the entryway, a woman at the pay phone is punching in numbers, and Theresa is there too, pressing the hang-up button, shaking her head at the woman who is smaller and turns and hurries back through the doors into the wind.

Fellas, please, fellas. A cook in white, his short mustache, his pink face. He stands behind the counter of still people, his arms half raised as if in surrender, but this is a scrap of paper ripping by in the wind, my work boot kicking again the kid with the knife, and I turn for the big one but he lies there as still as when I left him days ago, Liz standing now, words coming from her mouth, her eyes dry, and my vocal cords are strings about to break, these silent people Vinny walks by, his chest and shoulders rising and falling, and on the floor at the end of the counter, the legs of the other, his pants gray corduroy, his motorcycle boots flat on their sides, his body half behind the counter where there was no protection for him, no movement there or anywhere, just Sam standing in the wind that is

my sound that has never stopped, the boy curled at his feet. But there is
another sound now, a weeping, a woman's weeping.

She stands in front of the cook holding clasped hands to her breasts.
Her dark hair is streaked with gray. Eyeliner runs down her cheeks.
"Please, please, please." She is in a white blouse and black skirt, an apron
around her waist and hips, and her legs are in black stockings, her waitress
shoes white like Sam's mother's. "Please." She keeps shaking her head,
and her lower lip trembles and why is she so *scared*? The question stops
everything, the wind dying to nothing, no more sound coming out of me.
I want to say something to her, I want to calm her down, but when I step
forward she steps back, her hands tight fists against her throat.

Is she *afraid* of me? How can she be afraid of *me*?

"Time to go."

Vinny's voice, no others. The only sound is the sizzle of bacon, these
men and women watching us from the counter and from the booths,
faces I now turn away from. We walk past the kid curled in a ball. We
step over the big one who has not moved. *Is he gone?* The girls are outside
already. They stand together under the halogen haze of the security lights,
their breaths small clouds in the air, and Vinny and Sam and I are pushing open the first doors, then the second, the restaurant behind us so very
crowded, and so very quiet.

WE SHOULD'VE gone straight to Sam's Duster. We should've all climbed
in and driven to the hospital for Sam and his chin. We could have gone to
Vinny's then for coffee and omelets, the sun rising over the tree line and
frozen lake, but instead we took our time out in the parking lot. Maybe
Theresa and Liz wanted a cigarette first, or maybe we were waiting for one
of those shitheads to stagger outside. I felt weak and empty, my knuckles
starting to burn. Then two things happened at once: two police cruisers
pulled one after the other into the lot, their blue lights flashing, and like
dark ghosts, the three we'd left behind drifted out of Sambo's.

But it couldn't be them, could it? Five minutes ago all three lay on
the floor, out, or close to it, especially the big one, and how could he be
standing there with his blood-streaked face looking at us in the flashing
blue of real police lights?

There were cops' voices in the air. Vinny stepped over and flashed his Bradford security badge and started telling our story. I was relieved the big one wasn't dead. It was good I hadn't killed him or anyone, but I was also disappointed they were already well enough to be walking, and this weak emptiness in my arms and legs had to go away because Liz said something to the kid who'd pulled the knife and out of his face came, "Fuck you, you fuckin' cunt." And Vinny was halfway to him before I even moved, both cops tackling him, and now it was close to sunup and the five of us were at the Haverhill police station waiting for Sam's father.

After our arrests at the beach, it's the one thing he insisted Sam do if he ever got into trouble again: call him. Sam gave his name to the lieutenant on duty and asked if he could use his desk phone. "You the inspector's son? Sure, be my guest. Give him a call." He sat back in his chair and laced his fingers behind his head. He wasn't the only friendly one. The two cops who arrested Vinny offered us coffee, and one of them kept smiling and shaking his head, "You guys couldn't've picked a better trio to beat on. Believe me, those three are the lowest of the low."

Vinny was in a holding cell, and Theresa and Liz and I were sitting on a long wooden bench. The three cops were behind a half-wall of raised panel, deep scratches along its surface, a gouge in the corner. Sam stood there waiting. The whiskers of his chin were caked with dried blood, and I could see he was nervous about having woken his father for this. Then Mr. Dolan strolled through an office doorway and down the hall, this short Irishman in a hat and coat. He glanced at his son and us, then pushed open the swinging half-door to the police desks and moved easily through the room. He took off his hat and sat down in an oak chair beside a desk.

"Mornin', Sergeant."

"Morning to you, Sam."

Sam's father nodded in the direction of the other two. "Officers."

"Inspector."

"You've got a tough kid here, Sam."

"Oh sure, sure." There was more small talk, a laugh or two, and I could see Sam relax a bit as his father began to make a case for our friend Vinny and how he could lose his job over this and did any of us want that?

In minutes Vinny was out of his cell signing something at the counter. Then the five of us were thanking Mr. Dolan and climbing back into Sam's Duster for the short ride to the hospital. While his chin got stitched, I stood outside with Vinny near the ambulance bay. From the hill of Buttonwoods Avenue, we could see out over the river flowing east. The sky had lightened above the trees and houses, and across the water the stacks of the boxboard factory churned out smoke the color of ash. I looked farther up the hill to the middle school where from the asphalt playground I used to watch that smoke rise into the air, the school where I saw Russ Bowman chased and beaten by a grown man, and I could feel the soft thud of the big one's head against my boot again and again. Maybe to shake it off, I said, "Good fight."

Vinny lit up a cigarette. He blew smoke out his nose and smiled at me. "Fight? That was a fucking ambush."

We both laughed, but again there was the feeling I'd just gotten away with something, the cops treating us like rogue colleagues, Mr. D. scolding us not so much for the fight but for letting the police get involved. Vinny was still chuckling under his breath. He looked over at me. "And *you* are fuckin' crazy."

I smiled and shrugged and looked back out at the brown river. I had never hit a baseball with a bat in a game people I loved were watching; I didn't know what it felt like to slap a puck into a net or catch a football and run with it into a place called the end zone, but standing in the dawn's early light with Vinny it occurred to me this is what those acts must feel like: earned and glorious and edged with blood.

12

_____

I WAS ALONE IN Liz's bed. It was late afternoon and winter light lay in a path across the floor. There was laughter out in the hallway, a rich girl's laugh, chest-deep and ironic, and my right shin was sore from the ankle to the knee. I closed my swollen fingers into a fist, then opened them again. My clothes lay on the floor over my work boots, and stuck to the lower legs of my corduroys were bits of glass in ketchup and blood.

It was eight or nine in the morning when Sam dropped Liz and me off at the campus gate. We'd been up all night. The sky was gray and the air was flat and cold against my skin. It was a Sunday morning, the campus quiet, steam rising from a pipe on the roof of Academy Hall. A car drove slowly down the asphalt lane through the green between the student union and library. It was a European sedan of some kind, silver. Then the rear window rolled down and Pop smiled at me. The car stopped. His father-in-law was behind the wheel, a rich businessman from New York City. He was a handsome man in his fifties or sixties, his hair combed back, and his wife sat beside him, Peggy and Pop in the back. They were going out to breakfast somewhere, and Peggy's father nodded hello and was polite, but he looked like he wanted to get going and why did his son-in-law have to get out of the car to say hello to his son?

Pop may have seen something different about us, or felt it, but he gave

Liz a hug and stood there waiting like he knew I had something to tell him. Then it came out of me, Sam and Theresa getting pulled over, the sucker punch, the knife, then the five of us finding them, and now my heart was knocking against my ribs and all over again I was breaking the cup in the kid's face, pushing it into the other's, elbowing the big one in the chin—I was aware of my voice being louder now, of my steel toe kicking the air, of pointing out to my father the blood and ketchup and bits of glass on my lower pant legs, of Liz having gone inside Academy Hall. He studied me as I kept talking. His beard was perfectly trimmed as always, and I knew I had a good story for him, one he seemed to be taking in as just that.

"Wow," Pop said. He hugged me, said he wanted to hear more later, then he opened the rear door of his father-in-law's expensive sedan and said, "My boy just beat the shit out of three punks downtown."

The pride in his voice was unmistakable. And isn't that why I'd told him? To get just that back from him? But in the side view mirror I could see his father-in-law's expression—startled, then disapproving, then concerned: What kind of family had his daughter married into anyway? Who were these people?

Then they were gone and I was walking to Academy Hall. What did I care what this capitalist from Manhattan thought of me? My father was proud and even the cops who showed up couldn't be happier about what we did and who we'd done it to.

Only Liz treated me differently. In the days and weeks that followed, she was still affectionate but in a guarded way, as if she'd just discovered I had a serious defect of some kind, and she wasn't sure how much of herself she would allow to get close—not to me—but to *it*.

It was the wrong word, though, because *it* was nothing, a non-space inside me I moved through without restraints of any kind; I'd learned how to break through that invisible membrane around another's face and head, but now there was no more barrier inside me either. *It* was nothing. And Liz knew what I wasn't letting myself think about too much, that without her that night I had come so very close to kicking a man to death, a boy it turned out, a teenager like the other two, kids from the avenues where I'd roamed myself only five years earlier.

And there was revenge to think about. I'd knocked out Steve Lynch's teeth and gotten a carload of men at our door the same night. What would come of this one? Now the story was going around campus and Ronnie D.'s. Somebody started calling us "the Sambo Slayers." It was a kind of fame.

AS THE winter deepened, I began to feel far away from myself, as if I had somehow stumbled into someone else's life. Nothing I did from Sunday to Saturday seemed to have anything to do with me.

On the job, after months of work, we were close to finishing Trevor D.'s three-decker of new condominiums. All the finish carpentry was done, and he'd sent Doug and Jeb on to a new project two towns over while Randy and I stayed behind to paint. Trevor D. didn't want to share his profit with a realtor, so for any tour of his property he would change out of his contractor clothes and wear shined loafers, ironed khakis, and a collared shirt under a new wool sweater. He'd be clean-shaven and attentive and charming, leading young couples from one room to the next where Randy and I might be on a stepladder rolling a final coat onto the ceiling, or else on our hands and knees brushing paint in level strokes along a baseboard. They'd walk past us as if we were not there.

I didn't know what Randy thought of that, but it felt like the truth to me: *I* was not there. Or anywhere really; for a while, those early years when I began to change my body, and then later in Texas when my eyes were opened to all the cruelty down through the ages, my feet felt planted on a piece of ground with my name on it, or at least part of my name on it, and then this lengthened into a trail I'd followed, but now I was somehow in the brush, standing there surrounded by thorns I seemed to have agitated as if they were bees.

At night, when I wasn't at the gym, I still brewed tea and tried to read Weber and Marx and Engels and all the rest, but their language looked more abstract to me than ever, nearly indecipherable, and worse, irrelevant. What did Weber's "Theory of Bureaucracy" have to do with how in a restaurant or bar now I always sat against a wall with a view of the door? What did it have to do with how unmotivated I felt in the gym? The Golden Gloves competition was weeks away, and I still trained hard under Tony Pavone; I still shadowboxed and worked the bags and sparred with whoever was around, but every time I threw a punch in the direction of another fighter's face, I felt myself pull it a bit. I was jabbing less and getting punched more. Pavone would yell, "Set your feet and throw somethin'. *Fight.*" But it was like someone telling you to kiss your mother and feel excited about it; before, what had kept boxing from feeling like a fight was the absence of rage, but now I feared it would show up uninvited, and I began to wonder why I kept coming back to that dank underground room at all.

LIZ AND I were going to a movie. It was a Saturday night, and I had just driven over the Basiliere Bridge and up the hill of Main Street past the statue of Hannah Duston. Liz turned to me and asked if we could stop somewhere for a pack of cigarettes. In Monument Square I pulled in front of a convenience store, left the engine and heater running, and went inside.

The floor was dirty with people's slush and mud tracks, the overhead light fluorescent and too bright, and I was waiting my turn at the register when I saw him watching me, smiling as he walked up. He carried a carton of ice cream and a quart of Coke. I had on a sweater and a jacket, but he wore only a T-shirt, green Dickies work pants, and sneakers. He was taller than I was, lean, and his black goatee made him look sinister until he started talking in that high voice that hadn't changed since he'd told us he was hawny in the mawnin'.

"Andre, how ya doin', man?"

"Good, Cleary. Real good, you?"

He said he was living down in the avenues, that he was getting married soon. I said congratulations, then I was at the counter asking for a pack of Parliaments and he touched my shoulder, said to say hi to Jeb. I said I would. At the door I glanced back at him and watched him dig into his front pocket for crumpled bills. He nodded and smiled at me, winked even, and as I left the store, the cold tightening the skin on my face, I remembered the time his mother went to visit her sister in Nebraska for a whole month. I'd never understood why she went alone, why she'd leave her family like that to go off for a visit. Then someone told me it was detox she went to, some twenty-eight-day program in Boston. When I told him I knew, Cleary laughed and said, "Nah," but he swallowed twice and walked away to do nothing in particular.

In six months Cleary would send an envelope to our father's house on campus. Inside it would be two invitations to his wedding, one for me, and one for Jeb. We wouldn't go.

Four more years and Cleary would be dead.

I'd hear about it after he was buried. They said his wife stabbed him in the back. That was it; she stabbed him. But a year later, I'd be working as a bartender at McMino's Lounge on Route 110 near the Haverhill-Merrimack line and a customer from Seventh Ave would tell me what had really happened, that Cleary always thought his wife was cheating on him, that he was always beating her up. That final night he ran outside off the porch to go kill the guy he just knew she was fucking. This was down in the avenues, and he took the trail in back of his apartment house. But his wife opened his black-handled Buck knife and chased after him, screaming. She was short and small, barely five feet, and just as he reached the weeds she got to him and drove it in low, sinking the blade into his liver, snipping something called the portal artery. Cleary went down without a sound. He curled up in a heap. But his wife spent four hours at a neighbor's house crying before they called anyone, and then it was the cops, and Cleary was gone.

I sat back behind the wheel, handed Liz her cigarettes, and drove toward the highway. I didn't tell her I'd just seen an old friend, or that the farther we got from Monument Square the more I felt I was turning my back on him somehow.

IT WAS late on a Friday afternoon. Jeb and I had been painting in a closed room for hours. This was a one-day job, and Jeb hadn't wanted it. He was enjoying the one we were doing with Trevor D. and the crew in Swampscott, framing three new rooms and a roof onto a widow's house, her long snow-covered yard that sloped down to a stand of pines through which we could see barrier rocks and the ocean. I was the cut man, but under the winter sun I was also learning how to lay out the exterior walls and nail them together on the open plywood deck. Jeb was much faster than

I was, especially when it came to the math; he'd pull his tape along the bottom plate of a future wall, marking off studs and the center of rough openings for windows and doorways, going back to mark off where the jack studs would go to hold the headers, then the king studs beside them. A week or so before, Trevor D. had given us each another raise, an extra dollar per hour. He said, "Andre, you focus well but you're slow. Jeb, you have much more natural talent at this than your brother, but you could use more focus."

He was right about both of us, and the only reason I may have had more focus is because I *had* to just to keep up. I could feel myself gathering more skills, though, ones I wasn't sure I wanted. What did I care about condos and houses, about walls and windows and clapboards and shingles and paint? These were just material objects, weren't they? What did they have to do with people in the world? Isn't that who I was more interested in?

I didn't know. And on that Friday afternoon on that one-day job in that empty old house, something strange was happening. It was a white room to be made even whiter with paint that smelled like rubbing alcohol. Jeb and I had already painted the baseboards and walls and window trim, and I felt a little drunk. It occurred to me that lately I'd been taking too many shots to the head. But when I told Jeb this, he said he felt a little drunk, too. For some reason, we left it there and kept working.

Next came the ceiling; it was ornate with a fluted cornice going around the top of each wall, and in the center of it was a flat four-foot-wide medallion of carved flowers and angels around a hook that once held the chain of a chandelier. It'd been a long time since my brother and I had been alone together, and it was good just talking while we painted. He was a father, something I kept forgetting, and he spoke of his baby son Ethan. How much he loved holding him, feeding him, even changing his diapers. "You can't believe how much you can love, Andre. You can't *believe* it."

It was true, I couldn't; I was many years from having a child myself, and I only saw his young fatherhood through a dark lens; he'd knocked up a girl he hadn't known and was now living with and trying to love; instead of being in some art or music school, he was working construction, the nails of his picking hand no longer long and filed but short and chipped. And his years up in his room with the teacher had done something to him. He looked like a grown man, but there was something raw and childlike about him, as if some clock had stopped for him by staying in that room, a clock that would have kept ticking if he'd left it and gone out into the streets and been with people his own age. He was twenty years old. There was the vague and nagging pull of having failed him somehow. My head began to feel like a ball of gas.

Jeb took the cornice, and I rolled the staging under the chandelier fixture and climbed up there and lay on my back, dipping my brush into the open can of paint, jabbing white into the faces of angels. This made me laugh, but then I'd been laughing for a while, both of us had, and I couldn't remember when we'd started or why. The brush was heavy in my hand, then light, then heavy again, and when had Trevor D. come into the room? Why was he looking up at us and yelling something, and why did we keep laughing anyway?

There was the slamming of the door and it seemed so long ago he'd been in the room, but was it?

I was still on my back only a foot or two from the chubby angels and their flower garlands, but my arm was too short to reach them when it hadn't been before. Had I pissed them off?

"Do you think they're mad?"

"Who?"

"The angels. I think I pissed them off." I was laughing and Jeb laughed back. He was bent over the top of his stepladder, his scraggly hair covering his face. "Fumes, man. It's these fucking *fumes*."

Then the room was done and we were sitting outside on the front porch steps, waiting for Trevor D. to pick us up in the truck. We were no longer laughing, and I wasn't sure if what was happening was inside my head or out in the world, and it was like being boys again, tripping together up in my attic bedroom.

The sky was darkening. The snow on the ground was too white to look at directly, so I sat in the cold sobering air and watched my brother smoke a cigarette. I listened to him talk about his baby who I kept seeing as a pudgy angel in the ceiling I hoped I'd finished painting.

WE SHOULD'VE gone home. Jeb to his, me to mine. We should've eaten something and taken long hot showers and cleared our heads, but it was Friday, the day Trevor D. took his crew to the Hole in the Wall for pitchers of beer. We'd drink and throw darts, what he called arrows.

Trevor's pickup pulled to the curb. Tied to the rack was the British flag hanging off a broomstick that'd been there for weeks, ever since a British warship took the Falkland Islands back from Argentina who'd taken it back from them. I climbed into the cab of the truck, wedged between my brother and our imperialist-capitalist boss. He pushed the shifter into gear and said, "That's alcohol-based paint, mates. Those windows should've been cracked all day. Where's your common sense?"

And why were we now stumbling into the small, dark Hole in the Wall to drink beer when our brains were already stewed? And was it Doug and me against the rest? Or Randy? And did Trevor D. keep winning, or was he just laughing a lot because he'd sold one of his units and that's why he was buying us round after round? There was a voice in my head: *You should eat something. You should drink some water and eat something.* Then Liz's face, her brown hair and hazel eyes, how far away she'd gotten on me, how we didn't seem to be an us anymore.

The back roads were thin ribbons, and if I closed one eye it was easier to keep my balance. On either side were bare trees and black branches and white snow, sometimes the lights of a house or streetlamps, a convenience store, a gas station and sub shop, then darkness again, pierced by lights coming at me I kept my one eye away from, both hands on the steering wheel. *You shouldn't be driving. You shouldn't be fucking driving.* But now I was halfway to Haverhill. If I turned around and drove back, it would be as much driving as continuing on.

I rolled down the window, the air so cold it was hard, a constant slapping in my face, a constant rebuke. And I must've gone to the college first, right? Because I was in Haverhill now, walking in Lafayette Square, the flesh-and-bone memory of having walked earlier. Yes. Into Academy

Hall and up to Liz's room. A kind face, a woman I didn't know telling me, "She's at the 104 Club. A bunch of 'em went."

The fucking 104 Club. A street bar in Lafayette Square across from the statue of another dead soldier, around him the incessant lights of Store 24, a car dealership and liquor store, a martial arts studio, and beyond that the Little River foamy with industrial waste, black now, too polluted to freeze over. It was a bar where nothing good happened unless you were looking to cop some drugs or get into a brawl or get busted, and it's where girls from the college liked to go slumming, and how had Jeb gotten here? The two of us were walking side by side away from the car. He was talking, had been for a long time. In the car too, the whole one-eyed ride here, about music, about J. S. Bach and Rodrigo, Mozart and Beethoven and Andrés Segovia, smoking cigarette after cigarette, trying to teach me something, not about the music it seemed, but him. Because how could I know him if I knew nothing of what he cared so much about?

The plowed lot beside the bar was packed with cars, so we'd parked blocks away near the railroad trestle, beyond that the abandoned brewery we used to sneak into with Cleary, steal cans of beer and drink them right there on dusty wooden steps. There was that conveyor belt Cleary would turn on and we'd ride it drunk to the upper floors, then run back down the steps and do it again and again.

Jeb and I stepped over an iced-over snowbank and walked in the street back toward the square. My brother lit up another cigarette. I hadn't been inside a Haverhill bar with him since that night at the Tap, but tonight, instead of hand-knitted slippers, he had on work boots and paint-splattered jeans, a loose sweater with a hole in the elbow. He looked like what he did all day, and I knew we were walking on asphalt gritty with sand and salt from a city truck, but my legs and feet were like cotton, my torso and face some kind of drunken steam. Then we were inside the 104 Club under flat, bright light and a haze of cigarette smoke, men and women ten or twelve deep drinking at the bar or shouting out an order, laughing and talking and smoking. There were the smells of nicotine and damp leather, of denim and perfume and sweat and beer. High in the corner hung a color TV, a Muhammad Ali fight I'd forgotten about, Ali taking a shot to the chin, his head snapping back. From below came a deep masculine roar, blood-joy in the air, a happy happy place, and my eyes burned and I wanted to turn around and leave, but my shoulder was being squeezed, my upper arm too, Liz smiling up at me, drunk. Behind her were six or seven from the college, boys and girls I didn't know, and now this too-tight hug from her, almost as if she were apologizing, and I knew she was.

She was saying something, but I wondered which of the guys behind her she'd been fucking. I leaned in close. "You want a beer?"

She smiled and kissed my lips, her tongue apologizing too. I turned and stepped sideways through people I may have known or once known, and did I even care she was moving on? What did I know about love anyway? Did I even love her? Had she loved me?

Then I was standing at the bar, my hip against someone's hip, my shoulder against another's shoulder. I could see with two eyes now, but barely, and I raised my hand to slow the movement of one of the bartenders behind this long chipped bar covered with bottles and half-full glasses and overflowing ashtrays and peanut shells in spilled beer or wine. Five feet down, a woman's hand stubbed out a cigarette, a silver ring on each finger.

I ordered three Buds. Liz preferred Michelob, but I wasn't sure I could say that many syllables without slurring. I looked over the crowd for my brother. The hip against mine belonged to a blonde woman, a student from the college. I knew her and did not know her. A big man stood behind her talking to the back of her head, but she wasn't looking at him. Her nose was straight and perfect, her skin clear and unlined, her chin strong, her hair thick and shiny and with no sign of bleach or color or any of the shit girls from around here put in theirs. Her name was Hailey, and she must've taken off a sweater or something because she was wearing the dark blue T-shirt she'd had on when Liz had first introduced us on the red-carpeted stairs of Academy Hall. It was tight and showed off her breasts and small waist, her lean swimmer arms. And those small white letters above her left nipple: *LAGNAF*.

I drank from my beer, thought about talking to her, didn't want to talk to her. Didn't want to be here. Liz was behind me in the crowd somewhere, and she'd laughed on those stairs and told me what those

letters meant· *Let's All Get Naked and Fuck*. Five or six other girls wore
the same T-shirt. I wondered if any of them were here tonight, slumming too.

"*I'm **talking** to you.*" The man behind Hailey put his big hand on
her shoulder and she turned, her hair whipping. "I said to fuck *off*."
Just a string of words instantly swallowed up in the barroom noise. She
shrugged her shoulder away from him.

I'd never seen him before. Twenty-two or -three, over six feet, maybe
230, 240. He had a handsome face, all jaw and cheekbones, but there was a
dullness in his eyes, not stupid but predatory, and now maybe a little pissed
off too. He put his hand back on her shoulder. I rested my bottle on the bar
next to the two I hadn't delivered yet. Why should I do something? What
did Hailey and her friends with their secret T-shirts think they'd find down
here anyway? But she was clearly done with him and that should be it. That
should always be it.

"Hey, brother, she's all set."

I was shorter than he was, smaller, two things he took in as he was
taking in the main thing: that I was sticking my face into his business.

"I'm not your fuckin' brother."

"Outside then." I jerked my head toward the door.

"Let's *go*." These words the answer to a riddle floating down a river
I was also floating down, the crowd parting and moving, the red and
gold glow of a neon Miller sign above the door that opened for me on
its own. But my heart hadn't even woken up for this. I could be nodding
off somewhere; there was no fear, none of that marrow-electric jolt that
put something I needed into my arms and legs, no pounding heart and
shallow breath, no keen eye on any movement coming my way. There
was just the steady forward momentum of having broken through the
membrane—because the invitation to fight is a breaking too—and this
was the right thing to do, wasn't it?

It was school all over again. The crowd sensed the change in the air,
and now people were outside and ringed around us under the white light
over the door. I had both hands up, but my back foot kept slipping on ice
and I couldn't plant it but jabbed at him anyway, this pathetic move from

a boxing ring nobody used in a real fight, and how had I forgotten that? Why all of a sudden did I think there were some rules to this?

He feinted away from it, his head ramming into my chest, and I was lifted and there was the back-slap of pavement, a weight on my sternum. The first punches were almost a surprise, hard and fast from the right and left, sparks behind my eyes. I opened them, and there he was on my chest. His face was in shadow, and it was hard to breathe and he kept punching and my hands grabbed both his wrists and wouldn't let go.

"Kill him, man. Fuckin' **kill** *'em."*

There were more words out there in the air around us, men's voices, then Jeb's, "That's my *brother*." His hands on the shoulders of the one on me, but then other hands pulled him away and there was yelling, had been for a long time, from the one on me who had a handful of hair on both sides of my head, my fingers still locked around his wrists, and he began to lift my head and slam it back down, lift it and slam it, the concrete beneath me felt like a betrayal, and I tried to tense the muscles in my neck but that only slowed his momentum and at the corners of my eyes darkness welled and I tried to pull his hands from my hair but he was too strong. I began kneeing him in the back, but that only loosened my neck and he slammed harder, the back of my skull thinner now, more brittle, and I could only see the shadow of his face meeting more shadows, my eyes filling with them, and if I didn't keep him from this and if no one was going to pull him off, this would be it, *this will be it, this is it, this can't be it, this can't be it,* every muscle I'd ever worked going rigid, my neck a clamp, and maybe he was getting tired, but my fingers were now part of his wrists against the sides of my head and he could no longer move, and he was spitting, hawking and spitting into my face, this warm wet evidence of a street rage I'd either forgotten to bring along, or was too drunk to bring along, or could no longer summon, these thoughts not in my head but in my blood I could feel stiffening on my face beside his phlegm.

At first I thought it was another brawl. There was a whooshing movement to my right and people parted and were walking away quickly. There was a lightness in my chest, then something jerked from my fingers and

I was rolling onto my side as the cruiser pulled in tight to the snowbank inches from my face, the flash of blue lights in the air, my good, good friends, the Haverhill police.

I MAY have slept at Liz's that night, or at Sam's in his second-story bedroom on Eighteenth Avenue. I may have driven back to Salem and Lynn with Jeb. I don't remember. But these kinds of fights happened in Haverhill all the time, and the cops helped me up and told people to move along. The big one was gone, and there was no talk of pressing charges anyway. They may have asked if I wanted medical attention, and they probably went inside the 104 Club to make their presence known, but all I remember clearly is the next night Pop found out, and now Pop wanted revenge.

It was close to ten, a Saturday night, and I was standing in the small dining room of his campus house. Theresa sat at the table nursing a beer, and Sam stood with his back to the plate-glass window, outside so dark that we were reflected back at us, a woman and three men. My father stood in the center of the room in his corduroy shirt and leather vest, a drink in his hand. Peggy had gone to bed early, as was her habit, and my baby half-sister was asleep downstairs too.

Both my cheeks were swollen. My left eyelid was puffy, my lower lip split, and if I'd ever had a worse headache I couldn't remember it. My neck muscles were stiff and sore. Pop took a long drink off his Stolichnya. He drank it like the Russians, over ice with ground black pepper. He put it on the table and walked up to me and studied my face for the second time in five minutes. It was Vinny who'd told him what happened, Vinny who'd gotten the story from the rich girl Hailey I never saw again.

In the light from the kitchen Pop touched two fingers under my chin and tilted my face up. I could smell vodka and Old Spice. This gesture of his was new, and it made me feel like a boy, a feeling I both liked and hated.

"Who was this motherfucker? He's gotta be pretty tough to beat you."

I shook my head and shrugged. There was the earned sense I had reached a dry plateau on some long, steep climb up a mountain in the rain. I was more than happy to stay there now, no need to go to the top; I hadn't changed myself from what I was to what I'd become for my father, but it was good hearing he thought this of me. I also felt vaguely like a liar and an impostor, though, and he'd shown his street-naïvité for having said it: there were thousands of men tougher than I was, tens of thousands.

Sam was talking. He knew people who were at the 104 Club the night before, and he'd made a few calls and found out who'd beaten the shit out of me. It was Devin Wallace, someone who brawled in the bars regularly. I knew his older brother Ben. He had a severe underbite and was tall and sinewy and he drank all day, cruising around town in beat-up sedans, burning rubber at traffic lights, giving the finger to anyone who said a thing about it. Years later, he went on to serve multiple sentences at the state prison in Walpole, and he'd be dead of cirrhosis of the liver before he hit forty-five. Now my father wanted something done to his bigger, stronger, handsome brother, but I was through with it. I'd fought and lost, and wouldn't a movie be a good thing to do right now? Popcorn and cold Coke and a dark room full of strangers turning themselves over to the imaginations of others?

It was my fault I'd lost so badly anyway. Since when do you invite someone outside? *I'm not your fuckin' brother.* That was *his* invitation, which came first and which I should have followed with a straight right to his predatory face. But since Sambo's, something had changed in me, and now Pop's and Sam's plan was to go back to the 104 Club where the Wallaces and their crew hung out and then get him somehow, Sam and Theresa and my half-drunk and determined writer father, who, with his trimmed professor's beard, stood at the door and pulled on an insulated Red Sox jacket and one of his Akubra hats. They both reflected things he loved, finely made leather from Down Under, and a team of grown men who played a game called baseball. I'd seen him wearing them many times before, mainly walking his dog within the campus walls, but now I pictured him down at the 104 Club looking for a fight, and I felt protective of him and cowardly all at once for I was doing nothing to stop this; if I did, I would look like the weak little boy I'd been working all these years to kill.

POP AND Theresa went in his car, Sam and I in the black Duster. We were going to walk in separately and in twos; if Wallace wasn't there, then we'd stand on opposite sides of the bar and wait. Then what? Jump him? All four of us? Theresa, too?

Sam drove us out of the sanctuary of campus, my father's taillights ahead of us. Through the back window of Pop's car I could see the silhouette of his Akubra, and I was eleven years old again, standing at the window of our old rented house on Lime Street, watching my father admonish and warn Clay Whelan, his father Larry holding him back, this chained dog who would've surely killed Pop if he'd gotten free. And I couldn't let Pop get to Wallace before I did. If he got to him first, my father would begin things with words, with language, the one thing he was so good at, and probably in his Marine captain's chest-voice like he'd done at the Tap with the husband of the spurned wife, but that would give Wallace too much time and motivation, and he was so much bigger than my father, so much angrier. No, I needed to get there first: no words, no foreplay, no polite invitations. I'd just have to start swinging and hope the first one was hard enough to give me time for the second and the third and the fourth. I was tapping my foot, my tongue dry as shaved bark. I wanted that cold Coke.

Sam turned off Main and headed down a side street for the river. We were still in neighborhoods of large, comfortable houses, their shingles or clapboards in no need of paint, their covered porches spacious and level and free of trash and the clutter of discarded kids' toys. Christmas lights were draped along the fascia, and in the windows stood lighted trees behind wispy curtains. These were Bradford houses, nobody living in them on welfare or food stamps, many of them college-educated, their late-model cars parked neatly in plowed driveways.

Sam followed Pop's car over the river. There was the hum of tires on the steel grates, and the black water beneath us flowed east and I could see the dim white of snow on the mudbanks. Then we were on River Street passing lighted sub shops and package stores, a diner in Railroad Square. Soon we were in the dark gauntlet of the closed shoe factories where we passed the brewery and drove under the tracks again. In an abandoned weed lot a shopping cart lay on its side, rags spilling from it, and up ahead was the light of Lafayette Square, the exterior lamp over the door to the 104 Club a white star pulsing in my head.

The lot was only half full. While Pop parked, Sam did two loops around the statue of the dead hero.

"We'll give them time to get in first."

"Good."

"You all right?"

"Yep."

"Don't worry, we'll get him."

On the second loop I could see Pop and Theresa walking into the bar, Pop holding the door open for her. Theresa was only a year or two younger than his third wife, and they looked like a mismatched couple out on a date. Again there came the feeling this was not my father's world, that he was having too much fun right now, and that very soon the fun would stop.

Sam parked the Duster in the lot close to the street. I started to get out fast, but Pop and Theresa didn't know what Wallace looked like and they'd have to wait for us anyway. I glanced over the car at Sam. "Buddy, if he's there, he's gonna know why we are, too. I'll have to go right at him."

"*We'll* have to go right at him."

I didn't say anything. I wanted Sam's help and I did not want his help, but more than this, I didn't want to be here at all. In the cold air, my cheeks stung, my split lip too. It was going to hurt to get punched there again.

The 104 Club was as empty as it had been crowded the night before. Only one bartender was working, a thin man with a gray ponytail who stood at the far end watching the TV in the corner. Beneath it was a shuffleboard I hadn't seen the night before, and two couples sat beside it in wooden chairs drinking and smoking and talking. Four or five others stood at the bar, men and women, Pop and Theresa among them. But no Devin Wallace. The air smelled like cigarette smoke and disinfectant and popcorn from the machine.

Sam called the bartender over and ordered two Buds. Saturday nights always seemed to start slow. It was date night, people going out to dinner or the movies, maybe a dance club somewhere. Around ten they'd come in for a drink that would turn into two, then three, then by last call business would be as good as the night before. But now it was after ten and

still this place was quiet. Maybe all the regulars were as hungover as I was
and had stayed home. I didn't know, but I was relieved and took a sip
of the Budweiser that tonight was like drinking lighter fluid or chicken
grease. I put my bottle down. The door opened and four or five men
walked in with the icy air, Ben Wallace one of them. A dark wool cap was
pulled down around his ears and his whiskered chin jutted out, and as he
walked by me and Sam, he took us in and his eyes changed from expectant of a good time to something darker. I looked down the bar at Pop and
Theresa. Both of them were smoking a cigarette, but Pop's eyes were on
mine. I shook my head once, then tapped Sam on the hand. "If Devin
shows, we're way fucking outnumbered. This was a bad idea."

"See that tall one with Ben? I played hockey with him. What's he
doing with Wallace?"

Theresa stood in front of us. Somebody had put a quarter in the jukebox, and Huey Lewis & the News was singing about believing in love. She
leaned in close. "Is he one of them?"

Sam shook his head and drained his beer. "This isn't going anywhere.
Let's shoot up to Ronnie D's."

Theresa went back for Pop, and maybe that's what she'd told him,
that this wasn't going anywhere, which really meant it *was* going somewhere but not where we'd pictured it back in my father's small campus
house full of books, some precise act of revenge on one man, a big man at
that, one I was happy to concede to now.

Pop stood on the sidewalk under the light. His face was shadowed by
the brim of his Akubra. "Why're we leaving?"

"It's dead, Pop. Nobody's in there tonight. We're heading up to Ronnie D's. Maybe he's there."

Most likely Pop knew I was lying; bars had their regulars and Ronnie
D's across the river had never had a Wallace as one, but maybe Pop, too,
had come to feel this was all a bad idea.

He smiled at Theresa and held out his arm. "Let's go, darlin'."

Theresa laughed and hooked her arm in his, and Sam and I were
heading for the Duster, a strip of ice cracking under my boots, when
behind us the door to the bar swung back on its hinges and Ben Wallace
and his crew came walking fast into the lot. "Fuck you, Dubis. You're

down here waiting for my brother, you and your fuckin' friends." Spit arced out of his mouth, and he was already a few feet away from me, and I never realized how tall he was, taller than his handsome, stronger brother. On both sides of him stood men I did not know, but Sam moved toward them and was calling out the name of his hockey mate, calling it in the warm tone of an old friend glad to see another.

I said, "I'm just here for a beer, Ben."

"Fuck you, you are. My brother kicked the shit out of you last night, that's why you're here." He was closer to me now, a step away from punching range, but my body wasn't having anything to do with this. My weight was even on both feet, and there was no lightness in my hands, no flames running through my blood. I heard myself talking about Christmas.

"What?"

"It's Christmastime, Ben. Peace on earth, right?"

"Fuck *you,* my brother kicked your ass, and I'll fuckin' do it again right now."

But he wasn't moving any closer, and now Pop and Theresa were walking across the lot toward us. Pop had both hands in the pockets of his Red Sox jacket, and even with his thick beard and the twenty years he had on us all, there was something boyish about him.

"You're backing down 'cause you know I'll fuckin' kill you, Dubis."

"You're right, Ben. Merry Christmas."

Ben kept swearing at me, and now Sam turned to his hockey friend, a square-faced kid with an Irish name and shoulder-length hair. "Tell your buddy to calm down, Tim."

But Ben wasn't calming down. Our lack of reaction seemed to make him angrier, his chin jutting out, spit flying, and his friends seemed no more interested in a brawl than we did. They stood quietly behind him, looking from me to Sam, then at Pop, who stood a few feet back, his hands still in his pockets. He looked happy and relaxed and so awfully out of place. Wallace was threatening to kill me again and how new it was that I didn't care what he said, that he could go on and on, and it just did not matter. Because I noticed he still wasn't stepping any closer, and only when he glanced over at Pop and Theresa did my blood thin out a bit; I'd have to do something if he went after them in any way, especially my father who, it was clear now, had come downtown to see more of this part of my life. I opened the passenger door and waited for Sam whose hockey friend was speaking quietly into Ben's ear.

Ben threatened to kill me once more, but in minutes Sam and I were driving over the Merrimack River, Pop and Theresa ahead of us. My face ached, my neck too. I was looking forward to a bed somewhere, a long night's sleep. I thought we were heading for Ronnie D's but Pop steered for the campus. Then we were inside his house again, Pop creeping into his downstairs bedroom to hang his Akubra on its hook, Sam and Theresa and I sitting around the small dining room table. Theresa shook her head and laughed. "Your dad had a gun, you know."

"What?"

"When those guys ran into the parking lot, he reached right over me and took it out of the glove compartment. He had it in his pocket the whole time."

Sam looked at me and shook his head. Now I knew why Pop had really gone into his bedroom. It's where he kept his guns, on his closet shelf, and I pictured him swinging open the six-round chamber of the snub-nose and emptying the bullets into his cupped hand. Or he might be releasing the loaded clip of the semiautomatic, pulling back the slide and eyeing the bore for a straggler round. And I had a flash of him standing in the lot of the 104 Club with his hands in his jacket pockets, his relaxed smile, his right fingers cupped around something so lethal. My chest felt squeezed. *"Shit."*

"I asked him if he would've really used that. He said he'd just shoot in the air."

Like that would've stopped anyone. Like there was reason involved here. Like we would've all paused at the loud noise and cooled down right away and walked off in opposite directions because this had all gotten so obviously out of hand.

Pop was walking up the stairs. "Who wants a nightcap?" He was smiling widely, his cheeks flushed above his beard. His dog Luke followed him up to the lighted kitchen, and Pop opened the fridge and pulled out four bottles of beer. He twisted the cap off Theresa's first and walked over and handed it to her. She smiled up at him. "Put your gun away?"

"Yes, ma'am."

We all laughed, even me, and it occurred to me I'd gotten so brave in one way but had stayed so cowardly in another. When Pop handed me the bottle, I took it from him and then we four lifted our drinks to that dish best served cold, a revenge I knew I would never seek.

THE NEXT morning my father drove to Mass, and I had coffee with Peggy while she fed my baby sister. She was six months old and her name was Cadence and she had a shock of red hair that reminded me of the little bird Woodstock from Charlie Brown cartoons. After Peggy had burped and changed her, she asked if I wouldn't mind holding her so her mother could squeeze in some writing upstairs. "And your father should be back soon."

Cadence was lighter than a book of political theory, her entire bottom resting in my palm. She held her hands out from her sides but had a hard time holding her head up, so I fanned my fingers against the back of her tiny skull, smelled mashed pear and clean cotton and something I couldn't name. She was looking directly into my eyes, hers the color of a blue planet, her mouth open slightly, and how was it possible to be so young and small and utterly dependent on the love of the people you were born into, their constant care, their good judgment, for years and years?

I made patronizing baby sounds to make her smile, but she just kept looking into my eyes. It was as if she had me all figured out and wasn't quite sure she wanted to be held anymore by this man twenty-three years older than she was, her brother.

I was sitting with her at the dining room table when Pop came home. She'd fallen asleep against my shoulder. The sun shone across the floor and up the stairs where her mother was writing.

I heard Pop greet Luke downstairs, then he was walking up to where we were. He smiled right away. He was wearing the same corduroy shirt from the night before, that and a pair of jeans and black leather boots he'd ordered from a boot maker in Montreal. He'd gone to church to talk to Jesus. That's how he usually described prayer, as a personal conversation with Jesus Christ. This was something I had never done or even considered doing. Nor, as far as I knew, had my brother or sisters.

When Suzanne turned sixteen, she informed Pop she wasn't going
to church anymore and it was like a sandbag fell away, and soon Jeb and
Nicole and I were caught up in this lucky current that eventually meant
we got to sleep late on Sundays too. But Pop kept going to Mass six or
seven days a week, and now he was smiling at his second and fifth children. His beard was newly trimmed, his cheeks and throat shaved clean.
He stopped smiling and started scratching Luke behind the ears.

"That was wrong last night."

"What was?"

"Bringing the gun. That was bad."

I nodded, my hand pressed to the warm spine of his sleeping daughter. Peggy came downstairs for more coffee then. She held an empty mug,
a big one from which she drank café au lait, a habit she'd picked up during
a semester in Paris, and there was a far-off look in her eyes that reminded
me of Jeb whenever he used to come downstairs after hours of practicing
his guitar. Pop glanced at her as she passed. "Writing?"

"Yeah." She filled her cup with coffee and warm milk from a pan, said
to me quietly, "You can give her to your dad. He'll lay her in her crib."

She walked back up the stairs to her desk, and I stood and Pop came
over. With my palm against the back of his baby's head, I handed him my
sleeping sister. I could smell his hair, the sweet wafer of the Eucharist on
his breath, this thing he believed in so strongly and which got him to say
things like he'd just did. It was good he had something like that. Maybe
people needed something like that. Men in particular.

13

LIZ HAD A crush on a guy named Joe Hurka. He was in my father's fiction writing class with her, and whenever she talked about him, which was quite a lot, her eyes had more light in them, her skin more color, her hair more shine. She talked about how sensitive he was, how beautiful his writing, and that he even wrote songs and played the guitar. One day in class Pop asked him to sing them all something, and Joe did, and now Liz's crush looked like outright love to me. I hated Joe.

And I didn't. All the weeks she pined for him, I never met him. Whenever she talked about something new he'd written or sung, the jealousy I felt was a hot stone in my abdomen, but it was of two parts: the obvious, and that it was possible to be a young man and know what you were supposed to do with your time on earth. This guy Joe seemed to have that, and as much as I wished for him to pack up his guitar and short stories and move away somewhere, there was also a gnawing sense that he was a better man than I was and that I should just stand aside and let what was happening happen.

One Saturday before my weight workout with Sam, I walked into Liz's empty dorm room and saw a thin manuscript on her bed. The room smelled like shampoo, and she had probably just gotten dressed and was getting something to eat down in the dining hall. I sat on the mattress and picked up four or five stapled pages. It was a new story by Joe. My fingertips went numb. It was as if I'd found a love letter from him to her, an irrational thought, I knew. I turned the title page over and began to read.

The words were simple, clear and concrete, and soon I was no longer aware I was reading sentences written by Joe; instead, I became the story's protagonist, a teenage boy working as a dishwasher in a diner in a small town like Haverhill. I knew these things from the details, the abandoned mill building on the other side of the alley, the flickering light of the streetlamp over the broken sidewalk, the cigarette smoke of the boy's boss behind the counter. It's two or three in the morning and the boy is mopping the floor when two middle-aged prostitutes walk in from the cold. They're wearing too much makeup and not enough clothes and before they can even sit down the boy's boss yells at them to leave, yells that they're closed and he doesn't serve whores anyway. The women go without much of a fight, and the story ends with the boy mopping the floor, shaking his head and thinking, *That's not right, that's just not right.*

I laid the story back down on the bed. I sat there awhile. I wasn't thinking of Joe or Liz or me. I wasn't thinking at all. I was seeing that boy in that diner and even *feeling* what it might be like to be him in that moment when the world pulled him up against his own conscience, though this word was not yet in my head. It was like hearing a good song on the radio, that place it puts you where you weren't before. Or the movies, how they did that, too. And now Joe's story.

I wanted to read another one. I wanted to read whatever he'd written. But I was running late for my workout with Sam, and as I left Liz's room and walked down the worn carpet of Academy Hall, dorm room doors open and ten different albums playing on ten different record players, talk and laughter and a vacuum cleaner running somewhere, I felt more *here,* like water leaking from an ear you hadn't known was blocked, and then something warm and wet is on your skin and now you can hear.

THE GOLDEN Gloves were three weeks away. It was a weeknight, probably Wednesday, and all day long Jeb and Randy and I had hung Sheetrock in the rooms we'd built in the widow's house overlooking the water.

The ceilings came first. The day before, we'd started nailing spruce strapping into the joists sixteen inches on center and while Jeb finished that, Randy and I were hauling sheets of plaster board off the truck and stacking them against a wall in each of the three rooms. By coffee break, all the Sheetrock was unloaded and Jeb had finished the strapping. He was faster with measurements and cuts and handling the screw gun, so it fell to Randy and me to do most of the grunt work. We'd squat and lift a full sheet, carry it under where it would go, then we'd count off, "One, two, *lift*," and yank the sheet up from our sides and flat onto our heads, our fingertips on its smooth surface to keep it from buckling and cracking. We'd each step up onto a stool or lidded joint compound bucket, and together we'd press the four-foot-wide, twelve-foot-long sheet up against the ceiling strapping and there'd be the electric whine of the screw gun as Jeb went to work sinking black screws through plasterboard into spruce till we could let go and drop our arms and step down to do it again and again.

Now the day was over, and I was in my small apartment in Lynn pulling on sweats. The only light in my room was a bulb in the ceiling, stark and too bright, and outside the windows was blackness, a cold I was planning to run through on my way to the Boys' Club and Tony Pavone's boxing ring. My shoulders were fatigued from all the overhead work of the day, and it would be hard to keep my fists up, hard to throw punches. But I wouldn't allow this thought to stay in my head. Whatever good had come to me had come from my complete and utter disregard for my body's need for comfort. If I began to capitulate now, where would it end? In no time I'd be small and soft again, a boy who liked to read books and build tree forts with his brother. A boy easily stomped.

I pulled a second sweatshirt down over the first. For a moment or two I just stood there in my empty room. No posters or photographs on the walls. No desk or chair or couch or bed. Just my yoga mat on the floorboards under my sleeping bag, the two work boots stuffed into a pillowcase I called a pillow. Beside it was the stack of books I'd been laboring through all year, a composition binder I sometimes took notes in, the glossy brochure of the University of Wisconsin at Madison waiting for me in the fall. In the corner, propped up against the dusty baseboard, was the

AAU number I would soon pin to my trunks in the Golden Gloves, and it was time to move, time to get moving.

But in the kitchen I stopped at the door. I watched myself let go of the knob and turn and put a pan of water on the stove. I opened the flames under it all the way, then watched myself take an empty cup and drop a tea bag into it. I walked back to where I slept for the notebook and a pencil, and why did I set them on the small kitchen table? Why was I sitting there waiting for the water to boil for the tea when I should be running along an icy sidewalk in the night to train?

I began to feel too warm in my layered sweats, but I didn't move. I opened the notebook in front of me. The water began to bubble and I stood and poured it steaming into my cup, the tea bag jerking, then rising, and now I watched as I set the cup near the notebook and took my pencil and held it. What was I doing? And why? Why was I doing this?

For a short time or a long time, I stared at the page. I saw how consistently level the blue lines were from left to right, a quarter of an inch high, maybe five-sixteenths. I kept staring at them. Then a curtain lifted and I began to see a factory somewhere where these notebooks were made, men and women running big machines, cutting and printing and binding, and I saw a man like Randy working some press, his outlaw mustache, sweat in the corners of his eyes, then I was in the woods, woods I called Maine, the place Liz was from, and now a young woman who looked very much like her was half drunk on warm beer and was losing her virginity on the hood of a Pontiac. Then I *was* her, feeling the metal hood under my skin, the jabs into me that hurt, then didn't but did.

The boy she'd given herself to finished quickly, and it was as if I were a mist in the trees watching them sitting now in the front seat. They smoked cigarettes and neither of them spoke. A soft rain began to fall and the boy started the engine and put his car in gear and drove down the rutted road away from what they'd just done together. Away from me.

I put down my pencil. In front of me were just handwritten words, quite a few crossed out and replaced with others. I raised the cup of tea to my lips and blew on it, but it had cooled to the temperature of the room. Hadn't it just been steaming? How long had I been sitting here?

I blinked and looked around my tiny rented kitchen, saw things I'd never seen before: the stove leaning to the left, the handle of the fridge covered with dirty masking tape, the chipped paint of the window casing, a missing square of linoleum on the floor under the radiator.

I stood and closed the notebook. I picked up the pencil and set it on top like some kind of marker, a reminder to me of something important I shouldn't lose.

A FEW days later I was in the ring with someone new. He was my height with a bushy beard, a narrow chest and wide waist, his arms thin, his eyes cloudy above blotchy cheeks. He was too young to look like this, a drunk from one of the neighborhood barrooms, and as I stepped into the ring to spar him, I wondered why he was here.

Someone hit the bell and we tapped gloves. He kept his hands low like Bobby Schwartz, and I thought I'd just throw some jabs, that's all, and I threw one, a white canyon opening up in my head. My eyes cleared and there were the ropes wrapped in duct tape, the darkness on the other side where Tony Pavone said, "Good hook. But both a you, keep your hands *up*."

I must've dropped my right. I must've dropped it when I threw the jab and opened myself up. It was the hardest I'd ever been hit in the ring, and I didn't want to get hit again. A thousand bees were hovering now, their wings beating dully, and we were moving clockwise, our eyes locked. His still looked cloudy to me, the whites not white, his gaze unfocused. What he'd just thrown was luck, right? Tony yelled at him to hold his hands *up*, but he wasn't, so I stepped in and threw a right and a flower flamed up behind my eyes, the bees' wings hot and buzzing under my skin, and through a maroon haze, he was there again. I wished for headgear. I wanted to stop and ask him how he was getting to me so easily, what was I doing wrong? But a three-minute round was a three-minute round, and you didn't stop in the middle. You just didn't.

I tried to evade him with some footwork, something I was never too swift at. I planted my feet, jabbed, then began to move counterclockwise, a direction from which it was harder for me to throw a strong right. His eyes blinked and his right hand dropped and I shot a hook for his cheek, but a hammer smashed the bees into my skull where they kept drilling on their own and my eyes burned and I could hear a voice, one of the bees talking, its wings explaining something, *Finish him off. Throw a combination.* These words meant not for me, but for this man who looked like he was just getting started, this drunk who punched hard enough to kill somebody. And he was holding back, too. Each of his hooks had hurt me, and he had to have seen that, but he wasn't stepping in to end things. He wasn't doing what I'd learned to do, to hurt even more the one you've already hurt.

In the next two minutes he hit me six or seven more times. When the round ended, I thanked him for the session and ducked between the ropes and untied my gloves and unwrapped my hands. My fingers were clumsy and looked far away. Tony Pavone was saying something to me, his voice close, words of advice, it sounded like. Words I couldn't quite decipher.

The headache lasted ten days, a huge hand squeezing my temples between thumb and forefinger. At the edge of my vision was a green world that sometimes turned purple or brown, and whenever I read my tape measure I had to squint, the hand squeezing harder.

I WAS riding in the back of Peggy's Subaru. Pop was driving. We were pulling away from Kappy's liquor store with one of his buddies I didn't know well. He sat in the passenger side and had a beard as wild-looking as Fidel Castro's, and he kept talking about Romania and collective farming. It was a warm, gray afternoon. On both sides of Main Street the dirty snowbanks had melted into slush, its runoff sluicing into the drains, some of them clogged with damp leaves, empty cans or cigarette packs, damp sections of newspaper.

Pop elbowed his friend. "My boy's a Golden Glove boxer."

"What're you, a middleweight?"

"Yeah, no."

"No? You're not a middleweight?"

"I am, but not what he said."

Pop's eyes caught mine in the rearview. He was waiting for me to continue, and I could see that whatever I'd say next would be all right, that he was just curious, that's all; this was the collateral gift of him having been a father who'd always lived somewhere else, one who had never been part of any decisions we made or did not make about our lives; he'd always been absent, and it made the next thing easy to say. "The Gloves were last week. I didn't go."

"How come?"

"I don't know . . ."

"What?"

I could've told him about the beating I'd taken in the ring. I could've told him about the headache that wouldn't go away, or how I'd begun to see my skull as a container for my brains, one that had been designed to protect them so why was I encouraging people to punch it as hard as they could? Weren't there other things I could learn to do?

"I think I should be doing something more creative."

I did not say artistic, though I was thinking that. I did not say I'd started to write a short story for the first time and that each night after work I looked forward to that tea and to that table, to my pencil I would sharpen with the U-knife from my carpentry apron, the lined notebook I was slowly filling with words and sentences and paragraphs. I did not tell him that just doing this left me feeling pleasantly empty of something after, something I normally would have brought into the ring or the weight room.

Pop said, "Interesting." And he downshifted and drove the three of us along Main Street. We were heading off to a Bradford College faculty party somewhere, a dinner with grown men and women like the man beside Pop, people who had Ph.D.'s and taught and wrote, people who danced and painted and sculpted. Pop's friend was talking about Romania again, and I was looking out the window at this place that had become my hometown, the street Rosie P. had lived on, her sweet smile and naked brown legs. Columbia Park and the house my mother had worked so hard to keep us in, the longest we'd ever been anywhere, the tree house in the back made from stolen lumber, the attic turret I'd exiled myself to, the sidewalk in front where Tommy J. had punched my brother in the face and called my mother a whore. There were the worn apartment stairs beside Pleasant Spa where early in the morning kids from the avenues still waited for the bus and passed joints and drank Pepsis or Cokes. And Cleary's side street, his loving drunk mother.

Pop's friend was talking about Miles Davis now and we were driving through Monument Square, a new restaurant where I had nearly beaten a boy to death. My father was driving and he could keep driving. Then we were on the Basiliere Bridge over the Merrimack River, and as I watched the dark water flow east past the concrete floodwall and Captain Chris's Restaurant and the boxboard factory on the opposite bank, there was this recognition of movement, that like the currents below I was being pulled from what I had known to what I did not yet know, that for now I was suspended between two worlds.

IN MAY I finished writing a short story. It was set in Louisiana and was about a young man caring for his ailing grandmother. Every afternoon the grandmother's elderly friend brings fresh blackberries she's picked and the grandson takes them and puts them with the rest, but he's getting tired of baking blackberry cobbler and blackberry pie and blackberry bread and muffins, and he's about to throw them all out when one afternoon, as he's getting ready to serve the women coffee, he overhears the friend crying and telling his grandmother how unhappy she is because she lives with her son and daughter-in-law and grandchildren in their small house and she doesn't want to be a burden, doesn't want to be any trouble, and that's why she leaves the house every day with her empty coffee can to pick blackberries. But now the season's over, she weeps, and she doesn't know what to do with herself anymore. In the final scene, the grandson decides to keep all the blackberries she's picked, and he bakes for days.

It was an overwritten, sentimental story, something I wouldn't know till months had passed after finishing it. But as I wrote that last line my heart was thumping against my sternum and my mouth was dry and I felt pulled along by something larger than I was, something not in me but in this story that had come out of me.

It was a Saturday afternoon, warm enough I didn't need a jacket. I grabbed my workout clothes and left my apartment. The inside of my car smelled like sawdust and the leather of my carpentry apron on the backseat. For a few miles the day was too bright and real and I blinked at it from the dream I'd cast myself in with the two old ladies and the young man and all those blackberries. Then I was on the back roads heading west. Instead of playing the radio, hunting for that one good song, I drove along in silence. On both sides of the road were woods, but today, for the first time, I saw them as individual trees, each one different from the one beside it or in front of it or behind it. One was as bent with age and weight as an old man, another as thin and straight as a young girl, one pine, the other maple or elm or oak, and the sun seemed to shine on each sprouting leaf, on each needle, on the black telephone lines sweeping from pole to pole, on the veined creosote at their bases, on each pebble at the side of the road, each broken piece of asphalt, each diamond of glass from a smashed bottle or cracked mirror or discarded compact from a woman I would never meet. And I felt more like me than I ever had, as if the years I'd lived so far had formed layers of skin and muscle over myself that others saw as me when the real one had been underneath all along, and writing—even writing badly—had peeled away those layers, and I knew then that if I wanted to stay this awake and alive, if I wanted to stay *me*, I would have to keep writing.

SOMETIME LATER I gave Pop and Peggy a copy of my story, "Blackberries." Pop read it first, then Peggy. She said, "Writing's hard, isn't it?"

I nodded.

Pop said the story started to make him feel something. Then he said, "I had a hunch you were going to do this."

"What?"

"Write."

"I didn't."

"I know, but I did."

I nodded again. There was a change in the air, a shift in winds, and I wasn't sure any of this was a good thing.

"You should tend bar."

"Why?"

"It's a great job for a writer. You can write in the morning and work at night."

But I wasn't a writer. He was a writer. I didn't want to be a writer. I just knew I had to *write*.

"It's a good job for a graduate student, too. You'll need some pocket money working on that Ph.D."

It was strange to hear him offering such fatherly advice, but I knew he was right and I took it.

That summer he paid my way to the American Academy of Bartending in South Boston. It was in the same neighborhoods where my sister was raped, but I felt at home among the row houses and tin-sided apartment buildings, the overflowing dumpster beside the pool hall across from the barroom and sub shop and gas station where a black man in a greasy winter coat stood all day under the sun beside the shopping cart that held his life.

The bartending school was on the second floor above an Italian grocery and an Irish pub. It was a long damp room, and it held four bars the students were supposed to practice on. The carpet was a flattened orange shag, the walls fake white paneling between smudged windows looking out over the street. The instructor was from the same generation as Tony Pavone. He had a thick Dorchester accent and wore glasses with black frames, his graying hair combed back with Vitalis. During class, he wore a white shirt and a black bow tie and vest, its worn hem rubbing along the belt of his pants as he talked with his hands. He was from a time and place I knew nothing about, and over the next few days he taught five or six of us how to mix martinis and Manhattans, Brandy Alexanders, sidecars, and Rob Roys. He taught us how to open bottles of wine and how to pull a draft off the tap. He suggested we keep a lighter in our pocket in case a customer wanted to smoke, and he gave us a lecture on doing things right. Especially when it came to watching the till.

"You people are the money handlers for the whole operation, you understand? So be honest and don't tell no jokes when you're makin' change, all right?"

He made me think of resorts and casinos, all-night joints where Cadillac convertibles were parked under palm trees in a soft blue light. He made me think vaguely of organized crime.

At the end of the week I had my certificate proclaiming me a successful graduate of the American Academy of Bartending. That same week Trevor D. handed me my last check. We were standing in the sunlit yard of the widow's small home, larger now, something I'd always wondered about, this need of hers to expand when her life had gotten smaller and simpler, so why enlarge a house for only one?

"No jobs coming up, mate. I'll try to keep your brother working, but you don't have a kid so good luck to you." He shook my hand, his larger and more callused. I thanked him for all I'd begun to learn and drove away, the sun still high above the telephone lines and rooftops and trees. I'd started another story, this one set in New Hampshire and told from the point of view of a teenage girl whose family was moving when she didn't want to. She smoked a lot, often late at night among packed boxes in the dark living room, her family asleep upstairs. In the last writing session, she was drawing deeply on her Kool, its tip a bright ember she was thinking of putting to dry cardboard.

Rent was due and there was only a month left before I was to drive west for studies I was no longer pulled toward, so I left my apartment in Lynn and moved in with Pop, Peggy, Cadence, and Nicole. He gave me the spare room on the first floor, the same one he and I had broken into when he lived here with his second wife, Lorraine leaning against the doorframe in her nightgown, smoking, waiting for us. Except for those two weeks between women when he'd stayed with us on Columbia Park and slept in my room, I hadn't lived in the same space with him since I was a boy in the woods of New Hampshire. It was strange to share a house with him; I felt like some hovering ghost of the boy I had been.

Soon enough I owned a black vest and bow tie, a white shirt and black nylon pants and black shoes, all of which I'd bought in pieces in strip malls. I'd gotten a bartending job working for a small catering company who did private parties for people wealthy enough to cater parties. They were in Boston in neighborhoods where surgeons and bankers and corporate executives lived. Except for some of the bigger houses in Bradford, I had never even seen homes this big and comfortable. They were on wide quiet streets, the unbroken sidewalks shaded by maples and oaks, and many of the houses were behind tall walls of stone and thick green hedges ten feet high. Some had security gates, and my boss—a funny and warm man going bald at thirty-five who referred to himself as a bisexual Jew—would get out of the van and announce us into an intercom. A metal gate would slide open and we'd be directed to a service area, the place where I learned the cleaning people parked, the cook or nanny, the pool men, the gardener, and any tradesmen who'd come to work on the house.

It was a dry August and many of the parties were outside under cream-colored tents. We'd carry our bins of food and bags of ice and kegs of beer and cases of wine and liquor out to lawns that usually held a clay tennis court, a pool and pool house, a lush rose garden alongside hedges like those hiding the walls from the street. There would be tables set up under white linens, votive candles floating in glass bowls of water. I'd set up my bar in a corner of the tent or up on a veranda, and while I cut limes into wedges, as I emptied jars of olives and pearl onions and maraschino cherries into their respective dishes, as I cored lemons and sliced the skins into twists, I took in how the owners were usually polite enough but spoke to us all in the clipped and patronizing tones reserved for children or the mentally impaired. It was the same tone I would hear from owners on construction sites, the surprise the widow had shown when Jeb first saw her piano and mentioned he was a classical guitarist. She smiled and looked him up and down, his carpenter's apron and framing hammer hanging against paint-splattered jeans with the hole in one knee, his scuffed work boots, the two days of whiskers on his cheeks and chin. She clearly did not believe him, something which didn't seem to bother him the way it was bothering me, and I was glad he began to describe the piece he was teaching himself, something by J. S. Bach, and he was going on long enough about it her face began to soften, and a light came into her eyes that looked less like revelation and more like guilt.

At one function, I had set up my bar in a high-ceilinged room. There was gleaming furniture laid out on Oriental carpets, and the walls were a raised-panel oak I was admiring, waiting for the party to begin, when a woman five or six years older than I came up to the bar and stared at me. She was lovely, her blonde hair pulled up in a twist, her clavicle tanned above a black cocktail dress. She said, "Aren't you Andre Dubus's son?"

"Yeah, how'd you know that?"

"I work at Godine, your father's publisher."

I did not remember meeting her or any of Pop's publishers, but a

summer before there'd been a cookout at Pop's house, a few people there
from Boston. Maybe it was then. An older man stepped up beside her. He
was tall and wore a double-breasted blue suit, the room filling with guests
behind him. She smiled up at him and was about to say something, but
he put his hand on her elbow and ordered from me a Glenfiddich on the
rocks.

While I poured it, she said, "Dad, this is Andre. His father is with us
at Godine."

He gave me the once-over in my barman's uniform. "What is he, a
printer?"

"No, Dad, his father is one of our *authors*, one of the best short story
writers in the country."

"Oh." He took me in again, a slight shrug in his shoulders, this young
man before him getting paid to be subservient. "Nice to meet you."

"You too, sir."

His daughter apologized for her father, but I was already busy taking
orders from polite men and women in summer-weight suits and cocktail
dresses, clothes my mother and father had never owned or worn. These
were cheerful people in their forties, fifties, and sixties, so many of them
fit-looking and tanned, flashy watches on the men's wrists, delicate bracelets of gold or silver or turquoise and silver on the women's, their earrings
glittering, their teeth as straight and white as the rich girls I'd known at
Bradford College, and as pleasant as they were to each other and to me,
it was clear I was being put in the same category as all the other people
in their lives who performed services for them that made them feel more
comfortable, well-traveled, well-fed, well-housed, and soothed, services
they paid for with money the rest of us would never know. And it was like
waking from a dream of rain to find yourself wet and getting wetter.

But the outrage I'd had in Austin was largely gone; all night long I saw
these people not as a class, but as individual men and women. There were
no woods, only trees.

These people threw a lot of parties, too: for a judge retiring from the
bench; for a daughter or son going off to a job in some city; for weddings
and engagements; to celebrate a promotion; or—and there were many of
these—just to have a party, as if the summer itself was being celebrated.

And what was wrong with that? What was wrong with taking your money and spending it on a good time?

There was the twenty-fifth reunion of lawyers who had all gone to Harvard Law School, an institution I had never heard of until I found myself standing in my tie and vest behind an outdoor bar not far from a hot tub and swimming pool where a dozen men stood around drinking and laughing and shooting the shit. Most of them were in shorts and Bermuda shirts, and they all wore a heavy brass graduation ring on the ring finger of their right hands. Some were tanned and handsome, their temples beginning to gray, a few others pale and plump and bald, like they'd spent their entire lives sitting behind a desk in a suit in a dim office. But they seemed happy to me, or at least happy to be among one another again, each of them a rich lawyer. Behind them, their wives swam in the pool or soaked in the hot tub or sat in the shade of massive umbrellas at glass tables sipping from glasses of wine I'd poured for them.

The men drank beer or scotch on the rocks or vodka tonics I would squeeze a wedge of lime into, and one of the handsome ones, the host who owned the massive house beside us, he turned to one of the portly ones and said, "You hear about Rodney?"

"No, what?"

"He's banging nails now."

"*What?*"

"Yep, said he was fed up with it all. He had a very healthy practice, too."

"Banging *nails*? I can't believe it."

"Yep, banging nails. Says he's never been happier."

As if the slang of that one phrase could begin to capture the painstaking geometry of building safe, long-lasting structures of concrete and wood and glass. But hearing this story pushed me further down the stream of my thinking, that those on the top were human beings too, and not all of them were happy, were they? Who was I to judge them?

ANOTHER EVENT, a midafternoon in late August, and my car wouldn't start so I'd left Pop's house early and walked down side streets, then under the railroad trestle and past the gas station up to the roller-skating rink and the train depot behind it. It was hot. I was sweating in my black nylon pants and white button-down shirt, my black bow tie stuffed into one of my front pockets. I carried my black vest tucked under my arm, and I could smell the river—rust and oil and dried mud. I was a week from leaving for Wisconsin and this would be my last job working for the warm bisexual Jew who made me laugh and told me once he was really an abstract painter, that he loved the work of a man named Rothko. I did not tell him I was trying to teach myself how to write, but I felt closer to him when he told me that, and I thought of creative people having to earn a living like everyone else. How you had to work but needed time to create. My catering boss seemed to have given up on finding that time. Jeb, too. What was I going to do about that? What was *my* plan?

Now I was reaching for my wallet to buy a round-trip ticket, but all my money was in the bank whose account I was just about to close and there was just enough in my wallet for the fare and a one-way ride on the T. They usually fed us at these parties, though. Before guests arrived, my boss would fix me a plate of whatever they were serving. He'd have me eat in the corner of a kitchen or out on a back porch where no one could see me.

On the train I dozed in the heat, woke up thinking how I was always leaving places. Two hours later I was standing behind a rented bar in the living room of two white doctors from South Africa. He was some kind of surgeon, and she was an anesthesiologist. They were both small-boned and ruddy-faced, and it was clear from framed photographs on the walls that they ran marathons together. I spent long periods against the wall between a lamp and a bookcase doing nothing. My boss and the others were serving dinner outside on a patio beneath the deck, and from where I stood I could see the early evening sky, streaks of coral and purple that were already becoming bottom-lit from the city below. I could hear conversations, too. This was a small party of no more than thirty people, and most of them seemed to be like their hosts, married and in shape and doctors of some sort. Many spoke in that Afrikaans accent I had at first mistaken for Australian. They talked a lot about work, about long hours and the difficulty of collecting on insurance claims, about hospital bureaucracy, the ever-present threat of malpractice suits, a dull conference in a fun city. They talked about where their kids would be going to school in the fall, the lessons they were taking

in piano, dance, math, and horseback riding. Sometimes, there'd be a lowered voice, then laughter, and something vaguely sexual and extramarital
would be in the air, but not once did I hear any talk of their home country,
the one currently in flames; Mandela was withering away in prison, and the
agents of apartheid were massacring children in schoolyards, injecting resistance leaders with lethal drugs and throwing them out of helicopters. Rape
was being used as a form of mass torture, and in the townships black South
Africans had begun to murder anyone suspected of collaborating with the
white minority by necklacing them, forcing a gasoline-doused rubber tire
over their heads and lighting it on fire.

All of this and more I'd learned in Austin, Texas. Now I was serving the murderous ruling class in one of their homes, and of course they
weren't talking about it. They were free of it. They were here now. They
were Americans.

The party and our cleanup was over by nine o'clock. I tried to stay
polite to whoever talked to me, but it was like coming down with a fever
at a picnic and trying to pretend you felt fine. After I'd loaded my boss's
van with plastic bins of leftover food, the trash bags of half-eaten food, the
crates of china and cases of wine we hadn't opened, he handed me a check
and offered to drive me to North Station. I thanked him but told him I
needed some exercise, that the late train was still two hours away.

He gave me a half hug and wished me luck in Wisconsin, then he
drove off and I was walking down a hill street of more fine homes, my
bow tie in my pocket alongside my last paycheck, this money that may as
well have been stained with dried blood.

It was a Saturday night in late summer, and I could smell mown grass
and pool chlorine, citronella candles and cigarette smoke. From behind a
wall came the splash of water, a woman laughing. Jazz played on a record
player through an open window somewhere, and I imagined more doctors lived there, or professors, lawyers, businessmen and businesswomen,
anthropologists, psychologists, people with culture. People who read
books and knew things. All those full bookcases back in the South Africans' house: medical journals, yes, but also novels and collections of short
stories, books on art history, music, and world wars. Wasn't learning from
these just the beginning? Weren't we then supposed to *do* something?

At the bottom of the hill were the tracks of the subway train. One was just pulling away, its windows bright lighted squares of faces, most of them young and laughing and on their way to a good time. To the left was an intersection of streets and rail tracks where there were restaurants and bars, their doors open, rock and roll playing, a rising tide of voices and laughter, a horn honking, a shout, the smells of baked flour and oregano and the exhaust of a small imported car shooting past me for Kenmore Square where I was walking, this need to move and clear my head. But being in the midst of all this humanity could not possibly clear my head. Life, it seemed, was one big party, and what happened in faraway places or shadowy places at home or in places where people's skin was darker was just bad news nobody wanted to hear.

And did *I* really want to hear it? Didn't I want to be in one of those bars drinking a cold beer and watching all the pretty young women? Maybe talk to one of them? Maybe dance? Liz had been accepted to the University of Colorado at Boulder, and all summer she'd been renting an apartment in Boston. The day before she left, we stood under the sun in her parking lot. Her hair had blonde streaks in it from afternoons at Wollaston Beach, and she was tanned and looked happy.

Write me from Wisconsin.

Write me from Colorado.

I will.

Me too.

She gave me a kiss and a hug and I climbed into my car knowing these were lies we'd just told while smiling and waving goodbye. Who was I to feel above anyone? And now I was going off to study the work of dead men nobody read anymore.

But the thought of turning away from what was written about injustice would be like turning my back on a thousand little brothers, all of them standing there with their arms at their sides while grown men punched them in the face.

KENMORE SQUARE was a small pulsing city, a place I knew only as the subway stop that had gotten me here. A few hours earlier, it was a sunlit convergence of traffic from three directions, two- and three-story build-

ings on all sides that under the sun were like well-dressed grandfathers
dozing on park benches, but now the old men had been replaced by the
neon-electric young; the bottom floors were a wall of light—slashes of
yellow, orange, and blue—a record shop, an organic pizza joint, a beer
garden and Chinese takeout, an underground dance club called Rathskeller's, an Irish pub and Italian eatery, its doors and windows open, round
tables set up with candles burning in glass lanterns, Italian stringed instruments colliding with the bass thump of the dance club, the perpetual river
of cars and their engines, the talk and drunken yelps and falling and rising laughter of hundreds of college kids back in town just before Labor
Day. The girls were in shorts or skirts and spaghetti-strap tops, their hair
pulled up or cut short or flapping down their backs as they walked or ran
across the square from one buzzing spot to another. Many of the boys
were in shorts and sandals and the short-sleeve polo shirts they were all
wearing now, blue or pink, the collars pulled up, this street gang of investment bankers' kids. There were musicians playing guitars and fiddles and
saxophones. In the recessed doorway of a dry cleaning shop, a black kid
with drumsticks was tapping out a rhythm on an upside-down joint compound bucket, a coffee can in front of him overflowing with dollar bills.
Five punk rockers stood under a streetlamp in tight black leathers and
chains. The sides of their heads were shaved clean, and their Mohawks
rose from the tops of their skulls red and purple and white, these outfits
they could barely move in, this hair that was their art.

I smelled pot smoke, gum on concrete, and the warm granite of curb-
stones. Up in the hills, the ruling class was putting their white kids to bed,
and all the world was doing what all the world did, taking care of their
own desires and needs, and right now I needed air and quiet. I walked by
a bearded man wedged into a sandwich board. He said something to me
and held out a pamphlet, a bright portrait of Jesus Christ in robes looking
mournfully at the viewer. I shook my head and stepped past him into a
well-lit bookstore.

The air was cool in here, the carpet absorbing my footsteps. Something classical was playing, something with violins that sounded sweetly
melancholic, like a sick lover has finally died and the one left behind is on
the cusp of knowing she's relieved.

Older people browsed from aisle to aisle, and I did too. All these books. Thousands and thousands of them. On everything. You could live a dozen long lives just reading what's in this one store and still not be finished. Meanwhile, more were being written. Every day men and women across the earth were stealing time to find a quiet place to write. And some had to hide what they wrote. They could be shoved into a cell or put up against a wall and shot for these words coming out of them. And I'd written that morning. Sat at the desk in the borrowed room of Pop's small campus house. I'd been imagining the life of a girl who did not love her family the way she thought she should. Who would read this? And why? What *good* was this doing for anyone but me, the feeling it gave me every time, that somehow by escaping to the dream on the page I became more fully here.

So *what*.

I moved away from books with words in them to books of photographs. They were big and glossy and the largest ones were laid out on a table. On the cover of one was the black-and-white portrait of a bodybuilder standing in the same pose as the statue of David, except this man had so much more muscle, his skin oiled and shining. He'd probably spent his entire adult life achieving that. I thumbed through the pages, saw pictures of massively muscled men whose names I still knew. I had worked so hard to be one of them so no one would even think of trying to hurt me or anyone I loved.

I closed the book and slid it back into place. I hadn't been in a fight since Devin Wallace. I picked up the next book without really looking at the cover, opened it to the images of famous war photographers, some in color, others in black and white, all of human bodies shot or stabbed or burned or blown-up. The first one I had seen in a magazine on our kitchen table when I was a boy. It was the massacre at My Lai. Over five hundred villagers lying in the ditch where they'd been shot to death by American soldiers. Old men and women, women and their babies, boys and girls, a tangle of naked bloody flesh, each bullet hole a dark intrusion. Beneath this was the photo of a small Vietnamese man in baggy clothes. His hands were tied behind his back and his eyes were squinting as if he'd just been hit with a blast of air and not the bullet ripping through his brain from the handgun of the officer at his side executing him in the street.

I turned the page. My mouth had gone dry and there was a buzzing in my fingertips and here was another man at the precise moment of his death, his arms spread as he fell backwards, his rifle falling, the open sky behind him. There were the bodies of American soldiers on the beaches of Normandy. They lay facedown in the damp sand, and their rifles were half buried and the helmet of one still had a pack of cigarettes stuck in the band. There were the charred bodies of the men Jimmy Carter had sent into Iran to rescue the hostages, the melted pieces of their helicopter littered around their bodies like a broken promise. There was Mussolini hanging shot and upside down alongside his mistress. There was the photograph of the flag-raising at Iwo Jima, another of a bandaged Marine rushing through a defoliated stretch of mud to his wounded comrade. And there was one of a woman and her three young sons in El Salvador, all four of them lying dead outside the shack they'd lived in. The woman had dressed that day in a white cotton skirt and a blue sleeveless top. It looked like a man's T-shirt with the sleeves cut off, and she'd tied the hem tightly around her waist. Her hair was wrapped up in a red kerchief, and she was barefoot and her three boys were too, none of them older-looking than nine or ten. They wore shorts and were shirtless and they must've been huddling close to their mother and she must've tried to turn them away from the shots for now two lay on their stomachs and one on his side and her bare arms lay across all three of them, dark pools of blood in the dust beneath them. On the skin of the boys were small black marks. I looked closer and saw they were flies.

I closed the book and set it down and walked out of the store and across the square, a car honking at me and others, this sea of hopeful drunk youth from the land of my birth. That family had been murdered by a death squad armed by the government armed by us, paid for with the taxes of the mothers and fathers who had sent their children to this city to learn and to grow, to work hard and become successful people who would then make money and pay their taxes that would go where and do what?

I followed the crowd and walked down concrete steps to Rathskeller's. A live band was playing, the drums louder than the rest. A bouncer

glanced at us from his stool that propped open the door, and I could
see into the happy shadows of the club—a gang of boys downing shots,
couples dancing jerkily under a light the color of flames, a hundred yelled
conversations and crackling laughter, a crowded smoky haze the waitresses moved through. The bouncer wanted five bucks and I was glad I
didn't have it and turned and walked past a line of people my age I felt
so far away from, though gone were those barely suppressed feelings of
moral superiority. What I felt instead was uselessness. I had no use.

Only a year earlier it had been easy to see people as members of
classes, as groups that could then be influenced, steered, and changed.
But I no longer saw them that way, and why was I leaving for the Midwest
to continue studying them like this? How could a man aim his M-16 at
a young mother and her three boys? What part of himself did he have to
kill to kill them? How was it possible for a woman and her children to be
gunned down while elsewhere, at that exact moment, people laughed and
drank and ate and made love?

There was a dime in my pocket under my check and bow tie. Soon
I was standing in an outdoor phone booth dialing my father's number.
When he answered, I told him I wasn't coming home.

Why not?

I don't know, I'm just—I'm fucked up.

You been drinking?

No. The world's fucked up, Pop. It's just so fucked up.

Come home.

It was *his* home, his and his third family's, but hearing him say that
was like feeling his arm reach out and pull me in for a hug.

No.

Don't miss your train, son. Come home.

No, I can't. I just—I'll see you tomorrow.

Andre?

Yeah?

*Meet me at Fenway Park. It's where the Red Sox play. There's an after-
noon game and I've got tickets. I'll give one to you.*

A game. How could people play *games?*

Maybe.

I hung up and began walking away from the noise and bright lights and music and laughter. The night was cooling. Three blocks north was a concrete overpass. It had two levels of traffic coming and going, and on the other side were the brownstone apartments and mansions of the rich. I could see the glow of their windows, the nearly translucent curtains separating the city from their cooled rooms. Then I was standing on the sidewalk under the bridge. It was dark here, the only light coming from passing cars. Across the street a hooded homeless man sat on a guardrail beside a shopping cart. It was stuffed with bundles wrapped tightly in trash-bag plastic, and hanging from the front was a clear sack of empty bottles and cans. Taped to the cart's handle was a small flag jutting out at an angle, a rally flag of some kind, the soiled logo of a sports team or car racing team or college crew. Behind him and up a dirt embankment just under the overpass, four or five men were passing around a bottle. One of them was yelling about something, his words so slurred they sounded like a foreign tongue.

I turned and left the sidewalk and walked over matted grass. I climbed a rise to the concrete pad that held the footings that held the steel girders on this end of the bridge. There was broken glass here and old rags, a white sweater balled up beside a square of warped plywood, but no men or women. Down to my right a culvert of water flowed west under Storrow Drive and the jogging park beyond into the Charles River, MIT on the other side, Harvard, the best schools for the finest minds, and I stepped over broken glass and up the concrete incline till I could touch the steel of the girders. I smelled mud and dried urine and the sticky sweetness of cheap wine. In the shadows I could see how the steel plates were bolted into the concrete and between each beam was a six-foot gap. The footing they rested on was chest-high, and I reached out and brushed away a few pebbles, an empty beer can, a rotted sock. The underside of the overpass was sixteen or eighteen inches above where I'd just cleaned and as each car or truck rolled over me, I could feel a slight compression in the air, the tires a muted rumble.

I pulled myself up and kept my head low and lay down on my back. To the left was a concrete wall, at my feet and head was steel; the only way at me was from where I'd just come, and I turned on my side in that direction and curled my legs up and rested my head against my arm and pushed my fingers between my knees. The drunks sounded closer than before, but I could see them fifty or a hundred yards away huddled in the darkness on the other underside of this bridge. I could still hear the Saturday night noise of Kenmore Square, but it was muted now, and I closed my eyes, and there were the three dead boys, their mother's body doing all it could not do.

Then I was a boy again, curled in my bed across from Jeb's while downstairs Mom and Pop and their friends laughed and drank and argued, and all across the earth wars raged like fires, and not one of us seemed to know how to put them out.

I WOKE just an hour or two after dawn. Sometime in the night I must've rolled to my left because I opened my eyes to concrete, the embedded grain of the plywood forms it had been poured in. I started to roll away, but then remembered the five-foot drop. The traffic above my face was constant now, the roll and bump over the expansion joints of one car after another. My mouth tasted like dry iron and I was hungry and thirsty and turned to see a pale blade of sun shining onto the matted grass beside the culvert. Down the length of the overpass and up the other embankment the drunks were gone. I reached into my pocket for my boss's check, hoping to see a Boston bank written on it. There was, though it was also Sunday, wasn't it?

But I had a bank card in my wallet, and I knew there were bank machines in Harvard Square across from where men played chess under the trees in front of Au Bon Pain. An hour later, after a long walk, I had money and was eating a croissant at a small table there. The orange juice was cold and freshly squeezed and I began to feel grateful for these gifts, small as they were. The despair from the night before hadn't completely lifted, but was it wrong to feel grateful for the small gifts in my life? Wasn't I fortunate to have something in the bank? Wasn't I fortunate to have a plastic card I could push into a machine to get it? Now I was eating in the sunshine, watching men play chess in the shade. I'd played it once but wasn't good at it. With chess, you had to think ahead and weigh the probability of your opponent's countermoves. You had to be cool and rational and clear-headed, three qualities I just did not seem to possess.

I stood and brushed the crumbs off my pants. There was still grit there from sleeping under the overpass, and I slapped off as much as I could. On the sidewalk I stopped two guys my age, both of them in jeans and T-shirts. The taller one held a grocery bag under his arm, and I asked them where the Red Sox play.

"Today?" the shorter one said. "Home."

"Fenway Park, right?"

He narrowed his eyes at me, trying to decide whether I was fucking with him or not. "Where do they play when they're at *home*?"

"Yeah, I'm supposed to meet someone there."

"That's right, Fenway," the taller one said, and he started walking again. "It's right off Kenmore Square."

The short one shook his head and kept walking too, and so did I, back in the direction from which I'd come.

MY BEER was cold and the sun was hot on my face. It was the first baseball game I'd ever watched with my father, and the second I'd ever seen. He sat two seats away from me in the crowd, this living, breathing quilt I felt sewn into. He wore a red short-sleeve shirt and a baseball cap, its visor shadowing the sun, his thick beard lit by it. In one hand he held a plastic cup of beer, in the other a smoking pipe. He'd draw from his pipe, then sip his beer, his eyes intently on the men playing down in the field. Between him and me was Richard. He was a poet who ran the bookstore at Bradford College, and I'd always liked him because he was thoughtful and kind and quiet. I sat beside him in my dusty black pants and white shirt, my black vest stuffed under my seat, my pocket full of cash.

Then Pop and Richard and I were standing with all the others under the sun, cheering for a player who'd just hit the ball past another player out in the field. It was clear to me the runner was on our side and that's why we were rooting him on as he made it to the last base before home. We sat back down and Richard and Pop were talking about that player, something about his record for the season, a good word, I thought, though I associated it with falling leaves or snow or rain or heat. Every now and then Pop would glance over at me and take in my face and hair, my whiskers and wrinkled bartending clothes, and I'd catch the concern in his eyes before he winked at me; he must've told Richard something, too, because they were both treating me with the gentle reverence reserved for someone in trouble.

But that afternoon, drinking too much beer and sitting in the sun with my father and his friend, trouble was momentarily out there in the streets, away from the thousands of men, women, and kids watching these famous men play this famous game. Maybe the trick was to turn it all off sometimes. To concentrate on something comprehensible, though I knew it would take me years to understand this sport with all of its rules and apparently hidden strategies. I kept glancing over at Pop. He knew baseball and enjoyed every bit of watching it. He also spent his mornings writing deeply about men and women in some kind of pain. What was wrong with taking a break from all that?

There was the crack of the bat, its splintered echo throughout the sunlit park, then we were all standing again cheering for these men we did not even know, cheering as one of them sprinted home and tapped the plate, dust rising up from beneath it like smoke from some underground fire.

PART III

HOLYHEAD

14

———

THE PRE-PAROLE CENTER was three stories of rambling brick for convicts from Canon City Penitentiary. It used to be a sorority house just blocks from the University of Colorado campus. The south windows looked out over the yard and its live oaks, the brick fraternity houses on the other side of the street, the rise of the Flat Irons beyond. The city of Boulder was nestled at the base of them, these naked rock faces hundreds of feet high, left behind by a glacier thousands of years earlier. In their crevices grew aspen and columbine and blue spruce, and there were trails you could hike to the top and look west toward Nederland and the Rocky Mountains or east out over the plains toward Denver. Over a year had passed since I'd watched that baseball game with my father, and now I stood in an inmate's room, staring at the stars over the ridge of the Flat Irons.

I was doing a head count. It was long after lights-out, and when I opened the doors to their rooms, the light from the hallway spilled over men in bunks. Some would be curled under blankets like boys, others lying flat on their backs and snoring, a few more facedown, a bare arm hanging off the side of the mattress. It was hard not to think of their victims then.

There was Harlan G., who'd done five years for armed robbery. He committed most of his crimes in convenience stores during the day, and he wore no disguises. He liked to have security cameras pointing at him, maybe a customer or two in there as well, and the climax was always the same, sticking his loaded .38 in the face of the man or woman behind the counter just to see the terror in their eyes, to feel the absolute power he had over them as they did whatever he asked them to do, which was to empty the register into a paper bag he'd hand them. One time, though, he didn't even ask for money, just walked into a store on a June afternoon and pressed his pistol under the chin of a man who looked like his father, the man who'd beat him up regularly as a kid.

It was hard to imagine anyone beating up Harlan G. He was short and a lean 190 pounds of prison weight-room muscle. He had flat gray eyes and a flat crooked nose, and his only tattoos crawled up both forearms, two dragons, the one on the left breathing fire, the one on the right getting its head lopped off. But with Harlan G., who was quiet and kept to himself and who other inmates stayed away from, we never knew which part of him was the slayer or the slain. Was it the old Harlan getting its head lopped off? Or the new one, the man who worked for an HVAC contractor in Boulder and was forced to go to AA meetings and classes in anger management, the one who, as a condition of his parole, was not allowed to travel back to his old neighborhood in East Denver? It's where the projects were, and it's where he and a lot of the other inmates had been raised.

There was Dozer whose real name was Gil, a six-foot, 330-pound biker with the Sons of Silence. He'd done time for weapons violations and for dealing cocaine and crystal meth, and the first time I saw him was on a Friday night. He walked into the office without permission, swearing, two house-rule violations already. His voice was a booming rasp staccato, gun blasts from a rusty barrel. "Those fuckin' frat boys park in my fuckin' space one more fuckin' time I'll take a fuckin' bat to their motherfuckin' heads!" Dozer's hair was a gray two-foot braid down his back, his jacket black leather he had custom-tailored by an old woman down in Loveland. I later learned the inside pocket was reinforced to carry a 9-millimeter, something the state had forbade him from doing ever again. I was standing behind the desk under the fluorescent light of the office, the only C.T. in the room, the new one he hadn't met yet, and I was weighing whether or not to write Dozer up right then for walking in like this, for a verbal threat and for profanity, but Dozer's case manager, Buddy J., stuck his head in the office door and said, "Take a breath, Dozer, and come see me right now, please." Buddy J. was from New York City. He had long brown hair and a brown mustache and wore black a lot. The inmates respected him.

"The little motherfuckers." Dozer wiped his forehead with the back of his tattooed hand. He pulled off his leather and glanced down at me as if I should've done something for him by now. He wore a dark T-shirt, his arms an endless scrawl of blue and purple and green, his throat too. As he walked by I read the white lettering across his massive sagging chest: *Riding a Honda's Like Fucking a Faggot.* On his back was: *It Feels Good Till Somebody Sees You.*

Manny was older than my father, a handsome Latino with thinning hair and a graying mustache who liked to linger in the mess hall over cooling coffee and talk about the old days. It was winter now, a Sunday afternoon, and inmates who'd been denied weekend furloughs were allowed to lounge at the dining tables, playing cards or backgammon or dominoes. One of them was my age, a baby-faced kleptomaniac named Lenny. He'd sit in a corner and strum his guitar and sing mainly old Hank Williams. His favorite was "I'm So Lonesome I Could Cry," and even if he was a bit off-key now and then, the other men never told him to shut up. Instead they'd ask him to sing that one over and over again.

There were fifty-seven inmates in the house, but no more than a dozen or so would get weekend furloughs. Not because of any infractions weighing against them but because they were from neighborhoods that had forged them into the criminals they'd become. It was where their families lived—their wives and mothers, sons and daughters and brothers and aunts. But it's also where the inmates had learned the skills that had made them offenders, men and women who offend the rest of us with their stealing and dealing, their scamming and stabbing and shooting, with their rage.

That afternoon it had been snowing steadily for an hour or two, but now a wind had picked up, and we could see outside the windows of

the mess hall the snow blowing sideways at the oak and hedges border-
ing the street, everything white, and Manny was talking in his smooth
voice about Christmas. He sat across from Curtis, another inmate my
age, a frizzy-haired, bucktoothed armed robber who liked to read and
wanted to go back to school and be a horse doctor. Manny was telling
his Christmas story to Curtis, but he kept looking over at me. I had
one foot up on the dining table's bench, my clipboard and red pen resting on my thigh. I'd just finished a head count, and Manny must have
known I liked his stories because he raised his voice just enough for me
to hear him.

   "It was Christmas Day in Denver, brother." And Manny told us of
sitting at the bar just after noon sipping a V.O. and ginger, the only thing
he ever drank. He was drinking alone, thinking about business, about
people who owed him money and how hard it was to collect at Christmastime. He'd stepped into the bar because the air in the streets was so
cold it "froze my face, brother. You know, it hurt your *skin*."

   Curtis nodded and began talking about winters he'd known. In the
corner of the mess hall, the kleptomaniac was singing "Blue Eyes Crying
in the Rain," his voice high and plaintive, and Dozer was laughing too
hard as he won a hand, and Manny cut Curtis off about the ice storm that
had sealed a canyon in Curtis's youth. Manny kept talking: "It's Christmas, but the bar is full, man, full of sad-assed players like me." It was
warm and dark as a cave, and Freddy Fender was on the jukebox, and the
bartender was an older woman with big breasts she didn't mind showing
off in a low-cut sweater, two Santa earrings swinging at each ear. Manny
ordered another V.O. and ginger and was fishing in his pocket for some
cash when a man behind him jumped up from a table and ran outside.
From where he sat, Manny could see the whole scene out the oval window
of the front door, as if it had been framed like that just for him. And he
knew the man who'd rushed out to the street. It was Little Junior, a punk
in the neighborhood who was into everything but his own business. He
was small and always packing heat, and now he was pointing his finger an
inch from a big man's face, a black man Manny had seen around for years.
Manny turned to the barmaid who'd just finished mixing his drink, setting it on the bar in front of him, when four shots thumped through the

air outside and Manny turned to see through the oval frame Little Junior falling away, the black man out of sight.

"We all went out there. You know, we stood around Little Junior just looking at him 'cause he was gone, brother. You didn't have to take his pulse or nothing."

Little Junior lay flat on his back, his arms and legs spread like he was going to make a snow angel. Only there was no snow, just the frozen air, and all four shots had ripped through his chest and now Manny was getting to the end of his story, the point that made him tell us in the first place.

"There was steam rising out of them holes, man. You could see it coming out of him." Manny looked from Curtis to me. He shook his head. "I know that was the heat of his body, but it was Christmas Day, brother, so I seen that as his soul, Little Junior's dirty little soul, rising up over us all."

THERE WAS Brendan D., a recovering coke addict who'd done five years for possession and for stealing thousands and thousands of dollars to buy that white powder he could no longer go a day without. He was born the same year I was and had grown up the son of a banker. He was raised in a shiny world of shiny things, he said, and it was at his private high school on acres of protected green that he discovered the rush of snorting white lines up his nose that put him in a soft white world where everything made sense and he was never at a loss for words.

"I just couldn't not be high anymore." Brendan told me this on a Wednesday or Thursday night after all the counseling sessions and recovery meetings were through. I was making my rounds, and he stood near his bunk folding clothes he'd just pulled from the center's dryer down in the basement. He was in a white T-shirt and institutional green pajama bottoms, a pair he must've gotten in rehab somewhere. His roommate, Hernando, was taking a shower in the bathroom down the hall. These were the last two on my head-count sheet, so I leaned my shoulder against the doorjamb and waited for Hernando.

"These meetings keep reminding me of that, Andre. Sometimes you forget."

I asked Brendan if he still had the craving for it. He nodded, placed folded jeans on his mattress, and reached for a shirt. "But not enough to do time again."

Maybe there was something in my face that made him talk more. Maybe it was how close we were in age, I didn't know, but he began telling me how scared he was his first months inside. How it took him a while to learn the rules, that you never take a favor or even a cigarette from anyone or you'll owe a debt and if you don't pay it, you're fair game. That as a fish, a new prisoner, you're fair game anyway. Especially when you're eighteen years old, like he was, with a smooth face and lean body. That was the first thing he had to do, prove he wouldn't be taken easily. His first week behind the walls, a big con in the commissary said in a loud voice that he was going to make Brendan his little punk. Brendan turned and told him just as loud to fuck off. There were C.O.'s there, so nothing happened, but the next morning just before stepping out into the corridor for formation to the mess hall, a con from next door pushed a rolled newspaper at him.

"I thought he was giving me something to read." Brendan smiled and shook his head. Inside the paper was a shank, a broken length of aluminum from the machine shop that had been sharpened to a point on one end, the other folded back on itself for a handle. "Stick them papers under your clothes 'fore you fight."

Then the formation was moving down the corridor, men in front of him and behind him, and as Brendan walked along to keep up he pushed the shank into the waistband of his prison-issue pants and began stuffing pages of the newspaper up under his shirt over his chest and abdomen, then around the back to cover his kidneys. The formation started down the stairs and he pulled the shank away from his skin and pushed it between the newspaper and his pants, and he wanted to thank the inmate who was helping him, but he already knew that you can't show that kind of softness, and he prayed he didn't owe him anything for this.

In the mess hall he sat at a long crowded table, a bowl of watery oatmeal in front of him he couldn't eat. His mouth was dry and he kept scanning the tables for the big loud one who would make him his punk.

He looked for him for weeks.

"What happened?"

"The C.O.'s heard what he said. They moved him."

"Anyone else come after you?" I felt nosy, like hearing someone young has died and asking the bereaved how it happened.

"No, people knew I was shivved up now. There were other fish in the sea."

"Did you ever have to fight?"

"No. I've never been in a fight in my life." Brendan was looking straight at me. "How old are you, Andre?"

"Twenty-three."

"Me too. You go to college?"

"Yeah."

"What years?"

I told him.

"The same years I was in the joint. Good for you for staying out of trouble." He dropped a folded towel on his mattress beside the small neat pile of what he wore and used, and I wanted to tell him about trouble, that I hadn't stayed out of it. Not at all.

ALAN D. called the inmates many things: animals, nut jobs, whackos, bad people. He was tall and broad-shouldered and wore brightly colored sweaters over his shirts, the collar tucked in close to his throat. He worked the day shift and always had a big smile for me when I came in to relieve him at 4:45 p.m. He'd shake my hand, then shut both office doors to brief me on anyone I should keep an eye on. Unlike the case managers whose job it was to counsel inmates, our job was to keep them in line. At least that's how Alan saw it. When he spoke of the inmates, it was with a tone I remembered hearing as a kid from some of the cops back in Haverhill, that we were low-lifes, punks, and scum. Alan used that tone even when he talked *to* them, even the very dangerous like Dozer and Harlan G., both of whom would give him a look he didn't seem to see, that they were very much looking forward to the day or night they'd find him outside of this place, outside of his job, outside of their parole. A day they were counting on coming.

"THE INMATES like you too much." Duane was the director of this half-way house and the even bigger one in Denver. He weighed over 350 pounds and wore ties under v-necked sweaters that strained at his chest, shoulders, and gut. He had a whiskey-raw voice, and there was a haunted and intelligent light in his eyes above cheeks of broken purple capillaries. It was Monday, my off day, and he'd called me to come see him for a quick chat. We were in his office on the second floor. He sat behind his desk leaning back in an upholstered chair, and from where I sat in front of him I could see outside his window the bare branches of an oak tree, the pitched roof of a frat house on the other side of the street.

"Is that not good?"

Duane laughed. "No, that is not good. These are cons, kid. Once they get close, they'll con you. You want them to respect you, not like you."

But I found myself liking *them*, these people who'd done terrible things. "So what do I do?"

"You need to stop acting like you're one of them."

Heat crawled up my face and forehead; it was as if I were standing naked on a city street. "All right."

"That's all. It's your day off. Go have some fun."

I thanked him and shook his hand and left his office. At the base of the stairwell, Old Frances was dusting the treads, a hump in her back. She smiled up at me as I passed, this woman who'd been beaten and terrorized by her husband for three decades until one summer night she finally broke and took one of his many handguns, walked up to him as he sat at the dinner table, and shot him five times in the face.

Alan D. would call her a murderer, and legally speaking—and maybe even morally speaking—he was right. But as I smiled back at Frances, something I was going to have to stop doing so regularly now, I knew I didn't see her quite that way; I saw a woman who'd been hurt and hurt and hurt till she was so full of it she could only do two things: die of it, or push it all back out into the face of another. It was a nearly unavoidable flow of bad feeling, and as I stepped out into the cool spring air of this city in the foothills, I knew that's what joined me to these offenders, that shared ability to turn a wound into a wounding, one that might even kill another, the one who deserved it.

I HAD another job, too. On my off days and nights I worked for a private investigator who sometimes brought in wanted men for the bounty on

their heads. For this work he used more than one name and months earlier had given me a new one. It's what I used when he introduced me in
meetings with state and federal agents in a high-rise building in Denver.
It's where the U.S. marshalls all looked in shape and wore crisp shirts and
expensive ties, well-oiled handguns clipped to their belts above ironed
pants. The agents from the New York office of the DEA wore sweaters
or open-collared shirts, and they talked fast and chewed gum and one of
them kept looking me up and down, this twenty-three-year-old in corduroys and a leather jacket, this kid my boss introduced as his "associate."
The CBI agent was undercover, a big Latino in a dark T-shirt, his arms
wrapped in tattoos, and he sometimes glanced over at me in these meetings as if I were a potted plant in the corner somebody should water but
not him.

I didn't like my new name. It was monosyllabic and too common,
but I was glad to have it. My boss had a few aliases, but his real name was
Christof. At thirty-five he was over six feet and a sloping 230 pounds. He
wore a thick Western mustache and had dark circles under his eyes from
kidney damage he'd suffered in a car accident years before, and he lived
in the canyons above Boulder and drove a 1953 black Buick Skylark he'd
named Beulah.

I'd met him at the center where we both watched over men like Dozer
and Manny and Harlan G. Christof was friends with the supervisor, and
he'd asked him for a few shifts a week. We both started as correctional
technicians the same night. Christof probably needed the extra income,
or was keeping an eye on an inmate involved in a case he was working
on, I didn't know. But I liked how directly he spoke to everyone, how he
looked people in the eye deeper than anyone I'd ever seen before. This
made some people nervous, including me, but especially Alan D.

Briefing me and Christof in the closed office, Alan D. had a hard
time looking straight at him. Cristof would already be leaning back in the
chair at the main desk, a damp mukluk crossed over one knee, and he'd
give Alan his entire attention, his eyes narrowed slightly above those dark
rings above that thick mustache and pursed lips. Then he'd nod his head,
and Alan would turn to me and his cheeks would flush as if he'd just been
revealed in some way.

Christof gave the inmates that direct gaze too. It was a look that said he knew what they were capable of, both the good and the bad, but he also knew they could grow free of the bad, could rise to the higher parts of themselves he was seeing too. This seemed to scare the shit out of them. Most had a hard time looking him in the eye, and they'd sign in quickly at the half-door of the front office and head to their rooms. But I noticed, too, that on the nights he worked, far more inmates than usual dropped by. They'd knock on the door casing or stand there quietly before asking about their latest chore assignment or the time of their next case manager or AA meeting, or when they were to meet again with their P.O. down in Denver. These were questions most of them had the answer to already, and he would invite them into the office and have them sit on the chair in the corner facing him. He'd give them that look and start asking questions about their lives, and even cons like Harlan G. would start talking about being a kid again, just a kid who never thought this is what he would have become.

I'd leave the office around then because I knew what was coming next. Christof would pull his chair closer. His voice would deepen and he would get them to keep looking at his face and he'd somehow take them to places inside themselves that were broken and had been left like that for far too long. Sometimes I'd stand just outside the office and listen. It was hard to hear the actual words, but the sounds were clear; Christof's voice would be low, careful, and focused, the inmate's resisting, often defiant, a tone that seemed to have inherent flaws in it, fissures Christof moved into until there was a pause, then a yielding, then the inmate's voice would become higher and anguished, as if a small boy had been buried for years beneath the muscle and scarred flesh of a man who had finally turned around to see him standing there, looking up at him, waiting.

Later, I'd see a change in these people. It was subtle but the very air around them appeared cleaner and lighter, and they moved through it with a newly discovered purpose I could only call hope. Old Frances, the woman who'd shot her husband in the face, said Christof was a godly man, that God was talking through him.

I didn't know much about God, but I was learning more about mysteries. This came largely in the form of images, those in my daily writing, and those in the waking world that for me now were rarely as clear as the ones I dreamed. But I was learning, too, that some images on the page are mirages, that you can work hard as ever to make them real, reaching for the right words which are always the truest words, and still what you've written is some kind of lie, though you've told it well; I'd want to write about a man on a job site, but an old woman on the street would show up instead. I'd barely see her at all, just feel her outside the walls of the house my character was building, and I began to learn that that's where the story was, with that old woman I didn't even want to write about. I began to learn that some images were simply projections of what I hoped to write, and that what *I* wanted was completely beside the point anyway, that these things had a destiny of their own and my job was to *find* them. It took a while for me to start seeing it this way, and I resisted for this meant cutting weeks or months of work; but more than that, it meant falling into the unknown.

But it's what I'd done on my fourth day in Madison, Wisconsin. I walked to the office of the man who ran the department of Marxist social science, and I quit.

I drove straight to Austin and spent three weeks living with Kourosh in a small house he was renting not far from campus. I'd write every morning, then walk to the gym and lift weights, but it was different now. I didn't think much anymore about having to fight anyone. Fear and rage used to help me push that iron bar off my chest, but now it was just a good way to sweep all those words and sentences out of my head. The harder I worked in the gym, the emptier my head got, and the next morning seemed to go better. Writing was becoming as ingrained a habit as workouts, a private and necessary thing I had to do, but I did not see this as my work or my purpose. I didn't even appear to be any good at it, and whenever Kourosh asked me what I was doing with my life, I'd shrug my shoulders and say, "Man nehmiedoonam." I do not know.

I kept thinking of Liz in Colorado, kept seeing her under the sun in that parking lot in Boston. That night I called her, told her I missed her, asked if I could come see her awhile. Her tone went from cheerful to guarded to reluctantly yielding, but she said I could come stay with her and her roommate till I found a place of my own.

Six months later, Liz had dropped out and moved to California and I was living in a motel in the shadow of the Flat Irons working for Christof. There was the feeling I'd displaced her, had shown up and derailed her dream of getting educated in the Western mountains. In that time we drank too much, didn't talk enough, took refuge too often in our warm bodies till they cooled, her sweet roommate forgotten.

My room at the motel had a desk, a bed, a shower and toilet. No TV or radio. No shelves or pictures on the wall. I bought a coffeemaker that brewed one cup at a time, and each morning I'd drip some and stare out my window at the back of the pancake house, its blue dumpster set against a graying plank fence. On the other side was the street, the traffic slow and easy, beyond that a shopping plaza, then a rise of ground where split-level homes were set into the aspens and columbine, then the steep climb of the Flat Irons, these massive slabs of stone under a cold blue sky.

I'd pull the musty curtain closed and sit and sharpen my pencil and stare at what I'd written the day before. So much of this seemed to be staring, waiting really, waiting for something true, no matter how small, to reveal itself. I'd write the wrong words, the false or slightly false, and nothing substantial would come. I'd cross it out, this act of cutting a gesture of good faith that somehow summoned the glimpse of something real: the front tire of a red tricycle, a woman hanging up the receiver in a phone booth, a car pulling too fast out of a driveway— then there were only a few seconds to find the words to catch those images before they faded and I'd be left staring again. But if I caught one, then that thing led to the next to the next and some days it was hard to stop though I knew I had to; there should be something left in the well for the following day.

Ever since I was a boy running from other boys, I'd been making myself into a man who did not flee, a man who planted his feet and waited for that moment when throwing a punch was the only thing to do, waited for that invisible membrane around me to fall away and I'd gather

once again the nerve and will to shatter another's. But I had discovered a
new membrane now. The one between what we think and what we see,
between what we believe and what *is*.

ONE LATE morning, sitting alone at the desk in my motel room, I pushed
aside what I'd been writing. All my staring and waiting had brought scenes
that led to other scenes, but I'd felt little to nothing about the people in
them and I didn't know why until I read *The Stories of Breece D'J Pancake*. It
was clear Pancake not only knew the West Virginia hollows he was evoking
so well on the page, he *became* the men and women and kids living in them.
Maybe he even loved them. And he showed this by writing in a simple,
naked style that drew the reader's eye not to him but to *them.* It's what I had
not been doing. Somewhere along the way I had started trying to sound like
a real writer, something I did not see myself as, a contradiction between my
actions and my desire that seemed to put me in the worst stance possible
for writing honestly: I was staring at myself as much as I was staring at the
page; I had one eye on the mirror to see how I was doing.

Years later I would read this definition of sincerity in Nadine Gordi-
mer's novel *A Son's Story:* "Sincerity is never having an idea of oneself." I was
still the boy who could not bear being perceived a certain way, a boy who'd
learned to fight and get hurt or worse just so he would not be seen as weak.
But what did being *seen* have to do with writing well? It was time to start
seeing. I sat at that desk feeling small and self-absorbed and with little ability
to do this one thing I felt pulled to do. But this negative self-scrutiny was
just another form of insincerity; *I* had to disappear altogether.

It took a few days or a week or longer, but I seemed to be staring
at the page from someplace emptier than before, a place lower to the
ground and more open to whatever or whoever might come. And it was
an inmate, fresh out of prison and out on a date with a woman for the
first time in years. He's sipping coffee, listening to her talk, behind this
moment all those thousands and thousands of caged moments leading
to this one, and he can't keep them from entering the present with this
woman just inches away.

Then I was going back to the joint with him, living through being new in the prison yard, having to fight to save myself, even making a name as one not to fuck with, looking out for a smaller man in my cell block, all while counting the days till I'm free.

It took five weeks to write a beginning, a middle, and an end. When I wrote that final passage it was raining outside and my breath was high in my chest and I was tapping my foot under the desk, my hand and pencil joined together. The room was quiet. There was just my breathing and the ticking of rain against the glass.

OVER THE next few days, I typed the story on a black Royal typewriter I'd bought from a woman in Loveland. I'd found her through the classified ads of the newspaper and drove out to where she lived in an Airstream trailer in a brown valley in the shadow of a mountain. She had two type-writers to sell, both of them her father's. He'd been a journalist and war correspondent and had just died. She told me this almost cheerfully, this kind-faced woman in a smock and jeans, but when I pointed to the one I wanted, she began to cry. She shook her head and covered her mouth and apologized. She asked if fifty dollars was too much, and I paid her and we hugged each other as if we had both lost him, and now I was typing the last line of my story on her father's black Royal.

It was only seven pages long. I called it "Forky" and drove to a copy center across from campus, made six copies, then mailed five to maga-zines, one in Boston, three in New York City, and one in Chicago. It was the first time I'd done that. It was like throwing a rock over a cliff and waiting to see if it would make a sound.

The sixth copy I mailed to the only writers I knew, my father and his wife back East. Three days later, there was a knock on my door, a skinny drunk who lived across from the phone booth telling me I had a call.

It was Pop. "Son?"

"Yeah?"

"You're a writer, man."

He'd told me that once before and I'd deflected it, deflected the word itself, but hearing it now was different for I felt tied only to what gave birth to that word, the *writing*, the sweet labor of it, and now he was talk-ing about this new story, praising it far more than I thought it deserved.

But hanging up, I was grateful for the call, for my far more experienced father to take the time to see what I was doing and say something about it. This was something he had never done much of, and as I walked back down the hall to my room, there was the feeling I'd stepped into a river whose current was taking me to someplace good.

IT WAS night and I was back on Columbia Park again. The house was full of men drinking and smoking, trash-talking and yelling, laughing across rooms to one another through the noise from our stereo they'd cranked too loud. I was sick and weak, my mouth dust and ash, and my hands were unable to grasp anything though I was trying to yank men out of chairs and off our wicker couch. I was screaming to get out, get the fuck *out,* and I was kicking and throwing wispy punches that missed. I got only one or two men out the front door and off the porch, my face burning, my stomach rising up, then I was on my knees, my head resting against the cool seat of the toilet. I was in my bathroom in Boulder, and I'd been this way for days. It was some microscopic bug, but it felt like punishment. For everything. For keeping over fifty men in line with my clipboard and red pen. For never clearing anybody dangerous out of my house. For all the faces I'd punched.

I was tired of living alone a mile above sea level and so far from a beach or anyone who'd known me for a long time. I was tired of the inmates, of being one of the men who stood between them and freedom. And something had changed in me. I no longer wanted to be proving myself to myself over and over again. It was time to go back East. It was time to go home.

THREE WEEKS later I'd gotten back in the mail four of the stamped self-addressed envelopes I'd sent to Boston and New York City. Each of them came with a form letter, a note really, no more than three lines long. *Thank you for your interest in our magazine, but unfortunately this piece is not right for us. Sincerely Yours.* Only one of them had a name beneath that, and it came from an inked stamp, a scrawl of letters I couldn't read.

When the fifth one came I didn't open it right away. It was a manila envelope with my story in it, and I felt little about this, which told me I hadn't expected much in the first place. But I knew I'd send it out again. Why not? I was done with it.

I was checking my savings passbook. I had enough to gas up and drive two thousand miles east, to stay at a cheap place along the way if I had to, but there wasn't enough for first and last month's rent once I got there, and I didn't want to crash at Pop's place, or Jeb's, or Sam and Theresa's. It was late spring, early summer. I saw myself in Boston, maybe working in a halfway house, doing some kind of good while I lived alone and taught myself to write more honestly. I wanted to find a job at night so I could write all day.

Before I could leave, though, I'd have to work here longer. There were more jobs I could do for Christof. I'd trailed a diamond thief for him once, a tall black man in a brown suit I followed through the streets of Denver for two days. I watched him walk into one jewelry store after another, trying to switch real diamonds for zircons. I'd logged what I'd seen, passed it on to Christof and got paid three hundred dollars.

I picked up the fifth manila envelope and opened it. Clipped to my manuscript was a long typewritten letter. At first I thought it was a detailed criticism of why they wouldn't even think of publishing my story. But there were adjectives of praise, a few editing suggestions, and at the bottom of the page what they, *Playboy* magazine, planned to pay me for this story: two thousand dollars.

It was hard to imagine having that much money in my pocket, but my fingers were trembling and my feet were air, and I was running down the motel hallway to the pay phone to call someone, but who? *Who?*

I pushed a dime into the slot and pressed 0. A woman answered. She had the voice of a lover, and I asked her to make the following call collect to this number, and tell him I'll pay him back later. Tell my father I can pay every bit of it back.

15

———

I WAS LIVING ACROSS the river in Bradford Square in a one-room apartment above a fish market and a shoe repair shop. My apartment's heat never seemed to turn off, so I kept my windows open and could smell shoe polish and damp leather, fresh fish and the cool water of the lobster tank, car exhaust and the Merrimack, a smell I now associated with home. Two doors down from me was Ronnie D's bar, and on Friday and Saturday nights I could hear the bar noise out in the streets. Sometimes they'd keep the door propped open, and there was the din of talk and laughter, the jukebox thumping out a tune, a man shouting at a game on the TV. At last call, just before one in the morning, the regulars stood on the sidewalk out front smoking cigarettes or a joint, drunk and brain-happy and not wanting to go home. Some nights I was down there with them, standing with Sam and Theresa and maybe a woman I'd met. Pop would be down there too, looking for a party to go to next, or breakfast, or the Dunkin' Donuts across the river that he and one of his friends called "Dizzy Donuts" because they'd walk in there between two and four in the morning to sober up on crullers and coffee, flirt with the waitress under the flat fluorescent light.

But on this night I'd stayed in, and now it was after last call and I could hear a fight outside. *Yeah, mothuh****fucka****?* Then the dulled thump of a fist on flesh, a woman shrieking, *Kill him, Bryan! Fuckin'* ***kill*** *him!*

I looked out my window and there in the middle of Main under the dim flicker of the streetlights, one man lay curled on his side and another man was on one knee punching him in the face, but the man kept covering up with his arms and hands so the other stood and began kicking him in the chest and shoulders and head.

I told you, Joey! I fuckin' ***told*** *you!*

The kicker was my age. He wore jeans and work boots and a denim jacket that Big Pat Cahill grabbed and jerked backwards, the man pivoting to throw a punch till he saw it was Pat and dropped his hands. He was breathing hard. I knew him. It was Bryan F. He'd been one of the kids from the bus stop at the corner of Seventh and Main, one of the kids who'd sat on the steps beside Pleasant Spa toking on a joint from Nicky G., taking a hit off the Southern Comfort bottle from Glenn P.

Bryan's hair was shorter now and even from my second-story window I could see his three-day beard, a blue-black shadow of whiskers covering the same square jaw he'd had as a kid twelve years earlier. Cahill was telling him to get going, somebody had called the cops. The man Bryan had beat on was rising to his feet. He was a tall bundle of rags, a stoop-shouldered long-hair who slunk back into the bar crowd in front of Ronnie D's. Pat yelled at everyone to go the hell home, and Bryan was walking under my window now with someone I couldn't see.

"I just had to do that, man. I've been in a mood to fight all fuckin' day."

I moved away from my window and lay back down on my mat. My heart was twitching like a dreaming dog. *In the mood.* Fuck him. His day or life wasn't going well in one way or another, so now he wanted to pound on somebody. And despite what writing was doing to me, I wanted to pound *him.* I stared at the ceiling. Headlights swept across it in a flash, and it was like getting punched in the head. The light that shot into your brain, how it made you want to do the same to another.

PHOENIX EAST was a rambling halfway house in the lot behind the Haverhill police station and town hall, and I worked the overnight shift there two or three times a week. Afternoons I worked for a lady cleaning houses, and sometimes Sam Dolan's father, still the health inspector, would pay me twenty-five dollars to dig perk holes for him with a pick and shovel. It was enough to pay my bills and every morning I wrote.

Most of the residents of Phoenix East were recovering alcoholics and drug addicts, and most of them were between eighteen and twenty-five. They were the kids of broken families, the kids of single mothers who did what they could and often it just wasn't enough. Some of the residents drank too much coffee and were scrawny and smoked one cigarette after another. Others were heavy or obese and moved glumly through the day attending AA and NA meetings, working a day job in a fast food restaurant or for a cleaning company, getting rides to and from work in the house van. At the end of the week they signed their checks over to their counselor who then deposited it into the account that went to their court-ordered restitution, the payback for their crimes: shoplifting, burglary, writing bad checks, and there were always people on the other end who'd been made victims and wanted theirs.

There was one young woman in the house who kept having panic attacks and would carry a folded paper bag in her back pocket in case she hyperventilated. On the third floor, in a converted attic that smelled like horsehair plaster and old socks, lived three schizophrenics who rarely left the house. They were older, in their thirties and forties, and one of them was bald and all three had beards and wore glasses. Every few hours, the day counselors would climb the creaking stairs and hand each of them a cocktail of psychotropic drugs they washed down with a Dixie cup of water or weak Kool-Aid. There was a TV up there that never seemed to be off, and along the knee wall beneath the rafters were stacked dozens of paperbacks beside magazines and newspapers and notebooks one of them wrote in every day and night. We called them "the three wise men."

One early morning after my shift I was sitting on the steps of Phoenix East when I saw Crazy Jack walking across the lot from Main Street. For years he had been roaming the streets, walking up and down the sidewalks talking to himself, yelling and swearing. He had long brown hair and a beard and wore dark T-shirts and old jeans. In the winter I'd sometimes see him in a parka, the sleeves too short, or he'd be in a camouflaged hunting jacket, the sleeves too long, and all four seasons he wore a navy wool cap on his head.

One afternoon years before, I was walking through the parking lot of DeMoulas grocery. It was a weekend and mothers and their little kids were going into the place or leaving it, pushing their loaded carts ahead of them, the kids running beside it or jumping on it, and Crazy Jack stood in an empty parking space, his dark eyes on me. "How's it feel to be a *chickenshit*!? Huh?! How's it fuckin' *feel*?!"

I kept walking. That was the only way to deal with Crazy Jack, to ignore him, something the town had been doing for so long.

MY NIGHT shift started at eleven when all the residents were in bed and it was lights-out. The second-shift counselor would brief me on anything I needed to know, if one of them had "acted out" that day, or if there were any new issues in the air. The counselors I relieved were college-educated, well-meaning, young and white, and whenever I took the house log and shut the front door behind them, locking it twice, I felt between two planes: theirs, which I shared, and the young men and women lying in the dark upstairs.

Donny C. was twenty-two, clean and sober, and living by court order in Phoenix East. With his olive skin and thick black hair, he would've been handsome if it weren't for his flattened nose and that he smoked cigarette after cigarette and called people stinkbums. He'd grown up in South Boston and knew his father only from sporadic visits to the state prison in Walpole. His mother didn't have a car so Donny didn't see much of him. He said to a counselor once that it was his brother who raised him, his big brother Francis whom everybody called Frankie C.

When Donny was little, Frankie C. read him picture books at night. Walked him to and from school so nobody would mess with him. Taught him how to shoot a basketball and later how to smoke a cigarette and drink a few beers, though that's where he drew the line. Nothing harder was allowed. No liquor. No dope. But then Frankie C. got busted and sent to the same prison their old man had been paroled from.

Donny C. was thirteen and lived alone with his mother. She smoked too much and lived off government checks and hardly ever left their apartment she kept spotless, everything in place. Donny C. fell in with the gangs, started dealing, starting drinking liquor and snorting lines. He stopped going to school and was high all the time. Sometimes he wouldn't come home for over a week or more. After being up for days he'd crash on somebody's couch in the projects, or in a car or van parked on Mission Hill where he woke up worried about getting shot for being white. His mother never called the cops because she knew what he was doing and couldn't bear him being taken away from her, too, but when he'd finally stumble into their apartment she'd yell at him, tell him how worried she was and what if you die out there and nobody ever *tells* me?

Donny told his counselor he knew he was fucking up his life, and that he better fly right soon because Frankie was up for parole. Frankie would be coming home, and Donny didn't want to let him down. He was seventeen.

The day Frankie C. was granted parole, he called home to tell his mother and brother himself. Their mother cried and apologized to Frankie for not being at the hearing, said she couldn't find a ride out there and her breathing hadn't been too good lately. Donny got on the phone. He told his counselor how Frankie's voice was "like God" to him, the way He always knows what you're up to. He said to Donny, "I want to shoot hoops with you soon as I get home."

Donny hung up and kissed his mother and went out and partied one last time. He found his boys and drank vodka shots and cold forties. They smoked blunts and snorted lines and washed it down with more vodka and beer. They did this in an empty warehouse down by the water. They were celebrating. But that night, Donny told his counselor, he knew when to stop. That night he was going home, and then he was going to clean up. From the inside out. For Frankie C. For their mother. For *himself*.

When he stumbled home, his mother was crying on the sofa. Her hands were over her face, and the phone receiver was still in her lap. The TV was on. Donny turned it off. "*What*, Ma? What? What *happened*?"

And it was like your whole life laughing at you, Donny said. "Like I had no right to be happy for *one* fuckin' night, just one *night*."

She told him the news and he was screaming, pulling over the bookcase of her knickknacks, kicking them across the floor and stomping on them. He kicked the TV, the stereo, ripped it off its stand and threw it across the room. Her screams were in the air with his now and so was the recliner he heaved onto its side and began kicking till its legs broke off, and he picked one up and whipped it at the glass window his brother would never stand at ever again; he wouldn't sit here with him and Ma smoking and watching a show; he wouldn't sleep in the back room; and he wouldn't be shooting hoops with his little brother for God had been shanked, and now Donny's mother was quiet, her face gray, and she was pressing her palms against her chest, and she was dead before Donny was even finished breaking all he needed to break. She was gone and he'd done it to her, and why wouldn't he live in the streets after that? Sleeping under bridges and in dumpsters. Hustling his body. Dealing in whatever could be dealt. Getting drunk or high whenever he possibly could.

The night I found Donny C., I was sitting in the front room sipping weak coffee. The overhead light was kept on twenty-four hours a day and it shone on donated furniture and a linoleum parquet floor that was dusty and needed to be swept and mopped. I'd just made a round of the rooms upstairs and everyone was asleep, the boys and men in rooms facing Main Street, the girls and women in the back. The main job of the overnight counselor seemed to be to keep residents from walking off, and to keep them from fucking. Three of the five women upstairs were gay. A week earlier, one of them, a pale, dead-eyed girl from Lawrence, told me she probably wasn't gay but after all that had happened to her, well, she was now.

There were no shades or curtains over the windows in the front room. Across the empty asphalt lot was the back of the police station, a security lamp shining down on three cruisers. I'd brought a book with me and was looking for a place to sit when I heard out in the kitchen the tink of metal on metal. I put down my book and coffee and listened. There was the sound of a stifled giggle, like a man laughing with two hands pressed over his mouth. Somebody must've crept down the rear staircase and was stealing food from the fridge or cabinet, maybe one of the three wise men, and that's what I expected to see when I stepped into the kitchen.

Donny C. stood shirtless in boxer shorts crying as quietly as he could, his eyes squeezed shut, a butcher knife pressed to his throat just beneath his Adam's Apple.

"Donny?"

He shook his head, didn't look over at me.

"Donny, what're you doing, man?"

I stepped closer and he glanced at me, his eyes unseeing. In the dull light that shone from under the stove's vent I could see where a tattoo had been burned off his shoulder. His face was streaked with tears and he was shaking his head. "I've had it. I've fuckin' had it."

"Come talk to me, Donny."

He shook his head, the blade still pressed to his throat. "No, I can't do nothin' no more."

"Let's sit and talk. Bring the knife with you if you want." I backed into the front room. "C'mon, Donny."

He stayed in the kitchen staring at me over his shoulder, his biceps tensed, ready to drive in the blade. In Colorado, the kitchen and everything in it had been locked, and why wasn't this one? The phone was out in the hallway. I was thinking *911*. If he does it, I'll punch those numbers, then stuff a dish towel into the wound.

But now Donny was sniffling and walking toward me, the knife at his side like a tool he carried with him wherever he went. I sat on the edge of the couch, didn't let myself sink into it. I knew nothing about staying away from a jabbing knife. I knew nothing about talking to someone who wanted to die.

"What's got you all fucked up, Donny?"

He looked down at me. His chest was small. There was a tuft of black hair along the sternum, and his small gut protruded over his boxers. I could feel the blade there between us but tried not to look at it. Donny sat slowly, carefully, like a man with a broken leg easing into a bath of hot water. He rested the knife across his bare knee. "You just swore. If I swear like that they write me up. Two more a them and I'm back in fuckin' jail." He shot me a look. "You gonna write me up for that?"

"No."

"Yeah, right."

"I'm not worried about your swearing, Donny."

He looked down at the blade, the floor, the wall. "I can't breathe no more. They don't let me do nothin' I know how to fuckin' do."

"Who?"

"The *counselors*. They don't like how I talk, they don't let me get pissed off, and if I do I gotta use words without swearin' and without fuckin' yelling. They tell me I can't fight anymore. You know what would've happened to me if I didn't *fight*? Take these things away and I should just be dead 'cause I'm not fuckin' me anymore." His voice broke and he shook his head like what was rising up in him was a fly buzzing at his face. He wiped the back of his arm across his eyes, the knife flashing dully. He looked over at me as if he was expecting to see nothing at all.

The day counselors were doing what they could; they were trying to turn a pit bull into a collie, and they were probably doing it for him. No one in the safe, clean, and appropriate world wanted a pit bull around. But what happens to the streets that made Donny Donny? The ones that are still inside him, this young body in boxer shorts he now wanted to be free of?

"No disrespect to them, Donny, but I think they're wrong."

He turned his face to me. His back was slumped like an old man's, and I wondered if he looked like his dead mother or his long-gone father.

"No, they're right. I'm no fuckin' good."

"Then I'm no good either."

I didn't tell him any stories about myself. I didn't swear. Part of me felt I was betraying the trained people in this house, the good lady who hired me not to counsel anyone but to keep an eye out. But images were coming to me, and I was putting them into words I began to speak, Donny with a good job making good money, all dressed up and out on a date with a beautiful woman, walking down a city street at night when a man steps from the shadows to give them shit and Donny takes care of business before the man can even get started. Donny began to nod his head at this; I was talking about punching first and punching hard, no talk, no foreplay.

"That's right. That's fuckin' *right*." He was tapping his foot, the flat of the blade bouncing on his knee. I began to imagine the wooden toolbox Jeb built once for his block planes and chisels, his handsaws and hammers. I told Donny he had tools he should never lose: the street talk, not taking shit from anybody, the punching and kicking and anything else that had to be done. But now it was time to learn how to use some new tools, that's all. Not to toss out everything he knew, just *add* to what he knew.

"You're learning how to be around other kinds of people, Donny. To be in other kinds of places. But don't ever lose the old Donny. He got you this far, didn't he? You can't leave him behind now."

Donny's eyes were on mine and not on mine. He was nodding his head. Then he shook it once. "How come they never said that?"

"Different people carry different toolboxes, I guess."

He looked at me and laughed. "Where'd you fuckin' come from?"

"Beats the shit outta me. Put the knife back and go to bed, all right?"

He stood. "You gonna write me up for this?"

"No."

He looked like he didn't believe me but wanted to, *needed* to. He turned and walked back into the kitchen with the knife. There was the light clatter of metal on metal, the slide of the drawer, then the creak of one stair tread after another as Donny C. climbed back up to his bed in the men's wing of Phoenix East.

The next morning, the day staff showed up with their Dunkin' Donut coffees and called all the residents into the front room for the morning meeting. I pulled one of the counselors aside and told him about Donny. On the short ride back over the river, the sun glinting off its brown swirling surface and littered mudbanks, there was the feeling that maybe I'd gone too deep with him, that I had no business counseling someone, but I couldn't deny that some kind of truth had passed between us. I thought of Donny C.'s new toolbox, something I never could have told him about if I hadn't built one, too; since I'd begun to write a few years earlier, the hurt and rage that forever seemed to lie just beneath the surface of my skin was not gone but had been consistently directed to my notebooks. Jabs had become single words, a combination of punches had become sentences, and rounds had become paragraphs. When I was done, whether I had written well or not, something seemed to have left me, those same pent-up forces that would have gone into my fists and feet. But it was more than this; I was finding again and again in my daily writing that I had to become these other people, a practice that also seemed to put me more readily in another's shoes even when I wasn't writing. The way it had with Donny. Before this, a guy like him would have simply been an angry face I'd force myself to confront in the one way I'd learned how, my weight on my right foot, my hands in loose fists at my side. To see him as anything other than bad would have deterred me when I did not want to be deterred. But writing was teaching me to leave *me* behind. It required me to suffer with someone else, an act that made trying to hurt him impossible.

BECAUSE I lived in his neighborhood now, I saw a lot of Pop. By late afternoon his writing and running would be finished, and he'd stand on the sidewalk one story below my open window and yell up something like, "Hey, Andre, Random House called. They want your book." He was joking, of course, but he knew I was up there writing, and I could hear the pride in his voice, just as I had when he'd answered the phone months earlier, when he'd whooped like some Southern cowboy about my story being published in *Playboy*. I'd stick my head out the window. "Tell them I'm not done yet."

"Got time for a beer?" He'd be smiling up at me in his Red Sox jacket or his faded denim, an Akubra on his head, his beard thick and graying, and even if I was in the middle of a sentence it was hard to say no, and I'd meet him on the sidewalk and we'd go into the dim, smoky light of Ronnie D's for a beer.

Sometimes on the weekends, he'd roam from bar to bar with me and Sam and Theresa. It's what we all still did, though it was beginning to feel old to me, and some Fridays or Saturdays I'd drive into Boston instead, see a play if I had the money, or go to a museum or some film from another country.

One Saturday afternoon in late May, Pop and I were driving to the Am Vets on Primrose Street to meet Sam for a beer. Pop was driving, and he had Waylon Jennings playing on his cassette player. The windows were down as we drove along Water Street past the boarded-up Woolworth's building, past Mitchell's Clothes and Valhally's Diner where Jeb and Cleary and I would sit in a booth for hours drinking too much coffee with stolen money.

Pop had just sold a short story to a literary quarterly and he was in a good mood, tapping the steering wheel and singing along with Waylon Jennings about how being crazy had always kept him from going insane.

A warm wind blew against the side of my face, and I could smell car exhaust, the dried mudbanks of the river. My father downshifted past the post office, then headed north. On both sides of us were closed-up mill buildings. We passed Grant Street where Connolly's Gym used to be, its windows covered with plywood, and up ahead was the railroad trestle then Lafayette Square. It always felt strange to be on the Haverhill side with Pop, as if I were a tour guide who had to keep my mouth shut.

The Am Vets on Primrose Street wasn't far from Eighteenth Avenue. It's the street where Sam's parents still lived and where I'd insulted the drunk and he'd punched me in the face and Jimmy Quinn had nearly killed him. Across the lot was the long white building that held Pilgrim Lanes, a place Pop didn't even know about, and beyond that the strip plaza and pizza joint where Lee Paquette had the warm shotgun barrel pressed to his forehead. On the other side of the Am Vets was a lot for the city's trucks, most of them parked now in front of a mountain of gravel, and as Pop pulled into the lot I remembered Cleary and Jeb and me hopping onto the back of one late at night during a blizzard, how we held on to the iron ledge and cruised through the soft, white avenues like heroes in a ticker-tape parade.

The Am Vets bar was crowded and there was so much cigarette smoke in the air my eyes burned. Two TVs were going in the corners, the bartenders working without a break, pouring shots and opening bottles of Bud and serving draft beer in 16-ounce plastic cups to pile drivers and truckers, to off-duty waitresses and state cops, to plumbers and carpenters and unemployed millworkers. Big Jeff Chabot was there. He'd sold his flatbed truck and was buying us a round. This was his hangout, not far from where he and his pretty wife Cheryl had bought a house right after high school. He and Sam and my father were laughing about something, their laughter lost in all the bar noise, the TVs droning in the corners, the jukebox playing "Smoke on the Water." Pop was clearly enjoying the

company of my old friends—their size, their jocular good cheer—and I
was enjoying how much he was enjoying them. It was like showing him
something I had made, a drawing or essay for school, those moments that
had never really happened between us. But now he'd just gotten quiet and
was looking past the bar to four men sitting at a table against the wall.
They were in biker T-shirts, all of them long-haired and whiskered, and
I knew one of them. Dom Aiello was short and heavy and wore wire-
rimmed glasses too big for his face. He was one of those who'd lounge in
our house on a weekday afternoon, smoking a cigarette or a joint, looking
up at me whenever I walked in as if I should've knocked first. His sister
Robyn used to come around too. She was blonde and had green eyes and
high cheekbones. She looked like she'd been born into a wealthier class,
but she was a speed dealer, mainly Black Beauties and dots of Orange
Sunshine, and one afternoon in Cleary's alley she walked up and French-
kissed me as if she knew me. She tasted like bubblegum and nicotine, and
in ten years she'd be in prison for driving up Cedar Street and pointing a
pistol out her open window and firing a bullet into an old woman she'd
never met. Now my father was noticing something about her brother, and
he didn't like it.

"Is that a *swastika*?"

I looked through the smoke haze past the men and women at the bar.
On Aiello's upper arm was the tattoo of a swastika above an iron cross.
"Yep. Biker bullshit, Pop."

"My wife is Jewish. My *daughter's* Jewish."

Then my father was moving around the bar to the tables against the
wall. I stepped in between Sam and Jeff. "My old man's getting into it."
And I hurried to where he was, my friends behind me. Pop was pointing
his finger inches from Aiello's arm. "You think six million dead is *good*? Is
that what you're saying with that obscenity on your arm?"

Aiello was looking steadily up at Pop, then the three of us. Big Jeff
Chabot was smiling like this was the best time he'd had in a long while,
and Sam stood there in a tank top, his shoulders and arms thick as hams,
and Aiello's friends—one of them with a beard he'd braided into a fine
point—were staring hard at Aiello; it was his move and he wasn't doing
anything.

"Do you *know* what they did to those people?" Pop's voice was getting chest-deep, the Marines in it. A few people at the bar turned toward us.

"I want you to apologize to my wife and daughter."

Aiello's eyes were on his hand cupped loosely around his beer bottle. My father stepped closer to him. "You hear me?"

"Hey, I'm sorry, all right? I didn't mean nothin' by it."

Pop's forefinger was close enough to Aiello's tattoo to touch it. "Well this *means* something, son. This fucking *means*."

The others began to look restless. One of them could be carrying, and more than one probably had a knife, but that wasn't why I didn't want this to go any further; we'd been having a warmhearted afternoon, a place I hoped to stay a little while longer. I stepped closer and tapped my father's wrist. "That's good, Pop. Our beer's getting warm."

Pop kept his eyes on Aiello, but he let me turn him back the way we'd come, then we were at the bar, my father quiet, his cheeks flushed, his eyes still on those men at the table. Sam bought us a fresh round. I sipped my beer and wanted to tell Pop I knew that guy, that Suzanne had been his girl for a week or so years earlier. Instead I raised my cup and said to my big friends, "Here's to my old man kicking some Nazi ass." Chabot laughed and Sam was smiling and squeezing my father's shoulder, and Pop was shaking his head, "A fucking *swastika*." We lifted our beers and drank. I admired him for what he'd just done, but I was surprised a tattoo like that was news to him, and I thought it was good he didn't hang out in places like this very often.

Soon enough Aiello and his friends stood in the smoky light and made their way back outside to their bikes. Over the TVs and voices and talk and laughter came the rumble of their engines outside, then they faded to nothing, and in ten years Aiello would be strung out on heroin, HIV-positive on the streets of Haverhill, sleeping under trestles, wandering Main Street and the avenues like Crazy Jack.

ONE FALL weekend Pop and Peggy drove up to Montreal, and they asked me to stay at their campus house to look after their golden retriever Luke. Nicole lived in California now, a place she would stay for the next two decades, and that Saturday night I called Jeb and asked if he wanted to come over, cook a meal and have a few drinks. He brought his new girl-friend, Leigh, a student at Bradford, a sweet-faced rich girl from Califor-nia whose hometown was the same name as her family's

The three of us drank rum and Cokes, chatting and listening to some classical on Pop's stereo. It's all Jeb would ever listen to, these dead mas-ters he was still trying to teach himself to play on the guitar. Over the years we'd both learned to cook, and that night we made garlic bread and homemade tomato sauce and meatballs over a bed of linguine. Leigh tossed a salad and we were all a little drunk when we sat down to eat.

It was at a table Pop had just inherited from his mother in Lake Charles, Louisiana, a round hardwood brought over from Ireland by her ancestors. He told me he remembered playing under it as a small boy as his mother and father listened on the radio to the war in Europe. I remembered lying on the floor in that camp in the New Hampshire woods, playing with toy cowboys while my father watched and listened to news from another war.

Over the Mozart or Bach or Beethoven, Leigh was flirting with Jeb, winking at him and telling him about the great sex they should have that night in his father's bed. Jeb was smiling but he said, "No, we'll sleep on the floor upstairs." I knew why. Jeb wasn't supposed to be here at all. Pop, for now anyway, had washed his hands of him. My father and I argued about it one night late in his kitchen. I asked him why? Why do that to Jeb and not to me?

"Because you finished *school*. Because you don't walk away from *responsibility*."

"But he doesn't love her, Pop. He never did."

After two years of trying to make himself love the mother of his son, Jeb had moved out of their small house in Salem. This happened when I was in Colorado, and he'd asked Pop if he could stay with him for a while but Pop had refused, told Jeb he was a grown man and was on his own. For weeks, until he had first and last month's rent, Jeb lived in the woods behind Bradford College. During the day he did carpentry work. At night he slept under a lean-to he'd made out of pine boughs.

Pop stared at me, his voice sinking into the Marines. "I don't like the way he *lives*, Andre. He needs to become a *man*."

These may not have been his exact words, but they're close, and what I knew was this: In my father's eyes I had somehow found my way to being a man; was it because I'd finished school and had drifted into the writing life? Or was it because of what I'd learned to do with my fists, or both? I didn't know, but I stood there with the unspoken belief that wherever I was, I'd gotten here without much guidance from him, and if Jeb was having a hard time, why was his father blaming *him*?

I was tired and half drunk. Leigh and Jeb and I cleared the table and washed the dishes and got rid of the evidence of our time here together. They poured themselves some more rum and were soon kissing up against the table, and I said good night and went down the stairs to the spare room I had been given readily over the years but not Jeb.

A WHIMPER, a moan, a woman's voice calling my name, my arm and shoulder jostled and squeezed. "*Andre,* you have to come—" Razor panic in it, my eyes open to Leigh crying on her knees beside my bed. "He has a gun. Please, you have to *stop* him, he has a *gun.*"

I was up and following her into the dark hallway, a light on in Pop's bathroom, the house too quiet. I rushed past her. The bathroom was bright and empty, and its fluorescent light spilled over the floor of our father's den, the room where he wrote and lifted weights, where he kept all his handguns on a shelf in the closet and now it was open and my brother stood there facing it; he was naked, crying, Pop's .22 Colt in his right hand, its barrel in the palm of his left. Jeb's shoulders were jerking up and down, and he was studying the gun as if it were a problem he was not even close to solving. Words were coming out of me, my hand was on his back, his skin warm, the muscles bunching under it. I reached for the pistol, and he let me take it. He turned to me and dropped his head on my shoulder and I was hugging my naked crying brother, one arm around his back, the other heavy at my side with this pistol we'd both given our father.

LEIGH WRAPPED Jeb in a sheet and the three of us sat on the front stairs. Jeb kept crying. He'd shake his head and take a breath, then tell me how for years he'd taken refuge in thoughts of dying, ever since that first time when he was thirteen years old in the driveway at Columbia Park. When things got really bad, he said, that's where he went inside his head, to a dark door that immediately opened into a light, airy space, everything over, everything finished with.

"Have you tried it since then?"

He wiped his eyes, looked at me as if I'd never known him at all.

"A bunch of times." The last just a few months earlier. Pop hadn't washed his hands of him yet, and Jeb had stayed the night and woke up to find the house empty. For weeks he'd been standing at that door in his head, and now he hurried into Pop's writing room, took down from his shelf the .38 snub-nose and .380 semiautomatic, loaded both, then climbed the front stairs to the kitchen and walked out onto the small side deck. He pressed one gun up under his chin, the other to the side of his head. He was going to count to three and pull both triggers at once. *One, two—*

Sitting two steps below my brother, I could feel the ends of the barrels up under my jaw and against my temple. I held my breath, saw the scalding lead rip through my brother's passionate, inquisitive brain, and he told us of screaming, of pulling both guns away and emptying them into the trees. The door to the kitchen had been open, and the whole room had smelled of smoking cordite and scorched brass. He became afraid Pop would smell it when he got home. Jeb put the guns back on the closet shelf, then he found bacon in the fridge, put six slices on a skillet on the stove and turned up the heat till the air filled with pig smoke.

I squeezed my brother's knee. I stood and stepped past him and his girlfriend to the phone on the wall. I called information. I called Christof in the canyons north of Boulder.

IT'D BEEN less than twenty-four hours, and Jeb and I were greeting him at the airport in Boston. Christof had gained some weight and had a slight limp I'd forgotten about. The circles beneath his eyes seemed darker too, his mustache thick as ever. We hugged, and when I introduced him to my brother, Christof took his hand in both of his, looked down into his face and eyes the same way he always had with the inmates, as if he was seeing all that needed to be seen and now was the time for Jeb to see it, too.

It was near midnight. While I drove north up the highway, they talked, Christof turned sideways in the passenger seat, Jeb in the shadows in the back. Christof was asking my brother questions, and I felt like a voyeur listening to the answers. But already Christof's voice became deeper, more serious, and I could hear him work his way into the darkness my brother lived in.

Soon enough we were at the Haverhill line, and I was driving over the Merrimack River, the guardrail zipping by in our headlights. Up ahead was the exit for River Street and the Howard Johnson's where so many late nights Sam and Theresa and I would go for breakfast after last call. Christof had said earlier he needed to eat, so I slowed for the ramp, Jeb talking now, his voice small and high and anguished.

Down to the right a culvert was overgrown with weeds and beyond it was a new car lot, its sign lighted over what years ago had been a drive-in theater, one of those our mother would take the four of us to on a Friday night Mystery Ride. It's where I'd first seen *Billy Jack,* a misty rain spotting the van windows as he punched and kicked and broke bones.

I pulled into Howard Johnson's and parked in front of its windows. Most of the tables and booths were empty, a waitress leaning against the counter and talking to a cook in white. I cut off the engine. Christof was turned completely in his seat, one hand holding my brother's. In less than forty minutes he seemed to have taken Jeb back twenty years. In the rear-view mirror I could see his contorted face, and it was as if I were spying on someone's birth or death.

I left the car and walked into the bright fluorescence of Howard Johnson's. The air smelled like hot grease and cigarette smoke and disinfectant, and the waitress glanced over at me. She had short bleached hair and bad skin. I'd seen her around for years but didn't know her. She walked up to me, and I told her there would be three of us. She grabbed some menus and I followed her to one of the empty booths along the window. It was hard not to think of Sambo's then, of smashing ceramic cups into human faces, of kicking a boy in the head again and again. I sat in the booth but did not look outside. In the car, Christof was coaxing my brother to name all that had hurt him, a darkness he'd swallowed till it made him want to die. Sitting there waiting for them, I knew it was the same darkness I'd been pushing into the faces of boys and men for years.

CHRISTOF STAYED with Jeb a few days. Then my friend was back in the canyons two thousand miles west, and already my brother looked different. He walked straighter, his eyes were brighter, and a gray veil seemed to have lifted from him. Twenty-five years later, he's still free of it.

I never told my father about that night with Jeb and the .22 Colt. I never told him about that afternoon with the other guns, either. When trouble came, our father just was not the man we'd ever turned to; trouble was simply trouble, and who on this earth had ever escaped it anyway?

16

———

IT WAS AN early morning in July, the phone was ringing, and it was Peggy, her voice tentative. The night before Pop had been driving back from Boston. He'd stopped on the highway to help someone who'd been in an accident, and he'd gotten run over.

"What?"

"Your father got run over by a car. He's at Mass General."

My blood seemed to thin out in my veins. The air itself was easy to see. Later I'd learn that Pop had driven into Boston to meet a woman he knew who worked with prostitutes. He wanted to interview one for something he was writing. This was in the Combat Zone, a dusty cluster of massage parlors and peep shows and basement barrooms near the theater district. Before going there, Pop had armed himself; under his white cotton sports jacket he wore his leather side holster and its .380 semiautomatic. Four inches beneath that, he'd clipped to his belt the .38 snub-nose he'd bought Peggy, and into his right front pocket he'd dropped a small, single-shot derringer.

He met his friend, strolled the dim neon streets of the Combat Zone, talked to a couple of prostitutes on the corner, then walked his friend back to her car and headed home. It was a dry night, the stars out, and on a straight and lighted stretch of highway a car was stopped in the fast lane.

Pop slowed down. A young man and woman sat in the front seat, their faces bleeding. Then he saw the motorcycle they'd hit, most of it under their car, and he pulled ahead of them and cut left onto the median strip between the northbound and southbound lanes. He helped the young woman out of the car first. She had long dark hair and was crying, her accent Spanish. She told him how she and her younger brother were from Puerto Rico, that he spoke no English and they were passing a big truck, then saw a motorcycle lying in the passing lane and she'd hit it going so fast. Just now. She'd hit it.

It was after midnight, the highway quiet, and Pop wanted some help before he squatted and looked under the car to see the crushed motorcyclist. Later we found out there was none, that the driver of the bike was drunk and stumbling through the woods off the highway, that his wife had just left him and he'd gone to a bar and drank and drank, then raced up the highway on his motorcycle where he wiped it out, then walked away, this boy and girl plowing into it.

Now my father was helping the brother out of the car. He was lean and handsome. It looked like he'd broken his nose. Pop walked him around to where the young woman was. He stood there, one foot on the grass of the median, the woman between Pop and her brother, and Pop was trying to comfort them somehow, thinking about what he should do for them before going for help. A hundred yards north was an emergency call box he could see. That's when he also saw a car coming and he raised his arms to wave it down.

Maybe the woman driving that car was reaching for a new cassette tape, or maybe there was a glittering piece of debris in the road, we still don't know, but she swerved and drove straight for Pop and the brother and sister from Puerto Rico, Pop grabbing the woman's arm and pulling her away, an act which put him where she'd been standing and so she could only watch as the car shot into her brother and my father at fifty-eight miles an hour, a speed we know because a state trooper was driving down the southbound lane at that exact moment, a moment he clocked before switching on his siren and lights and driving across the grassy median where the boy lay dead on the hood of the woman's car and she was out and running across the highway screaming, "It's not my fault! It's not my fault!"

Pop lay on her trunk. His pants were around his knees. In his left front pocket a quarter was bent in half. The trooper was talking to him, words Pop barely heard because his dead mother was there, too. She was at his side, running her palm along his forehead and hair, telling him it wasn't his time, that he was going to go through something very difficult, but he had to stay strong because it was not yet his time.

Then she was gone, and Pop was lying there, not feeling anything, telling the trooper about his guns. He assured him that he was licensed to carry them, and he reached into his side holster and pulled out the semiautomatic. He ejected the magazine and handed it and the pistol to the trooper who rested the gun on the roof of the car and began to cover Pop with a light blanket, but my father was pulling free the .38 snub-nose now. He tried to unload it and the trooper gently took it from him, thanking him. He'd already called an ambulance. In the air were the cries of women, the sister of the dead boy and the woman who'd driven into them. Two or three cars had stopped and pulled over and their drivers were climbing out to investigate. Pop said, "There's one more in my pocket. I can't reach it. It's a derringer."

The trooper told Pop to stay still. He reached into my father's pants pocket for the third gun. Pop wanted him to pull his pants up, but the pain was beginning now, a black tidal wave of it sweeping through the village that once had been my father's body and his life in it. We learned later that he'd broken thirty-four bones, that both his legs were crushed, his right one so badly it would undergo ten operations before being amputated just below the knee, his left so pulverized he would never use it again.

When Peggy called me early the next morning and told me what had happened, she said his legs were broken pretty badly. I pictured my father in two casts, lying in bed a few weeks, then walking on crutches, then the casts coming off and having to walk with a cane. Then walking with no cane. Then being his old self again. He was only fifty. He was in good shape. He'd be fine.

But he wasn't. He'd broken so many bones that his bloodstream had filled with marrow and entered his lungs. Those first days there was the fear he would drown or that the marrow would drift to his brain and kill him as surely as a bullet. The doctors told us to call his sisters down in Louisiana, to call a priest too.

But overnight his lungs cleared. One of his doctors said she'd never seen anything like it. She shrugged and called it a miracle.

They put his shattered left leg in a cast and went to work trying to save his right. After two months of operations, though, it was no use. The day before the amputation I was in his hospital room at Mass General. The writer John Smolens was there. He was an old friend of Pop's, one of the men he'd shared an apartment with after the divorce. Pop had lost weight, and there seemed to be more gray in his beard, his hair thinner, but that afternoon there was color in his face, and he was cheerful and laughed easily and looked like a man who was just about to leave something terrible behind him.

It was early September. He was talking about hunting squirrels, how by November he'd be doing that with his new leg. I looked down at his right foot. It was bare, pink and healthy-looking, the toenails clipped, but his shin was pinned and wrapped, still an open wound since the summer, and I joked about all the times that foot had kicked me in the ass, which it never had, and I bent down and kissed his foot goodbye, Pop laughing, his buddy too. But I was thinking of us running together, my father waiting for me at the top of the hill, the mottled light across his smiling and sweaty face.

17

____

WAS RENTING A trailer on Plum Island. It was a beach town three miles east of Newburyport where I worked as a bartender in an Irish pub, saving each morning, the strongest time of the day, for writing. Five blocks east of the restaurant was Lime Street. Sometimes I'd drive up it and look at the tiny house we four kids had shared with our mother in 1970 and '71.

It was even smaller than I remembered it, but the front door still opened right onto the narrow sidewalk and street, the tiny yard in back surrounded by a tall plank fence. This one, though, was straight and plumb and had been treated for the weather, the house too, its old clapboards newly painted an eggplant purple, the trim sage. Fastened to the door casing was a shiny brass mailbox, red flowers spilling over two window boxes screwed under the sills. Across the street, instead of cars sitting on blocks getting worked on by Larry, there was a low white fence and a green lawn and a toddler's swing set and sandbox. A black Saab was parked in the paved driveway. All the houses on the street looked bigger and brighter, and farther up, where the Jackman School had been and where I'd seen Cody Perkins beat Big Sully down, the condemned brick building was gone and now there were swings and a jungle gym and a long slide down onto fresh chips of cedar. There was a basketball court too, its smooth surface used by men who'd been moving their families into the South End for years—orthodontists and realtors, accountants and software engineers and college teachers. The whole town had changed because of this: Market Square was no longer littered with abandoned cars and sprouting weeds; its brick mill buildings had been completely refurbished, every brick scrubbed and repointed, every window and slate roof made new, and on the street level were clothing boutiques, food and wine shops, a record store, jewelry store, and a bookstore. Restaurants and pubs stood on every half block. Hanging from each lamppost were potted flowers, and tourists would stop and have their picture taken beside one.

The lumberyard was gone, so was the Hog Penny Head Shop. Big leisurely boats sailed up the river from ports off Maine, Boston, Hilton Head, and Florida, sleek white boats you could live on but docked here long enough for its owners to take a stroll through this town people actually wanted to come to.

I knew this meant the poor people who'd lived here before had been forced out, that what happened to Newburyport was known as gentrification. Part of me missed the tall weeds on Fair Street the drunks used to live in, a lot that was now the new Salvation Army building, but it was as if what had happened to Newburyport had happened to me too. Instead of fighting guys from those old streets, they kept showing up in my dream world on the page, men up against it who only know one or two ways how to get free, both of which can hurt other people or themselves.

Some early mornings, after locking up the pub, I'd sit on my trailer's stoop with a beer and watch the sun rise over the dune across the street, a blooming lip of orange that would send me to bed. I'd sleep, then make coffee, then get to work on the novel I was trying to write. It was set in a milltown, and the main character was a boy living with his single mother, his two sisters and brother. There was no money and the neighborhood was run-down and dangerous, and no grown-up seemed to ever be around or in charge. In one scene, the boy dreams he and his family are in the bed of a pickup truck that's hurtling down the long hill of Main Street to Basilisere Bridge and the Merrimack River. The boy's father is there in the truck bed with them. He has a dark trimmed beard and his arm is around his young girlfriend and he's drinking and laughing, and the boy's mother is back there too, his brother and sisters as well, but the truck's cab is empty, no one driving it, and no adult seems to notice or care as the truck barrels down the hill for the slow-moving, dirty river. My character wakes up, pulls on his leather, then walks down into the avenues looking for a morning high.

I knew this was as autobiographical as it could be. I also thought I'd been writing long enough that I was aware of the creative dangers of basing fiction so closely on one's own life. Wasn't the biggest danger that I'd confuse the facts with the truth? That I'd feel compelled to put everything into my novel just because it had *happened*? And if I was aware of this danger, wasn't that enough to guard against doing this?

But what I wasn't seeing was a more obvious problem, that I was too emotionally close to this story to write honestly about it; a part of me felt sorry for that boy I'd been, and I was angry at his mother and father for not doing a better job of taking care of him and his brother and sisters. This anger was new, and it was a surprise to me.

After writing, I'd drive the ten miles to my father's house to try to do whatever had to be done. Peggy was pregnant with their second child, and she needed help caring for Pop, who was bedridden and in constant pain.

Before the accident, they'd moved to Rocks Village, the rural part of Haverhill, where they'd built a small house into the side of a hill overlooking acres of open field and a ridge of trees. Their paved driveway was long and steep, and because their front door was four feet off the ground, Jeb and I had had to rip out the steps and build a winding forty-eight-foot ramp for Pop's wheelchair. We did this two days before he came home from the hospital. Jeb and I lay out the ramp's angle which by law could be no higher or lower than one inch per foot. This allowed a crippled person to wheel himself up or down it without help from anyone else. We went to work digging three-foot holes for the posts, and because we thought this ramp was temporary, we skipped mixing and pouring concrete footings. Friends came over and pitched in, Sam Dolan one of them. When the sun went down, we turned on the porch light and set up a halogen lamp and aimed headlights and kept working. We lagged treated two-by-tens into the posts and nailed in crosspieces and ripped sheets of plywood and tacked them down. There was a hopeful, nearly festive charge to the air; there was nothing we could do to save Pop from what had happened to him, but we could do this. We were also still under the illusion that Pop would walk again one day, that his casted left leg was not nearly as damaged as it was, and that his main challenge would be learning how to walk on the new prosthetic leg for his right.

The first time I saw him home from the hospital he was lying on his living room couch, his casted leg propped on three pillows, the right leg of his sweatpants folded up under his stump. He wore a Red Sox T-shirt that used to be tight around his chest but now was loose, his upper arms thinner than I'd ever seen on a grown man. His beard, always trimmed, was long and shaggy, and his cheeks were gray, the whites of his eyes yellowed, but he was smiling up at me, raising his atrophied arms to hug me as I leaned down and kissed his cheek. It was rough with stubble, and he smelled like oily skin and damp hair and cotton bandages.

My five-year-old sister Cadence was talking to him, asking him about a drawing she'd done, did he like it? It was dusk and the TV was off and their golden retriever Luke lay on the floor in front of it. Peggy was cooking in the small kitchen.

Now it was a month later, and Pop hadn't even left the house. He lived in a haze of pain that never lifted and most of it came from his left leg. If it wasn't positioned in just the right place on the pillows, he told me it was as if sharp knives were slashing into his nerve endings across bone. Peggy was the one who took care of Pop, but when I was there I learned how to prop the leg at an angle that did not hurt him as much as another. Sometimes half an inch to the right or left or up or down is all it would take to make it far worse or far better, but like a neighborhood bully, the pain never quite went away. And he told me the phantom pain of his right was sometimes worse, that where his lower leg and foot had been, the actual *air* there hurt. Sometimes I'd see him reach down and pass his hand through it, this limb he no longer owned but haunted him like some disgruntled ancestor.

I laid a towel across his chest, took scissors and trimmed his beard. I lathered his cheeks and throat and shaved him. Sometimes I'd take over bedpan duty, a task Pop made easier by rolling onto his side and calling out in a weakened Marine Corps voice, "Get in there, boy, and *wipe* that ass!"

But there were times he clearly hated having to get help for this, and he would thank me more than once and I'd tell him not to worry about it. What I did not tell him was that I felt joy doing these things, an emotion I then felt guilty about because how could there be any human room here for joy at all?

In January my father and Peggy had their second child, his sixth. It was long after midnight at a hospital in Boston, and Pop was well enough to be in the delivery room, but there was no space for his wheelchair where the husband and father usually sat at the head of the operating table so he watched from the foot, and he and Peggy asked me to sit where the young father would. I was twenty-seven years old. Peggy was twenty-eight. I held her hand and watched over a raised blue sheet as the surgeon made an incision in her belly and parted the flesh and in seconds there was my crying infant sister being lifted from her mother's womb, the umbilical cord purple and wet, and I was crying too, saying, "It's a girl, you guys. It's a *girl.*"

Later, while Peggy was in recovery and my fourth sister, Madeleine, was being cleaned up and examined, Pop and I sat in a dark hallway sharing an illegal cigarette. It was just before dawn. The sky outside the windows was black, and down the street a traffic light turned green for no one. I didn't smoke, so I drew on the Marlboro as shallowly as I would a cigar. I'd been up all night with my father and his wife, and I should've been tired but I wasn't; I kept seeing my baby sister being pulled from her mother's womb, this completely formed, healthy human being two other human beings had made. I rarely thought of God or angels or anything otherworldly or good that may be among us, but in that hospital hallway with my father, I was feeling that something other than just us and our daily stumbling and striving may be here after all.

Pop looked beleaguered. In the delivery room he had smiled and there'd been tears in his eyes, but now he looked fatigued and gripped by a fresh pain he could barely tolerate. His torso was still weak with atrophy and both elbows rested heavily on his chair's armrests. He'd be starting physical therapy soon, and it was time to get him ready for that, time to build his upper-body strength back to where it was just so he could work the crutches, and later, a cane.

MONDAYS, WEDNESDAYS, and Fridays I'd drive to Haverhill and set up his old weight bench in the living room. This was the same bench his second wife, Lorraine, had dumped in our front yard on Columbia Park, and while Cadence played or read or drew, and Peggy breast-fed baby Madeleine or lay her down for a nap or went off to do errands, I'd help transfer Pop from his wheelchair to the weight bench, an act which required him to have the strong triceps and pectoral muscles he no longer had. He'd be pale and sweating before he even lay down on the bench, something he could only do with help. His left leg was no longer in a cast but it did not bend, and his right was a stump so he wasn't able to plant two feet on the floor on either side of the bench. This made this exercise far more difficult for him to do, but once he was in place and ready, we began anyway and with just the bar.

Before his accident and in the early years married to Peggy, Pop had worked himself up to a 200-pound bench press, but now this 20-pound bar had clearly taxed him by the eighth or tenth rep, and he set it back in its forks and looked up at me standing there behind them, looked up at his son's upside-down face. "I'm fucking *weak*."

"But muscle has memory, Pop."

I told him what I'd read in one of my muscle magazines years earlier, that once you've built muscles and then neglect them, each cell remembers what it once was, and so the lifter starting over is miles ahead of the one beginning for the first time.

"Muscle memory," Pop said the words slowly and to himself, the way he'd always done whenever he heard a line or phrase or human situation that intrigued him. Usually it would end up in a published story of his months or years later. One night he'd called me down in Austin just to shoot the shit. "Hey, it's your father who art in Haverhill." We talked awhile, then I told him about the gym where I was working out, about a bumper sticker on the locker of one of the powerlifters there: *I don't know how I feel till I hold that steel.*

"Wait," he said. "Tell me that again."

And I knew he'd just reached for the pen he always carried and was writing those words down. A few years later they became the opening line for his novella "The Pretty Girl."

But this time, as he lay crippled on the bench, ready to do his next set of presses, he seemed to be taking it in for his use only, words he would need, not to help build a character, but to build himself.

EIGHT WEEKS later his upper body was back to what it had been before the accident. We'd learned it was easier for him to bench-press only if his torso couldn't slide to the left or right, so we'd hook his leather weight belt under the bench and around his waist, cinching it in tight, and he stayed that way till his bench presses were done. For his shoulders he did overhead dumbbell work from his wheelchair. For his back I installed a chinning bar in his kitchen doorway that he could reach but could be taken down afterward. For his upper arms Pop did seated dumbbell curls and overhead triceps extensions, and with each passing week he got stronger and stronger.

One afternoon Pop told me that the day before his accident he'd gone out and bought a compass because he'd wanted to walk wherever he went, to get his exercise that way and learn more about where he lived.

"Can you believe that, man?" He was between sets and he glanced over at me and wiped the sweat off his forehead with the back of his arm. "I had plans to *walk*."

And now he wanted to do something for his heart and lungs, too. But what can a man without legs do? There was swimming, but his entire life he'd been afraid of water. There were those racing wheelchairs you could take out on a track somewhere, but Pop and the rest of us still held out hope that he'd walk again one day and the thought of buying another wheelchair was a dark one.

Then I remembered shadowboxing. I told him how it could wind even the fittest boxers, how you could probably do it in a sitting position, and I pulled up a chair beside him and showed him how to throw a few punches. I felt like I was lying to him, though, because these punches were not themselves without pivoting feet and legs and hips to power them. But Pop liked the movement, needed the movement, and he remembered boot camp in the Marine Corps, how much harder the running became when you had to count cadence too, when you had to sing "the D.I.'s fucking song." So Pop began singing. After his weight workouts, he'd put on some Sinatra or Ella Fitzgerald or Peggy Lee, and he'd shadowbox in his chair and sing from his diaphragm, *Fly me to the moon and let me play among the stars . . .* , his left leg sticking out straight from his chair, his right gone, his eyes closed as he hit notes and punched the air.

I'd drive down the hill feeling more joy than sadness. I had never grown anything before, never planted a seed and watered it till something blossomed that had been waiting there all along. At least I thought I hadn't. But I had. It was me I had built up. And I imagined that helping Pop get his strength back gave the kind of sustained creative satisfaction a gardener must feel, or a coach, or a father.

18

___

I T WAS THREE years later, and because of what I'd just done, a big man offered me his place in line, another squeezed my shoulder and said, "That's the way to do it," and the woman who took my boarding pass glanced at me quickly, her eyes passing over me as if she were trying to memorize something. My heart had finally slowed back down. My legs felt unsteady. I needed water.

It was a big plane, and I took my seat in the center row. Beside me sat a young woman in a Boston College T-shirt. She had long blonde hair, a thin gold bracelet clinging to her tanned wrist, and she was reading *Cultural Literacy*, which I'd just read. She glanced at me. I asked her if she liked the book, told her I thought it was pretty good, my voice still high and reedy from where the adrenaline had put it. She said she'd just started it, and she smiled and stared at my bare arm. She went back to her book.

I reached for both ends of my seat belt. I clicked them together and now saw what she had seen. They were the same size as the fine droplets of paint that come off a roller when working on a ceiling, that winter day Jeb and I painted that closed room, our accidental high, the drinking and driving and more drinking, Devin Wallace knocking my head against the concrete again and again. Covering the backs of both my hands and forearms were hundreds of dots of blood. It was as if I were exposing some

shameful part of myself, and I stood and stepped sideways past other pas-
sengers and rushed up the aisle and locked myself in the bathroom.

I pulled the faucet lever. The water was warm and I tried to make it
hotter than that, as hot as it could possibly get. I began to wash off the
man's blood. When it swirled down the drain I looked into the mirror so
close to my face. At first I didn't see me, only what I'd done, the men's
boom box breaking into pieces, the big one rising up from the floor and
swinging at me, a wild hook I'd ducked.

It was the Sunday after Thanksgiving in Miami International Airport,
its wide corridors filled with people walking in all directions, every seat in
the waiting areas taken, whole families sitting together. Some were tanned
or sunburned and heading back north or east. Others were already brown
and sat on the floor sharing sandwiches and salads from one of the food
stands. Spanish hung in the air, and Southern accents, New York and
New England, too. Every few minutes, neutral voices shot out of an invisible sound system calling out departing flights. It was late afternoon, and
on the other side of the tinted windows the tarmac and flashing planes
were still too bright to look out at.

In Key West I'd bought myself a bolo tie, its center a small TV screen
that kept scrolling black-and-white geometric shapes. I didn't watch TV
anymore, hadn't for years, but I liked the digital patterns that seemed to
rise up inside that screen like some positive and innovative future I was
part of. I'd just sold my first book, a collection of short stories I'd been
working on since Colorado. I'd gotten paid four thousand dollars for it,
and now I could afford to go visit my mother where she and Bruce lived
in Miami. She'd gone back to school and was studying for her master's in
social work. She and Bruce lived in a carpeted two-story condo in a gated
compound of palm trees and aloe vera, live oaks and Spanish moss.

There'd been a plan for all four of us grown kids to go down for the
weekend, but only Nicole and I were able to get there, Nicole from California where she, too, was earning a master's in social work, and me from
Boston. Bruce's drinking years were behind him now, and he was visiting
his seven kids and ex-wife up north, his grandkids too. It was the Friday
after Thanksgiving and outside my mother's condominium the Florida
sun shone on the live oaks and sable palms of her gated apartment com-

plex, a lime green lizard skittering across the concrete patio. Nicole and
Mom and I were sitting around the air-conditioned living room talking
about getting out and doing something.

Mom wore shorts and a blouse. She looked tanned and pretty and
younger than her forty-nine years. Nicole's red hair was cut short, and she'd
spent the morning studying, her focus still on what she'd been reading
though this talk of doing something seemed to jolt her into the present,
and she said she'd never been to Key West.

"Let's go there. We'll stay in some cheap motel."

"Oh, I can't afford that, honey." Mom's tone was sweetly matter-of-
fact, like she was stating the time of day or what she planned to cook for
supper. Not being able to afford things was a condition she and we had
always known, and I thought of her Mystery Rides when we were kids,
her ability to take nothing and make something fun out of it.

I thought, too, of the book money I still had in the bank, enough to
stay in a good hotel and eat well and drink well, which we did for the next
two nights in Key West. We found a resort on a beach, swam in its pool,
ate all our meals outside in the salt air under thatched umbrellas, and we
walked from shop to shop under the sun with other tourists, something
we'd never been before.

Mom and Nicole seemed to soak in this idleness as a much-needed
break from their graduate work, and I couldn't remember ever being this
happy before. There was the light-shouldered feeling that a kind of darkness was behind us for good, that we'd gotten through it and that from
here on out things would be better. But there was this, too: I was finally
taking care of my family the way I'd felt called to from the beginning,
since I was a boy and Pop had left the five of us in that cottage in the
woods.

And how sweet to be able to give my mother a Mystery Ride, to sit
with her and Nicole at a linen-covered table overlooking the sea, the sun
going down like some gloriously kept promise, to tell her to order whatever she wanted, to eat and drink her fill, how she looked at me once and
shook her head, her eyes shining.

On Sunday we drove straight from Key West to the airport in Miami.
The sun was brighter than ever, and I sat in the backseat squinting out

at marine supply stores and beach shacks and stretches of blue-green salt water. A cormorant swooped off a rotting post and disappeared into a thick stand of mangroves, and my face and arms were sunburned. With my new bolo tie and its digital screen, I felt like some aristocratic bohemian.

I was inside the airport only twenty minutes when I saw a woman crying near one of the shops. She was thirty-five or forty years old. She had curly black hair, and she was short and round, and three young women were comforting her. They wore the same waitressing uniform of a restaurant along the airport's corridor, a cotton dress the color of peaches, a white apron cinched in at their hips, these pretty Cubana girls asking the woman if she was all right. Did she call the police? Are those men still down there?

I stopped walking. People passed me by. A businessman's briefcase bumped the backpack over my shoulder, and he turned and apologized, a man in a blue button-down shirt and yellow tie, his cologne lingering in the air. The woman was saying, "No, they're still there, and I'm afraid to walk to my *gate*."

I was stepping toward the women. I said, "What happened? Do you need some help?" All four of them looked me over, a sunburned tourist in jeans and a short-sleeve shirt and electronic bolo tie, a leather book bag over his shoulder. The woman sniffled and told me her story. She'd just hurried here from another gate, and she'd been pulling her suitcase on wheels behind her. Two men were sitting on the floor against the wall, and one of them called out to her, "Hey, lady, quit dragging your ass." He pointed to her suitcase and the two men laughed, and the woman stopped and told them off.

"What'd you say to them?"

"I said they had no business talking to me like that and then one of them stood up and bent my arm behind my back and *kicked* me—" Her voice broke. She put her hand over her mouth and looked down at the crowded gates and shook her head.

Two of the other women had drifted back to work. One remained, her hand on the woman's shoulder. "Wait for security. They should be here soon."

But they weren't here, and I was saying to the woman, "Let's go. I'll walk you to your gate."

She thanked me, her accent New York City. She sniffled once more and grabbed the handle of her suitcase and pulled it as I walked beside her. Up ahead of us were hundreds of people heading home after sharing Thanksgiving with their families, and most of them seemed to be families, mothers and fathers and grandmothers, little kids dozing in their laps or sitting two to a chair sharing a book or a bag of chips. Most of the kids were in a T-shirt and shorts like their parents, others were dressed up. In the center of the terminal was a decorative dividing wall ten or twelve feet high and built out of glass block. Across from it four young black girls in pink dresses laughed and played some invisible game between two rows of people sitting and waiting.

Cutting through the din of all this were the jolting electric guitars of ZZ Top. The woman said, "There they are, right there." She kept her voice low, and she sounded scared, and I looked over and saw where the music was coming from. At the base of the glass wall two men sat against it drinking Heineken from cans. Between them was a blocky silver boom box, their music too loud, an audio *fuck you* to the rest of us. One was white, the other Latino. The white one wore jeans and a turquoise T-shirt with a blue marlin across the front. His legs were crossed at the ankles, and he wore black cowboy boots, and he was tanned and looked gym-hard, and he was nodding his head in time to the beat. He took a long pull off his beer and glanced up at me and the woman. I put my hand on her shoulder and took in his friend and kept walking.

The woman's gate was fifty yards beyond the glass wall. There was no seat for her, so she stood by one of the tinted windows near the Jetway, both hands on her suitcase handle. She smiled up at me. I told her to have a safe flight, but I was already walking away, this movement necessary, my body having slipped into a gear it had not been in in a long time. My gate was on the other side of the glass wall. The waiting area, like all the rest, was crowded with people heading north. The digital screen above the gate's desk said my flight had been delayed fifteen minutes. I took this as a sign, some cosmic green light that I had permission to do what I was now doing.

I reached up to my bolo tie, loosened it, pulled it over my head, and pushed it into the front pocket of my jeans. Everything that happens began to happen: a light sheen of sweat broke out on my palms and the back of my neck. My breath was shallow and even, my heart a pulsing stone, and I was on the other side of the glass, but the music was loud even here. I walked fast. My arms and legs became the air around me. Just ahead was the long wide corridor where I'd first seen the woman, no sign of security officers or police, and I took this as another sign. There was just no one here to do what had to be done.

I slipped my backpack off my shoulder and rested it against a chrome trash bin, then I was walking down the other side of the glass wall to the heart of the thumping music. It was a song I happened to like, but not here and not this loud, all these kids, all these old women dressed for the weather they'd be flying to, sweaters around their shoulders or folded in their laps. And did I hate anyone more than a man who would punch or kick a woman?

I was standing directly in front of the boom box, talking.

"What?" The white one squinted up at me. He reached over and turned down the music, not all the way, but enough. His friend was long and thin, his hair as dark and curly as the woman they'd assaulted. I said, "Do you *like* kicking women?"

Somewhere in the shadows of myself, a small quiet voice said, *That's enough. Just leave it here. Don't do anything unless they do. Wait for the cops.* But the man was sneering up at me, or maybe he wasn't, maybe it was fear I saw, or appeasement, but I'd forgotten how hard it is to stop the movement once it has started, and I didn't want to stop anyway, and so let it begin with this searing in my shin, the air finally quiet as the boom box rose up in two pieces, the man jumping to his feet. He swung and I ducked under the wind of it and shot a right into his face, his arms dropping as I hooked him in the cheek, his head snapping sideways into another right, then another, and now he fell to the floor and I was charging his friend, screaming, "Let's go, mother*fucker!*" He was taller than I was by a foot, and he had both hands up, saying, "Take it easy, take it easy, take it easy," and I could see he was afraid of me, this stranger who had just hurt his friend, who was yelling such terrible language in front of all these old women and mothers and fathers and little kids.

There was the sound of leather soles slapping the polished granite floor, the bounce of holsters against hips, a shout, then another, five or six men in uniform running down the corridor straight for us. Somehow the woman was standing beside me now. I was breathing hard, my knees oil, my breath high in my mouth. Off to my left the tall friend paced and waited. At my feet the other one lay on his back. His lower face was a mask of blood, and I couldn't tell if his eyes were open or shut, and the police were getting closer so now was the time to stand perfectly still and be very quiet, something the woman seemed to know too, that these men in uniform had no idea what they were running into.

Just before they got to us, the woman looked up at me. In her eyes I could see guilt and a kind of dark pleasure, too.

"Thank you," she said.

"You're welcome." But as the cops finally reached us, all of them breathing hard, one of them already on a radio calling for an ambulance, I stood there feeling depleted and ugly and wrong.

THE POLICE interviewed us separately, the tall friend near the glass wall, and the woman and me close to the entrance of the wide shining corridor. They wore green uniforms and 9-millimeters, and an older one with three yellow stripes stenciled onto his short sleeve was getting the woman's story, telling her to slow down. The sergeant had a deeply lined face, his skin dry and brown, his voice a chain dragging across gravel. On the other side of the woman, a policeman with no stripes on his sleeve was taking notes.

The sergeant kept nodding his head. Every few seconds he'd glance down at me. Fifty feet away, the tall friend was gesticulating to another cop taking notes, and then he was pointing at me, and two EMTs had loaded the other man onto a white gurney and were pushing him on wheels past the crowd who'd gone quiet, the four black girls in pink dresses huddled around a woman who could be their grandmother. Moments earlier, they'd looked jubilant; now they looked scared.

"'Scuse me," the younger policemen said. He nodded at me. "So that's when this one started the fight? After he walked you over to your gate?"

"Well, that's when the fighting started, yes. But he was helping me."

"But ma'am, you're saying this man was the perpetrator—"

"He's no perp," the sergeant said. "This man's a witness."

"But she just said—"

"Put him down as a witness. The man's got a plane to catch."

The younger cop looked like he wanted to say more, but he shook his head and crossed something out and kept writing. The sergeant turned to me. He wasn't smiling, but his eyes were warm and approving. He rested his hand on my shoulder. "Just give us all your information, and you're on your way."

He squeezed hard, then let go, and the woman thanked me again. The younger cop said nothing. He took my driver's license and wrote down information, then flipped his notebook shut and followed the sergeant to the others who stood in the center of the corridor waiting for an arrest that wouldn't come.

At the chrome trash bin I picked up my book bag and hooked it over my shoulder. Many people were watching me. My plane was boarding, and now a man in line was letting me go before him, another winked and said, "That's the way to do it."

I could see the respect in their faces, though others took me in dubiously. It was the same contradictory look Billy Jack had gotten from some of the townspeople in that film so long ago. It was the look Buford Pusser had gotten in *Walking Tall*. It was the look Clint Eastwood got aimed at him in the *Dirty Harry* movies. It was a mix of admiration and fear, revulsion and titillation, and as I sat on the plane next to the pretty student from Boston College, it's what I'd felt too. That boy who Clay Whelan had chased through the streets of the South End felt proud and vindicated and accomplished and brave. But the young man I was, the one who wrote daily and tried to capture the many conflicting layers of living a life, knew better; when my mother and sister had dropped me off, we'd been talking about Pop, and whatever was being said had opened up old hurts and the bitterness of the semi-abandoned. I don't know what was said about him or by whom, just that that surprising anger was rising up in me again, that same anger that fired up whenever I'd read whatever I'd just written in this novel I was slowly filling notebooks with in that trailer on the beach only miles from Lime Street where I'd been beaten up daily as a boy. And the anger felt old, as if it had been coiled in some Mason jar on a basement shelf and each scene I wrote turned the jar's lid another revolution and now the lid was off and it was the boy in me who was screaming, not the twenty-seven-year-old man who loved and admired his father and treasured being one of the ones to help bring him back, but the boy who wanted to know one thing: Where were you when I needed *you*?

This was not a conscious question. I'd be too ashamed to know it was there, for I wasn't the one who'd been run over and crippled trying to help someone. And I knew where he'd been. He'd been living on the other side of that river doing the best he knew how to do. I knew that his monthly child support payments often left him with ten dollars to get him through the last two weeks of the month. I knew he'd lived in small rented apartments and drove that used Lancer he'd bought for a hundred dollars. I knew he sometimes went months between girlfriends and got lonesome. I knew he strove every morning to create art.

I knew all these things, but I also knew he knew little about us. We children were in our twenties now: Suzanne had left her husband and was thinking about going back to school. Jeb no longer craved death and had weekend custody of his son. He was living in a mill downtown, working as a self-employed carpenter, practicing guitar at night, painting, trying to pay all his bills and go back to school and be the artist he'd always been. Nicole had moved to Santa Cruz for college. She owned a mobile home and was living with a woman and would soon have an advanced degree she'd earned with help from no one. And I was writing and living in the very town I thought I'd never return to; on the skin of things, it looked like we were all doing all right and would continue to do all right.

There was an afternoon cookout, maybe a birthday celebration for one of us. It was at Pop and Peggy's before the accident. Mom was there, Bruce too, and most of us grown kids with our girlfriends or boyfriends, our baby half-sister Cadence being passed from one of us to the next. There was a lot of tickling and laughing and cuddling.

Mom was scanning the room, taking us all in. Brubeck was playing.

Behind her was the wall of windows looking out over that rise of field and ridge of trees, and the sun was sinking low beneath their trunks, the sky a low-burning fire. She said: "Oh, I just wish we could have done more for them."

Pop smiled over at her. "They had all they needed. What're you talking about?"

"Oh, you know, I just—" Somebody jumped in and changed the subject. It may have been me, it may have been Suzanne or Jeb, but what lingered for me was Pop's surprise at what she'd said. It was the same surprise in his face when he'd thrown a baseball to me for the first time when I was fourteen, when he saw that playing ball, playing at anything, was not part of my boyhood the divorce had taken him from.

Now I was a grown man, and I wanted to tell him about that boyhood. He and I were close, not like a father and son really, but more like two buddies who work out together, then drink together. That's how it had been between us. Surely I could sit down with him sometime and tell him how it was. Surely he'd want to know.

But over the years, one of us would mention not having had something—a belt, a second pair of shoes, a good winter coat—and his cheeks would redden and his voice would become Marine-deep, and he would get loud about having done the best he possibly could. And how could he be anything but right about this? How could this frustration and rage be anything but a signal to us all that he had, in fact, nothing left to give?

But still, that boy in me needed to tell him how it was.

Before his accident, there were moments when I came close to doing this. We'd be at Ronnie D's drinking a beer, or running together along the streets near the campus, and he might bring up something he'd read in the paper, once about some local thug who'd just gotten out of Walpole and was already back in, and I said I knew him and he looked over at me as if I were cracking a joke, and I said, "No, I mean it. He lived a block away down on Seventh."

He'd nod, and we'd keep running, sweating together, breathing easily though these things felt uneasy between us. One morning when I stopped by his and Peggy's house, he had just finished the paper, and he looked up from the column he'd been reading.

"This black woman in Boston, she's poor and has no lawn but every day she rakes the dirt in her yard. Isn't that something? She keeps the dirt *neat.*" Pop's eyes were full. This was my favorite part of him, his compassion for others, his love for humanity, his capacity to feel so deeply so quickly about things other people don't let in or even see.

I nodded. "I used to rake our dirt yard, too."

"No you didn't."

"Yeah, I did. On Lime Street." That tiny yard of dried earth I would sometimes rake clean after sweeping the concrete stoop, the dirt rising against the plank fence I'd nailed shut.

"You're exaggerating. You had *grass.*"

We were headed to a place where only hurt feelings could surface, both of us misunderstood, a universal human plight, it seemed. I changed the subject. But I told myself that he and I would have to talk openly about this one day. And what *was* this anyway?

On one run together, we were talking about his time in the Marines, how much he admired the D.I.'s, how they could stay up all night drinking and playing cards, then kick everyone's asses out of bed before dawn to hump hills for fifteen miles in full gear under a cruel sun.

"I needed that. They made a man of me." He glanced over at me. "Joining the track team was your Marines."

I nodded, taking this in, but it felt off to me. He was talking about becoming a man, about severing that cord between the boy you were and the man you must be. I'd studied enough to know that cultures throughout history had devised rites of passage for this, elaborate rituals where the men in the community would take the sons away from the women and girls and younger children, where the boys would be put through physical pain of some sort, a praying of some sort, a joining of sons and fathers and grandfathers back through time. In modern America, there were no rites of passage like this. But there was the Marine Corps, and other arms of the military. There were the team sports I'd mostly had nothing to do with, and there was stepping into your fear instead of running from it; there was learning to break that membrane around another's face and head. There was learning how to fight the sons and fathers and grandfathers back through time.

That scared and crying woman had been the perfect opportunity to take this out on a man, for all I knew, who had a story to tell as well; she had seemed genuinely shaken and frightened, but I never even gave those two men a chance to talk. Who's to say she wasn't delusional in some way? Or paranoid? Maybe it hadn't happened the way she said it had. And even if it had happened just as she'd described, how had my putting a man in the hospital helped anything? If he truly *was* a woman beater, now he would fly home even angrier than he was before. For I'd learned this much about physical violence: One hurt demanded another.

I was still in the airplane's bathroom. The faucet lever had shut off again and I pushed it one more time. I ran hot water along my forearms and hands, clean now, no sign of blood anywhere. I'd been staring at my face the way I'd done years earlier when I was fourteen, my brother bleeding in the kitchen, his teacher girlfriend and our mother tending to him after having been called a fucking whore. I'd told my face what I'd told it, and now I was telling it something else.

You should've just walked her to the gate, that's it. And don't think you did any of this for her because you didn't. You did it for you. And you need to stop. You need to stop doing this.

19

—

SUZANNE AND I were living together back in the South End of New-buryport. It was a hot, dry summer, and we lived at the foot of Federal Street across from the Tannery, an L of mill buildings that had been boarded up when we lived here as kids but was now a thriving plaza of boutiques and shops and a dance studio. Late-model cars filled the parking area, and in the air was the hopeful charge of commerce and innovation and a hard-earned well-being.

Pop's third marriage had ended the winter before. Peggy had moved out with the girls, so now Suzanne was taking care of him full-time and he was paying her enough to live on until she found something else. Suzanne and I had been roommates for a year. I was still working at the Irish pub, and all summer long my older sister had been depressed. When she wasn't working, she kept playing Mozart's *Requiem* over and over again. She'd listen to it curled up on her bed in her shade-darkened room, the revolving fan blowing wherever it blew.

I thought this was a deep and honest way to be depressed, much deeper and more honest than the novel I'd been working on for over two years. It was called *Lie Down and Make Angels,* and for months I'd been dreading going to it daily. I told myself this was because the story kept bringing me back to some bleak years from my own life, that's all, but one bright August morning I couldn't write another word before reading the entire thing from the start. I had the windows open but no fan. About two hours into my reading, I began to sweat, and it wasn't just the hot, stale air of my room. Down on the street an occasional car drove by. A delivery truck or van would pull into the Tannery parking lot, its brakes squeaking. There were voices calling to one another, the cry of a gull, the smell of asphalt and the Merrimack and the ocean. Living things and dead things.

From behind Suzanne's door came the barely muffled chorus of women, their voices high and strident, then urgent and accusatory, a string section sweeping in like scythes and cutting them down like wheat. Or maybe the women were doing the wielding and the cutting. I didn't know. What I did know is that this novel was dead and I had killed it. I'd been trying too hard to *say* something—about poverty, about over-whelmed single mothers, about absent fathers and tough neighborhoods and all the trouble that could be found there, but most of all I'd been try-ing to make the reader feel sorry for the children, especially the teenage boy I'd based solely on me. I'd been talking and talking but not listening. The result were scenes that did not ring true, characters who felt more like marionettes than people, a story whose rising arc felt contrived and predictable and false.

The room was a cell, and I pulled off my T-shirt and began to pace. A sick sweat began to roll down my back, and I made myself read more. Scenes I'd thought I'd liked, I now despised. Sentences I had worked and worked and worked were built on a foundation of lies. Why hadn't I seen this sooner? How could I have not known how rigidly I'd been trying to control this story from its very first line?

In Suzanne's room, buffeting violins pushed the chorus of women out onto a precipice; they were calling *Rex! Rex!* In the heart of it a woman screamed. It was off-key and I hadn't heard it before, and now the chorus seemed to retreat, calling lower and with less urgency, as if they were los-ing their resolve, but the woman screamed louder, a shriek this time, and I dropped my notebook and stepped to my window and slid up the screen. At the bottom of the street, across from the antiques dealer's shop, a man was pulling a woman by her hair onto the sidewalk. She was crying and had both hands around his wrists and he was yelling and swearing, spit flying. He yanked her hard and I lost sight of them around the corner of the house, then I was running through Mozart's final work, a polyphony of rising and falling voices, both male and female, one wielding a sword that were the slicing notes of a violin, and I was out in the sun and off our deck, taking the wooden stairs barefoot and two at once, running down the hot sidewalk, grit under my feet. In the window of the antiques shop, the owner stood next to a woman, both of them watching something play out around the corner of the building I had not yet reached. The woman's hand was pressed to her mouth.

Don't hurt anyone. Don't hurt anyone.

Fifty feet down the sidewalk the woman sat crying on the concrete, her long hair gripped in the yelling man's fist. He wore frayed cutoff jeans and was shirtless, his arms shadowed with tattoos, and I was still running, calling to him to back off, "Back off!"

He punched her in the face, her eyes a squint, a whimper coming out of her. Still, there was this voice: *Just get him off her.* He punched her again, this barefoot woman in a blue T-shirt and white shorts and long, white legs. Her eyes were squeezed shut and blood sprang from her nose and when I finally reached him and grabbed his shoulders and yanked him back, even then came the voice, *Just hold him so she can get away.* But touching him did something to me, his body healthy and unhurt while hers was not, and so when he swung around to see who had interrupted him, I planted my feet and tore through that membrane that separated us, and he soon became far bloodier than she was and he stumbled away, then ran, his long stringy hair swaying dully under the sun.

I moved to the woman and helped her up. She was crying softly, blood and snot across her lips. She wiped them with the back of her arm. She tucked her hair behind her ears and started walking in the direction she'd come from. I tried to keep up beside her. I told her to call the cops, to get some help. She screamed, "Get the fuck *away* from me!" And she ran across Federal Street and past the antiques shop and kept going. In front of the store, the owner was smiling widely. He called out, "Hey, *Rocky*. Good job. Good *job*."

But I was already walking fast up the sidewalk under the sun. The concrete was an iron under my feet. My shoulder ached. Did it bother the shopkeeper that he had done nothing but watch? Or did he simply tell himself it was none of his business and he could get hurt? Maybe he'd called the cops and was waiting for them. What was wrong with that?

But no, somebody should have at least kept that man from punching that woman in the face. And why not me? *Because you hit him and hit him because you could and because it felt good to let go of all the bad feeling that came from seeing a woman punched in the face, but admit it, your novel is dead and somebody must pay and how sweet to have had a wife beater in the neighborhood today. How fortuitous really.*

From Suzanne's window drifted a slow-building duet, a conversation between a man and a woman, each of them, it seemed, looking down on me like two disappointed gods wondering where and how this would ever end.

I WAS back on Columbia Park again. The house had never had more strangers in it. Each room was an ear-ringing, eye-stinging party, drunk men in black leather, brown leather, sleeveless T-shirts that showed puffy muscles. Their loud talk and laughter was a freight train speeding over a trestle over the river and somewhere lost in all this were my sisters and brother and mother. I was yelling harder than I ever had. I was grabbing jacket collars and the fronts of T-shirts. I was yanking men into the front hallway and trying to kick them out the door. But every single one of them was so much bigger than I was, so much older and tougher, so I began punching faces as hard as I could, and this helped a little; they seemed to leave more quickly then, very few of them fighting back, but they didn't take me seriously either. They left with smirks and a shrug of the shoulders. They left because they were ready to go anyway. I was grown but not grown. They peered down at me over their drinks and bottles of beer like I was an oddity of some kind, a kid who should be put to bed.

Now I was bellowing at them till the veins in my forehead pulsed and my throat burned. I was in the foyer, my back to the staircase, then I was surrounded by twelve big men. Not one of them was under six feet eight or 300 pounds, and they were all wearing suits and ties, their hair cut short as Marines, but in this dream I thought they played football for the University of Texas at Austin, these giants I would sometimes see on campus. But now they were in my family's front hallway, backing me against the staircase balusters, and for a second I planted my feet to start throwing punches, to create a hole for myself to slip through, but there was no way through them, these young men who were *born* stronger than I was, who were far superior physically to me in every way. I began to panic and looked behind me. Maybe I could climb over the stair rail, but sitting on the treads was Fontaine, my wife of nearly two years.

The first time I saw her, a girlfriend had taken me to a modern dance show at Bradford College. I'd never seen modern dance before, these athletes who made art with their bodies. My girlfriend and I had sat side by side, neither one of us touching the other, our end within sight down the road like a break in the trees or something burning. Still, I felt guilty for staring at the dark-skinned dancer in the middle of the troupe. But how could anyone not stare at her? And it wasn't her wildly curly black hair or her muscular thighs, her small waist and large breasts; it was the way she moved through the air like an angry spirit, then a joyful one, then one who will never need anything from anyone, some lone hunter disappearing over a rise, her bow and quiver of arrows slung over her shoulder, her feet leaving no prints.

Over a year later, I was behind the bar at the Irish pub just before the lunch crowd came in. It was a weekday, an October sun laying coolly out on the street, the pub in shadows, and she walked in with a seat cushion for one of the booths. She nodded at me and said hi and I said hi back, and I tried not to stare at her as she placed the cushion where it went, her wild curly hair pulled back loosely behind her, this dancer who made her living upholstering furniture.

The following spring Pop invited me to give a reading with him in New York City. He was driving down in his new handicapped-accessible Toyota with the enclosed wheelchair rack on the roof. He was going with friends who would be driving with him, so I went with two of mine, one of whom was close with this Greek dancer named Fontaine. She wanted to come along and take a Luigi class and visit a friend, and when she climbed into the backseat of the car, I was sitting there too. For the five-hour ride south to New York, we talked without a break. After a while, I asked her what she wanted to do with her life.

"I'm already doing it."

"What's that?"

"Dancing and drawing."

She looked at me, her brown eyes seeing not only me but what she'd just said and accepted fully as her life. There was a stillness to her that seemed to come from somewhere other than here, and I had to look away for a recognition was rising up in me from before I was born.

She'd grown up in Salisbury, the town across the river from Newburyport. It was a cracked asphalt strip of tattoo parlors and gun shops, of country western bars and used truck dealerships and trailer parks under the pines. She'd gotten her first job at thirteen working as a chambermaid for one of the motels on the road to the beach, and she made beds and emptied ashtrays and threw out used condoms and empty beer cans. Her father, who'd lived in Greece as a boy, owned a linen delivery business and a laundromat, though there never seemed to be much money. She lived with her twin sister, her mother and father and widowed grandmother in a small ranch house down a street where some of the kids at the bus stop called Fontaine and her sister niggers.

When she got older, she spent her summer days at Salisbury Beach, not far from where I'd been arrested for fighting under the Frolics. She dated boys from Haverhill, some of whom I'd fought. Whenever I talked to her about that part of my life, she nodded as if this was normal and to be expected. I'd lived in many houses, but if I'd had a home, I still wasn't able to locate it; with her I felt I'd found it, this embrace that had nothing to do with walls and windows, a roof or locked door.

Now she was in my dream, sitting on the stairs behind white balusters. Blocking my way were those giant men in suits, and there was someone new in the middle of them, a black man closer to my size and better dressed than them all. He was in his middle age, just the beginnings of curled gray at his temples. In his right hand he held a Bible to his chest, and I was still struggling to get free and he was saying something to me that I was ignoring and I swung around and shot a look at Fontaine through the balusters in the stairs. Her face was still and accepting of my fate; there was nothing she could do, and I dropped back onto my right foot and scanned these towering Christians for the one I'd have to hit, my last chance. Then the preacher's voice rose above the masculine noise of the house, his words amplified somehow. I could look nowhere but at his brown face, the dark light of urgency in his eyes as he shook his head and yelled, "You're gonna *die*."

I opened my eyes to blackness. The preacher's last words hung in the air like an echo. I peered into the dark for him, for surely he must be here in this room where even coming out of sleep I had heard him.

*You're gonna **die**.*

Seconds before, when I was still in the dream, I'd begun to hear these words as a warning that I must change, but no more: this was a predictor of my immediate future; I would die here in England where I lay next to my wife in a soft bed on the second floor of this stone cottage in the country outside Oxford.

I sat up against the headboard. We were staying in her cousin's house, and out the second-floor window there was no moon, no streetlights, no stars. I opened my eyes wider but could only begin to see the pale plaster of the wall. With a sick dread opening up in my abdomen and chest, I knew I would probably die today or maybe the next and it would have to be violent, wouldn't it? Isn't that what the black preacher's eyes were telling me? That violence begets violence, no matter who you claim you're defending or protecting?

But I didn't want to die. I was thirty-one years old. I was in love with my wife. We wanted to make a family. We wanted all those things people want before they, too, are cut down.

If I'd thought I'd felt terror before this I was wrong. The man I'd lived long enough to become fell away and I was a boy again, one who was not going to make it. Beside me, Fontaine slept curled on her side. We'd made love before falling asleep, and now I wanted to wake her, I wanted to tell her my dream, I wanted her to tell me that's all it was.

The month we got married, troops in Bejing marched on the peacefully protesting students of Tiananmen Square. They bludgeoned and ran over and shot to death hundreds. In the heart of the crowd was one of the leaders and his girlfriend. She was young and lovely and smart, and she could see now that most of the advancing soldiers were their age, young people from outside the city, the sons of farmers and truck drivers. One of them raised his weapon and shot her boyfriend in the head. She screamed, *"Why?! Why?! Why?!,"* and the next round tore through her face and out the back of her skull and she collapsed dead across her boyfriend's body next to the bodies of the others who had tried to change their world.

This moment was witnessed by a journalist, and long after reading it I kept hearing the young woman scream *Why? Why? Why?* This was true innocence, wasn't it? Innocence is asking why to brutality. But when innocence is gone, you don't ask why anymore; one merely expects it and either fights it or runs from it or does something in between.

There was no reason to wake Fontaine. Sometimes fate *is* cruel and clearly mine was to die on this two-week trip to Europe. How could she comfort me? Why ruin her good night's sleep? There was nothing she could do.

I'd partly brought it on myself anyway. Earlier that night, Fontaine's cousin Helena had taken us to a pub. It was small and dark and working-class, and it brought me back to the bars along the Merrimack River three thousand miles west. I sipped my Guinness and told Fontaine's cousin this. She was older than we were and had grown up south of Boston in a mansion, her father a wealthy businessman, one of the few in Fontaine's family. She was loving and intelligent and close to getting a graduate degree in Jungian analysis, and maybe that's why I began to tell her about fighting in places like this. I told her about knocking teeth out, about the time I almost kicked someone to death and the time I nearly had my skull caved in. I told her about these things and more, and a part of me could hear the lie in everything I was saying: I was making it sound too romantic and heroic, the kind of thing some neighborhood boys just learned to do and I was one of them. I left out how small and afraid and passive I'd been for years. I left out my constant fear that I'd become some kind of runaway train, that I was incapable of resolving conflict with another man except through throwing that first clean punch. I left out that I often walked around with the feeling I'd gotten away with something for a long time but that one day I was going to get caught. I left out that all these stories made me big to the boy but small to the man.

Before dozing off, Fontaine already asleep beside me, I lay there thinking of fight after fight: a man on a beach in Texas at sundown, how he was chasing his screaming wife and I set my feet and punched him through his beard, his arms at his sides like my little brother years before, blood dripping from his chin into the sand. There was a gray-haired bar customer who drank four hot toddies in one hour and when I shut him off he reached across the bar and yanked my tie till I couldn't breathe and I hit him with a straight right, this man thirty years older than I who fell to the floor. I dragged him up, hauled him outside, and when he came after me I punched him again. There was a night party in a marshy field in old Newburyport, a gauntlet of cars facing each other, their headlights on, four or five radios going at once, dozens of football players and their girlfriends drinking and laughing and talking loud, and I was drunk with Sam and a few others from Haverhill, walking down the center of that headlit lane, yelling, "I want to fight! Who wants to fuckin' *fight*!?" And then I was being tackled and rolled into the weeds, Sam Dolan on top of me throwing punches into the ground near my face. "I'll fight you!" Then his cheek close to mine, his voice low. "Keep your mouth shut. You want to *die* here?"

Now the dream preacher was my black crow on a limb. My time was up, and why shouldn't it be after all these years of raging and then the glo-rification I'd practiced the night before? Still, I was terrified of what was coming and how it would come and there was no one to call and nothing to do but wait for it.

I needed something right then. Anything. A book to read. Other lives to fall into away from my own that would soon end. But the reading light was on Fontaine's side of the bed, and the only book was a pocket-size New Testament she read briefly most every night. It was another thing about her I admired, her private and necessary faith in something inef-fable, though I'd never felt any pull toward it myself. It all seemed man-made and preposterous to me, but now it was the only book in the room, one that had always given my wife solace, and I reached over her shoulder and grabbed it and sat up straight in the darkness and opened it to the middle of the book. I narrowed my eyes at two dim pages, the words on them indecipherable lines of shadow. I flipped the pages over two at a time, stopping every other heartbeat and squinting down at sentences I could not make out as words. I turned over more pages, then started back again from the beginning. Now I held the book inches from my face. I could smell the worn fake leather of its cover, the long-dried sweetness of its ink, then there was a name, *Matthew,* and beneath it, a short sentence I could see now as if a small door had opened and a thin crack of light shone across just this one line: *Love one another.*

I blinked my eyes and brought the book closer. I wanted to read more. I wanted to read the entire page, but now I could no longer see those words. The page was back in darkness. I turned it toward the window that sliver of light must have come from, but there was no light.

I closed the book and lay back down and held it to my chest. Was this a possible reprieve? If I worked harder at loving the other, would I live?

WHEN I woke the next morning Fontaine was downstairs with Helena. I could smell toast and brewing tea. On the other side of the windowpane, through thin leafy branches, was a shock of blue sky and I stared at it like a man with a noose around his neck; the black preacher's face was as clearly behind my eyes as if he'd always been there, his words too. Since when does a night dream not fade with the morning but grow stronger? Was this my last morning? Or would I get one or two more? I had other questions like this, and I began to feel my family back home like some warm planet I would soon fall away from.

Sweat broke out along my hairline, my mouth was old paper. *Love one another.* Of all the words in the New Testament, why was I only able to see those three? *Was* there some invisible presence guiding us? And if there was, why was I finding it only now, just before it would all end?

Downstairs Helena laughed. I dressed quickly and hurried barefoot down the dark wooden stairwell to the sunlit kitchen and the comforting voices of my wife and her cousin.

I TOLD Fontaine and Helena my dream. Fontaine listened as if I had just read to her from a passage of fiction and she was interested to read more on her own. Helena looked concerned, not about the content of the dream but that I had taken it so literally. She made me some tea from herbs she said were calming. She talked to me about symbolic death versus literal death, how the dream was suggesting an old part of me was giving way to something new, that's all.

I sipped my tea with two hands and listened. This was a logical and more sophisticated reaction than mine had been. But she hadn't seen the preacher's face when he looked at me. She hadn't seen the urgency in his eyes. She hadn't heard his voice.

No, she was wrong. I was going to die soon. It was just a matter of hours now, or days.

DAYS PASSED and I didn't die, but sometimes dreams come back like fevers, and you deny that first pricking along the skin just before your eyes ache and your flesh burns once more and you sink back into a malevolence you thought you'd put behind you.

We were on an overnight ferry crossing the Irish Sea, a ferry of loud, drunk men on their way home from beating a British team in one of those games with a ball in it. The boat smelled like beer and vomit, and there was no place to sit that was not in a crowd of them, laughing and yelling and raising paper cups of ale and calling the Brits a bunch of *focking conts*. We were on the main deck, an enclosed space with the chairs and tables bolted to the floor, the tops of them strewn with empty cups and cans, sweaters and caps, a spilled pack of cigarettes left behind in a pool of wine.

It was after two in the morning and Fontaine and I sat up against the wall in a corner. She was one of the only women on the ferry, and every now and then one of the Irish fans would glance over at her, then at me, and I'd stare at him and try to leave enough on my face he would look away without thinking he'd been challenged. There were so many of them and they did not remind me of my dream, they *were* the dream, and so this is where it would happen, late at night on the black Irish Sea.

Fontaine's friend Audrey lived in a farmhouse on twenty acres of land on the west coast of Ireland. Once we got to Dublin, we were going to rent a car, then drive five hours across the country to Audrey in County Galway. We were going to spend our last week with her. That was the plan. But sitting in that smoky, pulsing crowd, it was clear to me these things would probably never happen. What mattered then was protecting my wife, and I was relieved when she curled up on the plastic bench seat and lay her head in my lap and now when one or two or three looked over, they saw only me.

After a while, there was sleep. The bar never closed and the crowd kept drinking, and there was the soft tilt and roll of the boat and all the loud, raucous *focking conts,* the roaring laughter of young men, the victorious blood in it, and now a shouting match broke out somewhere back near the smudged windows, darkness on the other side, and I woke Fontaine and nudged her under the bolted table where we lay down side by side on the thin carpet between the metal legs. After a while we closed our eyes. Above the din came more shouts, then a muffled thud, then another, and I pulled Fontaine into me, her cheek and ear resting against my arm. I could smell her hair—sweat and Helena's shampoo—and the musty carpet: seawater, dried vinegar, and dust.

Then there was the ship's horn, a long mournful honk, and the room was empty and bright with daylight from the windows. We were up and trudging down the gangplank with all the subdued half-drunk boys, their hair tousled, their cheeks and chins stubbled and pale.

So I would not die on that boat, but where would it happen then? Maybe the dream had been just that, a dream, and now its afterimages were stranded in another country on the other side of the Irish Sea.

ON THE return trip, the day was cool and gray, the damp air smelling of peat moss, cow dung, and woodsmoke. In Dún Laoghaire Fontaine and I boarded the ferry back to Holyhead where we would buy tickets for a train to London. The cheapest was for an overnight ride across England, and just before midnight we found our seats in a car of old couples and thirty-five schoolgirls from Germany. They were twelve or thirteen years old. Their teachers were two women in their forties, and one of them sat across the aisle from Fontaine. She told my wife they were on the train because of what had happened over Lockerbie two and a half years earlier. The mothers and fathers of these girls did not want them in the air.

In the seat across from her sat a retired Irish carpenter and his wife.

They both wore white wool sweaters and she was reading a book while he and I talked about the differences between building materials here and in the United States, how a tradesman in the U.K. worked less with wood and more with stone and brick and plaster. The car was new, well-lit, and warm, and as soon as the train pulled away from the station, the two schoolteachers had their students stretch out in the aisles on blankets and pillows they'd brought with them. Soon they were curled up toe to head all along the floor between the seats, and when the conductor came by for tickets he smiled down at them and stepped carefully, punching a hole in our tickets and wishing us all a good sleep. Our car felt as safe as a fairy-tale grandmother's home, infused with good-hearted warmth, soft edges everywhere, and soon it seemed that only the old carpenter and I were awake. He was reading a book. I was revising a novel I'd just finished. Fontaine dozed beside me, her cheek on my shoulder, and there was the comforting chug and sway of the train, the cool glass of the window to my right. Every few minutes I'd look up to think deeper than the page would allow me, and the old carpenter would nod and smile at me over his book. I'd smile back and keep writing.

THEY CAME in loudly and all at once. There was the rattle of the outer door, then the jerking slide of the inner door, three men in their twenties walking in and laughing mid-joke. Each of them held a cup of beer from the bar car and one wore black wool, the other two denim. The shortest of them said, "Look, mates, it's a fuckin' slumber party." They laughed and walked down the aisles, stepping between the sleeping girls, grabbing the backs of seats to balance themselves, spilling beer here and there, laughing as they reached the opposite door and jerked it open, the short one draining his cup and tossing it behind him.

I closed my notebook. My heart was beating in the tips of my fingers. The inner door opened again and two more stood there looking at the schoolgirls blocking their way. Some of them were awake now and lifted their heads from their pillows, blinking at the light.

These two were tall and scrawny, pierced and tattooed, one of them with a blue Mohawk, the sides of his head newly shaved. His dull eyes were lit with the surprise of the happy drunk who has just stumbled through the wrong door into somebody's living room, not a drink in sight, but instead of turning around he and the other started forward in their hobnail boots. One of the teachers stood and said, "Please, gentlemen, there are girls sleeping. Can you go to another car?"

The one with the blue Mohawk raised his hand in a gesture that was both placating and threatening, his fingers long and white, the nail of the middle finger bruised or painted black. "We're just seeing a friend, luv." And they lurched forward down the aisle, their hands grabbing the seat backs. Most of the girls were awake now, and one or two were crying softly. It was the sound of children waking from a bad dream, the solitary misery of it, but it was what they had woken to that scared them, and the rear door rattled open as these two left and the first three made their drunken way back over the students. "Hush, girls. Hush now. Be *good*. Be *good*." A laugh, then the dirty fingernails of a hand on Fontaine's headrest inches from her hair, then they were at the door, sliding it open, a chest-deep *whoop* as it closed behind them. In it was the joy of the addict about to get just what he craves, the drunk who's been promised a brand-new tab; there was only one more car behind this one, and it was clear that in it someone was dealing dope, for now the other two were already stepping over the girls, most of them awake, a few of them sitting up and leaning away from the boots and legs of these men who did not speak this time, just seemed intent to get out of this grandmother's kiddie car to where the party was farther down the train.

Both teachers stood and spoke in German to the girls. Their tone was consoling and instructional. As the last two men reached the doors, one turned and winked flirtatiously down at the schoolgirls, then they were gone, and something was pressing against my ribs. There were whispered words in my ear.

"Honey, *do* something."

Ahead of us the outer door was already opening again. Through two sets of glass, I could see it was one man this time. Blond hair and black leather, the dull flash of silver. I glanced past Fontaine to the nearest teacher. Her eyes were on mine, and the old carpenter's were too, alert beneath white eyebrows. The inner door was jerking open. I was already up and squeezing past my wife, but it was like stepping into a cold, black

cave, a final place that had been foretold in my youth. I stepped over a
brown-haired girl lying on her side. Her eyes were as alert as the old man's,
and I was struck with a razored dread and a cosmic wonder too; of all the
cars in this train, how was it possible that I had chosen one where I was
the only young man, the one in front of the dealer's car, the one filled
with old people and frightened children? The preacher knew my fate and
had given me time to pack my bags: why hadn't I? Instead of working on
my mediocre novel, why hadn't I written letters home? To my mother
in Miami, to my father in his wheelchair in Haverhill, to my sisters and
brother? I would have told them I loved them, that I wished I'd been a
better son and brother. I could have written to my friends and to former
lovers. I could have written to anyone I'd ever hurt, and I could have
apologized. I could have begun to atone for all the harm I'd learned to do.
My dream had delivered me the bill, and now was the time to pay up.

The inner door slid closed and the man's eyes passed over the school-
children in the aisle and he kept walking forward without slowing. He
was a parody of street-mean; his head was nearly shaved, his nose and ears
pierced with silver. Draped over his beefy torso was a black leather jacket
festooned with giant safety pins and hooks, a metal chain hanging across
his heart. At the base of his throat was the green tip of a dragon's tail, the
rest down under his T-shirt and across his chest.

I stood in the aisle, the brown-haired girl directly behind me. The
man kept coming and I held up my left hand, my weight on my back
foot, my right hanging loosely at my side. "This car's closed."

The man stopped. I could see he was five or six years younger than
I was, his face contorting into a mask of instant hatred I'd seen so many
times before.

"You don't tell *me* what to do. Fuck you and your fuckin' *closed* car,
I'll cut your head off and stick it down your fuckin' *throat.*"

Now was that half second in which to move. Now was that flash
of time to tear through the membrane around his yelling face, to drop
him where he stood. He stepped closer. My fingertips touched his chest
beneath his T-shirt—flesh and muscle and bone—and he was yelling
louder, like seeing a chained German shepherd, hearing its chest-croaking
bark, sincere and unrepentant, and he smelled like beer and nicotine and

the sweat of the unwashed. Why did my right hand stay still? Why was I letting him go on like this in front of all these watching people?

"You *hear* me? I'll fucking *kill* you."

Behind us one of the girls whimpered. There were hoarse whispers from the old.

"Fine, but this car's closed."

My mouth was dry, my tongue thick. He yelled more words back, every other one *fuckin'* or *cunt,* and I wanted to get him away from the girls. I could hear some of them crying in the aisle behind me, and I nodded at every insult and threat he spit into my face. It was like opening my mouth and swallowing whole the ugliest part of him. He assured me he was going to murder me, how easy it would be to do it, and I nodded and agreed with him. I said, "Let's continue this outside."

"Happy to, mother*fucker.* Bleedin' fuckin' *happy* to." And he backed up, his eyes on mine. He reached behind him for the handle and flicked the door open. I could see he was strong, that confrontation was nothing new to him. Under the pale fluorescent light between the two doors, he glanced back at the platform separating the train cars and he flicked open the outer door, his eyes still on me, and I followed him out into the cold roar of speeding air and the train's wheels clicking over the ties and a deep darkness on both sides of us beyond low steel rails.

"Who the fuck are you to tell me what to do? *No one* tells me what to fuckin' do. You hear that?" His face was inches from mine. In the dim light from both cars I could see his eyes were brown, a life in them somewhere, one he'd lived over here while I'd lived mine over there. I wasn't going to let him throw me off this train, but I noticed I was standing normally too, my weight even on both feet. And I did not care if he truly believed he could easily beat me up, kill me, make me disappear.

I leaned one shoulder against the outer wall, felt its shifting sway, and I stared at this man I'd filled so immediately with rage. I stared and I waited.

It's what I did every morning. Tried to sit and stare at the page without expectation, without judgment. In order for something true to come, I had to disappear.

He was still yelling. I was aware of the black English countryside falling away behind his back and behind mine. There was the smell of diesel, the scorched iron of steel wheels zipping along steel rails. His brown eyes, two slits as he yelled, were ringed with moisture, and it was clear how much he needed me to know he was not one to be dominated by anyone else. He was not one to be fucked with, couldn't I see that? Was I *blind*?

He did not say these words, but they were in the dark sheen of his eyes, and they looked to me now like a young boy's, and I said, "So then you would do the same thing I'm doing, wouldn't you?"

"*What?*"

"You'd protect those girls, too."

"You're bloody fuckin' right I would. I wouldn't let anyone fuck with them girls."

"Then we're on the same side, aren't we?"

He didn't answer. He glanced back at the car of children and old people. He looked at me.

"D'you know what I've fucking seen in my life?"

"No."

It was as if he'd never asked anyone that question before, or maybe he hadn't quite asked himself. He began to talk. He told me of getting kicked out of his house when he was thirteen. He told me of his father's drinking, his mother's "fucking around." He told me of bumming all over Europe, living homeless in Madrid, Marseille, and Rome. He told me he'd done things he wasn't proud of, bad things, only because of the bad things done to him. He told me he hated people who did bad things to little kids. "Bleedin' fucking *hate* them."

"Me too. I'm just doing what you would've done." He'd been talking a long while. I was shivering.

"Fuckin' right." He looked tired now, the beer fading, the rage dissipated. His shoulders were slumped under his black leather, and he was smiling at me. "Where're you from anyway, mate?"

"America."

"You're a fuckin' *Yank*? What the Christ you doing in the U.K.?"

"Talking to you."

He nodded slowly, like I'd said more than I just had. The train was hugging a curve and I grabbed the door handle to keep from leaning into him. He squeezed my shoulder. "Look me up in Trafalgar Square, mate. You can't fuckin' miss me."

There was only one door into the car he'd come from, and he turned and pulled it open and walked down the fluorescent-lit aisle. The door didn't close, and I watched him move down the length of the car. In that light I could see how dirty his jeans were, a rip in them beneath the hem of his leather jacket. His skin there looked pinkish and vulnerable, then he turned and walked deliberately up the aisle. I thought he might be coming back to talk some more, but he wasn't even looking ahead and out the door he'd opened that still hadn't shut. It was colder than before, loud with wind and spinning iron wheels, but in the front row sat two elderly ladies, one in a gray cardigan sweater, the other under a train blanket she'd pulled up to her chin. They were awake and at first looked startled to see him, but soon they were nodding and smiling.

He straightened up, blond bristles on his head glistening under the light, and he moved down the aisle, stopping every few seats to kneel and say something quietly to somebody—a middle-aged man, a woman old enough to be the mother he hadn't seen since he was a kid, two plain young women, both of whom he'd woken to say what he had to say.

"Isn't this remarkable?" the lady in the cardigan said. "He's apologizing to everyone. He's *apologizing*."

I stepped over and pulled the door shut. It was two or three in the morning, and my fingers were numb as I slid open the outer door, then the inner. Fontaine smiled sleepily at me from her seat. I tiptoed around the brown-haired girl on the floor. She lay curled under covers, her cheek resting on a pillow, her eyes no longer alert but closed. Her teachers were asleep, too, slumped in their seats across from the Irish couple. The wife was snoring slightly, her head leaning against the window, her reading glasses at the tip of her nose, and her husband still had his book open. He was looking over at me. He nodded and winked. I smiled and nodded back and sat down next to my wife who apparently would not be a widow just yet.

She lay her head on my shoulder. I stared straight ahead for a long while. I couldn't remember ever feeling this good. Not just about what I'd somehow done by not doing something else, but about people, the stories inside every one of us, the need for them to be *known*. And the boy in that young man's eyes; he was all I saw after he began to talk, he was the only one I could hear.

THE DOORS were opening again and three new young men were stomping into the car. I stood and stopped them just before the pillow of the brown-haired girl. I was met with the same resistance, the same threats, and now there were three, but I heard myself pointing out all the sleeping children, I heard myself appealing to the young boys inside them they used to be. I complimented them on their size and strength and told them I knew they'd be doing the same thing I was doing if this was their car, wouldn't they?

Right, mate.

Right.

Cheers.

They turned and were gone, and I was halfway back to my seat when the outer door rattled again and now came two in rugby shirts, later one in a long brown coat, after that three more, drunker than the rest, the tallest one slurring "Ficku, ficku," trying to slide past me, his breath bile and whiskey, and I was somehow able to talk him and all the rest back to where they'd come from. *How* was I doing this?

With the first one, as I'd stood normally between the train cars, there was the vague sense I was being guided by something greater than me and my own fears, a presence that began to flicker inside the man who'd promised to cut off my head and stick it down my throat. It flickered inside him and it flickered inside me, then it was a steadily burning flame, a found warmth I'd been inviting intruder after intruder into, but now, three or four in the morning, my limbs were heavy and my eyes were burning and it began to feel like some cosmic run of good luck was about to go dry: I knew this was still an unreasonable world; I knew I could not keep this train car clear all night long with words alone.

I sat heavily in my seat. Fontaine lay asleep against the window. I heard the doors slide open once more, and I looked up to where I'd been rising since after midnight, but the rattle and swoosh had come from behind and I turned and he was already at my side.

"Someone in this car's not letting me friends through. Now who would do *that*?"

He spoke in a full voice, his accent working-class British. He stood in a crouch, must've leapt over each girl to get to my seat.

The girl with the brown hair opened her eyes and looked up at him. He squinted down at her as if she were misbehaving and would now have to be punished.

The girl pushed her face back into her pillow.

He was deep into his forties, his dark hair slick and long, his side-burns shaved into a point halfway down his cheek. He wore a tight black shirt open at the chest, the skin there pale and nearly hairless. If his buyers weren't getting through, how did he know why?

"That was me." I tried to state this as evenly as I could. I tried to state this from the larger warmth of the world I'd somehow stumbled into tonight, but my voice sounded defiant to me, and scared, for smiling side-ways at me, his teeth gray and yellow, was the death I'd been waiting for.

"Who are you to keep my friends from visiting *me*? What gives you the fucking right, mate?" The dealer's voice was lower now, his face too close to mine, and I could feel him taking me in: I felt young and weak and exposed: Who *was* I to keep anyone from moving freely up and down this train? What *did* give me the right? My hatred of cruelty? My nearly pathological need to protect others, one I could follow all the way back to my youth? How was my problem all of a sudden everyone else's?

I stood and said, "People are sleeping. Let's talk somewhere else."

"I'm not talking, mate. I'm not here to fucking talk."

He said it calmly. He stepped back between the girls so I could walk ahead of him and out the doors.

He was not large or well-built, but he moved with the cocky ease of the truly dangerous. So it would be a knife then, wouldn't it? I'd die the way Cleary had six years earlier, his wife stabbing him in the lower back, my friend collapsing into the weeds and slowly bleeding to death.

I kept my back to the windows. I stepped sideways through both doors out into the perpetual noise between both trains. The air was colder, and in the zipping darkness on the other side of the steel rail a porch light came and went. The dealer had taken a moment longer to follow me

through the doors, and I was sure this was to pull the knife he would start
jabbing at me very soon. My left hand hovered six inches away from my
hip, my weight sinking back onto my right foot, locking me, the way it
always had, into what would happen now.

He stepped in front of me, but he stood in his own fight stance, his
hands low and empty, and I began to talk; it was like getting in the first
punch without the punch, and I talked more than I wanted to. I told him
I hadn't asked to be put in this train car. I told him I'd rather be sleeping
than doing this. I told him I was tired and if there were no children trying
to sleep in the aisles, I wouldn't give a shit who was walking up and down
this train. And it wasn't just so the girls could sleep, it was so they would
stop being scared.

"Because some of your friends are scary-looking to kids."

While I talked he'd crossed his arms over his chest. He leaned against
the wall and scrutinized me. In the pale fluorescence from the cars, with his
long hair and sideburns, the narrow face and deep eyes, he was every street-
tough I'd ever known: he was Cody Perkins about to knock out Sully; he
was Clay Whelan just before he chased me down; he was Kenny V. punching me while Ricky J. beat on Cleary; he was Dennis Murphy slapping the
old lady with the thin branch; he was Tommy J. walking away from my
bleeding brother, and he was Steve Lynch the second before I threw my
first punch. Except now I wasn't going to throw a punch, even if the dealer
was to step away from the wall and square off to shut me up; I wasn't going
to fight him either, and it was as if, in my explanation to him, I had stood
between those trains and taken off all my clothes, then began to pull away
every muscle I'd ever built: I ripped off the plate of my pectorals, dropping
them at my feet. I reached up to each shoulder and unhooked both deltoids
and let them fall, too; then I reached around for the muscles of my upper
back, the first to show up years earlier, and dropped them at the feet of the
dark dealer, speaking to him all along as if I'd never learned to do anything
but talk, as if this armor I'd forged had never been needed because I could
trust the humanity of the other to show itself. *Trust.* I was going to trust this
stranger, this man who had entered my train car and not to talk. I was going
to trust him to see and to listen and to do the right thing.

A part of me was watching myself do this, the same part that watched my fictional characters say and do things. And when they did that apart from me and my authorial wishes for them, they were more truly themselves. As I was now, standing before the dealer in the whisking cold, more truly myself. No armor, no sword.

He lit a cigarette, the lighter's flame extinguishing in the wind. He took a deep drag and said, "You're just protecting the girls then." The words came sideways out his mouth, slipping through a stream of smoke.

"That's all."

His eyes were two slits of shadow. He held the cigarette to his lips. He nodded. It was as if he were seeing all the unfolding years that had brought me here with him between these two train cars and it was a story he knew well, one he'd already written and discarded and wasn't up to being reminded about.

He blew smoke through both nostrils. "Fuck it, the night's done anyway, right, mate?" He flicked the smoking butt over my shoulder into the black wind. I knew what this action meant, I knew what he was saying he had chosen not to do to me, but I didn't care one way or another. A part of me seemed to have died anyway, and what remained watched myself walk behind the dealer through both doors, through the outer and then the inner, into the warm and quiet car of safe and sleeping girls.

20

————

THE LAST TIME I saw my father alive, we were both watching two men fight each other in the ring. It was February, near midnight, and I sat in damp work clothes on his couch in his house on the hill. In the past twelve years, Pop had learned how to live in a wheelchair, and there were signs of him and it all over the house: just weeks after his accident, one of his friends—a professor, Vietnam veteran, and Marine captain—had come over with one of his daughter's boyfriends and built a ramp spanning the two steps of the dining room down to the living room. Neither men were carpenters, but the pitch was right and the two-by-four railing didn't shake much, and twelve years later its top rail was worn smooth as bone from my father's hands.

Along both walls of the corridor to his bedroom we'd screwed in wood rails and he'd grab one on each side of his chair and pull himself rolling fast into the room where he slept and wrote on a desk he'd hired me to build, one he could roll up to, one that his surviving leg wouldn't bump underneath. Three years after his accident, Pop had taken out a loan and hired Jeb and me and some mutual friends, Beau Mullen and Jack Herlihy, to remodel his house. If we hadn't needed the work, we would've done it for free, but we did need the work so five days a week for two and a half months, we changed his home from what it was to what he now needed.

Jeb did the design, and we cut away and hauled off the old deck, we poured new footings then tore out walls and ripped away half the roof. We built a larger living room with a small deck he could wheel out to, one that looked over the wading pool he'd had installed. We built a larger bedroom for Cadence, a brand-new one for little Madeleine. We tore out the wall separating what used to be his and Peggy's bedroom and their library, and now his bed sat up against a wall of floor-to-ceiling books and there was more natural light streaming in from the windows facing the hill of poplars behind his house.

Later Jeb and I poured concrete footings for the posts of the long, staggered exterior ramp, and we ripped up the plywood decking and nailed stronger, much longer-lasting pressure-treated two-by-sixes. As the boards aged and bowed slightly, his wheels would make a clacking sound over them not unlike a far-off train's.

Pop had made peace with his crippling. Once, sitting straight in his wheelchair, he'd looked over at me in his small dining room and said, "I'd stop on that highway again. Even knowing what I was going to lose, I would."

"Why?"

"Because I've learned so much."

I couldn't pretend to know what he'd learned, but I and others had seen a change in him that was not solely physical. When I was a boy, my memory of him then is of a man in constant motion, even when he was sitting. It was there in his eyes, a dark and restless intelligence and a kind of hunger, too. When he wasn't sitting—which was reserved, it seemed, only for writing and reading and eating—then he was running or mixing a drink or he was talking and talking, carrying books out to his car to drive to a classroom where he would talk some more.

Then he was gone, and when we saw him once a week, when we four kids sat with him in a restaurant he could not afford, there was still that restlessness, that hunger, his body poised as if he could stay just a little while because there was work to do, so much to get done.

And he got it done too. Despite three broken marriages, four children from the first, two ex-stepkids from the second, and two daughters from the third, he got it done, and it was art. Whenever I read his work, I was pulled easily into a vision that was both bleak and redemptive, one illuminated with a kind of ancient love and compassion I could only associate with the divine. My father's work was a deeply compelling blend of the profane and the sacred, like a drunk confessing his sins to a good priest only to go out and commit them once more but this time not as unconsciously, not as cruelly, and not as if that would forever be his fate.

Off and on throughout the years, my father had said in passing that he'd always saved the best part of himself for his work, that he relaxed with his friends and family. But since getting run over on the highway, that no longer seemed to be the case. He still wrote every morning. He woke, transferred himself to his wheelchair, wheeled himself first to the bathroom, then the kitchen where he put water on the stove for tea. He wheeled himself back down the hall, laid out clothes on his mattress—almost always sweatpants and a cotton shirt—and transferred onto the bed to get dressed lying down. Then he sat up, which wasn't always easy, and transferred into the chair where he folded the empty right pant leg over his stump and tied a rolled bandanna around it. He wheeled down the long corridor to his tiny kitchen and the boiling water, poured it into a cup over a tea bag and honey, then carried it balanced on his lap back down to the bedroom where he'd sit at his desk and write longhand in pen.

By midmorning he'd be done. He'd count how many words he'd gotten and record the number. After each total, whether it was fifteen hundred or fifty, he wrote: *Thank you.*

My father would then transfer back to his bed. He'd dress in workout clothes he'd tossed there from a drawer, transfer once again down into his chair, an act he did countless times every day and every night, one that required strong upper-body muscles, and he'd put on some Sinatra or Ella Fitzgerald or Waylon Jennings and he'd sing and shadowbox the air, he'd lift light dumbbells, he'd strap his surviving leg to his weight bench and do abdominal crunches till his muscles burned.

Crippled or not, he was still living the rituals he'd established for himself since he was a young man, but what was different was how he was afterward. Gone was that subtle look that his time with you was something to do between writing sessions, that you were a pleasant or unpleasant distraction. Now, when he spoke to me, usually looking up into my face from his chair, his thin hair clean and combed back, his beard nearly white now but trimmed as neatly as it had always been, he looked directly into my eyes, and he did this not just when *he* was talking, but when I was too, and it made me want to tell him more about myself. It was as if he'd been gone for thirty years and had finally wandered back home, and now was the time to know each other while we could. Now was the time to do things together.

We did, too; for ten years nearly every other Sunday, Pop would host a family potluck dinner at his house and we grown kids and our girl-friends or boyfriends, later our spouses, and then later our kids, would come share an afternoon together, eating chili or stew or fried fish or something from Pop's grill out back. Jazz or classical would be playing on his stereo, little children running around our feet. Three of them were mine and Fontaine's, and at age five our oldest, Austin, liked to push Pop in his wheelchair all the way up and down the hall from his bedroom back to the dining room. Sometimes Jeb would sit in the corner and play a piece on his guitar. Somewhere along the way he'd gotten into the New England Conservatory of Music, and he lived in Boston and had a German girlfriend who sang opera. Then more years passed and he was married to Victoria, a pretty young woman he'd met while she was babysitting our two half-sisters, Cadence and Madeleine. If it was a weekend when they weren't with their mother, then the girls would be there too, sitting on the couch reading books to the younger kids or outside on the swing Jeb had built.

Pop had begun to worry about the possibility of a house fire. If he couldn't get to the front door and the staggered ramp down to his car, how would he get away? So Jeb and his carpentry partner, Bob, had framed a long deck off the small one in the rear. It ran the entire length of Pop's wading pool and because of the hill Pop lived on, the end of this new deck was fifteen feet off the ground and they built a square sitting area there with room for a grill. We called it "the Cajun Boardwalk," a nod to our Louisiana roots we four adult kids had never lived, and every Sunday that we gathered, if the weather was good, just about all of us would end up out there. My mother would come, too. She'd moved up from Florida and now lived with Bruce in the woods of western Massachusetts. Over the years she'd gained a little weight and her hair had begun to go gray, but she was still a beauty, still the kind of woman a man would hit on if she were to sit alone in a bar, which she never did.

To see her and Pop together was to see a couple. They teased each other and laughed. Sometimes she'd make him a plate of food and bring it to wherever he sat, and he'd smile up at her brightly and squeeze her hand, sometimes lift his face for a peck on the cheek. Whatever had ended their marriage was scar tissue no longer even sensitive to the touch, and Bruce was fine with this; he'd been living with my mother thirty years, three times longer than my father ever had. He'd go get his own plate of food, and some of us would sit at Pop's small dining room table, others on chairs against the wall or on the couch beside the wheelchair ramp. There'd be Jeb and his wife Victoria. Suzanne and her husband Tom. A few times a year Nicole would fly out from California with her girlfriend, then later her baby son Theo. There would be me and Fontaine, our three kids, Austin, Ariadne, and Elias, who over the years, one at a time, Fontaine would be breast-feeding while she ate. Cadence and Madeleine might be sitting in the laps of one of us older brothers or sisters, and friends would drop by: Lori, Jack and Joe, Sam and Theresa, and their son and daughter too.

My father's house would be loud with talk and laughter, Ella Fitzgerald singing on the stereo, the phone ringing, the clank of silverware, the toilet flushing, the hollow roll of sliding doors opening out to the deck where Pop and Jeb and Mom might go to smoke. There was the creak of the oven door, the spray of water on dirty plates, the smell of coffee and wine and hot olive oil. There was the late-afternoon light coming through the bank of windows that looked out over Pop's pool and the road below, the rising field of wheat-colored grass, the ridge of bare trees. In Pop's small house, the light was the color of fire, the kind that came from a hearth this family sat around as if we'd never been fractured, as if we'd never been broken up into pieces that had also, somehow, found their way back home.

ON ONE of those Sundays, Pop and Jeb and I sat at the end of the Cajun Boardwalk sipping drinks and shooting the shit. The sky was gray, the leaves beginning to yellow. The air smelled like rain and the cigarettes my brother and father were smoking. Pop had just written a new short story that was also a western, and Jeb and I were teasing him about some of the practical details being off: in the story, the protagonist builds a coffin for a dead man, then digs his grave near a stand of trees, and he does it all in a three-hour afternoon.

We told him that even with power tools, there was no way his character could build a coffin so fast. And that six-foot grave was near trees with *roots*. The hole alone would take two to three days for one man to dig with a pick and shovel.

"Old man," Jeb said, smiling, "do you even *know* what real work is?"

"Not *man*work," I said. Jeb and I shook our heads and sipped our drinks, and Pop was laughing, clearly enjoying himself. "Well, I'm declaring poetic license, damnit. All the wood and tools were already in that barn ready to go, and there was sand near those trees."

Sand. Jeb and I kept shaking our heads.

"And when I die you boys can build my coffin and dig my grave and then you can see how long it takes." He laughed and raised his drink and sipped from it, his eyes bright and mirthful, his cheeks a deep red, his whiskers thick and gray and white.

IT WAS true, he never had done any work with his hands. We never once saw him push a lawn mower or even change a lightbulb. But he seemed proud that his sons were carpenters, and now it was late at night in February, and I was sitting on his couch in damp clothes because I'd been working the wet saw most of the night in Suzanne's new house five miles down the river. It was a project Jeb and I—and even Pop—were doing together.

Suzanne had bought a house in Amesbury up the hill across from a brick hat factory on the Merrimack. Her house was old and only had three rooms. Its sills were rotted, and most of the first-floor joists were too. When you stepped into the dark, mildewed bathroom you could feel the floor sink an inch under your feet, the toilet shifting off its wax ring in the floor, the smell of sewage seeping from the pipe. There was a chimney stack in the kitchen that needed to go, and a leaking roof and drafty doors, and all these just had to be addressed before she could move in; Pop offered to pay for the materials, Jeb and I signed up to contribute the work, and this is what we three did together the last months of Pop's life.

I had just sold my third book and had enough in the bank I could do this, but Jeb had to turn his back on his bills for this job. Like always, it was good working with him again. He did the design and layout of what turned into a new kitchen and bathroom, a new floor frame and rear outside wall, and I went to work with him cutting and nailing and driving into place. Many days after we'd been working four or five hours already, the noon sun high over the Merrimack and the hardwoods on the other side, Pop would drive up in his Toyota with its handicapped controls, and he'd tap the horn and hold up a bag of Dunkin' Donuts and a tray of coffees in Styrofoam cups. We'd walk out thirsty and hungry in our leather tool belts, sawdust in our hair and across our forearms. We'd thank him but say, "You just get up, writer boy? It's lunchtime. Where're the *subs*?"

He'd laugh, and we'd eat our doughnut lunch under the sun in front of Suzanne's small new house.

Once a week or so, I'd swing by his place for a check for the lumberyard, and he'd write one out at the dining room table. One morning, he was finishing up praying with his rosary beads, something I didn't know the first thing about. He looked up at me and said, "I was praying to my father."

"Your real father?"

"Yep."

"I didn't know you could pray to dead people."

"Oh yes, son. I talk to my daddy all the time."

Over the years Pop had written and talked about him. I knew he'd been a surveyor and a good provider for his wife and two daughters and baby son. I knew he'd golfed every Saturday, then played cards with his friends. I knew he used to ridicule my father for being a dreamer, "All you're good for is shooting Japs in the backyard." I knew that Pop had joined the Marine Corps to prove to his own father he was a man. I knew that my grandfather had never told my father he loved him and my father had never said those three words back.

This is all I knew, and it wasn't much.

ONE AFTERNOON, Pop pressed the button that activated the electric winch that lowered his wheelchair from its metal container bolted to his roof. He transferred to his wheelchair, and Jeb or I backed him to Suzanne's door and pulled him into her house where we pushed aside tools and scraps of lumber and showed him our latest progress. He looked up at the vaulted ceiling we'd just framed in the kitchen, at the new skylight, a square of blue sky above. He said, "Y'all are doing holy work for your sister. This is holy work."

IT WAS after eleven o'clock and I'd been working at Suzanne's house since eight that morning. The sky was clear and the stars shone over the hat factory and the ice floes drifting down the Merrimack for Newburyport and the black Atlantic. Hard snow covered the ground, the tree branches bare and frozen, and when the wind picked up they sounded like dry bones knocking together. The following day I was flying to the West Coast to start a book tour for my new novel, a story I'd written about a woman who loses her father's house to an Iranian colonel, a proud man who tells himself he always puts his family first. This had taken me four years to write. When I began it, Fontaine was pregnant with Austin. Now, two days before its publication, we had three kids. These had been the most joyous years of my life, but this book was shot through with bitterness and loss, and I was dreading the reviews.

Earlier in the day I had hung two doors and hadn't gotten to the bathroom till sundown. It was a small space, but I wanted to get all the full pieces set into mortar, then the cuts too, something a real tile man would take two days for. I was to be gone for over a week, but the plumber couldn't do his finish work till the floor was down, and I'd arranged for somebody to come grout the tiles on Monday. I had to get done tonight.

Suzanne's house was unheated. In the halogen light I worked under I could see my breath, but now the night had gotten so cold the mortar was setting up too fast so I'd turned on the oven in the kitchen and opened its door and rested the bucket of mortar on the floor in front of it. Beside my wet saw the growing stack of tile scraps were framed with slivers of ice.

The night before I hadn't slept much. This was something I'd grown used to since we'd started having kids six years earlier. It wasn't simply the duties that came with caring for babies and young children—getting up to carry my infant son or daughter to Fontaine's breast for a feeding, burping them after, maybe changing a diaper; it wasn't only that one of them was older now and had had a bad dream or needed to be carried to the bathroom through our dark bedroom; it was that since becoming a father, I now slept like a soldier on watch in enemy territory. It had been ten years since that hot afternoon and Mozart's *Requiem* and the scream-ing woman on the sidewalk, but the world had never seemed so danger-ous. Anybody or anything could hurt my kids at any time, a gut-sick feeling every mother and father knew. It was the shadow side of a love so large my body could not hold it all, and I was beginning to believe in the soul.

The phone rang as I knelt at the wet saw and fed a full tile through the spinning blade. Icy water sprayed my fingers, hands, and wrists. I usually wore a mask for this, but I was beyond tired and wanted to get home, my lungs sore now from a fine mist of porcelain dust. I coughed and flicked off the saw, wiped my cut tile dry, and answered the phone.

"Hey. You coming over?"

"Pop?"

"Yeah, it's on soon. You almost done?"

"What's on soon?"

"The fight, man. De La Hoya."

Five or six times a year Pop would host a poker night, or if there was a major fight on pay-per-view, we'd do that. Jeb and I would come over, his son-in-law Tom, Sam Dolan, the Haley brothers, Jack Herlihy and others from over the years, mainly friends of his sons who'd become his friends too. We'd drink beer and whiskey, smoke cigars and tell bad dirty jokes, Pop sitting happily at the head of the table in his wheelchair, everybody at the same height.

On fight nights we'd crowd into his narrow living room, some of us standing on the wheelchair ramp and leaning on the railing, others sprawled on the couch or standing near the dark windows with a beer. Pop would always be in his chair close to the TV, and I found myself explaining the smaller things to him, how the corner man rubs Vaseline on the fighter's face to help prevent cutting, how each fighter will try to combat that by throwing punches with a twisting motion to more easily tear open the greased skin of his opponent, how hard it is to find your punching range when the other has good feet and can bob and weave, how truly hard it is to take a punch or a flurry of them, not only to keep your cool, but to keep your fear locked in some tiny room deep down inside.

"I forgot that was tonight, Pop. Who else is there?"

"Nobody." He told me a few had called and said they couldn't make it. The others just hadn't shown up this time. "You coming?"

I pictured him sitting alone in his small house on the hill, an expensive pay-per-view fight on to watch by himself. "I can't, Pop. I've got to get this floor done. I'm leaving tomorrow."

"I think you'll regret it. It looks like it's going to be a good one."

"I'll try, but I don't think I can, Pop."

He told me he thought I should come over anyway, and we hung up.

I was in Suzanne's bathroom, pushing my cut pieces into mortar when the phone rang again. I took my time answering it. I had to first clear the mortar from between the tiles so it wouldn't harden there and make grouting difficult. I did this with the end of my combination square, dragging it through the eighth-inch gap between tiles, then wiping it off with a cold rag. My eyes stung from fatigue, and I had at least another hour of this floor ahead of me. The ringing phone was a nail tapping into my skull.

"Hello."

"You've got to come over. You're missing all the prefight footage, man. This is going to be a *fight*."

"I've been here fourteen hours, Pop, and I'm still not done. I just don't think I can make this one."

"You're going to regret it."

"I know."

"You see De La Hoya? Man, he looks in great shape."

I imagined Pop in front of the TV in his wheelchair, watching the hype I too loved to watch. I told him maybe I'd make it over if he stopped interrupting my damn work.

"Good," he said, and we hung up.

Thirty seconds later the phone rang again. I had just knelt at the wet saw and flicked it on. I left the blade whirring and picked up Suzanne's phone.

"They're saying this could be one of the *great* fights. You're going to regret it if you don't come over."

"Pop, let me work and maybe, *maybe,* I can come over."

He said more things about what he was watching. The blade kept spinning. The mortar was hardening in its bucket in front of Suzanne's open oven.

"Pop, stop *calling.*"

He laughed, and we hung up again and in the next twenty minutes he called two more times. If I hadn't been so tired, this might have been funny. Each conversation went the same way and ended the same way, Pop excited and intent, nearly urgent in his request for me to come over, me tired and cranky and barely able to hold a respectful tone.

After he called a fifth time, I hung up but kept my hand on the receiver. My lungs were raw and the overhead light was too bright and my ears were ringing slightly. Suzanne's kitchen was almost warm now from the oven, and the air had the wet-stone scent of drying mortar, the damp cotton of my sweatshirt, the broken bone of cut porcelain. I hadn't seen Fontaine or the kids all day and night, and soon I'd be thousands of miles away from them and gone for days, but Pop had used the same word each time he'd called. Standing alone in Suzanne's quiet house I could hear his voice saying in my ear: *You're going to regret it if you don't come. I think you'll regret it, son.*

I walked over to the oven. I shut the door and turned off the heat. I stepped into the cold bathroom, glanced at the section of subfloor I'd yet to cover, and switched off the light. In the front room where my wet saw was set up, I unplugged it and the halogen lamp and left my hand tools where they were. Normally, I'd clean up the site; I'd empty the wet saw tray and wipe down the motor, blade, and frame; I'd roll up cords and dump the tile debris into a barrel and sweep the floor and put away my tools. I sure wouldn't leave wet mortar in a bucket where it would dry and harden and have to be tossed. I wouldn't leave a floor undone that I'd promised my grouter and plumber would be ready. But I did. I turned off the kitchen light and locked the door and left everything just the way it was. Then I drove to my father's house.

HE GREETED me at the door smiling in his wheelchair. He was wearing charcoal sweatpants and a black jersey made from some kind of shiny material not unlike satin. This was something Jeb and I would tease him about, that he liked to wear soft clothes and sleep in satin sheets.

He reached up and hugged me and slapped my back. "I have one beer. You want it?"

I did. I cracked it open and followed him in his wheelchair down the short ramp into his living room. He positioned himself in front of the flickering TV. The volume was low, and two boxing commentators in tuxedos were speaking earnestly into the camera. I sat on the couch in my work clothes, still damp from the porcelain mist, and I took a long drink from my beer and was glad I had come; Suzanne's bathroom would just have to wait till I got back. In the morning I'd make some calls before I left for the airport.

Pop said, "Who's going to win this?"

"De La Hoya."

"I think so too."

We talked awhile about the fight, about who had the reach advantage and who might be hungrier for this, Trinidad or De La Hoya? This was the only sport we could talk about because it was the only one I'd ever done and most of the knowledge my father had of it had come from these talks. Before them, he'd had only a passing interest in boxing, but now it was more than that for him, and it seemed to come from my passion for it, the way my eventual and late interest in baseball would come from my sons.

Pop had never seen me box. We'd had that night at the Tap together twenty years earlier, but my father had been on the floor and hadn't seen me knock down the man trying to make peace. Over the years, he'd heard the fight stories about me to the point where they had taken on the mantle of myth, and this often left me feeling like a poseur and a liar, even though I *had* been in those fights. I had done those things.

Not long before this night, the editor of a magazine wanted to do a story on my father and me. Pop kept calling my house to hear when I could do the interview. I told him of the work yet to be done on Suzanne's house, of my commitments at home. "I don't know, Pop, I might not be able to make this."

"You have to, man. It's about the two of us. It'll be fun."

I loved my time with my new father. I loved our easy rapport, but I did not want to do this interview partly because it was my book coming out, not his. Once he'd been interviewed by a woman who began to talk at length about one of the stories in my first book. Later he mentioned that to me. He said that he'd almost said to her, "Hey, lady, whose work are we talking about right now anyway?"

"I get that all the time, Dad."

That's where we'd left it. But why *shouldn't* every journalist I'd ever talked to bring up my father and his masterful work? I was his firstborn son with the same name writing fiction, too. What did I expect? In these interviews, I was treated with a vaguely disguised pity: how hard it must be to follow the footsteps of a real master, a writer's writer, to share his name and probably not his gifts, an assumption I shared but honestly did not think much about. Sometimes there was outright irritation that there would be two Andre Dubuses now. One journalist, a woman in her thirties who smoked one cigarette after another and wrote in shorthand, said, "God, don't you want to do something *different* from your father? Why don't you go into another *field*?"

But I had never thought about writing as a field or a career. These were not words that came to me. Ever since that night in my apartment in Lynn when—instead of running to the gym to box—I'd sat down with tea and a pen and a notebook, writing had given me *me,* and this was the only reason I'd kept doing it. Only when I published something was I aware there was now a reflection of me, however small, in some cultural mirror. When my first novel was published, it got a favorable review in

Library Journal, but the reviewer wrote that this was a novel by my father and listed his books. I felt the violation of the robbed, but I also felt protective of my father's name. Was it fair to him that people would think he, a master, had written the prose of an obvious apprentice? Wasn't it time I wrote under a new name? But my first name was Andre and my last name was Dubus, and I just could not bear to paint a fake name over the truths writing had carried me to; there had been Alexandre Dumas, *père*, and Alexandre Dumas, *fils*; there was Hank Williams and Hank Jr. and Hank III. Now there were two Andre Dubuses, that's all.

It was not this simple, though. Pop kept calling me about doing that interview and I kept resisting, but it wasn't because I did not want to share time and attention for a book I had just finished, nor was it to avoid sitting in the long shadow of his substantial body of work either. No, it seemed to go beyond work and "career" into something far deeper, into blood and bone and spirit and what comes after we all leave this earth: it was having to be joined to him forever by name, the way the Alexandres were, and the Hanks, as if the sons had never separated from the fathers and become fathers themselves. What got lost in this public reflection of us were deeper truths, not just of my life so far, but his too. And what got lost was my mother, who had stayed.

In the end I drove to Pop's house for that interview. My resistance had begun to feel too self-serving, and I was glad I went. The editor was my age, an affable and intelligent guy, and the three of us sat in Pop's narrow living room for six hours and talked and talked and laughed and talked some more. Around the fourth hour, we switched from tea and coffee to Jack Daniel's on the rocks. Then we were talking trash the way men drinking often do. Pop brought up my fighting, and again, I could hear the pride in his voice, and I fell into telling a few stories like some drunk asshole telling shopworn jokes, but even as we all got louder, the testosterone rising in the air, my eyes caught Pop's above his beard and that small voice we all seem to have inside us like some eternal flame, said, *You need to tell him how it was. He still thinks this was just a sport for you. He'll listen now. Tell him how it was.*

But sitting there alone with him in front of the De La Hoya fight, to tell him how my boyhood really was was to tell him how it was not, and I did not want to hurt this man who'd been run over and crippled for stopping on the highway to help someone. I did not want to hurt this man in black sitting in his wheelchair. But this seemed to be the moment given us, didn't it? How could all eight or nine men who would usually be here *not* be here now? Wasn't this the time to tell my father that since that night train in England, a story I'd told no one, I'd been on a new road, and one I preferred? With physical violence there was always the wreckage after, not just the bruises and lacerations, the chipped teeth or fractured bones, there was a hangover of the spirit, as if all those punches and kicks had pushed you into a gray and treeless landscape where love and forgiveness were hard to find.

I was a father now. All day and all night of every week of every month of every year since becoming one, I'd felt surrounded by love, responsible to it, careful not to hurt it, and so grateful to get it. To punch another man in the face was to punch another father, was to punch some father's son.

As much as I admired the heart and the skills of the two fighters we were watching, for me it was like a recovering alcoholic sitting at a bar with a glass of soda water while his friends drink tequila shots. I wanted to tell Pop this. My crippled father, the new one, the one who looked at me and listened more fully now, he would hear all this if I told him. And maybe he wouldn't feel blamed. Maybe the younger father in him, the one who had had so much work to get done and so little time in which to do it, maybe he would listen too.

Soon the fight was over, and De La Hoya lost. Pop and I sat there surprised. He muted the TV's volume and in its pale glow we talked awhile about the judges' decision. We talked about how hard both fighters had fought, how really, it could have gone to either one of them. Halfway through the fight Pop had poured us each a cognac and I sipped from my glass and felt myself lean forward. It was close to two in the morning. My clothes had dried and felt stiff against my skin. I could feel the word *Pop* rising up my throat. There was that itch in my chest that I needed to set the record straight. I needed to tell him about the lives his children had really led on the other side of that river. I needed to tell him about the boy in the mirror.

Was I being greedy? What I had with my father was already so much more than he'd ever had with his. We sat before the muted blinking shine of the TV, and my father started talking about his boyhood. He was with friends in a car sitting outside a whorehouse. It was a summer night outside Lafayette, the vanilla scent of camellias in the air. His friends had French and Irish names, and they got their nerve up and left the car and climbed the steps and went inside.

"But I couldn't go."

"Why not?"

"I'd just gone to Mass. I didn't want to ruin how I felt."

"How did you feel?"

"Holy." He smiled. In the gray-white light of the TV, there was a puffiness around my father's eyes I hadn't noticed before. He didn't look well. He had both elbows on the arms of his wheelchair, his shoulders hunched, and he told me of his friend who came down after and couldn't stop shaking. He had just sinned and could not keep his hands and fingers still. As Pop drove them away from the house, the shaking one began to pray to himself prayers Pop knew by heart.

He began talking about his own father, and while I don't remember one detail of what he said, I can still hear Pop's voice, the acceptance in it, the forgiveness, and it brought me immediately to one of those weekends when I'd spent the night at his and Peggy's house on campus. When I woke in the spare room late in the morning, Pavarotti was singing and I knew my father was in his room writing. He sometimes played opera as he wrote, and lately he'd wear a Japanese kimono at his desk.

But when I climbed the stairs to the kitchen, he was standing in his kimono at the countertop, a cup of steaming tea there, and he was crying. I asked him if he was all right. Did something happen?

He glanced at me, his eyes shining. "I've been writing about my old man." He shook his head. "I'm more like him than I ever thought I was." He lowered his chin and cried and I hugged my father and he hugged me back.

Maybe my father's forgiveness for his father had begun then, maybe later or earlier, but as I sat on Pop's couch at nearly three in the morning, my glass long empty, Pop talked about his own father as if he were simply another man in the world like he was, just another man climbing out of bed each day to try and do the best he knew how to do. I listened and I nodded. I said little and did not need to say much. That had been true of my father too, hadn't it? He'd done the best he'd known how to do, and if it wasn't enough, then we still had this, didn't we?

Across from me in the window was my reflection lit by the artificial light of the TV, a grown man sitting near another man in a wheelchair. Nine miles down the river, my own children slept in a house without me, and tomorrow I was leaving.

I stood and told my father it was time for me to go.

"All right, man." He smiled up at me and raised his arms for a hug. I leaned down, the glass in my hand, and hugged him with one arm. His back felt broad and thick, and I could smell his Old Spice, the dried cognac on his whiskers. He held on and looked into my face and said to me what he said to all six of his children all the time, those three words his father had never said to him. I said them back and kissed him on the lips.

He took my glass and rested it in his lap with his, then he turned his chair around, gripped the railings, and pulled himself up the plywood ramp into his dining room and kitchen. He switched on the overhead light. I put on my jacket and opened the door. The stars were out, the air so cold my lungs ached with the first few breaths. Pop followed me out in just his black shirt and sweatpants. He stopped at the end of the landing before the descent of the first ramp. He was talking about this new novel I'd written, his tone generous and encouraging, the way it was with most young writers, including me.

I turned and waved and headed down the first ramp, then the second, third, and fourth. From the driveway I could see him in his wheelchair beneath his porch light, his breath thin and white, rising into the air where it vanished. Beyond him was the steep hill behind his house, the bare poplars in snow, their upper branches against the stars.

Pop was talking, and while I couldn't make out his words, his tone was upbeat, and I knew he was still speaking about me and my new work.

"I'll call you from the road, Pop."

He called out something else I couldn't hear. I started my car and didn't give it enough time to warm up. I backed it to the frozen snowbank, drove down the hill, and away.

21

———

THE COFFIN WAS a simple pine box with a domed lid and it took Jeb and me all night to build. Even with power tools it took two men twelve hours, though our work was interrupted by visits from people who'd come for the funeral—Pop's agent, Philip Spitzer, who was like a brother to him, his wife Mary, Reverend Bob Thompson from Exeter, others too. Jeb and I would be at the table saw or the chop saw, or we'd be clamping and gluing pieces of pine together on the worktable, when the front door of Jeb's shop would open and people would move slowly toward us down the long concrete corridor. We'd stop and walk over to them. There'd be long tight hugs, a shake of the head, tears and sometimes even a teasing or two. Jeb would describe his design, that he'd decided on a coffin with no nails, just glue and dowels. He'd show them the cardboard template he'd sketched to get the arc of the domed lid, how he'd used that to trace the final shape onto pine boards he then cut on the band saw. My main job was to rip the forty staves we would need to cover those supports for the finished cover.

We told them this, and we told them other things, and we listened to whatever they had to say. Our father's body lay in a funeral home in Haverhill not far from the courthouse and police station, but as his coffin began to take shape in Jeb's shop, people who loved Pop would stand before it and lower their voices. They looked from the coffin to Jeb and me then back at the coffin. Before leaving, they'd take a small scrap of pine we no longer needed, pushing it into their coat pockets or holding it in one hand. They hugged us once more and walked back down the concrete corridor out into the night.

For long stretches Jeb and I were alone. In many ways it felt like old times. Jeb was the artist at this; I was the slow, careful, mostly competent worker. While Jeb glued and clamped the planks of the side panels, a smoking cigarette between his lips, three-day-old whiskers across his chin and cheeks, I was cutting the shorter lengths for the end panels. Sometimes we'd glance over at each other at the same time, and our eyes would catch and we'd shake our heads and well up. Other moments, we'd be busting each other's balls the way you did on a job: "You call that *square*? What a butcher." More than once, one of us would pass closely by the other on the way to a new tool or task and we'd reach out and squeeze a shoulder or upper arm, then pull each other in for a quick hug.

Many times during the night—pine dust in the air, smoke from Jeb's Marlboros, the heated electric engine smell of the power tools—one of us would shake his head and say, "Three hours, my ass."

Just before dawn, we began to tire but not much. We had just screwed the lid to its long piano hinge when the shop door opened and against the gray light stood the silhouettes of two men. One of them pulled the door shut behind them and they came walking down the corridor, a cooler over the shoulder of the shorter one, a bag under the arm of the other. Walking into the light were Sam Dolan and Kourosh, who had flown all night from Seattle, and they'd brought beer and sandwiches. There were hugs and some laughter, quiet words that got quieter as we stood back and looked at my father's nearly finished coffin. It was long and straight, the corner joints tight and clean, a router bead running the length of the closed lid whose arc was slight, all forty staves glued tightly together and sanded smooth, this new pine the color of bone.

We four sat against the wall. We ate our sandwiches and drank cold beer. Maybe we talked about the wake that would start in less than twelve hours. Maybe about the funeral the next day and how the ground was too frozen for the burial and we'd have to wait till spring for that, Pop's body to be kept in a vault in a local cemetery until then.

While we talked and ate and drank, I kept looking at the coffin sitting over on the worktable, this last project for our father. I stood and brushed the crumbs and sawdust off my legs. I walked up, opened the lid, climbed onto the table, then stepped inside and lay down. I asked Jeb to close it, told him I wanted to make sure there was enough room for a body inside. These are the words I said, and part of me was thinking that, but another part of me had to feel what our father would not, had to see what he would not, the new lid closing, then the darkness, the nearly milk-sweet scent of drying glue, the sap and sawdust, the walls of this final box at my shoulders and toes.

When the call came, I'd been standing in the lobby of my hotel in San Francisco. It was cocktail hour. Business men and women sat around a small fireplace sipping complimentary wine, talking quietly to one another or on their cell phones. Jazz was playing softly on the sound system, light brushwork on cymbals, a throbbing bass, a lone horn. Outside, on the other side of the street, candles burned in the windows of a restaurant, and I stood near the revolving glass door with my new book in my hand, this novel that was now being reviewed around the country, the response overwhelmingly positive. It was strangely hard to take, all this good news, and earlier that day, cold and sunlit, I'd walked up and down Nob Hill, I'd walked through Chinatown and Ghirardelli Square, I'd looked for gifts to buy my kids, and I felt blue. Nothing good ever comes for free and something bad was going to happen and when would it come knocking?

This was neurotic and self-absorbed, I knew, but as I stood in that lobby, just minutes from walking out the door and down to the Clean Well-Lighted Place bookstore to read, it was as if I hung suspended in this membrane I'd learned all those years ago to break, this barrier between what was and what would be, and now came the ringing of the phone at the front desk, then my last name being called in the air. It was from the man who'd checked me in hours earlier. He was older, his hair short and gelled, his tie in a snug Windsor at his throat. He held his hand over the receiver as if it were a home phone. "There's a call for you, sir." Then I was standing at the desk, the jazz and cocktail chatter behind me. Fontaine was crying so hard she couldn't get her breath to speak.

"Honey, what? *What?*"

I saw my children's faces—six-year-old Austin's deep brown eyes, swollen from allergies, his curly hair; Ariadne and how she'd make a face at me and laugh, as if she were fourteen and not four; two-year-old blue-eyed Elias, his big hands and feet, his patient sweet stillness—which one, which *one*. "Fontaine—"

She kept crying and couldn't stop.

"Just tell me. Tell me."

There was the shudder of her breath. "Your dad—"

Relief jabbing into my heart, a half-breath of gratitude, then the knowing and a right cross of black grief before I even asked the words and she confirmed them, and I was climbing carpeted marble stairs, the stairwell bright and quiet, a sound coming from me from so long ago, Pop's breath in the air just three nights before, just three nights, and I was unlocking my door, then I was facedown on the mattress crying *Daddy Daddy*, a word I hadn't used since I was a young boy and in it was mine but also the voices of my own children calling for me, and my father's voice for his father, too. I had lived thirty-nine years without ever losing someone this close, so fortunate really, so blessed, so why did it feel so familiar? Why did this feel like the second punch following the first?

Then I saw it, Pop's back as the four of us followed him down the porch stairs, Mom crying inside the house. There was the glint of frost on gravel, Pop tousling my hair, then his old Lancer driving down the hill and Jeb running after it, *You bum! You bum! You bum!*

Jeb opened the lid and I climbed out. I was blinking in the light at my friends, at my younger brother who held out his hand.

THE LADY I'd bought the plot from said her men would dig as soon as the thaw began. I asked her if she owned her own backhoe. She said no, they dig it themselves.

I could feel the blood descend into my hands. "Would you mind if we did that then? His sons?"

"No, I don't mind."

But we would have to wait over two months, Pop's body kept in a concrete crypt in that same cemetery behind the old Hale Hospital and the doctor's office Mom had rented for us at the base of Nettle Hill. Life continued. Despite this black grief, I was working on something new and needed to do some research at the local county jail. I called them and soon was standing in a glassed-in walkway twenty feet over the main population. Below us, over a hundred men sat in orange or tan jumpsuits at tables and benches bolted to the concrete floor. They were playing cards or checkers, reading newspapers, or watching one of the TVs hung high in the corners of the room. From where I stood behind thick protective glass, I could see a lot of shaved heads and homemade tattoos, some of the men sitting with their legs spread wide and their chins up, an unlit cigarette between their lips. Others, narrow-shouldered or obese, sat off to themselves and avoided making eye contact. The public affairs officer beside me, an easygoing and talkative man in his late fifties who'd worked here for years, was brimming with stories. He was doing his best to give me good material, though I wasn't looking for any; one of my characters had found himself in a jail like this, and I just had to see it for myself.

The man from public affairs pointed out one inmate after another. "That big one there? He kidnapped his own wife. You don't even want to know the rest of that story. See those two under the TV? That old man and the other one? Uncle and nephew, only they never met each other till they got in here at the same time."

I nodded and listened. The uncle was no more than fifty, his graying hair tied back in a ponytail, his nephew a foot taller and half-black or half-Latino. The officer kept talking about them, about the good story their lives would make, but ten feet away from them sat someone I knew.

He was thin. His hair was short, the color of old tea, and he was playing checkers or dominoes with a bald man. The one I knew said something, and I could see the chipped front tooth, that wise-ass mouth in a lined and pallid face.

"'Scuse me." I pointed down to him. "I know that guy."

"Who?" The public affairs officer followed my arm and finger. "Murphy? How do you know him?"

Dennis Murphy, his pine branch flicking out and slapping the old woman in the face. "We're from the same town."

"Yeah? Good story about him." And the man from public affairs told me how two or three Thanksgivings ago, all four Murphy brothers were in at the same time, some awaiting a hearing or trial, others serving a sentence. "And Frankie, the bank robber—he's dead now, by the way— he comes up and asks us since it's Thanksgiving and all the brothers are together, would it be all right for their mother to bring them a turkey dinner? What the hell, we allowed it. We even had the kitchen make up some side dishes for them. So there's Ma Thanksgiving Day, sitting down there at one of the big tables with all her boys. They had a good feed, too."

He laughed and shook his head. I stared at Dennis Murphy. Except for the desiccated hair and yellowed skin, the lines around his mouth, he'd changed little since we were teenagers and his brothers were in their twenties and the four of them would walk into house parties down on the avenues and do whatever they felt like, later cruising by my gas station booth on Winter Street looking for revenge.

I followed the public affairs officer off the walkway for the rest of the tour, one concrete room and corridor after another. In the mess hall a gang of men in white jumpsuits were on a cleaning detail. They scrubbed tables and swept and mopped the floor, their faces hard, their bodies too, but they looked like boys to me, and when one or two of them glanced up at us—two men in suit jackets and pressed pants—in their eyes was the dull light of resignation, not, it seems, to the time they'd yet to serve, but to this, two village fathers walking by without a nod or a word, as if these young men were not right here in front of them, as if they never had been.

IT WAS a weekend in April, the sun high in a cold sky, and Jeb and Sam and I wore sweatshirts and sweaters and had been digging for three hours. We were only down two and a half feet. Nearly halfway through the day, our mother showed up with water and sandwiches she'd made herself.

One of the caretakers of the cemetery had cut into the grass the shape of the grave we were to dig: four feet wide, eight feet long, and we were to go down six feet. I'd brought two picks, two long-handled spade shovels, and two short. I'd brought work gloves and a jug of water, too.

The cemetery was less than a mile from Pop's house. There were nearly as many hardwoods and pine trees in it as there were graves, and most of those went back before the Civil War. Sam started in first with the pick, tearing up the brown earth, then he stepped back and Jeb and I began shoveling into a pile the clumps of dirt and leaf-rot and lingering turf. After ten inches or a foot of this, we hit rock and it took all three of us two hours taking turns with both picks to get through it. When we finally got back to dirt, we'd only gone down another foot and a half. We stopped and passed around the water jug. Not far off, someone was burning a trash pile, the woodsmoke drifting through the pines behind us. The air was still and cool, and high overhead a chicken hawk soared south toward the Merrimack.

I wiped the sweat off my forehead. We went back to work. Less than an hour later, it was a sweet surprise to see Mom's tired red Mitsubishi pull up to the cemetery gate, to see her walking toward us with a picnic basket and more water. She was wearing sweatpants and a black wool sweater, her hair blonde and gray. We hugged and thanked her. We dropped our pick and shovels, pulled off our gloves, and sat on the ground to eat.

Two months earlier, just minutes after the coffin was done, she and Fontaine had walked down that long corridor carrying measuring tapes, scissors, a staple gun and staples, a roll of cording, and the beige satin sheet off Pop's bed. While Jeb and I and our friends went home for a few hours' sleep, my mother and wife lined the inside of Pop's pine box with the same sheet he'd slept in the last night of his life.

Now Mom was sipping her water, her eyes on the grave of her ex-husband. She was sixty years old. I'd been in her life since she was twenty. In the coming months she would lose her mother, then Bruce, but this recent loss was enough. Over eight hundred people had come to Pop's funeral: his two older sisters from Louisiana, their grown daughters and sons, cousins of ours we barely knew. There were writer friends from his time in Iowa City, ex-girlfriends and two ex-wives, Peggy singing "Summertime" up in the balcony. There were hundreds of students from over the years, drinking buddies from Ronnie D's, retired professors from Bradford, waitresses and bartenders and former cops. And there were his six kids from forty-year-old Suzanne down to twelve-year-old Madeleine.

Pop had eaten life, and his death had left a cavernous, gnawing hole in the air we moved through.

Many times over the years, my mother had told me that Pop had been the one love of her life. "He was a self-absorbed son of bitch, and we could never stay married, but he was the one." She still had Bruce, her man of thirty years, but sitting on that grass with us she looked to me like a widow.

The night of Pop's death, Jeb and his building partner were coming over to watch a movie. Bob got to Pop's first, heard the water running in the shower. He knocked on the bathroom door but got no answer. He opened it and found our father slumped under running water that had turned cold. Bob pulled him out and did what he could, but Pop was gone.

A slight wind had picked up. It was sifting some of the dirt back into the hole, and it was hard not to think of those last moments, my father soaping himself on his shower bench, the hot water coming down, then whatever the first signs were, a final pain I did not want to think about him suffering alone. I stood and walked back through the gravestones.

So many of the names were French or Irish. There was one with the image of an electric guitar etched into it. Beside that marker, another with a man's name. He'd died in his early thirties, and next to his birth and death dates were the words: *A Loving Husband and Father*. But the *H, u,* and *s* of *Husband* had been chiseled away at the corners, the work, the caretaker lady later told me, of the dead man's grieving girlfriend. I kept walking past stones that were spread farther apart. Beyond them lay a pile of faded memorial wreaths, plastic flowers, deflated balloons, and soggy teddy bears. Just west of it, in the shadow of a thick stand of blue spruce, lay the graves of babies.

I turned around to get back to work. I could see Mom putting away what was left of our lunch. Sam and Jeb were already standing with their shovels. I took a different route back to them, and there it was carved into the back of a granite slab: *CLEARY.* I slowed and walked around to the front of it. There was my old best friend's first name, his dates, born two years after me and dead at twenty-five. I called Jeb over, and he joined me and we stood there staring at the stone, the three of us together again, roaming downtown and the avenues. I looked back at our father's deepening grave. Sam stood in it, swinging the pick down over his shoulder again and again, and there was the dirt alley and Cleary's small asbestos-sided house, his mother drunk on the couch, his father's big Chevy down in Boston. My once-a-month visits with Pop on the other side of the river when I'd tried to wash the smell off me—the dope, the alley dust, the trash of dumpsters we searched through for something to drink or break or eat. I took long showers and washed and dried my clothes. I tied my hair back as tightly as I could. At my father's apartment, I tried to stand straight, my chest out, and speak as if everything was all right and under control. I tried my best to flush away our friend and all we did together. And now here he and Pop would lie in the same stretch of ground, any past secrets exposed and irrelevant.

Mom waved goodbye from her car, and we three kept digging. After nearly eight hours we finally got down to six feet, the surface of the ground a couple inches above my head. Jeb gave Sam ten fingers to step in and he climbed out. He turned around and extended his hand and Jeb grasped it and Sam, still as strong as he'd always been, pulled him up and out of the hole.

It was just me now. Sam offered his hand, but I said, "Wait, buddy," and I lay down at the bottom of my father's grave. It seemed so much deeper than six feet, the dark walls of earth at my sides and head and feet, a blue rectangle of sky so far above. I smelled clay and cool stone. I closed my eyes for just a second, but it was too dark, too eternally dark, and I stood and climbed fast out of that hole.

WE HELD the burial on Fenway Park's Opening Day. While thousands of fans streamed into those seats surrounding that green field in Boston, a small group of us gathered to lower Pop's pine box into the earth. The sun was out, but it was cold enough you could see your breath in front of you. Sam had helped me find a Catholic priest who'd known our father. From the yellow pages I hired a bagpipe player, then called the local Marine Corps recruiting office in Lawrence. They sent a young captain and seven Marines, and while we gathered at the foot of Pop's coffin and open grave, these eight young men in dress blues stood at attention alongside it. The captain was a handsome young Latino, his eyes shadowed beneath the visor of his head cover, his white-gloved hands stiff at his sides. The priest, graying and respectfully jocular, had finished a prayer and was talking about Pop, how even in a wheelchair he'd make it to Mass, how when he couldn't a layman would drive out to his house to administer the sacrament of the Eucharist. This was language from the church Pop had turned to and used his entire life, and I was glad they were out in the air over his body and grave.

East Broadway lay thirty yards behind us on the other side of a chain-link fence. The priest was just finishing up, and I could hear it back through the trees behind me, a car coming fast down the asphalt, its engine upshifting and getting the gas. The priest was asking us to say the Lord's Prayer, and I didn't want to give this car any of my attention, but now it came into view as it sped west, a blue lowrider, the center of its spinning wheels a flash of chrome. A kid leaned out the passenger window and yelled at us: "Fuckin' *faggots!*"

Then they were gone, the driver downshifting for the drop of the hill through the trees. The priest smiled and shook his head: "Our Father who art in heaven, hallowed be Thy name." I began reciting the words with everyone else, but my tongue had become my beating heart and my hands had turned oily and light, and that old rage sat up inside me as if it had just lain down for a short nap. "Thy kingdom come. Thy will be done." I didn't move but saw myself running in my overcoat and suit to my car, starting it up and tearing down East Broadway through the pines. "On earth as it is in heaven." They'd be a half mile ahead of me by now, maybe more. "Give us this day our daily bread." These little punks with no respect for anyone, my eyes scanning for any flash of blue. "And forgive us our trespasses." At the stop sign at the end of East Broadway, Charlie's Variety Store across the street, I'd cut right and accelerate for downtown. Soon I'd be on River Street, on my left the rusted guardrail and bare trees, the Merrimack River flowing east, the boxboard factory on the other side, gray smoke unfurling from its stacks. I'd pass the hill street where the hospital used to be, the emergency room where they'd stitched up Sam's chin and Vinny smoked under the awning, his eyes on me. Farther up the street, the base of Nettle Hill, Russ Bowman on his

back in the classroom, his face getting punched over and over. Then I'd
be on Water Street, Captain Chris's Restaurant a gay bar now, that back
kitchen where Charlie Pierce had sprayed me with scalding water and
I'd gone after him, this killer of kids like me. "As we forgive those who
trespass against us." No blue car yet, to my right the concrete retaining
wall for the parking lot of the shopping plaza where Crazy Jack had yelled
on a warm, crowded Sunday afternoon, *How's it feel to be a chicken**shit**?!*
Then the traffic lights at the intersection where ten years after that night
at the 104 Club, a loaded .38 in my father's Red Sox jacket pocket, Ben
Wallace, drunk behind the wheel of a dented sedan, had seen me walking
along the sidewalk and he revved his engine till the chassis vibrated and
yelled, *You still want to go at it, Dubis?!* And I'd drive straight through
the intersection, the Basiliere Bridge to my left, Bradford shimmering on
the other side, and if there was still no blue ahead of me, I'd head deep
into downtown, on the river side the old Woolworth's building, Valhally's
Diner, Mitchell's Clothing Store where our mother had put clothes for us
on layaway she still could not afford, past Casey's Office Supplies and the
post office in Washington Square, then the bars of Washington Street—
the Lido, the Chit Chat Lounge, the Tap and Steve Lynch swallowing his
front teeth. "As we forgive those who trespass against us." At the black
trestle of Railroad Square, I'd turn right and upshift past the old leather
tanneries, the berm of the Boston and Maine rail line to my left, the abandoned brewery coming up, the turn under the iron trestle for Lafayette
Square, Devin Wallace straddling my chest, knocking my head against
concrete again and again, the martial arts studio and Haffner's Gas, the
brown rush of the Little River flowing through drainage pipes beneath
cracked asphalt, no blue yet, no blue, the shadow of another trestle above
me as I downshifted up Winter Street, the booth where I pumped gas
and waited for the Lynches and the Murphys to come get me, gone now,
an empty concrete lot, a chain-link fence halfway around it, and before
the Greek church there'd be the sharp left for the avenues, of course the
avenues, still poor, abandoned cars on the sidewalks, but now I'd see sat-
ellite dishes screwed to the vinyl sides of some of the houses, now I'd see
security lights and bred pit bulls. The lumberyard still there, the concer-
tina wire coiled at the top of the fence and gleaming in this April sun, my

brother and our dead stabbed friend passing me two-by-fours, and look, a flash of blue gunning up Fourth Avenue. "And lead us not into temptation." And me following in my family car, an old used Toyota wagon, the booster seats of my two youngest still strapped in the back, their raging father in his suit and tie accelerating after the boys he'd been, hoping he'll find them, hoping he won't.

"But deliver us from evil. Amen."

There was the young captain's orders in the air, the report of seven rifles firing three times each. The acrid smells of hot brass and cordite. A sob from one of my sisters or my mother. Then the low mournful wheeze of the bagpipe, its nearly frantic search for the notes becoming "Amazing Grace," the man in his kilt walking slowly off into the trees where we heard the last note without him, like some lovely echo we all one day leave behind.

ACKNOWLEDGMENTS

I'd like to thank Alane Salierno Mason, once again, for helping me to find the true book within the one I'd first written. I would especially like to thank my family for allowing me to write so openly from my memory of our mutual past: my sister Suzanne, a national leader in the field of domestic violence prevention; my brother Jeb, an inspired and inspiring architectural designer of homes and restaurants and public spaces; my sister Nicole, a professor and licensed therapist who works with families not so different from the one she came from; and my mother Patricia, who after thirty-five years working with and for the poor, is now, at age seventy-two, a newly certified Montessori teacher for young children. I am honored to be her son.

And here's to my father who, when I first began to write in my early twenties, told me not to do what he did. "Don't wait till your mama and I are dead before you write about us, son. Just go ahead and write."